1982

SIR THOMAS BROWNE

SELECTED
WRITINGS

SIR THOMAS BROWNE

SELECTED WRITINGS

Edited by SIR GEOFFREY KEYNES

THE UNIVERSITY OF CHICAGO PRESS

The University of Chicago Press, Chicago 60637
Faber and Faber Limited, London WC 1, England

Library of Congress Catalog Card Number 68 - 55536

CONTENTS

CONTENTS

ILLUSTRATIONS

INTRODUCTION

Sir thomas browne was born in London in 1605, the
only son of Thomas Browne, a silk mercer, who had come
south from Chester in the last decade of the sixteenth
century. Thomas Browne the elder died in 1613, and his widow
soon afterwards married a soldier and adventurer, Sir Thomas
Dutton. Her first husband having left Lady Dutton with adequate means for the support and education of her son and three
daughters, young Thomas began his education at Winchester
College and at the age of eighteen went on to Broadgates Hall,
Oxford. A year later, in 1624, this institution was given the
name and status of Pembroke College and the youth was chosen
to deliver one of the inaugural Latin speeches. Evidently the
authorities thought well of his attainments as a classical
scholar. His principal at Pembroke was Thomas Clayton,
regius professor of physic, and his tutor was Thomas Lushing-
ton, a broadminded cleric, who afterwards moved to Norwich
as Prebendary at the Cathedral. These men are likely to have
influenced Browne's choice of medicine as a career and of Norwich as the scene of his professional life. Having graduated as
M.A. in 1629, Browne was not yet ready to begin the practice
of medicine. He is known to have visited Ireland with his step-
father on a tour of inspection of the English government's
military installations, and this probably took place soon after
his graduation. Thereafter he is likely to have started on his
course of medical training on the Continent. No dates of his
various moves are known, but it is certain that he studied at the
medical schools of Montpellier and Padua before finally achiev-
ing the degree of M.D. at Leyden in 1633. It has been claimed
that he began the practice of medicine in Yorkshire while living
at Upper Shibden Hall near Halifax, but this is unlikely to be
true. It is more probable that he worked for a while as assistant
to a doctor somewhere in Oxfordshire until he was incorporated

M.D. at the University in 1635. In the following year he settled in Norwich. Clearly these years of study abroad were of great importance in the formation of his mind, but we know few details of his early life beyond hints contained in his writings.

From the time of his leaving Oxford, Browne's two careers as medical practitioner and author ran parallel, though his fame as a writer has tended to overshadow the importance of his background as a family doctor in Norwich. He was also very active as a naturalist, becoming the leading expert in the fauna and flora of Norfolk and Suffolk. He is not known ever to have left his East Anglian territory after 1636 for the rest of his life. He died in 1682. This limitation did not interfere with the growth of his reputation in either career, which culminated in the knighthood bestowed on him in 1671 by King Charles II as the most distinguished citizen of the great City of Norwich. In 1641 Browne had married Dorothy Mileham, daughter of Edward Mileham of Burlingham St. Peter, a village near Norwich, and so became connected with several of the county families of Norfolk. Although he had regretted in his *Religio Medici* that men could not 'procreate like trees without conjunction', the Brownes had twelve children, only four of whom survived their parents, the others dying in infancy or youth. The elder son, Edward, followed his father in medicine, becoming a distinguished practitioner in London, though he had no pretentions to rivalling him as a literary artist.

The task of making a selection of Browne's writings is simplified by the obvious propriety of including the whole of several of his shorter works, each of these being too definite an entity as a work of art to permit of any interference with its structure. This decision must account for nearly half the space allotted for the whole selection. The remaining portion has to accommodate the passages chosen from what is in fact the great bulk of his collected works, if the miscellaneous writings and letters, none of which was published during his lifetime, are taken into account. This disproportion is justified by the purpose of a selection; it is intended to serve as an introduction to the author's writings and must present in the first place those works generally accepted as the main evidence on which his reputation is founded.

RELIGIO MEDICI

Browne's *Religio Medici*, his first and most celebrated book, was written during leisure hours about the year 1636, when he first came to Norwich. It was composed, as he explained in a preface 'To the Reader', for the gratification of himself and an unnamed friend, but, as copies multiplied in manuscript, it became 'common unto many', until finally it attracted the attention of a London publisher, Andrew Crooke, who printed it without the author's knowledge in 1642. As soon as he became aware of this, Browne protested that the text was full of errors, but he forgave the publisher his act of piracy and provided him with a partially revised text, printed in 1643. Yet, although his text was still imperfect, it seems that Browne let it go at this, and made no further revisions in any subsequent edition, of which there were many published during his lifetime. The edition of 1643 has therefore been taken as the basis of the most recent recension of the text, the version printed here being founded on the elaborately critical text prepared by Dottoressa Vittoria Sanna of the University of Cagliari, Sardinia (1958). No manuscript in Browne's hand has survived, though it is believed that he made three, or even four, versions. Yet eight manuscript copies in other hands are known, all different in detail, so that the preparation of an entirely authentic text is hardly possible. Some idea of the manifold variations can be gathered from the footnotes in the present edition gathered from all the available sources, the existing manuscripts being arbitrarily designated by letters.[1]

The first printing of 1642 immediately attracted the attention of Sir Kenelm Digby, author, philosopher and diplomatist, who wrote a critical commentary published in 1643. The book was also quickly translated into Latin and published at Leyden in 1644. The numerous reprints both in English and Latin published during the seventeenth century provide evidence of the popularity of the book both at home and abroad. By the age of

[1] These are: L (British Museum, Lansdown MS); P (Pembroke College, Oxford, claimed by J.-J. Denonain to be the earliest form known); J (St. John's College, Cambridge); N (Norwich Record Office, Wilkin MS, II); R (Rawlinson MS, Bodleian Library, Oxford); O (Osler Library, McGill University, Montreal); H (Dr. Haviland Hall MS, Lehigh University Library); W (Norwich Record Office, Wilkin MS, I).

forty Browne was already a famous writer, and his attitude to life, religion and philosophy was being seriously discussed in many countries. Although the book was entitled 'The Religion of a Doctor', Browne's attitude to religion has been found hard to define. His views were humane and latitudinarian, and his lack of theological dogma soon involved him in accusations of atheism. The book was consequently condemned by the Roman Catholic Church and was placed on the *Index of Prohibited Books* in March 1645. Though neglected in the eighteenth century, Browne's account of his 'religion' (in the widest sense) has stimulated increasing attention and discussion during the last 150 years, beginning with the delight in his style expressed by Charles Lamb, S. T. Coleridge and William Hazlitt. They liked also the attractive personality portrayed by the author in the course of this candid exposure of his beliefs and prejudices.

PSEUDODOXIA EPIDEMICA

Browne's *Pseudodoxia Epidemica: or, Enquiries into Very many received Tenents And commonly presumed Truths*, his longest work by far, was licensed in March 1645 and published in 1646. Its composition must therefore have been begun long before the authorized edition of *Religio Medici* had been published or his fame carried abroad by the Latin translation. Commonly known as Browne's *Vulgar Errors*, since it was designed to combat the popularity of a large variety of erroneous beliefs, so bulky a book can only have been based on many years of patient thought, reading, observation and experiment. Browne was forty in 1645 when the book was finished, and had lived in Norwich for eight years, much of which must have been spent accumulating the notes in commonplace books from which the *Vulgar Errors* were quarried. The manuscripts he used are not known, though enough material of a similar kind is among the Sloane MSS in the British Museum fully to illustrate his method. He had defined his attitude towards philosophical problems in *Religio Medici*, saying: 'In philosophy, where truth seems double-faced, there is no man more paradoxical than myself, but in divinity I love to keep the road.' The reader of *Vulgar Errors* would therefore expect to find much that was daring, though little that was dangerous, and the many editions published during his life have proved that his public was not disappointed. Successive editions were revised and augmented up to 1672, when readers were informed that the work was now 'compleat and perfect'. Contemporary opinion, as illustrated by references in other books, regarded the work with great respect. It opens with a long discussion of the causes of popular errors and of the authors who have helped to perpetuate them. This occupies the First Book; the succeeding Six Books deal systematically with errors concerning mineralogy, botany, the animal world, and man himself; with those in pictures, in geography and history, and finally with those derived from Holy Scripture. The extent of the work is so great that a selection for the present volume can only be a small proportion of the whole. Enough, however, has been included to give a good sample of Browne's method, and his address 'To the Reader' sets out his purpose in characteristic style. The extracts printed here are placed after the more complete works with the miscellaneous writings.

A LETTER TO A FRIEND

It is probably right to place next in order of composition, if not of publication, the short work entitled *A Letter to a Friend upon the Death of an Intimate Friend*, not published until 1690. This remarkable piece has long been recognized as a literary elaboration of a clinical report on an actual patient who had died of phthisis under Browne's care, but the individuals concerned were not identified until some sixteen years ago, when Professor F. L. Huntley of the University of Michigan found what seemed to be a convincing solution of the riddle. It was formerly supposed, on the strength of a reference given by Browne, that the tract had been written about 1672, ten years before his death. Professor Huntley has collected evidence for believing that the sick man was Robert Loveday of Cheston, a village in East Suffolk. Loveday was a talented writer, who had translated part of La Calprenède's *Cléopâtre* (1647), but lived to complete only five of the twelve parts of this long prose romance, which he published in 1652 as *Hymen's Præludia, or Love's Masterpiece*. The older friend, for whom Browne was writing his report, is believed to have been Sir John Pettus, squire of Cheston, though he lived at Rackheath, near Norwich.

He held the appointment of deputy-governor of the royal mines in Wales, and, when Loveday died in December 1656, was absent on his duties. Pettus was certainly a friend of Browne and of Loveday, and, allowing for a certain degree of literary licence, the facts accord closely enough with the evidence provided by the text of the *Letter*. Browne certainly revised the text once or twice, and on one of these occasions had introduced the reference giving rise to the later dating. The concluding passages of the published text consisted of serious advice to the recipient on the conduct of his life, and these would have made publication inappropriate as long as Pettus was alive. He died in 1690, and the manuscript, which had come into the keeping of Dr Edward Browne, the author's elder son, was forthwith printed as a folio pamphlet suitable for binding with the sheets of Browne's *Collected Works*, published in 1686. This text, with a few corrections, has been printed here. A shorter and different version is now among the Sloane MSS in the British Museum. Browne's fertile imagination and his erudition playing around the clinical and pathological themes combined to form a composition of a most unusual and interesting kind. If it is assumed that these identifications are correct, *A Letter to a Friend* must be supposed to have been written early in 1657. The admonitory passages at the end of the *Letter* may have been added later and were used again in Browne's last work, *Christian Morals*, presently to be described.

HYDRIOTAPHIA AND GARDEN OF CYRUS

In 1658 Browne published *Hydriotaphia. Urne-Buriall* in a small octavo volume together with *The Garden of Cyrus*, each work having a dedicatory letter addressed to a friend living in the neighbourhood of Norwich. The first friend was Thomas le Gros of Crostwick Hall, head of an old Norfolk family; the second was Nicholas Bacon, grandson of Sir Nicholas Bacon, created premier baronet by James I. Internal evidence suggests that *Hydriotaphia* was written in 1656 or early in 1657. *The Garden of Cyrus* was probably written in the early part of 1658, the whole volume being published later in the year. An interval of some ten years, therefore, had elapsed between the publication of *Vulgar Errors* and the composition of this new volume. Browne's style was already shewing in the larger work his tendency to write elaborate prose with Latinization of his words. In the new volume this became accentuated, and in many celebrated passages Browne's 'full organ notes' can be heard. This musical comparison is justified because the grandeur and rhythm of his periods can be best appreciated by hearing them read aloud. It seems evident that both works were more consciously composed with a view to artistry and effect than anything else he wrote, and he certainly achieved his aim. The cinerary urns discovered at Walsingham near Norwich were supposed by Browne to be of Roman, that is, Romano-British, origin. The engraved illustration of four of them used in the early editions of the book shews that they were in fact Saxon and therefore of much later date, but this does not invalidate Browne's observations. He was using them only as an excuse for elaborating solemn and learned reflexions suggested to him by their discovery. His theme was the inevitability of death and the futility of ritual commemoration, thus demonstrating the superiority of a Christian belief in immortality over pagan vainglory.

Hydriotaphia is based largely on antiquarian enquiry and illustration. *The Garden of Cyrus*, on the other hand, named after the Emperor of Persia reputed to have made the famous hanging gardens of Babylon, is a fantastic elaboration of mathematics in nature, as seen in the quinary arrangements found in various plants. Browne claimed that the ancients had imitated the system in planting their trees by fives, so making the 'quincunx', or network formation, in their plantations. He was carried away by this idea and, as S. T. Coleridge exclaimed, came to see 'Quincunxes in Heaven above, Quincunxes in Earth below, and Quincunxes in the water beneath the Earth; Quincunxes in Deity, Quincunxes in the mind of Man; Quincunxes in bone, in optic nerves, in Roots of Trees, in leaves, in petals, in everything'. The two treatises have very seldom been printed separately, and, as pointed out by Professor Huntley, there can be little doubt but that Browne fully intended their close conjunction. The first dealt with Time, the second with Space; the first with Death, the second with Life; the first with Accident, the second with Design. They are contrasted by their association, and so illustrate Browne's philosophy of past and present. It has often been asked why Browne remarked in the closing passage of *The Garden of Cyrus* that 'The huntsmen are up in America', when it would have been more accurate to say 'in India', as indeed he himself observed in *Pseudodoxia Epidemica*, Book vi, chapter 2. Perhaps he found that *America* suited the rhythm of his sentence better than *India*, his instincts as an artist in words overcoming his love of truth.

Browne did not, as far as we can judge from inscriptions in his books, give away many copies of most of them. With *Hydriotaphia*, however, he was more generous than usual. Twelve are known which were probably gifts, each containing several, or sometimes a great many, corrections made by his own hand. These have helped in establishing the ideal text edited by John Carter in 1958 and followed here. No part of the book now exists in manuscript.

MISCELLANY TRACTS

Browne's three remaining works, *Miscellany Tracts*, *Repertorium* and *Christian Morals*, were all published after his death in 1682. *Miscellany Tracts* covers subjects in botanical history, scriptural history, music, philology and archaeology. They were written as occasion arose in answer to questions raised by friends at home or by distinguished correspondents, such as Nicholas Bacon, Sir William Dugdale, and John Evelyn. Of the thirteen tracts three are reprinted here, namely those on falconry and on the Oracle at Delphi, together with *Musaeum Clausum*, a whimsical piece listing books, pictures and rarities never seen by any living man, either being lost or having never existed. Browne had kept transcripts of his learned 'letters', and these were handed by Dr Edward Browne soon after his father's death to Thomas Tenison, rector of St. Martins-in-the-Fields and later Archbishop. Tenison had been a close friend of Sir Thomas Browne and was a suitable editor; two years later he supervised the printing of the *Collected Works*. The *Tracts* were published in 1684 with a portrait of the author.

Repertorium was an account of the monuments and tombs in Norwich Cathedral first published in *Posthumous Works*, 1712, with a reprint of *A Letter to a Friend*, notes on Browne's life by his friend John Whitefoot, and other minor pieces. It has no literary pretentions and is not printed here.

CHRISTIAN MORALS

Christian Morals, 1716, consists of a long series of short essays and moralizings on detached themes. It is a kind of moralistic anthology, and was edited jointly by Elizabeth Lyttelton, Browne's eldest daughter, and John Jeffery, Archdeacon of Norwich. It was dedicated to the Earl of Buchan, ancestor through Browne's second daughter, Anne Fairfax, of the only representatives of his line living at the present time. When Dr Samuel Johnson reprinted *Christian Morals* in 1756, prefixing a biographical account of the author, he criticized Browne on the ground that 'there are passages from which some have taken occasion to rank him with the Deists, and others among Atheists'. Johnson concluded, however, 'that Browne was a zealous adherent to the faith of Christ, that he lived in obedience to his laws and died in confidence of his mercy'. Many of the sections of *Christian Morals* bear evidence of the truth of this. The book is divided into three parts and it seems sufficient to print only the second part in this selection. Much of the first part and the last section of the third part have already been printed, though with many variations, in the concluding passages of *A Letter to a Friend*.

OTHER WRITINGS

Browne left among his manuscripts, most of which are now in the British Museum, a large collection of miscellaneous notes on natural history, anatomy, chemistry, ancient history, and so on. These are mostly not in the form of literary compositions. An exception is a short essay 'On Dreams', included here with miscellaneous pieces in verse; Browne was no poet, but his few metrical writings are characteristic and have an interest both biographical and literary. Two others have already found a place in *Religio Medici*, one of these being the well-known 'Dormative I take to bedward'. Lastly, a few letters have been chosen from the large number written to members of his family and to his friends. First there is a short series to his promising younger son, Thomas, who had served with distinction in the navy as a midshipman under Lord Sandwich, but died from an unknown cause soon afterwards. One letter was addressed to some young man evidently contemplating the study of medicine. It is possible that the recipient was Browne's younger friend, Henry Power, who afterwards practised as a doctor in Halifax, and the letter used to be conjecturally dated 1646. Recently evidence has come to light suggesting that it was in fact written in 1653, by which date Power had been for some time settled in practice, so that the real recipient remains in doubt. In conclusion a commendatory letter to Daniel King, compiler of a work on the County Palatine of Chester, has been printed as an example of a more formal and elegant style than was usual with Browne.

For readers of this selection wishing to make further acquaintance with Browne a short list of books covering the subject is added. Much attention has been given to him in recent years by writers of literary history, such as Basil Willey in *The Seventeenth Century Background*, London, 1934, and Douglas Bush in *English Literature in the Earlier Seventeenth Century*, Oxford, 1962. Books dealing more specifically with Sir Thomas Browne are:

The Works of Sir Thomas Browne, edited by Geoffrey Keynes, 4 vols., London, 1964.

A Bibliography of Sir Thomas Browne, by Geoffrey Keynes, Oxford, 1968.

Sir Thomas Browne. A Doctor's Life of Science and Faith, by J. S. Finch, New York, 1950.

Sir Thomas Browne, A Biographical and Critical Study, by F. L. Huntley, University of Michigan Press, 1962.

Sir Thomas Browne, by Joan Bennett. Cambridge University Press, 1962.

GEOFFREY KEYNES

RELIGIO MEDICI

A true and full coppy of that which was most
imperfectly and Surreptitiously printed before
vnder the name of: Religio Medici.
Printed for Andrew Crooke. 1643.

TO THE READER

CERTAINLY that man were greedy of life, who should desire to live when all the world were at an end; and he must needs be very impatient, who would repine at death in the societie of all things that suffer under it. Had not almost every man suffered by the presse; or were not the tyranny thereof become universall; I had not wanted reason for complaint: but in times wherein I have lived to behold the highest perversion of that excellent invention; the name of his Majesty defamed, the honour of Parliament depraved, the writings of both depravedly, anticipatively, counterfeitly imprinted; complaints may seeme ridiculous in private persons, and men of my condition may be as incapable of affronts, as hopelesse of their reparations. And truly had not the duty I owe unto the importunitie of friends, and the allegeance I must ever acknowledge unto truth prevayled with me; the inactivitie of my disposition might have made these sufferings continuall, and time that brings other things to light, should have satisfied me in the remedy of its oblivion. But because things evidently false are not onely printed, but many things of truth most falsly set forth; in this latter I could not but thinke my selfe engaged: for though we have no power to redresse the former, yet in the other the reparation being within our selves, I have at present represented unto the world a full and intended copy of that Peece which was most imperfectly and surreptitiously published before.

This I confesse about seven yeares past, with some others of affinitie thereto, for my private exercise and satisfaction, I had at leisurable houres composed; which being communicated unto one, it became common unto many, and was by transcription successively corrupted untill it arrived in a most depraved copy at the presse. He that shall peruse that worke, and shall take notice of sundry particularities and personall expressions therein, will easily discern the intention was not publick: and being a private exercise directed to my selfe, what is delivered therein was rather a memoriall unto me then an example or rule unto any other: and therefore if there bee any singularitie therein correspondent unto the private conceptions of any man, it doth not advantage them; or if dissentaneous thereunto, it no way overthrowes them. It was penned in such a place and with such disadvantage, that (I protest) from the first setting of pen unto paper, I had not the assistance of any good booke, whereby to promote my invention or relieve my memory; and therefore there might be many reall lapses therein, which others might take notice of, and more that I suspected my selfe. It was set downe many yeares past, and was the sense of my conceptions at that time, not an immutable law unto my advancing judgement at all times, and therefore there might be many things therein plausible unto my passed apprehension, which are not agreeable unto my present selfe. There are many things delivered Rhetorically, many expressions therein meerely Tropicall and as they best illustrate my intention; and therefore also there are many things to be taken in a soft and flexible sense, and not to be called unto the rigid test of reason. Lastly all that is contained therein is in submission unto maturer discernments, and as I have declared shall no further father them then the best and learned judgements shall authorize them; under favour of which considerations I have made its secrecie publike and committed the truth thereof to every ingenuous Reader.

THOMAS BROWNE

RELIGIO MEDICI

THE FIRST PART

FOR my Religion, though there be severall circumstances
that might perswade the world I have none at all, as the
generall scandall of my profession, the naturall course of
my studies, the indifferency of my behaviour, and discourse
in matters of Religion, neither violently defending one, nor
with the common ardour of contention opposing another; yet
in despight hereof I dare, without usurpation, assume the
honourable stile of a Christian: not that I meerely owe this title
to the Font, my education, or [the] Clime wherein I was borne,
as being bred up either to confirme those principles my Parents
instilled into my unwary understanding; or by a generall
consent proceed in the Religion of my Countrey: But [that]
having in my riper yeares, and confirmed judgement, seene and
examined all, I finde my selfe obliged by the principles of Grace,
and the law of mine owne reason, to embrace no other name but
this; neither doth herein my zeale so farre make me forget the
generall charitie I owe unto humanity, as rather to hate then
pity Turkes, Infidels, and (what is worse) [the] Jewes, rather
contenting my selfe to enjoy that happy stile, then maligning
those who refuse so glorious a title.

BUT because the name of a Christian is become too generall to
expresse our faith, there being a Geography of Religions as well
as [of] Lands, and every Clime distinguished not onely by their
lawes and limits, but circumscribed by their doctrines and rules
of Faith; To be particular, I am of that reformed new-cast
Religion, wherein I dislike nothing but the name; of the same
beliefe [which] our Saviour taught, the Apostles disseminated,
the Fathers authorised, and the Martyrs confirmed; but by
the sinister ends of Princes, the ambition & avarice of Prelates,

PART I and the fatall corruption of times, so decaied, impaired, and fallen from its native beauty, that it required the carefull and charitable hand of these times to restore it to its primitive integrity: Now the accidentall occasion whereon, the slender meanes whereby, the low and abject condition of the person by whom so good a worke was set on foot, which in our adversaries begets contempt and scorn, fills me with wonder, and is the very same objection the insolent Pagans first cast at Christ and his Disciples.

Section 3 YET have I not so shaken hands with those desperate Resolutions, who had rather venture at large their decaied bottome, then bring her in to be new trim'd in the dock; who had rather promiscuously retaine all, then abridge any, and obstinately be what they are, then what they have beene, as to stand in diameter and swords point with them: we have reformed from them, not against them; for, omitting those improperations and termes of scurrility betwixt us, which onely difference our affections, and not our cause, there is between us one common name and appellation, one faith, and necessary body of principles common to us both; and therefore I am not scrupulous to converse or live with them, to enter their Churches in defect of ours, and either pray with them, or for them: I could never perceive any rationall consequence from those many texts which prohibite the children of Israel to pollute themselves with the Temples of the Heathens; we being all Christians, and not divided by such detested impieties as might prophane our prayers, or the place wherein we make them; or that a resolved conscience may not adore her Creator any where, especially in places devoted to his service; where, if their devotions offend him, mine may please him; if theirs prophane it, mine may hallow it. Holy water and [the] Crucifix (dangerous to the common people) deceive not my judgement, nor abuse my devotion at all: I am, I confesse, naturally inclined to that, which misguided zeale termes superstition; my common conversation I do acknowledge austere, my behaviour full of rigour, sometimes not without morosity; yet at my devotion I love to use the civility of my knee, my hat, and hands, with all those outward and sensible motions, which may express or

PART I

promote my invisible devotion. I should cut off my arme rather then violate a church window, then deface or demolish the memory of Saint or Martyr.[1] At the sight of a Crosse or Crucifix I can dispence with my hat, but scarce with the thought and memory of my Saviour; I cannot laugh at, but rather pity, the fruitlesse journeys of Pilgrims, or contemne the miserable condition of Friers; for though misplaced in circumstance, there is something in it of devotion: I could never heare the *Ave Maria* Bell* without an elevation, or thinke it a sufficient warrant, because they erred in one circumstance, for me to erre in all: that is in silence and dumb contempt. Whilst therefore they directed their devotions to her, I offered mine to God, and rectified the errour of their prayers by rightly ordering mine owne. At a solemne Procession I have wept abundantly, while my consorts, blinde with opposition and prejudice, have fallen into an eccesse of scorne and laughter: There are questionlesse both in Greek, Roman, and African Churches, solemnities, and ceremonies, whereof the wiser zeales doe make a Christian use, and stand condemned by us; not as evill in themselves, but as allurements and baits of superstition to those vulgar heads that looke asquint on the face of truth, and those unstable judgements that cannot consist in the narrow point and centre of vertue without a reele or stagger to the circumference.

* A Church Bell that tolls every day at 6. and 12. of the Clocke, at the hearing wherof every one in what place soever either of house or street betakes him to his prayer, which is commonly directed to the *Virgin.*

Section 4

AS there were many Reformers, so likewise many reformations; every Countrey proceeding in a peculiar Method[2] according as their nationall interest together with their constitution and clime inclined them; some angrily and with extremitie, others calmely, and with mediocrity; not rending, but easily dividing the community, and leaving an honest possibility of a reconciliation; which, though peaceable Spirits doe desire, and may conceive that revolution of time, and the mercies of God may effect; yet that judgement that shall consider the present antipathies between the two extreames, their contrarieties in condition, affection and opinion, may with the same hopes expect an union in the poles of Heaven.

[1] *1643 has*: I should violate my owne arme rather then a Church, nor willingly deface the memory of Saint or Martyr. *The above version is in the MSS and unauthorized editions.*

[2] *1643 has*: in a particular way and method. *Emended from the MSS.*

BUT to difference my self neerer, & draw into a lesser circle: There is no Church wherein every point so squares unto my conscience, whose articles, constitutions, and customes seeme so consonant unto reason, and as it were framed to my particular devotion, as this whereof I hold my beliefe, the Church of *England*; to whose faith I am a sworne subject, and therefore in a double obligation subscribe unto her Articles, and endeavour to observe her Constitutions; [no man shall reach my faith unto another Article, or command my obedience to a Canon more]¹: whatsoever is beyond, as points indifferent, I observe according to the rules of my private reason, or the humour and fashion of my devotion, neither believing this, because *Luther* affirmed it, nor disapproving that, because *Calvin* hath disavouched it. I condemne not all things in the Councell of *Trent*, nor approve all in the Synod of *Dort*. In briefe, where the Scripture is silent, the Church is my Text; where that speakes, 'tis but my Comment; where there is a joynt silence of both, I borrow not the rules of my Religion from *Rome* or *Geneva*, but the dictates of my owne reason. It is an unjust scandall of our adversaries, and a grosse error in our selves, to compute the Nativity of our Religion from *Henry* the eight, who though he rejected the Pope, refus'd not the faith of *Rome*, and effected no more then what his owne Predecessors desired and assayed in ages past,

[In their quarrels with Pope Paul the fifth.] and was conceived the State of *Venice** would have attempted in our dayes. It is as uncharitable a point in us to fall upon those popular scurrilities and opprobrious scoffes of the Bishop of *Rome*, [to] whom as a temporall Prince, we owe the duty of good language: I confesse there is cause of passion betweene us; by his sentence I stand excommunicated, Heretick is the best language he affords me; yet can no eare witnesse I ever returned to him the name of Antichrist, Man of sin, or whore of *Babylon;* It is the method of charity to suffer without reaction: those usual Satyrs, and invectives of the Pulpit may perchance produce a good effect on the vulgar, whose eares are opener to Rhetorick then Logick, yet doe they in no wise confirme the faith of wiser beleevers, who know that a good cause needs not to be patron'd by a passion, but can sustaine it selfe upon a temperate dispute.

¹ *This passage is added from the MSS and unauthorized editions. It was possibly omitted by the author in 1643 as redundant.*

I COULD never divide my selfe from any man upon the difference of an opinion, or be angry with his judgement for not agreeing with mee in that, from which perhaps within a few days I should dissent my selfe: I have no Genius to disputes in Religion, and have often thought it wisedome to decline them, especially upon a disadvantage, or when the cause of truth might suffer in the weakenesse of my patronage: where wee desire to be informed, 'tis good to contest with men above our selves; but to confirme and establish our opinions, 'tis best to argue with judgements below our own, that the frequent spoyles and victories over their reasons may settle in our selves an esteeme, and confirmed opinion of our owne. Every man is not a proper Champion for Truth, nor fit to take up the Gantlet in the cause of Veritie: Many from the ignorance of these Maximes, and an inconsiderate zeale unto Truth,[1] have too rashly charged the troopes of error, and remaine as Trophees unto the enemies of Truth: A man may be in as just possession of Truth as of a City, and yet bee forced to surrender; tis therefore farre better to enioy her with peace, then to hazzard her on a battell: If therefore there rise any doubts in my way, I doe forget them, or at least defer them, till my better setled judgement, and more manly reason be able to resolve them; for I perceive every mans owne reason is his best *Oedipus*, and will upon a reasonable truce, find a way to loose those bonds wherewith the subtilties of errour have enchained our more flexible and tender judgements. In Philosophy where truth seemes double-faced, there is no man more paradoxicall then my self; but in Divinity I love to keepe the road, and though not in an implicite, yet an humble faith, follow the great wheele of the Church, by which I move, not reserving any proper poles or motion from the epicycle of my owne braine; by this meanes I leave no gap for Heresies, Schismes, or Errors, of which, at present, I hope I shall not injure Truth to say, I have no taint or tincture; I must confesse my greener studies have been polluted with two or three, not any begotten in the latter Centuries, but old and obsolete, such as could never have been revived, but by such extravagant and irregular heads as mine;

[1] *PL have:* Many out of zeale unto truth, more conscious of their desires than abilityes.

PART I

★ [That loos-
eth itselfe in
Greece and
riseth again
in Cilicie.]

★ A revolution
of certaine
thousand
yeares when
all things
should re-
turne unto
their former
estate and he
be teaching
again in
his schoole as
when he
delivered
this opinion.

for indeed Heresies perish not with their Authors, but like the River *Arethusa*,★ though they lose their currents in one place, they rise up againe in another: one generall Councell is not able to extirpate one single Heresie, it may be canceld for the present, but revolution of time and the like aspects of Heaven, will restore it, when it will flourish till it be condemned againe; for as though there were a *Metempsuchosis,* and the soule of one man passed into another, opinions doe finde after certaine revolutions, men and mindes like those that first begat them. To see our selves againe wee neede not looke for *Platoes* yeare,★ every man is not onely himselfe; there have beene many *Diogenes,* and as many *Tymons,* though but few of that name; men are lived over againe; the world is now as it was in ages past; there was none then, but there hath been some one since that parallels him, and is, as it were, his revived selfe.

Section 7

N O W the first of mine was that of the Arabians, that the soules of men perished with their bodies, but should yet bee raised againe at the last day; not that I did absolutely conceive a mortality of the soule; but if that were, which faith, not Philosophy, hath yet throughly disproved, and that both entred the grave together, yet I held the same conceit thereof that wee all doe of the body, that it should rise againe. Surely it is but the merits of our unworthy natures, if wee sleepe in darkenesse, untill the last alarum: A serious reflex upon my owne unworthinesse did make me backward from challenging this prerogative of my soule; so I might enjoy my Saviour at the last, I could with patience be nothing almost unto eternity. The second was that of *Origen,* that God would not persist in his vengeance for ever, but after a definite time of his wrath hee would release the damned soules from torture; Which error I fell into upon a serious contemplation of the great attribute of God, his mercy, and did a little cherish it in my selfe, because I found therein no malice, and a ready weight to sway me from that other extream of despaire, wherunto melancholy and contemplative natures are too easily disposed. A third there is which I did never positively maintaine or practice, but have often wished it had been consonant to Truth, and not offensive to my Religion, and that is the prayer for the dead; wherunto I was inclined from

some charitable inducements,[1] whereby I could scarce containe
my prayers for a friend at the ringing [out] of a Bell, or behold
his corpes without an oraison for his soule: 'Twas a good way
me thought to be remembred by Posterity, and farre more
noble then an History. These opinions I never maintained with
pertinacity, or endeavoured to enveagle any mans beliefe unto
mine, nor so much as ever revealed or disputed them with my
dearest friends; by which meanes I neither propagated them in
others, nor confirmed them in my selfe, but suffering them to
flame upon their owne substance, without addition of new fuell,
they went out insensibly of themselves; therefore these opinions,
though condemned by lawfull Councels, were not Heresies in
me, but bare Errors, and single Lapses of my understanding,
without a joynt depravity of my will. Those have not only
depraved understandings but diseased affections, which cannot
enjoy a singularity without a Heresie, or be the author of an
opinion, without they be of a Sect also; this was the villany of
the first Schisme of *Lucifer*, who was not content to erre alone,
but drew into his faction many Legions of Spirits; and upon this
experience hee tempted only *Eve*, as well understanding the
communicable nature of sin, and that to deceive but one, was
tacitely and upon consequence to delude them both.

THAT Heresies should arise we have the prophecy of Christ, Section 8
but that old ones should be abolished wee hold no prediction.
That there must be heresies is true, not onely in our Church,
but also in any other; even in Doctrines hereticall there will be
super-heresies, and Arians not onely divided from their Church,
but also among themselves: for heads that are disposed unto
Schisme and complexionally propense to innovation, are naturally indisposed for a community, nor will ever be confined unto
the order or oeconomy of one body; and therefore when they
separate from others they knit but loosely among themselves;
nor contented with a generall breach or dichotomie with their
Church, do subdivide and mince themselves almost into Atomes.
'Tis true that men of singular parts and humors have not beene

---

[1] *The MSS and unauthorized editions have*: whereunto I was inclined by an
excesse of charitie, whereby I thought the number of the living too small an
object for my devotion.

PART I   free from singular opinions and conceits in all ages; retaining something not onely beside the opinion of their own Church or any other, but also any particular Author: which notwithstanding a sober judgement may doe without offence or heresie; for there are yet after all the decrees of counsells and the niceties of the Schooles, many things untouch'd, unimagin'd, wherein the libertie of an honest reason may play and expatiate with security and farre without the circle of an heresie.

Section 9   AS for those wingy mysteries in Divinity and ayery subtilties in Religion, which have unhindg'd the braines of better heads, they never stretched the *Pia Mater* of mine; me thinkes there be not impossibilities enough in Religion for an active faith; the deepest mysteries ours containes, have not only been illustrated, but maintained by syllogisme, and the rule of reason: I love to lose my selfe in a mystery, to pursue my reason to an *o altitudo*. 'Tis my solitary recreation to pose my apprehension with those involved aenigma's and riddles of the Trinity, with Incarnation and Resurrection. I can answer all the objections of Satan, and my rebellious reason, with that odde resolution I learned of *Tertullian, Certum est quia impossibile est.* I desire to exercise my faith in the difficultest points, for to credit ordinary and visible objects is not faith, but perswasion. Some beleeve the better for seeing Christ his Sepulchre, and when they have seene the Red Sea, doubt not of the miracle. Now contrarily I blesse my selfe, and am thankefull that I lived not in the dayes of miracles, that I never saw Christ nor his Disciples; I would not have beene one of the Israelites that passed the Red Sea, nor one of Christs Patients, on whom he wrought his wonders; then had my faith beene thrust upon me, nor should I enjoy that greater blessing pronounced to all that believe & saw not. 'Tis an easie and necessary beliefe to credit what our eye and sense hath examined: I believe he was dead, and buried; and rose againe; and desire to see him in his glory, rather then to contemplate him in his Cenotaphe, or Sepulchre. Nor is this much to beleeve, as we have reason, we owe this faith unto History: they only had the [happiness and] advantage of a bold and noble faith, who lived before his comming, who upon obscure prophesies and mysticall Types could raise a beliefe, and expect apparent impossibilities.

'TIS true, there is an edge in all firme beliefe, and with an easie
Metaphor wee may say the sword of faith; but in these obscurities I rather use it, in the adjunct the Apostle gives it, a
Buckler; under which I perceive a wary combatant may lie
invulnerable. Since I was of understanding to know we know
nothing my reason hath beene more pliable to the will of faith;
I am now content to understand a mystery without a rigid
definition in an easie and Platonick description. That allegorical
description of *Hermes*,* pleaseth me beyond all the Meta-   * [Deus est]
physicall definitions of Divines; where I cannot satisfie my   Sphæra cuius
reason, I love to humour my fancy; I had as leive you tell me   centrum
that *anima est angelus hominis, est Corpus Dei*, as *Entelechia; Lux est*   ubique, cir-
umbra Dei, as *actus perspicui*: where there is an obscurity too   cumferentia
deepe for our reason, 'tis good to sit downe with a description,   nullibi.
periphrasis, or adumbration; for by acquainting our reason how
unable it is to display the visible and obvious effects of nature,
it becomes more humble and submissive unto the subtilties of
faith: and thus I teach my haggard and unreclaimed reason to
stoope unto the lure of faith. I [do] believe there was already a
tree whose fruit our unhappy parents tasted, though in the
same Chapter, where God forbids it, 'tis positively said, the
plants of the field were not yet growne; for God had not caused
it to raine upon the earth. I beleeve that the Serpent (if we shall
literally understand it) from his proper form and figure, made
his motion on his belly before the curse. I find the triall of the
Pucellage and Virginity of women, which God ordained the
Jewes, is very fallible. Experience, and History informe me, that
not onely many particular women, but likewise whole Nations
have escaped the curse of childbed, which God seemes to
pronounce upon the whole Sex; yet doe I beleeve that all this is
true, which indeed my reason would perswade me to be false;
and this I think is no vulgar part of faith to believe a thing not
only above, but contrary to reason, and against the argument
of our proper senses.

IN my solitary and retired imaginations, (*Neque enim cum*
porticus aut me lectulus accepit, desum mihi) I remember I am not
alone, and therefore forget not to contemplate him and his
attributes who is ever with mee, especially those two mighty

ones, his wisedome and eternitie; with the one I recreate, with the other I confound my understanding: for who can speake of eternitie without a solœcisme, or thinke thereof without an extasie? Time we may comprehend, 'tis but five dayes elder then our selves, and hath the same Horoscope with the world; but to retire so farre backe as to apprehend a beginning, to give such an infinite start forward, as to conceive an end in an essence that wee affirme hath neither the one nor the other; it puts my reason to Saint *Pauls* Sanctuary; my Philosophy dares not say the Angells can doe it; God hath not made a creature that can comprehend him, 'tis the priviledge of his owne nature; *I am that I am,* was his owne definition unto *Moses;* and 'twas a short one, to confound mortalitie, that durst question God, or aske him what hee was; indeed he only is, all other things have beene or shall be, but in eternitie there is no distinction of Tenses; and therefore that terrible terme, *Predestination,* which hath troubled so many weake heads to conceive, and the wisest to explaine, is in respect to God no prescious determination of our estates to come, but a definitive placet of his will already ful-filled, and at the instant that he first decreed it; for to his eternitie which is indivisible, and altogether, the last Trumpe is already sounded, the reprobates in the flame, and the blessed in *Abrahams* bosome. Saint *Peter* spoke modestly, when hee said, a thousand yeares to God are but as one day: for to speake like a Philosopher, those continued instants of time which flow into a thousand yeares, make not to him one moment; what to us is to come, to his Eternitie is present, his whole duration being but one permanent point without succession, parts, flux, or division.

THERE is no Attribute that adds more difficulty to the mystery of the Trinity, where though in a relative way of Father and Son, we must deny a priority. I wonder how *Aristotle* should conceive the world eternall, or how he could make good two Eternities: his similitude of a Triangle, com-prehended in a square, doth somewhat illustrate the Trinitie of our soules, and that the Triple Unity of God; for there is in us not three, but a Trinity of soules; because there is in us, if not three distinct soules, yet different faculties, that can, and doe

subsist apart in different subjects, and yet in us are so united
as to make but one soule and substance; if one soule were so
perfect as to informe three distinct bodies, that were a petty
Trinity: conceive the distinct number of three, not divided nor
separated by the intellect, but actually comprehended in its
Unity, and that is a perfect Trinity. I have often admired the
mysticall way of *Pythagoras,* and the secret Magicke of numbers;
Beware of Philosophy, is a precept not to be received in too large
a sense; for in this masse of nature there is a set of things that
carry in their front, though not in capitall letters, yet in steno-
graphy, and short Characters, something of Divinitie, which
to wiser reasons serve as Luminaries in the abysse of knowledge,
and to judicious beliefes, as scales and roundles to mount the
pinnacles and highest pieces of Divinity. The severe Schooles
shall never laugh me out of the Philosophy of *Hermes,* that this
visible world is but a picture of the invisible, wherein as in a
pourtract, things are not truely, but in equivocall shapes, and
as they counterfeit some more reall substance in that invisible
fabrick.

THAT other attribute wherewith I recreate my devotion, is   Section 13
his wisedome, in which I am happy; and for the contemplation
of this onely, do not repent me that I was bred in the way of
study: The advantage I have of the vulgar, with the content
and happinesse I conceive therein, is an ample recompence for
all my endeavours, in what part of knowledg soever. Wisedome
is his most beauteous attribute, no man can attaine unto it, yet
Solomon pleased God when hee desired it. Hee is wise because hee
knowes all things, and he knoweth all things because he made
them all; but his greatest knowledg is in comprehending that
he made not, that is himselfe. And this is also the greatest knowledge in man. For this do I honour my own profession and
embrace the counsell even of the Devill himselfe: had he read
such a Lecture in Paradise as hee did at *Delphos,*★ we had better   ★ γνῶθι
knowne our selves, nor had we stood in feare to know him. I   σεαυτόν
know he is wise in all, wonderfull in what we conceive, but   nosce·te-
far more in what we comprehend not, for we behold him but   ipsum.
asquint upon reflex or shadow; our understanding is dimmer
than *Moses* eye, we are ignorant of the backparts, or lower side

of his Divinity; therefore to pry into the maze of his Counsels, is not onely folly in Man, but presumption even in Angels; [there is no thread or line to guide us in that Labyrinth];[1] like us, they are his servants, not his Senators; he holds no Councell, but that mysticall one of the Trinity, wherein, though there be three persons, there is but one minde that decrees, without contradiction; nor needs he any, his actions are not begot with deliberation, his wisedome naturally knowes what's best; his intellect stands ready fraught with the superlative and purest Idea's of goodnesse; consultation and election, which are two motions in us, are not one in him; his actions springing from his power, at the first touch of his will. These are Contemplations Metaphysicall; my humble speculations have another Method, and are content to trace and discover those impressions hee hath left on his creatures, and the obvious effects of nature; there is no danger to profound these mysteries, no *Sanctum sanctorum* in Philosophy: The world was made to be inhabited by beasts, but studied and contemplated by man:[2] 'tis the debt of our reason wee owe unto God, and the homage wee pay for not being beasts; without this the world is still as though it had not been, or as it was before the sixt day when as yet there was not a creature that could conceive, or say there was a world. The wisedome of God receives small honour from those vulgar heads, that rudely stare about, and with a grosse rusticity admire his workes; those highly magnifie him whose judicious enquiry into his acts, and deliberate research of his creatures, returne the duty of a devout and learned admiration. Therefore,

> Search while thou wilt, and let thy reason goe
> To ransome truth even to the Abysse below.
> Rally the scattered causes, and that line
> Which nature twists be able to untwine.
> It is thy Makers will, for unto none
> But unto reason can he ere be knowne.
> The Devills doe know thee, but those damned meteours
> Build not thy glory, but confound thy creatures.

[1] *Added in PL.*

[2] *PL have:* was made not so much to be inhabited by man, as to be contemplated, studied or known by man.

Teach my endeavours so thy workes to read,
That learning them, in thee I may proceed.
Give thou my reason that instructive flight,
Whose weary wings may on thy hands still light.
Teach me to soare aloft, yet ever so,
When neare the Sunne, to stoope againe below.
Thus shall my humble feathers safely hover,
And though neere earth, more then the heavens discover.
And then at last, when homeward I shall drive
Rich with the spoyles of nature to my hive,
There will I sit, like that industrious flye,
Buzzing thy prayses, which shall never die
Till death abrupts them, and succeeding glory
Bids me goe on in a more lasting story.

And this is almost all wherein an humble creature may endeavour to requite, and someway to retribute unto his Creator; for if not he that sayeth *Lord Lord; but he that doth the will of the Father shall be saved;* certainly our wills must bee our performances, and our intents make out our actions; otherwise our pious labours shall finde anxiety in our graves, and our best endeavours not hope, but feare a resurrection.

THERE is but one first cause, and foure second causes of all things; some are without efficient, as God; others without matter, as Angels; some without forme, as the first matter; but every Essence, created or uncreated, hath its finall cause, and some positive end both of its Essence and operation; This is the cause I grope after in the workes of nature, on this hangs the providence of God; to raise so beauteous a structure, as the world and the creatures thereof, was but his Art; but their sundry and divided operations with their predestinated ends, are from the treasury of his wisedome. In the causes, nature, and affections of the Eclipse of [the] Sunne and Moone, there is most excellent speculation;[1] but to profound farther, and to contemplate a reason why his providence hath so disposed and ordered their motions in that vast circle, as to conjoyne and obscure each other, is a sweeter piece of reason, and a diviner

PL *add*: and most sweet philosophy.

PART I point of Philosophy; therefore sometimes, and in some things there appeares to mee as much divinity in *Galen* his Books *De usu partium,* as in *Suarez* Metaphysicks: had *Aristotle* beene as curious in the enquiry of this cause as he was of the other, hee had not left behinde him an imperfect piece of Philosophy, but an absolute tract of Divinity.

Section 15 *NATURA nihil agit frustra,* is the onely indisputable axiome in Philosophy; there are no *Grotesques* in nature; nor any thing framed to fill up empty cantons, and unnecessary spaces; in the most imperfect creatures, and such as were not preserved in the Arke, but having their seeds and principles in the wombe of nature, are every-where where the power of the Sun is; in these is the wisedome of his hand discovered; Out of this ranke *Solomon* chose the object of his admiration; indeed what reason may not goe to Schoole to the wisedome of Bees, Aunts, and Spiders? what wise hand teacheth them to doe what reason cannot teach us? ruder heads stand amazed at those prodigious pieces of nature, Whales, Elephants, Dromidaries, and Camels; these I confesse, are the Colossus and Majestick pieces of her hand; but in these narrow Engines there is more curious Mathematicks, and the civilitie of these little Citizens, more neatly[1] sets forth the wisedome of their Maker; Who admires not *Regio-Montanus* his Fly beyond his Eagle, or wonders not more at the operation of two soules in those little bodies, than but one in the trunck of a Cedar? I could never content my contemplation with those generall pieces of wonder, the flux and reflux of the sea, the encrease of Nile, the conversion of the Needle to the North; and [therefore] have studied to match and parallel those in the more obvious and neglected pieces of Nature, which without further travell I can doe in the Cosmography of my selfe; wee carry with us the wonders, wee seeke without us: There is all *Africa,* and her prodigies in us; we are that bold and adventurous piece of nature, which he that studies wisely learnes in a *compendium,* what others labour at in a divided piece and endlesse volume.

Section 16 THUS there are two bookes from whence I collect my Divinity; besides that written one of God, another of his servant Nature,

[1] *PL have:* doe more powerfully and neatly set forth.

that universall and publik Manuscript, that lies expans'd unto
the eyes of all; those that never saw him in the one, have
discovered him in the other: This was the Scripture and
Theology of the Heathens; the naturall motion of the Sun made
them more admire him, than its supernaturall station did the
Children of Israel; the ordinary effects of nature wrought more
admiration in them, than in the other all his miracles; surely
the Heathens knew better how to joyne and reade these mysticall
letters, than wee Christians, who cast a more carelesse eye on
these common Hieroglyphicks, and disdain to suck Divinity
from the flowers of nature. Nor do I so forget God, as to adore
the name of Nature; which I define not with the Schooles, the
principle of motion and rest, but, that streight and regular line,
that setled and constant course the wisedome of God hath
ordained the actions of his creatures, according to their severall
kinds. To make a revolution every day is the nature of the
Sun, because [it is] that necessary course which God hath
ordained it, from which it cannot swerve, but by a faculty from
that voyce which first did give it motion. Now this course of
Nature God seldome alters or perverts, but like an excellent
Artist hath so contrived his worke, that with the selfe same
instrument, without a new creation hee may effect his obscurest
designes. Thus he sweetned the water with a wood, preserved
the creatures in the Arke, which the blast of his mouth might
have as easily created: for God is like a skilfull Geometrician,
who when more easily, and with one stroke of his Compasse, he
might describe, or divide a right line, had yet rather doe this,
[though] in a circle or longer way, according to the constituted
and forelaid principles of his art: yet this rule of his hee doth
sometimes pervert, to acquaint the world with his prerogative,
lest the arrogancy of our reason should question his power, and
conclude he could not; & thus I call the effects of nature the
works of God, whose hand & instrument she only is; and therefore to ascribe his actions unto her, is to devolve the honor of
[God], the principall agent, upon the instrument; which if with
reason we may doe, then let our hammers rise up and boast
they have built our houses, and our pens receive the honour of
our writings. I hold there is a general beauty in [all] the works
of God, and therefore no deformity in any kind or species of

PART I creature whatsoever: I cannot tell by what Logick we call a Toad, a Beare, or an Elephant, ugly; they being created in those outward shapes and figures which best expresse the actions of their inward formes; and having past [with approbation] that generall visitation of God, who saw that all that he had made was good, that is, conformable to his will, which abhors deformity, and is the rule of order and beauty. There is [therefore] no deformity but in monstrosity, wherein notwithstanding there is a kind of beauty, Nature so ingeniously contriving those irregular parts, as they become sometimes more remarkable than the principall Fabrick. To speake yet more narrowly, there was never anything ugly, or mis-shapen, but the Chaos; wherein notwithstanding, to speake strictly, there was no deformity, because no forme; nor was it yet impregnate by the voyce of God: Now nature is not at variance with art, nor art with nature; they being both the servants of his providence: Art is the perfection of Nature: Were the world now as it was the sixt day, there were yet a Chaos: Nature hath made one world, and Art another. In briefe, all things are artificiall, for Nature is the Art of God.

Section 17 THIS is the ordinary and open way of his providence, which art and industry have in a good part discovered, whose effects wee may foretell without an Oracle; To foreshew these is not Prophesie, but Prognostication.[1] There is another way full of Meanders and Labyrinths, whereof the Devill and Spirits have no exact Ephemerides, and that is a more particular and obscure method of his providence, directing the operations of individualls and single Essences; this we call Fortune, that serpentine and crooked line, whereby he drawes those actions [that] his wisedome intends in a more unknowne and secret way. This cryptick and involved method of his providence have I ever admired, nor can I relate the history of my life, the occurrences of my dayes, the escapes of dangers, and hits of chance with a *Bezo las Manos* to Fortune, or a bare Gramercy to my good starres: *Abraham* might have thought [that] the Ram in the thicket came thither by accident; humane reason would have said that meere chance conveyed *Moses* in the Arke to the sight of *Pharaohs* daughter; what a Labyrinth is there in the story of

---

[1] *PL have*: a bare Prognostication.

Joseph, able to convert a Stoick? Surely there are in every mans PART I
life certaine rubs, doublings and wrenches which pass a while
under the effects of chance, but at the last, well examined, prove
the meere hand of God: 'Twas not dumbe chance, that to
discover the Fougade or Powder Plot, contrived the letter.[1]
I like the victory of 88. the better for that one occurrence which
our enemies imputed to our dishonour, and the partiality of
Fortune: to wit, the tempests and contrarietie of winds. King
Philip did not detract from the Nation, when he said, he sent
his Armado to fight with men, and not to combate with the
winds. Where there is a manifest disproportion between the
powers and forces of two severall agents, upon a maxime of
reason wee may promise the victory to the superiour; but when
unexpected accidents slip in, and unthought of occurrences
intervene, these must proceed from a power that owes no
obedience to those axioms: where, as in the writing upon the
wall, we behold the hand, but see not the spring that moves it.
The successe of that pety Province of Holland (of which the
Grand Seignieur proudly said, That if they should trouble him
as they did the Spaniard, hee would send his men with shovels
and pick-axes and throw it into the Sea) I cannot altogether
ascribe to the ingenuity and industry of the people, but to the
mercy of God, that hath disposed them to such a thriving
Genius; and to the will of his providence, that dispenseth her
favour to each Countrey in their preordinate season. All cannot
be happy at once; for, because the glory of one State depends
upon the ruine of another, there is a revolution and vicissitude
of their greatnesse, which must obey the swing of that wheele,
not moved by intelligences, but by the hand of God, whereby
all States arise to their Zenith and verticall points, according to
their predestinated periods. For the lives not onely of men, but of
Commonweales, and the whole world, run not upon a Helix that
still enlargeth; but on a Circle, where, arriving to their Meridian,
they decline in obscurity, and fall under the Horizon againe.

THESE must not therefore bee named the effects of fortune, Section 18
but in a relative way, and as we terme the workes of nature.

[1] *1643 has*: contrived a miscarriage in the letter. *PL have*: that in the discovery of the Powder Plot contrived the letter to a hard vizard.

PART I It was the ignorance of mans reason that begat this very name, and by a carelesse terme miscalled the providence of God: for there is no liberty for causes to operate in a loose and stragling way, nor any effect whatsoever, but hath its warrant from some universall or superiour cause. 'Tis not a ridiculous devotion, to say a Prayer before a game at Tables; for even in *sortilegies* and matters of greatest uncertainty, there is a setled and preordered course of effects; 'tis we that are blind, not fortune: because our eye is too dim to discover the mystery of her effects, we foolishly paint her blind, & hoodwink the providence of the Almighty. I cannot justifie that contemptible Proverb, *That fooles onely are fortunate;* or that insolent Paradox, *That a wise man is out of the reach of fortune;* much lesse those opprobrious Epithets of Poets, *Whore, Baud,* and *Strumpet:* 'Tis, I confesse, the common fate of men of singular gifts of mind, to be destitute of those of fortune; which doth not any way deject the spirits of wiser judgements, who throughly understand the justice of this proceeding; and being enriched with higher donatives, cast a more carelesse eye on these vulgar parts of felicity. 'Tis a most unjust ambition, to desire to engrosse the mercies of the Almighty, not to be content with the goods of [the] mind, without a possession of those of [the] body or fortune: and 'tis an errour worse than heresie,[1] to adore these complementall & circumstantiall pieces of felicity, and undervalue those perfections and essentiall points of happinesse, wherein we resemble our Maker. To wiser desires 'tis satisfaction enough to deserve, though not to enjoy, the favours of fortune; let providence provide for fooles: 'tis not partiality, but equity in God, who deales with us but as our naturall parents; those that are able of body and mind, he leaves to their deserts; to those of weaker merits hee imparts a larger portion, and pieces out the defect of [the] one by the excesse of the other. Thus have wee no just quarrell with Nature, for leaving us naked, or to envie the hornes, hoofs, skins, and furs of other creatures, being provided with reason, that can supply them all. Wee need not labour with so many arguments to confute judiciall Astrology; for if there be a truth therein, it doth not injure Divinity; if to be born under *Mercury* disposeth us to be witty, under *Jupiter* to be wealthy, I doe not owe a

[1] *PL have:* Tis a heresie more than an errour.

knee unto these, but unto that mercifull hand that hath [dis-
posed and] ordered my indifferent and uncertaine nativity unto
such benevolous aspects. Those that held that all things were
governed by fortune had not erred, had they not persisted there:
The Romans that erected a Temple to Fortune, acknowledged
therein, though in a blinder way, somewhat of Divinity; for,
in a wise supputation, all things begin and end in the Almighty.
There is a neerer way to heaven than *Homers* chaine; an easie
Logick may conjoyne heaven and earth in one argument, and
with lesse than a Sorites resolve all things into God. For though
wee Christen effects by their most sensible and nearest causes,
yet is God the true and infallible cause of all, whose concourse,
though it be generall, yet doth it subdivide it selfe into the
particular actions of everything, and is that spirit, by which
each singular essence not onely subsists, but performes its
operations.

THE bad construction and perverse comment on these paire
of second causes, or visible hands of God, have perverted the
devotion of many unto Atheisme; who forgetting the honest
advisoes of faith, have listened unto the conspiracie of Passion
and Reason. I have therefore alwayes endeavoured to compose
those fewds and angry dissentions between affection, faith, and
reason: For there is in our soule a kind of Triumvirate, or Triple
government of three competitors, which distract the peace of
this our Common-wealth, not lesse than did that other the
State of Rome.
    As Reason is a rebell unto Faith, so Passion unto Reason: As
the propositions of Faith seeme absurd unto Reason, so the
Theorems of Reason unto passion, and both unto Faith;[1] yet
a moderate and peaceable discretion may so state and order the
matter, that they may bee all Kings, and yet make but one
Monarchy, every one exercising his Soveraignty and Prerogative in a due time and place, according to the restraint and limit
of circumstance. There are, as in Philosophy, so in Divinity,
sturdy doubts, and boysterous objections, wherewith the
unhappinesse of our knowledge too neerely acquainteth us.
More of these no man hath knowne than my selfe, which I

    [1] *JW, 1642, and 1643 have:* reason; *but the sense seems to require* Faith.

PART I   confesse I conquered, not in a martiall posture, but on my knees. For our endeavours are not onely to combate with doubts, but alwayes to dispute with the Devill; the villany of that spirit takes a hint of infidelity from our Studies, and by demonstrating a naturality in one way, makes us mistrust a miracle in another. Thus having perus'd the Archidoxis and read the secret Sympathies of things, he would disswade my beliefe from the miracle of the Brazen Serpent, make me conceit that image work'd by Sympathie, and was but an Aegyptian tricke to cure their diseases without a miracle. Againe, having seene some experiments of *Bitumen*, and having read farre more of *Naphta*, he whispered to my curiositie the fire of the Altar might be naturall; and bid me mistrust a miracle in *Elias* when he entrench'd the Altar round with water; for that inflamable substance yeelds not easily unto water, but flames in the armes of its Antagonist: and thus would hee inveagle my beliefe to thinke the combustion of *Sodom* might be naturall, and that there was an Asphaltick and Bituminous nature in that Lake before the fire of *Gomorrha*: I know that Manna is now plentifully gathered in *Calabria*, and *Josephus* tels me, in his dayes 'twas as plentifull in *Arabia;* the Devill therefore made the *quere,* Where was then the miracle in the dayes of *Moses?* the Israelites saw but that in his time, the natives of those Countries behold in ours. Thus the Devill playd at Chesse with mee, and yeelding a pawne, thought to gaine a Queen of me, taking advantage of my honest endeavours; and whilst I labour'd to raise the structure of my reason, hee striv'd to undermine the edifice of my faith.

Section 20   NEITHER had these or any other ever such advantage of me, as to incline me to any point of infidelity or desperate positions of Atheisme; for I have beene these many yeares of opinion there was never any. Those that held Religion was the difference of man from beasts, have spoken probably, and proceed upon a principle as inductive as the other: That doctrine of *Epicurus,* that denied the providence of God, was no Atheism, but a magnificent and high-strained conceit of his Majesty, which hee deemed too sublime to minde the triviall actions of those inferiour creatures: That fatall necessitie of the Stoickes, is nothing but the immutable Law of his will. Those that heretofore denied the Divinitie of the holy Ghost, have beene condemned but as Heretickes; and those that now deny our Saviour (though more than Hereticks) are not so much as Atheists: for though they deny two persons in the Trinity, they hold as we do, [that] there is but one God.

That villain and Secretary of Hell, that composed that miscreant piece of the three Impostors;* though divided from all   * [Moses, Religions, and was neither Jew, Turk, nor Christian, was not   Christ, and a positive Atheist. I confesse every Countrey hath its *Machiavell,* every age its *Lucian,* whereof common heads must not heare, nor more advanced judgements too rashly venture on: 'tis the Rhetorick of Satan, and may pervert a loose or prejudicate beleefe.

I CONFESSE I have perused them all, and can discover no- Section 21 thing that may startle a discreet beliefe: yet are there heads carried off with the wind and breath of such motives. I remember a Doctor in Physick of Italy, who could not perfectly believe the immortality of the soule, because *Galen* seemed to make a doubt thereof. With another I was familiarly acquainted in France, a Divine and [a] man of singular parts, that on the same point was so plunged and gravelled with three lines of Seneca,*   * Post mortem that all our Antidotes, drawne from both Scripture and Philo- nihil est, sophy, could not expell the poyson of his errour. There are a   ipsaque mors set of heads, that can credit the relations of Mariners, yet   individua est question the testimony of Saint *Paul;* and peremptorily main- noxia cor- taine the traditions of *Ælian* or *Pliny,* yet in Histories of Scrip- pori, Nec pa- ture, raise Quere's and objections, beleeving no more than they   — Toti mori- can parallel in humane Authors. I confesse there are in Scripture   mur, nulla- stories that doe exceed the fables of Poets, and to a captious   manet No- Reader sound like *Garagantua* or *Bevis:* Search all the Legends of   399, etc.] times past, and the fabulous conceits of these present, and 'twill bee hard to find one that deserves to carry the buckler unto *Sampson;* yet is all this of an easie possibility, if we conceive a divine concourse or an influence but from the little finger of the Almighty. It is impossible that, either in the discourse of man, or in the infallible voyce of God, to the weakenesse of our apprehension, there should not appeare irregularities, contradictions, and antinomies: my selfe could shew a catalogue of

PART I doubts, never yet imagined nor questioned [by any], as I know, which are not resolved at the first hearing; not queries fantastick, or objections of ayre: For I cannot heare of Atoms in Divinity. I can read the story of the Pigeon that was sent out of the Ark, and returned no more, yet not question how shee found out her mate that was left behind: That *Lazarus* was raised from the dead, yet not demand where in the interim his soule awaited; or raise a Law-case, whether his heire might lawfully detaine his inheritance, bequeathed unto him by his death; and he, though restored to life, have no Plea or title unto his former possessions. Whether *Eve* was framed out of the left side of *Adam*, I dispute not, because I stand not yet assured which is the right side of a man, or whether there be any such distinction in Nature; that she was edified out of the ribbe of *Adam* I believe, yet raise no question who shall arise with that ribbe at the Resurrection; whether *Adam* was an Hermaphrodite as the Rabbines contend upon the letter of the Text, because it is contrary to [all] reason, [that] there should bee an Hermaphrodite before there was a woman, or a composition of two natures, before there was a second composed. Likewise, whether the world was created in Autumne, Summer, or Spring, because it was created in them all; for whatsoever Signe the Sun possesseth, those foure seasons are actually existent: It is the nature of this Luminary to distinguish the severall seasons of the yeare, all which it makes at one time in the whole earth, and successively in any part thereof. There are a bundle of curiosities, not onely in Philosophy, but in Divinity, proposed and discussed by men of most supposed abilities, which indeed are not worthy [of] our vacant houres, much lesse our [more] serious studies; Pieces onely fit to be placed in *Pantagruels*

* In Rabelais [the French author.] — Library,* or bound up with *Tartaretus De modo Cacandi.*

Section 22 THESE are niceties that become not those that peruse so serious a Mystery. There are others more generally questioned and called to the Barre, yet me thinkes of an easie, and possible truth. 'Tis ridiculous to put off, or drowne the generall Flood of *Noah* in that particular inundation of *Deucalion:* that there was a Deluge once, seemes not to mee so great a miracle, as that there is not one alwayes. How all the kinds of Creatures, not

only in their owne bulks, but with a competency of food &
sustenance, might be preserved in one Arke, and within the
extent of three hundred cubits, to a reason that rightly examines
it, will appeare very forcible. There is another secret, not
contained in the Scripture, which is more hard to comprehend,
& put the honest Father to the refuge of a Miracle; and that is,
not onely how the distinct pieces of the world, and divided
Ilands should bee first planted by men, but inhabited by Tygers,
Panthers and Beares. How *America* abounded with beasts of
prey, and noxious Animals, yet contained not in it that necessary creature, a Horse. By what passage those, not onely Birds,
but dangerous and unwelcome Beasts came over: How there
bee creatures there, which are not found in this triple Continent;
all which must needs bee stranger unto us, that hold but one
Arke, and that the creatures began their progresse from the
mountaines of *Ararat*. They who, to salve this, would make the
Deluge particular, proceed upon a principle that I can no way
grant; not onely upon the negative of holy Scriptures, but of
mine owne reason, whereby I can make it probable, that the
world was as well peopled in the time of *Noah* as in ours, and
fifteene hundred yeares to people the world, as full a time for
them as foure thousand since have beene to us. There are
other assertions and common tenents drawn from Scripture, and
generally beleeved as Scripture; whereunto, notwithstanding,
I would never betray the libertie of my reason. 'Tis a postulate
to me, that *Methusalem* was the longest liv'd of all the children
of *Adam*, and no man will bee able to prove it; when from the
processe of the Text I can manifest it may be otherwise. That
Judas perished by hanging himself, there is no certainety in
Scripture, though in one place⋆ it seemes to affirme it, and by   ⋆ [Matt.
a doubtfull word hath given occasion [so] to translate it; yet   27.5]
in another place, in a more punctuall description, it makes it
improbable, and seemes to overthrow it. That our Fathers,
after the Flood, erected the Tower of *Babell*, to preserve themselves against a second Deluge, is generally opinioned and
beleeved; yet is there another intention of theirs expressed in
Scripture: Besides, it is improbable from the circumstance of
the place, that is, a plaine in the land of *Shinar*.[1] These are no

[1] *In place of* That Judas . . . the land of Shinar, *P has:* That Judas hanged

PART I points of Faith, and therefore may admit a free dispute. There are yet others, and those familiarly concluded from the Text, wherein (under favour) I see no consequence. [To instance in one or two: as, to prove the Trinity from the speech of God, in the plural number, — faciamus hominem, Let us make man, which is but the common style of Princes, and men of Eminency; — he that shall read one of his Majesty's Proclamations may with the same logick conclude, there be two kings in England. To inferre the obedient respect of wives to their husbands from the example of Sarah, who usually called her husband Lord, which if you examine you shall finde to be no more than Seigneur or Monsieur, which are the ordinary language all civill nations use in their familiar compellations, not to their superiours or equalls, but to their inferiours also and persons of lower condition].¹ The Church of Rome confidently proves the opinion of Tutelary Angels, from that answer when Peter knockt at the doore, '*Tis not he but his Angel;* that is, might some say, his Messenger, or some body from him; for so the Originall signifies, and is as likely to be the doubtfull Families meaning. This exposition I once suggested to a young Divine, that answered upon this point, to which I remember the *Franciscan* Opponent replyed no more, but, That it was a new and no authentick interpretation.

Section 23 THESE are but the conclusions, and fallible discourses of man upon the word of God, for such I doe [verily] beleeve the holy Scriptures; yet were it of man, I could not choose but say, it is one of the most singular, and superlative Pieces that hath been extant since the Creation; were I a Pagan I should not refraine the Lecture of it; and cannot but commend the judgement of *Ptolomy,* that could not think his Library compleate without it: the Alcoran of the Turks (I speake without prejudice) is an ill composed Piece, containing in it vaine and ridiculous errours in Philosophy, impossibilities, fictions, and vanities beyond

himself 'tis an absurdity and an affirmation that is not expressed in the text, but quite contrarie to the words and their externall construction. With this paradoxe I netled an angrie Jesuite who had that day let this fall in his sermon, who afterwards, upon a serious perusall of the text, confessed my opinion, and prooved a courteous friend to me a stranger, and no enemy.

¹ *This passage from* To instance *to* England *is in the MSS and the unauthorized editions: the remainder is in P only.*

laughter maintained by evident and open Sophismes, the policy
of Ignorance, deposition of Universities, and banishment of
Learning, that hath gotten foot by armes and violence; This
without a blow hath disseminated it selfe through the whole
earth. It is not unremarkable what *Philo* first observed, That
the law of *Moses* continued two thousand yeares without the
least alteration; whereas, we see, the Laws of other Commonweales to alter with occasions; and even those that pretended
their originall from some Divinity, to have vanished without
trace or memory. I beleeve, besides *Zoroaster*, there were divers
that writ before *Moses*, who notwithstanding have suffered the
common fate of time. Mens Workes have an age like themselves;
and though they out-live their Authors, yet have they a stint
and period to their duration: This onely is a Worke too hard for
the teeth of time, and cannot perish but in those generall flames,
when all things shall confesse their ashes.

I HAVE heard some with deepe sighs lament the lost lines of
Cicero; others with as many groanes deplore the combustion of
the Library of *Alexandria;* for my owne part, I think there be
too many in the world, and could with patience behold the
urne and ashes of the *Vatican*, could I with a few others recover
the perished leaves of *Solomon*, [the sayings of the Seers, and the
Chronicles of the Kings of Judas].[1] I would not omit a Copy of
Enochs Pillars, had they many neerer Authors than *Josephus*, or
did not relish somewhat of the Fable. Some men have written
more than others have spoken; *Pineda** quotes more Authors in   * *Pineda* in his
one worke, than are necessary in a whole world. Of those three   *Monarchia
great inventions* of *Germany*, there are two which are not without Ecclesiastica*
their incommodities, and 'tis disputable whether they exceed   quotes one
not their use and commodities. 'Tis not a melancholy *Utinam* of   thousand and
mine owne, but the desire of better heads, that there were a   fortie
generall Synod; not to unite the incompatible differences of   Authors.
Religion, but for the benefit of learning, to reduce it as it lay   * [Gunnes,
at first in a few and solid Authours; and to condemne to the   Printing, the
fire those swarms and millions of *Rhapsodies*, begotten onely to   Mariner's
distract and abuse the weaker judgements of Scholars, and to   Compass.]
maintaine the Trade and Mystery of Typographers.

[1] *Added by P only.*

I CANNOT but wonder with what exceptions the *Samari-tanes* could confine their beliefe to the *Pentateuch*, or five Books of *Moses*. I am amazed[1] at the Rabbinicall Interpretations of the Jews, upon the Old Testament, as much as their defection from the New: and truely it is beyond wonder, how that contemptible and degenerate issue of *Jacob*, once so devoted to Ethnick Superstition, and so easily seduced to the Idolatry of their Neighbours, should now in such an obstinate and peremptory beliefe, adhere unto their owne Doctrine, expect impossibilities, and in the face and eye of the Church persist without the least hope of conversion: This is a vice in them, but were a virtue in us; for obstinacy in a bad cause, is but constancy in a good. And herein I must accuse those of my own Religion; for there is not any of such a fugitive faith, such an unstable belief, as a Christian; none that do so oft transforme themselves, not into severall shapes of Christianity and of the same Species, but into more unnaturall and contrary formes of Jew and Mahometan; that from the name of Saviour can descend to the bare terme of Prophet; and from an old beliefe that he is come, fall to a new expectation of his comming: It is the promise of Christ to make us all one flock; but how and when this union shall be, is as obscure to me as the last day. Of those foure members of Religion wee hold a slender proportion; there are I confesse some new additions, yet small to those which accrew to our Adversaries, and those onely drawne from the revolt of Pagans, men but of negative impieties, and such as deny Christ, but because they never heard of him: But the Religion of the Jew is expresly against the Christian, and the Mahometan against both; for the Turke, in the bulke hee now stands is beyond all hope of conversion; if hee fall asunder there may be conceived hopes, yet not without strong improbabilities. The Jew is obstinate in all fortunes; the persecutions of fifteene hundred yeares have but confirmed them in their errour: they have already endured whatsoever may be inflicted, and have suffered, in a bad cause, even to the condemnation of their enemies. Persecution is a bad and indirect way to plant Religion; It hath beene the un-happy method of angry devotions, not onely to confirme honest Religion, but wicked Heresies, and extravagant opinions. It

[1] *1643 has*: ashamed. *PRJN have*: amazed.

was the first stone and basis of our Faith, none can more justly
boast of persecutions, and glory in the number and valour of
Martyrs; For, to speake properly, those are true and almost
onely examples of fortitude: Those that are fetch'd from the
field, or drawne from the actions of the Campe, are not oft-
times so truely precedents of valour as audacity, and at the best
attaine but to some bastard piece of fortitude: If wee shall
strictly examine the circumstances and requisites which *Aristotle*
requires to true and perfect valour, we shall finde the name
onely in his Master *Alexander,* and as little in that Roman
Worthy, *Julius Cæsar;* and if any, in that easie and active part,[1]
have done so nobly as to deserve that name, yet in the passive
and more terrible piece these have surpassed, and in a more
heroicall way may claime the honour of that Title. 'Tis not
in the power of every honest faith to proceed thus farre, or
passe to Heaven through the flames; every one hath it not
in that full measure, nor in so audacious and resolute a temper,
as to endure those terrible tests and trialls, who notwithstanding in a peaceable way doe truely adore their Saviour, and have
(no doubt) a faith acceptable in the eyes of God.

NOW as all that die in warre are not termed Souldiers, so
neither can I properly terme all those that suffer in matters of
Religion Martyrs. The Councell of *Constance* condemnes *John
Husse* for an Heretick; the Stories of his owne party stile him a
Martyr; He must needs offend the Divinity of both, that sayes
hee was neither the one nor the other: There are questionlesse
many canonized on earth, that shall never be [called] Saints in
Heaven; and have their names in Histories and Martyrologies,
who in the eyes of God, are not so perfect Martyrs as was that
wise Heathen,★ that suffered on a fundamentall point of Religion, ★ [Socrates]
the Unity of God. I have often pitied the miserable Bishop★ that ★ [Virgilius]
suffered in the cause of *Antipodes,* yet cannot choose but accuse
him of as much madnesse, for exposing his living on such a
trifle, as those of ignorance and folly that condemned him. I
think my conscience will not give me the lie, if I say, there are not
many extant that in a noble way feare the face of death lesse than
my selfe; yet, from the morall duty I owe to the Commandements

[1] *Thus in PRJN; 1643 has:* way.

D

PART I of God, and the naturall respect that I tender unto the conservation of my essence and being, I would not perish upon a
Ceremony, Politick point or indifferency: nor is my beleefe of
that untractable temper, as not to bow at their obstacles, or
connive at matters wherein there are not manifest impieties:
The leaven therefore and ferment of all, not onely Civill, but
Religious actions, is wisedome; without which, to commit our
selves to the flames is Homicide, and (I feare) but to passe
through one fire into another.

Section 27 THAT Miracles are ceased, I can neither prove, nor absolutely
deny, much lesse define the time and period of their cessation;
that they survived Christ, is manifest upon record of Scripture;
that they out-lived the Apostles also, and were revived at the
conversion of Nations, many yeares after, we cannot deny, if
wee shall not question those Writers whose testimonies wee
doe not controvert, in points that make for our owne opinions;
therefore that may have some truth in it that is reported of[1] the
Jesuites and their Miracles in the Indies, I could wish it were
true, or had any other testimony then their owne Pennes: they
may easily beleeve those Miracles abroad, who daily conceive
a [far] greater at home; the transmutation of those visible
elements into the body and blood of our Saviour: for the conversion of water into wine, which he wrought in *Cana*, or what
the Devill would have had him do in the wildernesse, of stones
into Bread, compared to this, will scarce deserve the name of a
Miracle: Though indeed, to speake strictly,[2] there is not one
Miracle greater than another, they being the extraordinary
effects of the hand of God, to which all things are of an equall
facility; and to create the world as easie as one single creature.
For this is also a miracle, not onely to produce effects against, or
above Nature, but before Nature; and to create Nature as great
a miracle, as to contradict or transcend her. Wee doe too
narrowly define the power of God, restraining it to our capacities. I hold that God can doe all things, how he should work
contradictions I do not understand, yet dare not therefore
deny. I cannot see why the Angel of God should question
Esdras to recall the time past, if it were beyond his owne power;

---

[1] *Thus in PRJN; 1643 has:* by.   [2] *Thus in RJN; 1643 has:* properly.

or that God should pose mortalitie in that, which hee could not
performe himselfe. I will not say God cannot, but hee will not
performe many things, which wee plainely affirme he cannot:
this I am sure is the mannerliest proposition, wherein notwithstanding I hold no Paradox. For strictly his power is [but] the
same with his will, and they both with all the rest doe make
but one God.

THEREFORE that Miracles have beene I doe beleeve; that
they may yet bee wrought by the living I doe not deny: but
have no confidence in those which are fathered on the dead;
and this hath ever made me suspect the efficacy of reliques,
examine the bones, question the habits and appertinencies of
Saints and even of Christ himselfe: I cannot conceive why the
Crosse that *Helena* found and whereon Christ himself died
should have power to restore others unto life; I excuse not
Constantine from a fall off his horse, or a mischiefe from his
enemies, upon the wearing those nayles on his bridle which our
Saviour bore upon the Crosse in his hands: I compute among
your *Piae fraudes*, nor many degrees before cosnecrated swords   ✓ Sp.
and roses, that which *Baldwin* King of Jerusalem return'd the
Genovese for their cost and paines in his warre, to wit the ashes of
John the Baptist. Those that hold the sacntitie of the soules
doth leave behind a tincture and sacred facultie on their bodies,
speake naturally of Miracles, and doe not salve the doubt.
Now one reason I tender so little devotion unto reliques is,
I think, the slender and doubtfull respect I have alwayes held
unto Antiquities: for that indeed which I admire is farre before
antiquity, that is Eternity, and that is God himselfe; who
though hee be stiled the Antient of dayes, cannot receive the
adjunct of antiquity, who was before the world, and shall be
after it, yet is not older then it: for in his yeares there is no
Climacter, his duration is' eternity, and farre more venerable
then antiquitie.

BUT above all the rest, I wonder how the curiositie of wiser
heads could passe that great and indisputable miracle [of] the
cessation of Oracles: and in what swoun their reasons lay, to
content themselves and sit downe with such far-fetch'd and

PART I ridiculous reasons as *Plutarch* alleadgeth for it. The Jewes that can beleeve the supernaturall solstice of the Sunne in the dayes of *Joshua*, have yet the impudence to deny the Eclipse, which even Pagans[1] confessed at his death: but for this, it is edevint

In his Oracle of Augustus. beyond all contradiction,* the Devill himselfe confessed it. Certainly it is not a warrantable curiosity, to examine the verity of Scripture by the concordance of humane history, or seek to confirme the Chronicle of *Hester* or *Daniel*, by the authority of *Megasthenes* or *Herodotus*. I confesse I have had an unhappy curiosity this way, till I laughed my selfe out of it with a piece of *Justine*, where hee delivers that the children of *Israel* for being scabbed were banished out of Egypt. And truely since I have understood the occurrences of the world, and know in what counterfeit shapes & deceitfull vizzards times present represent on the stage things past; I doe beleeve them little more than things to come. Some have beene of my opinion, and endeavoured to write the History of their own lives; wherein *Moses* hath outgone them all, and left not onely the story of his life, but as some will have it of his death also.

Section 30 IT is a riddle to me, how this [very] story of Oracles hath not worm'd out of the world that doubtfull conceit of Spirits and Witches; how so many learned heads should so farre forget their Metaphysicks, and destroy the Ladder and scale of creatures, as to question the existence of Spirits: for my [owne] part, I have ever beleeved, and doe now know, that there are Witches; they that doubt of these, doe not onely deny them, but Spirits; and are obliquely and upon consequence a sort, not of Infidels, but Atheists. Those that to confute their incredulity desire to see apparitions, shall questionlesse never behold any, nor have the power to be so much as Witches; the Devill hath them already in a heresie as capitall as Witchcraft, and to appeare to them, were but to convert them: Of all the delusions wherewith he deceives mortalitie, there is not any that puzleth mee more than the Legerdemain of *Changelings;* I doe not credit those transformations of reasonable creatures into beasts, or that the Devill hath the power to transpeciate a man into a horse, who tempted Christ (as a triall of his Divinitie) to convert but stones

[1] *Thus in PRJ; 1643 has:* every Pagan.

into bread. I could beleeve that Spirits use with man the act of carnality, and that in both sexes; I conceive they may assume, steale, or contrive a body, wherein there may be action enough to content decrepit lusts or passion to satisfie more active veneries; yet in both, without a possibility of generation: and therefore that opinion, that Antichrist should be borne of the Tribe of *Dan* by conjunction with the Devill, is ridiculous, and a conceit fitter for a Rabbin than a Christian. I hold that the Devill doth really possesse some men, the spirit of melancholy others, the spirit of delusion others; that as the Devill is concealed and denyed by some, so God and good Angels are pretended by others, whereof the late detection of the Maid of Germany* hath left a pregnant example.[1]

* [That lived without meat upon the smell of a Rose.]

AGAINE, I beleeve that all that use sorceries, incantations, and spells, are not Witches, or as we terme them, Magicians; I conceive there is a traditionall Magicke, not learned immediately from the Devill, but at second hand from his Schollers; who having once the secret betrayed, are able, and doe emperically practice without his advice, they both proceeding upon the principles of nature: where actives aptly conjoyned to disposed passives, will under any Master produce their effects. Thus I thinke a great part of Philosophy was at first Witchcraft; which being afterward derived from one to another, proved but Philosophy, and was indeed no more than the honest effects of Nature: What invented by us is Philosophy, learned from him is Magicke. Wee doe surely owe [the honour of] the discovery of many secrets both to good and bad Angels. I could never passe that sentence of *Paracelsus* without an asterisk or annotation; *Ascendens constellatum multa revelat, quærentibus magnalia naturæ*,* i. e. *opera Dei*. I doe thinke that many mysteries ascribed to our owne inventions, have beene the courteous revelations of Spirits; for those noble essences in heaven beare a friendly regard unto their fellow-natures on earth; and therefore [I] beleeve that those many prodigies and ominous prognostickes which forerun the ruine of States, Princes, and private persons, are the charitable premonitions of good Angels, which more carelesse enquiries terme but the effects of chance and nature.

Section 31

* Thereby is meant our good Angel appointed us from our nativity.

[1] 'The Maid of Germany' *was Eva Flegen of Mörs.*—Ed.

NOW, besides these particular and divided Spirits, there may be (for ought I know) an universall and common Spirit to the whole world. It was the opinion of *Plato*, and it is yet of the *Hermeticall* Philosophers; if there be a common nature that unites and tyes the scattered and divided individuals into one species, why may there not bee one that unites them all? However, I am sure there is a common Spirit that playes within us, yet makes no part of us, and that is the Spirit of God, the fire and scintillation of that noble and mighty Essence, which is the life and radicall heat of spirits, and those essences that know not the vertue of the Sunne; a fire quite contrary to the fire of Hell: This is that gentle heate that brooded on the waters,* and in six dayes hatched the world; this is that irradiation that dispells the mists of Hell, the clouds of horrour, feare, sorrow, [and] despaire; and preserves the region of the mind in serenity: whosoever feels not the warme gale and gentle ventilation of this Spirit, (though I feele his pulse) I dare not say he lives; for truely without this, to mee there is no heat under the Tropick; nor any light, though I dwelt in the body of the Sunne.

[Spiritus Domini incubabat acquis Gen. 1.]

> As when the labouring sun hath wrought his track,
> Up to the top of lofty Cancers back,
> The ycie Ocean cracks, the frozen pole
> Thawes with the heat of that celestiall coale;
> So when thy absent beames begin t' impart
> Againe a Solstice on my frozen heart,
> My winters ov'r, my drooping spirits sing,
> And every part revives into a Spring.
> But if thy quickning beames a while decline,
> And with their light blesse not this Orbe of mine,
> A chilly frost surpriseth every member,
> And in the midst of June I feele December.
> [Keep still in my horizon, for, to mee,
> 'Tis not the Sun, that makes the day, but thee].[1]
> O how this earthly temper doth debase
> The noble Soule, in this her humble place!
> Whose wingy nature ever doth aspire
> To reach that place whence first it took its fire.

[1] *These two lines omitted in* 1643.

These flames I feele, which in my heart doe dwell,
Are not thy beames, but take their fire from hell:
O quench them all, and let thy light divine
Be as the Sunne to this poore Orbe of mine.
And to thy sacred Spirit convert those fires,
Whose earthly fumes choake my devout aspires.

THEREFORE, for Spirits I am so far from denying their existence, that I could easily beleeve, that not onely whole Countries,
but particular persons have their Tutelary, and Guardian
Angels: It is not a new opinion of the Church of *Rome*, but an
old one of *Pythagoras* and *Plato;* there is no heresie in it, and if
not manifestly defin'd in Scripture, yet is it an opinion of a good
and wholesome use in the course and actions of a mans life, and
would serve as an *Hypothesis* to salve many doubts, whereof
common Philosophy affordeth no solution: Now, if you demand
my opinion and Metaphysicks of their natures, I confesse them
very shallow, most in a negative way, like that of God; or in a
comparative, betweene our selves and fellow creatures; for there
is in this Universe a Staire, or manifest Scale of creatures, rising
not disorderly, or in confusion, but with a comely method and
proportion: betweene creatures of mere existence and things of
life, there is a large disproportion of nature; betweene plants
and animals or creatures of sense, a wider difference; between
them and man, a farre greater: and if the proportion held on,
betweene man and Angels there should bee yet a greater. We
doe not comprehend their natures, who retaine the definition★ ★ [Essentia
of *Porphyry*, and distinguish them from our selves by immortal- rationalis im-
ity; for before his fall, man also was immortall; yet must wee mortalis.]
needs affirme that he had a different essence from the Angels:
having therefore no certaine knowledge of their natures, 'tis
no bad method of the Schooles, whatsoever perfection we finde
obscurely in our selves, in a more compleate and absolute way
to ascribe unto them. I beleeve they have an extemporary
knowledge, and upon the first motion of their reason doe what
we cannot without study or deliberation; that they know things
by their formes, and define by specificall difference, what we
describe by accidents and properties; and therefore probabilities
to us may bee demonstrations unto them; that they have

PART I knowledge not onely of the specificall, but [of the] numericall formes of individualls, and understand by what reserved difference each single *Hypostasis* (besides the relation to its species) becomes its numericall selfe. That as the Soule hath a power to move the body it informes, so there's a Faculty to move any, though informe none; ours upon restraint of time, place, and distance; but that invisible hand that conveyed *Habakkuk* to the Lions den, or *Philip* to *Azotus*, infringeth this rule, and hath a secret conveyance, wherewith mortalitie is not acquainted; if they have that intuitive knowledge, whereby as in reflection they behold the thoughts of one another, I cannot peremptorily deny but they know a great part of ours. They that to refute the Invocation of Saints, have denied that they have any knowledge of our affaires below, have proceeded too farre, and must pardon my opinion, till I can thoroughly answer that piece of Scripture, *At the conversion of one sinner the Angels of heaven rejoyce.* I cannot with[1] that great Father securely interpret the worke of the first day, *Fiat lux*, to the creation of Angels, though (I confesse) there is not any creature that hath so neare a glympse of their nature, as light in the Sunne and Elements; we stile it a bare accident, but where it subsists alone, 'tis a spirituall Substance, and may bee an Angel: in briefe, conceive light invisible, and that is a Spirit.

Section 34 THESE are certainly the Magisteriall & master pieces of the Creator, the Flower (or as we may say) the best part of nothing, actually existing, what we are but in hopes, and probabilitie; we are onely that amphibious piece betweene a corporall and spirituall essence, that middle frame that linkes those two together, and makes good the method of God and nature, that jumps not from extreames, but unites the incompatible distances by some middle and participating natures; that wee are the breath and similitude of God, it is indisputable, and upon record of holy Scripture; but to call our selves a Microcosme, or little world, I thought it onely a pleasant trope of Rhetorick, till my nearer judgement and second thoughts told me there was a reall truth therein: for first wee are a rude masse, and in the ranke of creatures, which only are, and have a dull kinde of

---

[1] *Thus in all MSS and 1642. 1643 has*: cannot with those in that.

being, not yet priviledged with life, or preferred to sense or PART I
reason; next we live the life of plants, the life of animals, the life
of men, and at last the life of spirits, running on in one mysterious nature those five kinds of existences, which comprehend
the creatures not of the world, onely, but of the Universe; thus is
man that great and true *Amphibium*, whose nature is disposed
to live not onely like other creatures in divers elements, but in
divided and distinguished worlds; for though there bee but one
[world] to sense, there are two to reason; the one visible; the
other invisible, whereof *Moses* seemes to have left [no]¹ description; and of the other so obscurely that some parts★ thereof are   ★ [The Ele-
yet in controversie; and truely for those first chapters of *Genesis*,   ment of fire.
I must confesse a great deale of obscurity, though Divines have
to the power of humane reason endeavoured to make all goe in
a literall meaning; yet those allegoricall interpretations are also
probable, and perhaps the mysticall method of *Moses* bred up
in the Hieroglyphicall Schooles of the Egyptians.

NOW for that immateriall world, me thinkes we need not   Section 35
wander so farre as the first moveable; for even in this materiall
fabricke the spirits walke as freely exempt from the affections
of time, place, and motion, as beyond the extreamest circumference; doe but extract from the corpulency of bodies, or resolve
things beyond their first matter, and you discover the habitation of Angels, which if I call the ubiquitary, and omnipresent
essence of God, I hope I shall not offend Divinity; for before the
Creation of the world God was really all things. For the Angels
hee created no new world, or determinate mansion, and therefore they are every where his essence is and doe live, at a
distance, even in himselfe: that God made all things for man,
is in some sense true; yet not so farre as to subordinate the
creation of those purer creatures unto ours, though as ministring
spirits they doe, and are willing to fulfill the will of God in these
lower and sublunary affaires of man; God made all things for
himself, and it is impossible hee should make them for any other
end than his owne glory; it is all he can receive, and all that is
without himselfe; for honour being an externall adjunct, and
in the honourer rather than in the person honoured, it was

¹ no *added only by* P.

PART I necessary to make a creature, from whom hee might receive this homage, and that is in the other world Angels, in this, man; which when we neglect, we forget the very end of our creation, and may justly provoke God, not onely to repent that hee hath made the world, but that hee hath sworne hee would not destroy it. That there is but one world, is a conclusion of faith. *Aristotle* with all his Philosophy hath not beene able to prove it, and as weakely that the world was eternall; that dispute much troubled the pennes of the antient Philosophers [who saw no further than the first matter];[1] but *Moses* [hath] decided that question, and all is salved with the new terme of a creation, that is, a production of something out of nothing; and what is that? Whatsoever is opposite to something or more exactly, that which is truely contrary unto God: for he onely is, all others have an existence with dependency and are something but by a distinction; and herein is Divinity conformant unto Philosophy, and generation not onely founded on contrarieties, but also creation; God being all things is contrary unto nothing out of which were made all things, and so nothing became something, and *Omneity* informed *Nullity* into an essence.

Section 36[2] THE whole Creation is a mystery, and particularly that of man; at the blast of his mouth were the rest of the creatures made, and at his bare word they started out of nothing: but in the frame of man (as the text describes it) he played the sensible operator, and seemed not so much to create, as make him; when hee had separated the materials of other creatures, there consequently resulted a forme and soule; but having raised the wals of man, he was driven to a second and harder creation of a substance like himselfe, an incorruptible and immortall soule. For these two affections we have the Philosophy, and opinion of the Heathens, the flat affirmative of *Plato*, and not a negative from *Aristotle:* there is another scruple cast in by Divinity (concerning its production) much disputed in the *Germane* auditories, and with that indifferency and equality of arguments, as leave the controversie undetermined. I am not of *Paracelsus*

---

[1] *These words added by P.*
[2] *In 1643 this section was again numbered 35, the subsequent sections being also misnumbered.*

minde that boldly delivers a receipt to make a man without
conjunction; yet cannot but wonder at the multitude of heads
that doe deny traduction, having no other argument to confirme
their beliefe, then that Rhetoricall sentence, and *Antimetathesis** * [A figure in
of *Augustine, Creando infunditur, infundendo creatur*: either opinion Rethoricke
where one
will consist well enough with religion; yet I should rather incline word is into this, did not one objection haunt mee; not wrung from verted upon
another.]
speculations and subtilties, but from common sense, and
observation; not pickt from the leaves of any author, but bred
among the weeds and tares of mine owne braine. And this is a
conclusion from the equivocall and monstrous productions in
the copulation of man with beast; for if the soule of man bee
not transmitted and transfused in the seed of the parents, why
are not those productions meerely beasts, but have also an
impression and tincture of reason in as high a measure as it can
evidence it selfe in those improper organs? Nor truely can I
peremptorily deny, that the soule in this her sublunary estate,
is wholly and in all acceptions inorganicall; but that for the
performance of her ordinary actions, is required not onely a
symmetry and proper disposition of Organs, but a Crasis and
temper correspondent to its operations; yet is not this masse of
flesh and visible structure the instrument and proper corps of
the soule, but rather of sense, and that the hand of reason. In
our study of Anatomy there is a masse of mysterious Philosophy, and such as reduced the very Heathens to Divinitie; yet
amongst all those rare discoveries, and curious pieces I finde
in the fabricke of man, I doe not so much content my selfe as
in that I finde not, that is, no Organ or instrument for the
rationall soule; for in the braine, which we tearme the seate of
reason, there is not any thing of moment more than I can
discover in the cranie of a beast: and this is a sensible and no
inconsiderable argument of the inorganity of the soule, at least
in that sense we usually so receive it. Thus are we men, and we
know not how; there is something in us, that can be without us,
and will be after us, though it is strange that it hath no history,
what it was before us, nor can tell how it entred in us.

NOW for the wals of flesh, wherein the soule doth seeme to be Section 37
immured before the Resurrection, it is nothing but an ele-

PART I mentall composition, and a fabricke that must fall to ashes; *All flesh is grasse,* is not onely metaphorically, but literally true, for all those creatures [which] we behold, are but the hearbs of the field, digested into flesh in them, or more remotely carnified in our selves. Nay further, we are what we all abhorre, *Antropophagi* and Cannibals, devourers not onely of men, but of our selves; and that not in an allegory, but a positive truth; for all this masse of flesh which wee behold, came in at our mouths: this frame wee looke upon, hath beene upon our trenchers; In briefe, we have devoured our selves [and yet do live and remaine our selves].[1] I cannot beleeve the wisedome of *Pythagoras* did ever positively, and in a literall sense, affirme his *Metempsychosis,* or impossible transmigration of the soules of men into beasts: of all Metamorphoses and transformations,[2] I beleeve onely one, that is of *Lots* wife, for that of *Nabuchodonosor* proceeded not so farre; In all others I conceive there is no further verity then is contained in their implicite sense and morality: I beleeve that the whole frame of a beast doth perish, and is left in the same state after death, as before it was materialled unto life; that the soules of men know neither contrary nor corruption, that they subsist beyond the body, and outlive death by the priviledge of their proper natures, and without a miracle; that the soules of the faithfull as they leave earth, take possession of Heaven: that those apparitions, and ghosts of departed persons, are not the wandring soules of men, but the unquiet walkes of Devils, prompting and suggesting us unto mischiefe, bloud, and villany; instilling, & stealing into our hearts, that the blessed spirits are not at rest in their graves, but wander solicitous of the affaires of the world. That those phantasmes appeare often, and doe frequent Cemiteries, charnall houses, and Churches, it is because those are the dormitories of the dead, where the Devill like an insolent Champion beholds with pride the spoyles and Trophies of his victory in *Adam.*

Section 38 THIS is that dismall conquest we all deplore, that makes us so often cry (O) *Adam, quid fecisti?* I thanke God I have not those

---

[1] *These words are added in all MSS except P.*
[2] *R J NW have:* transformations. *P, 1642, 1643 have:* transmigrations.

strait ligaments, or narrow obligations to the world, as to dote
on life, or be convulst and tremble at the name of death: Not
that I am insensible of the dread and horrour thereof, or by
raking into the bowells of the deceased, [or the] continual sight
of Anatomies, Skeletons, or Cadaverous reliques, like Vespilloes
or Grave-makers, I am become stupid, or have forgot the apprehension of mortality; but that marshalling all the horrours, and
contemplating the extremities thereof, I finde not any thing
therein able to daunt the courage of a man, much lesse a well
resolved Christian. And therefore am not angry at the errour
of our first parents, or unwilling to beare a part in this common
fate, and like the best of them to dye; that is, to cease to breathe,
to take a farewell of the elements, to be a kinde of nothing for a
moment, to be within one instant a spirit. When I take a full
view and circle of my selfe, without this reasonable moderator,
and equal piece of justice, Death, I doe conceive my selfe the
miserablest person extant; were there not another life that I
hope for, all the vanities of this world should not intreat a
moments breath from me; could the Devill worke my beliefe to
imagine I could never[1] dye, I would not out-live that very
thought; I have so abject a conceit of this common way of
existence, this retaining to the Sunne and Elements, I cannot
thinke this is to be a man, or to live according to the dignitie of
humanity; in expectation of a better I can with patience embrace this life; yet in my best meditations doe often desire[2]
death; [It is a symptom of melancholy to be afraid of death, yet
sometimes to desire it; this latter I have often discovered in
my selfe, and thinke no man ever desired life as I have sometimes
death].[3] I honour any man that contemnes it, nor can I highly
love any that is afraid of it; this makes me naturally love a
Souldier, and honour those tattered and contemptible Regi-
ments that will die at the command of a Sergeant. For a Pagan
there may bee some motives to bee in love with life; but for a
Christian that is amazed at death, I see not how hee can escape
this Dilemma: that he is too sensible of this life, or hopelesse
of the life to come.

[1] *PJN, 1642 have* : never. *RW, 1643 have* : ever.
[2] *All MSS, 1642 have*: desire. *1643 has*: defie.
[3] *These words are added in the MSS.*

SOME Divines count *Adam* 30 yeares old at his creation, because they suppose him created in the perfect age and stature of man; and surely wee are all out of the computation of our age, and every man is some moneths elder than hee bethinkes him; for we live, move, have a being, and are subject to the actions of the elements, and the malice of diseases in that other world, the truest Microcosme, the wombe of our mother; for besides that generall and common existence wee are conceived to hold in our Chaos, and whilst wee sleepe within the bosome of our causes, wee enjoy a being and life in three distinct worlds, wherein we receive most manifest graduations: In that obscure world and wombe of our mother, our time is short, computed by the Moone, yet longer than the dayes of many creatures that behold the Sunne; our selves being yet not without life, sense, and reason; though for the manifestation of its actions it awaits the opportunity of objects; and seemes to live there but in its roote and soule of vegetation: entring afterwards upon the scene of the world, wee arise up and become another creature, performing the reasonable actions of man, and obscurely manifesting that part of Divinity in us, but not in complement and perfection, till we have once more cast our secondine, that is, this slough of flesh, and are delivered into the last world, that ineffable place of Paul, that proper *ubi* of spirits. The smattering I have [in the knowledge] of the Philosophers stone, (which is something more then the perfect exaltation of gold) hath taught me a great deale of Divinity, and instructed my beliefe, how that immortall spirit and incorruptible substance of my soule may lye obscure, and sleepe a while within this house of flesh. Those strange and mysticall transmigrations that I have observed in Silkewormes, turn'd my Philosophy into Divinity. There is in those workes of nature, which seeme to puzle reason, something Divine, and [that] hath more in it then the eye of a common spectator doth discover. [I have therefore forsaken those strict definitions of death, by privation of life, extinction of naturall heate, separation etc. of soule and body, and have framed one in an hermeticall way unto mine owne fancie: *est mutatio qua perficitur nobile illud extractum Microcosmi*; for to mee that consider things in a naturall and experimentall way, man seemes to be but a diges-

tion, or a preparative way unto that last and glorious Elixar PART I
which lies imprisoned in the chaines of flesh, etc.].[1]

I AM naturally bashfull, nor hath conversation, age, or travell, Section 40
beene able to effront, or enharden me; yet I have one part of
modesty, which I have seldome discovered in another, that is
(to speake truly) I am not so much afraid of death, as ashamed
thereof; tis the very disgrace and ignominy of our natures, that
in a moment can so disfigure us that our nearest friends, wives
and Children stand afraid and start at us. The Birds and Beasts
of the field that before in a naturall feare obeyed us, forgetting
all allegiance begin to prey upon us. This very conceite hath in
a tempest disposed and left me willing to be swallowed in the
abysse of waters; wherein I had perished unseene, unpityed,
without wondring eyes, teares of pity, Lectures of mortality, and
none had said, *quantum mutatus ab illo!* Not that I am ashamed
of the Anatomy of my parts, or can accuse nature for playing
the bungler in any part of me, or my owne vitious life for
contracting any shamefull disease upon me, whereby I might
not call my selfe as wholesome a morsell for the wormes as any.

SOME upon the courage of a fruitfull issue, wherein, as in the Section 41
truest Chronicle, they seem to outlive themselves, can with
greater patience away with death. This conceit and counterfeit
subsisting in our progenies seemes to mee a meere fallacy,
unworthy the desires of a man, that can but conceive a thought
of the next world; who, in a nobler ambition, should desire to
live in his substance in Heaven rather than [in] his name and
shadow on earth. And therefore at my death I meane to take a
totall adieu of the world, not caring for a Monument, History,
or Epitaph, not so much as the bare memory of my name to be
found any where but in the universall Register of God: I am
not yet so Cynicall, as to approve the Testament* of *Diogenes*,   * Who willed
nor doe I altogether allow that *Rodomontado* of *Lucan*;   his friend
                                                                    not to bury
                                                                    him but to
    Cælo tegitur, qui non habet urnam.   hang him up
    He that unburied lies wants not his Herse,   with a staffe
    For unto him a tombe's the Universe.   in his hand to
                                                                    fright away
                                                                    the crowes.

     [1] *These sentences are found only in P.*

PART I But commend in my calmer judgement, those ingenuous intentions that desire to sleepe by the urnes of their Fathers, and strive to goe the nearest way unto corruption. I do not envie the temper of Crowes and Dawes, nor the numerous and weary dayes of our Fathers before the Flood. If there bee any truth in Astrology, I may outlive a Jubilee;* as yet I have not seene one revolution of *Saturne*,* nor hath my pulse beate thirty yeares, and yet, excepting one, have seene the Ashes, and left under ground all the Kings of *Europe*, have beene contemporary to three Emperours, foure Grand Signiours, and as many Popes; mee thinkes I have outlived my selfe, and begin to bee weary of the Sunne; I have shaken hands with delight in my warme blood and Canicular dayes; I perceive I doe Anticipate the vices of age, the world to mee is but a dreame, or mockshow, and wee all therein but Pantalones* and Antickes to my severer contemplations.

* [The Jewish computation for 50 yeares.]

* [The Planet of Saturne makes his revolution once in 30 yeares.]

* [A French word for Antickes.]

Section 42 IT is not, I confesse, an unlawfull Prayer to desire to surpasse the dayes of our Saviour, or wish to out-live that age wherein he thought fittest to dye; yet if (as Divinity affirmes) there shall be no gray hayres in Heaven, but all shall rise in the perfect state of men, we doe but out-live those perfections in this world, to be recalled unto them by a greater miracle in the next, and run on here but to be retrograde hereafter. Were there any hopes to out-live vice, or a point to be super-annuated from sin, it were worthy [of] our knees to implore the dayes of *Methuselah*. But age doth not rectifie, but incurvate our natures, turning bad dispositions into worser habits, and (like diseases) brings on incurable vices; for every day as we grow weaker in age, we grow stronger in sinne, and the number of our dayes doth but make our sinnes innumerable. The same vice committed at sixteene, is not the same, though it agree in all other circumstances, at forty; but swels and doubles from the circumstance of our ages, wherein besides the constant and inexcusable habit of transgressing, the maturity of our Judgement cuts off pretence unto excuse or pardon: every sin, the oftner it is committed, the more it acquireth in the quality of evill; as it succeeds in time, so it proceeds in degrees of badnesse; for as they proceed they ever multiply, and like figures in Arith-

meticke, the last stands for more than all that went before it:[1]
And though I thinke no man can live well once but hee that
could live twice, yet, for my owne part, I would not live over
my houres past, or beginne againe the thred of my dayes: not
upon *Cicero*'s ground, because I have lived them well, but for
feare I should live them worse; I find my growing Judgement
dayly instructs me how to be better, but my untamed affections
and confirmed vitiosity make mee dayly doe worse; I finde in
my confirmed age the same sinnes I discovered in my youth;
I committed many then because I was a child, and because I
commit them still I am yet an Infant. Therefore I perceive a
man may bee twice a child before the dayes of dotage, and stand
in need of *Aesons* bath before threescore.

AND truely there goes a great deale of providence to produce
a mans life unto threescore; there is more required than an able
temper for those yeeres; though the radicall humour containe
in it sufficient oyle for seventie, yet I perceive in some it gives
no light past thirtie; men assigne not all the causes of long life
that write whole books thereof. They that found themselves
on the radicall balsome or vitall sulphur of the parts, determine
not why *Abel* liv'd not so long as *Adam*. There is therefore a
secret glome or bottome of our dayes; 'twas his wisedome to
determine them, but his perpetuall and waking providence
that fulfils and accomplisheth them, wherein the spirits, our
selves, and all the creatures of God in a secret and disputed way
doe execute his will. Let them not therefore complaine of im-
maturitie that die about thirty; they fall but like the whole
world, whose solid and well composed substance must not
expect the duration and period of its constitution; when all
things are compleated in it, its age is accomplished, and the last
and generall fever may as naturally destroy it before six thousand, as me before forty: there is therfore some other hand
that twines the thread of life than that of nature; wee are not

---

[1] *The remainder of this section and the whole of the next are wanting in the unauthorized editions and the MSS. These have instead*: The course and order of my
life would be a very death to others: I use myself to all dyets, humours, ayres,
hunger, thirst, cold, heate, want, plenty, necessity, dangers, hazards; when I
am cold, I cure not myself by heate; when sicke not by physicke; those that
know how I live, may justly say, I regard not life, nor stand in feare of death.

PART I onely ignorant in Antipathies and occult qualities, our ends are as obscure as our beginnings, the line of our dayes is drawne by night, and the various effects therein by a pencill that is invisible; wherein though wee confesse our ignorance, I am sure we doe not erre, if wee say, it is the hand of God.

Section 44 I A M much taken with two verses of *Lucan,* since I have beene able not onely, as we doe at Schoole, to construe, but understand [them]:

> *Victurosque Dei celant ut vivere durent,*
> *Felix esse mori.*
> *We're all deluded, vainely searching wayes,*
> *To make us happy by the length of dayes;*
> *For cunningly to make's protract this breath,*
> *The Gods conceale the happiness of Death.*

There be many excellent straines in that Poet, wherewith his Stoicall Genius hath liberally supplyed him; and truely there are singular pieces in the Philosophy of *Zeno,* and doctrine of the Stoickes, which I perceive, delivered in a Pulpit, passe for currant Divinity: yet herein are they in extreames, that can allow a man to be his owne *Assassine,* and so highly extoll the end and suicide of *Cato;* this is indeed not to feare death, but yet to bee afraid of life. It is a brave act of valour to contemne death, but where life is more terrible than death, it is then the truest valour to dare to live, and herein Religion hath taught us a noble example: For all the valiant acts of *Curtius, Scevola* or *Codrus,* do not parallel or match that one of *Job;* and surely there is no torture to the racke of a disease, nor any Poynyards in death it selfe like those in the way or prologue unto it. *Emori nolo, sed me esse mortuum nihil curo,* I would not die, but care not to be dead. Were I of *Cæsars* Religion I should be of his desires, and wish rather to goe off at one blow, then to be sawed in peeces by the grating torture of a disease. Men that looke no further than their outsides thinke health an appertinance unto life, and quarrell with their constitutions for being sick; but I that have examined the parts of man, and know upon what tender filaments that Fabrick hangs, doe wonder that we are not alwayes so; and considering the thousand dores that lead to

death doe thanke my God that we can die but once. 'Tis not
onely the mischiefe of diseases, and the villanie of poysons that
make an end of us; we vainly accuse the fury of Gunnes, and
the new inventions of death; 'tis in the power of every hand to
destroy us, and wee are beholding unto every one wee meete
hee doth not kill us. There is therefore but one comfort left, that
though it be in the power of the weakest arme to take away
life, it is not in the strongest to deprive us of death: God would
not exempt himselfe from that; the misery of immortality in
the flesh he undertooke not, that was in it immortall. Certainly
there is no happinesse within this circle of flesh, nor is it in the
Opticks of these eyes to behold felicity; the first day of our
Jubilee is death; the devill hath therefore fail'd of his desires;
wee are happier with death than we should have beene without
it: there is no misery but in himselfe where there is no end of
misery; and so indeed in his owne sense, the Stoick is in the
right: Hee forgets that hee can die who complaines of misery,
wee are in the power of no calamitie, while death is in our owne.

NOW besides this literall and positive kinde of death, there
are others whereof Divines make mention, and those I thinke,
not meerely Metaphoricall, as Mortification, dying unto sin
and the world; therefore, I say, every man hath a double Horoscope, one of his humanity, his birth; another of his Christianity,
his baptisme, and from this doe I compute or calculate my
Nativitie; not reckoning those *Horæ combustæ*,* and odde dayes,   * [That time
or esteeming my selfe any thing, before I was my Saviours, and   when the
inrolled in the Register of Christ: Whosoever enjoyes not this   moone is in
life, I count him but an apparition, though he weare about him   conjunction,
the sensible affections of flesh. In these morall acceptions, the   and obscured
way to be immortall is to die daily; nor can I thinke I have the   by the Sun,
true Theory of death, when I contemplate a skull, or behold a   the Astrolo-
Skeleton with those vulgar imaginations it casts upon us; I   gers call *Horæ*
have therefore enlarged that common *Memento mori*, into a more   *Combustæ*.]
Christian memorandum, *Memento quatuor novissima*, those foure
inevitable points of us all, Death, Judgement, Heaven and Hell.
Neither did the contemplations of the Heathens rest in their
graves, without a further thought of *Rhadamanth* or some
judiciall proceeding after death, though in another way, and

PART I upon suggestion of their naturall reason. I cannot but marvaile from what *Sybill* or Oracle they stole the prophesy of the worlds destruction by fire, or whence *Lucan* learned to say,

> *Communis mundo superest rogus, ossibus astra*
> *Misturus.*
> There yet remaines to th' world one common fire,
> Wherein our bones with stars shall make one pyre.

I [do] beleeve the world drawes near its end, yet is neither old nor decayed, nor will ever perish upon the ruines of its owne principles. As the Creation was a worke above nature, so is its adversary, annihilation; without which the world hath not its end, but its mutation. Now what fire[1] should bee able to consume it thus farre, without the breath of God, which is the truest consuming flame, my Philosophy cannot informe me. Some beleeve there went not a minute to the worlds creation, nor shal there go to its destruction; those six dayes so punctually described, make not to them one moment, but rather seem to manifest the method and Idea of that great worke in the intellect of God, than the manner how hee proceeded in its operation. I cannot dream that there should be at the last day any such Judiciall proceeding, or calling to the Barre, as indeed the Scripture seemes to imply, and the literall commentators doe conceive: for unspeakable mysteries in the Scriptures are often delivered in a vulgar and illustrative way, and being written unto man, are delivered, not as they truely are, but as they may bee understood; wherein, notwithstanding the different interpretations according to [the] different capacities, [they] may stand firme with our devotion, nor bee any way prejudiciall to each single edification.

Section 46 NOW to determine the day and yeare of this inevitable time, is not onely convincible and statute madnesse, but also manifest impiety; How shall we interpret *Elias* 6000 yeares, or imagine the secret communicated to a Rabbi, which a God hath denyed unto his Angels? It had beene an excellent quære, to have posed
* [The Oracle the devill of *Delphos** and must needs have forced him to some
of Apollo.] strange amphibology; it hath not onely mocked the predictions

---

[1] *Thus in PJN. 1643 has:* force.

of sundry Astrologers in ages past, but the prophecies of many **PART I**
melancholy heads in these present, who neither reasonably
understanding things past, nor present, pretend a knowledge of
things to come; heads ordained onely to manifest the incredible
effects of melancholy, and to fulfill old prophesies, rather than
be the authors of new; [In those dayes there shall be warres and In those
rumours of warres],[1] to me seemes no prophesie, but a constant dayes there
truth, in all times verified since it was [first] pronounced: There lyers and
shall bee signes in the Moone and Starres; how comes he then false pro-
like a theefe in the night, when he gives an item of his comming? phets.
That common signe drawne from the revelation of Antichrist is
as obscure as any; in our common compute he hath beene come
these many yeares, but for my owne part to speake freely,
[omitting those ridiculous Anagrams*], I am half of Paracelsus * [Whereby
opinion, and thinke Antichrist the Philosophers stone in men labour
Divinity, for the discovery and invention whereof, though Pope Anti-
there be prescribed rules, and probable inductions, yet hath christ, from
hardly any man attained the perfect discovery thereof. That making up the
generall opinion that the world drawes neere its end, hath number of the
possessed all ages past as neerely as ours; I am afraid that the Beast.]
Soules that now depart, cannot escape that lingring expostulation of the Saints under the Altar, *Quousque Domine? How long,
O Lord?* and groane in the expectation of the great Jubilee.

THIS is the day that must make good that great attribute of Section 47
God, his Justice; that must reconcile those unanswerable doubts
which torment the wisest understandings, and reduce those
seeming inequalities, and respective distributions in this world,
to an equality and recompensive Justice in the next. This is that
one day, that shall include and comprehend all that went before
it, wherein, as in the last scene, all the Actors must enter to
compleate and make up the Catastrophe of this great peece.
This is the day whose memory hath onely power to make us
honest in the darke, and to bee vertuous without a witnesse.
Ipsa sui pretium virtus sibi, that vertue is her owne reward, is but
a cold principle, and not able to maintaine our variable resolutions in a constant and setled way of goodnesse. I have practised
that honest artifice of *Seneca,* and in my retired and solitary

---

[1] *This passage is printed within brackets in 1643.*

PART I imaginations, to detaine me from the foulenesse of vice, have fancyed to my selfe the presence of my deare and worthiest friends, before whom I should lose my head, rather than be vitious; yet herein I found that there was nought but morall honesty, and this was not to be vertuous for his sake who must reward us at the last. I have tryed if I could reach that great resolution of his, to be honest without a thought of Heaven or Hell; and indeed I found upon a naturall inclination, and inbred loyalty unto vertue, that I could serve her without a livery, yet not in that resolved and venerable way, but that the frailty of my nature, upon an easie temptation, might be induced to forget her. The life therefore and spirit of all our actions, is the resurrection, and stable apprehension, that our ashes shall enjoy the fruits of our pious endeavours; without this, all Religion is a Fallacy, and those impieties of *Lucian, Euripides,* and *Julian* are no blasphemies, but subtile verities, and Atheists have beene the onely Philosophers.

Section 48 HOW shall the dead arise, is no question of my faith; to beleeve onely possibilities, is not faith, but meere Philosophy; many things are true in Divinity, which are neither inducible by reason, nor confirmable by sense; and many things in Philosophy confirmable by sense, yet not inducible by reason. Thus it is impossible by any solid or demonstrative reasons to perswade a man to beleeve the conversion of the Needle to the North; though this be possible, and true, and easily credible, upon a single experiment unto the sense. I beleeve that our estranged and divided ashes shall unite againe; that our separated dust after so many pilgrimages and transformations into the parts of mineralls, Plants, Animals, Elements, shall at the voyce of God returne into their primitive shapes, and joyne againe to make up their primary and predestinated formes. As at the Creation, [of the world] there was a separation of that confused masse into its species, so at the destruction thereof there shall bee a separation into its distinct individuals. As at the Creation of the world, all the distinct species that wee behold, lay involved in one masse, till the fruitfull voyce of God separated this united multitude into its several species: so at the last day, when these corrupted reliques shall be scattered in the wildernesse of

formes, and seeme to have forgot their proper habits, God by a PART I
powerfull voyce shall command them backe into their proper
shapes, and call them out by their single individuals: Then shall
appeare the fertilitie of *Adam,* and the magicke of that sperme
that hath dilated into so many millions. [What is made to be
immortall, Nature cannot, nor will the voyce of God, destroy.
Those bodies that we behold to perish, were in their created
nature immortall, and liable unto death but accidentally and
upon forfeit; and therefore they owe not that naturall homage
unto death as other bodies doe, but may be restored to immortality with a lesser miracle and by a bare and easie revoca-
tion of course return immortall].[1] I have often beheld as a
miracle that artificiall resurrection and revivification of *Mercury,*
how being mortified into [a] thousand shapes, it assumes againe
its owne, and returns to its numericall selfe. Let us speake
naturally, and like Philosophers: the formes of alterable bodies
in these sensible corruptions perish not; nor, as wee imagine,
wholly quit their mansions, but retire and contract themselves
into their secret and inaccessible parts, where they may best
protect themselves from the action of their Antagonist. A plant
or vegetable consumed to ashes, to a contemplative and schoole
Philosopher seemes utterly destroyed, and the forme to have
taken his leave for ever: But to a sensible Artist the formes are
not perished, but withdrawne into their incombustible part,
where they lie secure from the action of that devouring element.
This is made good by experience, which can from the ashes of a
plant revive the plant, and from its cinders recall it into its stalk
and leaves againe. What the Art of man can doe in these inferiour
pieces, what blasphemy is it to affirme the finger of God cannot
doe in these more perfect and sensible structures? This is that
mysticall Philosophy, from whence no true Scholler becomes an
Atheist, but from the visible effects of nature, growes up a reall
Divine, and beholds not in a dreame, as *Ezekiel,* but in an ocular
and visible object the types of his resurrection.

NOW, the necessary Mansions of our restored selves are those Section 49
two contrary and incompatible places wee call Heaven and

[1] *This passage is added in all the MSS and the unauthorized editions.*

PART I Hell; [for] to define them, or strictly to determine what and where they are, surpasseth my Divinity. That elegant Apostle which seemed to have a glimpse of Heaven, hath left but a negative description thereof; Which neither eye hath seen, nor eare hath heard, nor can enter into the heart of man: he was translated out of himself to behold it, but being returned into himself could not expresse it. Saint *Johns* description by Emeralds Chrysolites, and pretious stones, is too weake to expresse the materiall Heaven we behold. Briefely therefore, where the soule hath the full measure, and complement of happinesse, where the boundlesse appetites of that spirit remaine compleatly satisfied, that it cannot desire either addition or alteration, that I thinke is truely Heaven: and this can onely be in the enjoyment of that essence, whose infinite goodnesse is able to terminate the desires of it selfe, and the insatiable wishes of ours; wherever God will thus manifest himselfe, there is Heaven, though within the circle of this sensible world. Thus the soule of man may bee in Heaven any where, even within the limits of his owne proper body, and when it ceaseth to live in the body, it may remaine in its owne soule, that is its Creator. And thus wee may say that Saint *Paul*, whether in the body or out of the body, was yet in Heaven. To place it in the Empyreall, or beyond the tenth Spheare, is to forget the worlds destruction; for when this sensible world shall bee destroyed, all shall then be here as it is now there, an Empyreall Heaven, a *quasi* vacuitie [or place exempt from the naturall affection of bodies], where to aske where Heaven is, is to demand where the presence of God is, or where wee have the glory of that happy vision. *Moses* that was bred up in all the learning of the *Egyptians,* committed a grosse absurdity in Philosophy, when with these eyes of flesh he desired to see God, and petitioned his Maker, that is truth it selfe, to a contradiction. Those that imagine Heaven and Hell neighbours, and conceive a vicinity between those two extreames, upon consequence of the Parable, where *Dives* discoursed with *Lazarus* in *Abrahams* bosome, do too grossely conceive of those glorified creatures, whose eyes shall easily outsee the Sunne, and behold without a Perspective, the extremest distances: for if there shall be in our glorified eyes, the faculty of sight & reception of obiects, I could thinke the visible species

there to be in as unlimitable a way as now the intellectuall. PART I
I grant that two bodies placed beyond the tenth Spheare, or
in a vacuity, according to *Aristotles* Philosophy, could not behold
each other, because there wants a body or Medium to hand
and transport the visible rayes of the object unto the sense;
but when there shall be a generall defect of either Medium to
convey, or light to prepare & dispose that Medium, and yet a
perfect vision, wee must suspend the rules of our Philosophy,
and make all good by a more absolute piece of Opticks.

I CANNOT tell how to say that fire is the essence of hell; Section 50
I know not what to make of Purgatory, or conceive a flame that
can either prey upon, or purifie the substance of a soule; those
flames of sulphure mentioned in the Scriptures, I take to be
understood not of this present Hell, but of that to come, where
fire shall make up the complement of our tortures, & have a
body or subject wherein to manifest its tyranny: Some who
have had the honour to be textuaries in Divinity, are of opinion
it shall be the same specificall fire with ours. This is hard to
conceive, yet can I make good how even that may prey upon
our bodies, and yet not consume us: for in this materiall world,
there are bodies that persist invincible in the powerfullest
flames, and though by the action of fire they fall into ignition
and liquation, yet will they never suffer a destruction: I would
gladly know how *Moses* with an actuall fire calcin'd,* or burnt   * [Calcina-
the golden Calfe into powder: for that mysticall mettle of gold,   tion, a
whose solary and celestiall nature I admire, exposed unto the   Chymicall
violence of fire, grows onely hot and liquifies, but consumeth   terme for the
                                                                  reduction of
not [either in its substance, weight or vertue]: so when the   a minerall
consumable and volatile pieces of our bodies shall be refined into   into Powder.
a more impregnable and fixed temper like gold, though they
suffer from the action of flames, they shall never perish, but lie
immortall in the armes of fire. And surely if this frame must
suffer onely by the action of this element, there will many bodies
escape, and not onely Heaven, but earth will not bee at an end,
but rather a beginning; For at present it is not earth, but a
composition of fire, water, earth, and aire; but at that time,
spoyled of these ingredients, it shall appeare in a substance
more like it selfe, its ashes. Philosophers that opinioned the

PART I worlds destruction by fire, did never dreame of annihilation, which is beyond the power of sublunary causes; for the last and powerfullest action of that element is but vitrification or a reduction of a body into Glasse; & therefore some of our Chymicks facetiously affirm, [yea, and urge Scripture for it], that at the last fire all shall be crystallized & reverberated into glasse, which is the utmost action of that element. Nor need we fear this term of annihilation or wonder that God will destroy the workes of his Creation: for man subsisting, who is, and will then truely appeare a Microcosme, the world cannot bee said to be destroyed. For the eyes of God, and perhaps also of our glorified senses, shall as really behold and contemplate the world in its Epitome or contracted essence, as now they doe at large and in its dilated substance. In the seed of a Plant to the eyes of God, and to the understanding of man, there exist, though in an invisible way, the perfect leaves, flowers, and fruits thereof: (for things that are in *posse* to the sense, are actually existent to the understanding). Thus God beholds all things, who contemplates as fully his workes in their Epitome, as in their full volume, and beheld as amply the whole world in that little compendium of the sixth day, as in the scattered and dilated pieces of those five before.

Section 51 MEN commonly set forth the tortures of Hell by fire, and the extremitie of corporall afflictions, and describe Hell in the same manner as *Mahomet* doth Heaven. This indeed makes a noyse, and drums in popular eares: but if this be the terrible piece thereof, it is not worthy to stand in diameter with Heaven, whose happinesse consists in that part which is best able to comprehend it, that immortall essence, that translated divinity and colony of God, the soule. Surely though wee place Hell under earth, the Devils walke and purlue is about it; men speake too popularly who place it in those flaming mountaines, which to grosser apprehensions represent Hell. The heart of man is the place the devill dwels in; I feele somtimes a hell within my selfe, *Lucifer* keeps his court in my brest, Legion is revived in me. There are as many hels as *Anaxagoras* conceited worlds; there was more than one hell in *Magdalen*, when there were seven devils; for every devill is an hell unto himselfe: hee

holds enough of torture in his owne *ubi*, and needs not the PART I
misery of circumference to afflict him, and thus a distracted
conscience here is a shadow or introduction unto hell hereafter;
Who can but pity the mercifull intention of those hands that
doe destroy themselves? the devill, were it in his power, would
doe the like; which being impossible, his miseries are endlesse,
and he suffers most in that attribute, wherein he is impassible,
his immortality.

I THANKE God, and with joy I mention it, I was never afraid Section 52
of Hell, nor ever grew pale at the description of that place;
I have so fixed my contemplations on Heaven, that I have
almost forgot the Idea of Hell, and am afraid rather to lose the
joyes of the one than endure the misery of the other; to be
deprived of them is a perfect hell, & needs me thinkes no addition
to compleate our afflictions; that terrible terme hath never
detained me from sin, nor do I owe any good action to the name
thereof: I feare God, yet am not afraid of him, his mercies make
me ashamed of my sins, before his judgements afraid thereof:
these are the forced and secondary method of his wisedome,
[and] which he useth [not] but as the last remedy, and upon
provocation: a course rather to deterre the wicked, than incite
the vertuous to his worship. I can hardly thinke there was ever
any scared into Heaven; they goe the surest[1] way to Heaven,
who would serve God without a Hell; other Mercenaries that
crouch unto him in feare of Hell, though they terme themselves
the servants, are indeed but the slaves of the Almighty.

AND to be true, and speake my soule, when I survey the Section 53
occurrences of my life, and call into account the finger of God,
I can perceive nothing but an abysse and masse of [his] mercies,
either in generall to mankind, or in particular to my selfe; and
whether out of the prejudice of my affection, or an inverting and
partiall conceit of his mercies, I know not, but those which
others terme crosses, afflictions, judgements, misfortunes, to
me, who enquire farther into them than their visible effects,
they both appeare, and in event have ever proved the secret
and dissembled favours of his affection. It is a singular piece of

---

[1] *Thus in PRJN. 1643 has:* fairest.

PART I wisedome to apprehend truly, and without passion the workes of God, and so well to distinguish his justice from his mercy, as not to miscall those noble attributes [of the Allmighty]; yet it is likewise an honest piece of Logick so to dispute and argue the proceedings of God, as to distinguish even his judgements into mercies. For God is mercifull unto all, because better to the worst, than the best deserve, and to say he punisheth none in this world, though it be a Paradox, is no absurdity. To one that hath committed murther, if the Judge should onely ordaine a boxe of the eare,[1] it were a madnesse to call this a punishment, and to repine at the sentence, rather than admire the clemency of the Judge. Thus our offences being mortall, and deserving not onely death, but damnation, if the goodnesse of God be content to traverse and passe them over with a losse, misfortune, or disease, what frensie were it to terme this a punishment, rather than an extremitie of mercy, and to groane under the rod of his judgements, rather than admire the Scepter of his mercies? Therefore to adore, honour, and admire him, is a debt of gratitude due from the obligation of our natures, states and conditions; and with these thoughts, he that knowes them best, will not deny that I adore him; that I obtaine Heaven, and the blisse thereof, is accidentall, and not the intended worke of my devotion, it being a felicitie I can neither thinke to deserve, nor scarce in modesty expect. For these two ends of us all, either as rewards or punishments, are mercifully ordained, and disproportionally disposed unto our actions, the one being so far beyond our deserts, the other so infinitely below our demerits.

Section 54 THERE is no salvation to those that beleeve not in Christ, that is, say some, since his Nativity, and as Divinity affirmeth, before also; which makes me much apprehend the end of those honest Worthies and Philosophers which died before his Incarnation. It is hard to place those soules in Hell whose worthy lives doe teach us vertue on earth; methinks amongst those many subdivisions of hell, there might have bin one Limbo left for these: What a strange vision will it be to see their poeticall

---

[1] Boxe of the eare *found only in* P. R*J*N*W have*: whipping. *1642, 1643 have*: Fine.

fictions converted into verities, & their imaginary & fancied PART I
Furies, into reall Devils? how strange to them will sound the
History of *Adam,* when they shall suffer for him they never
heard of? when they [that] derive their Genealogy from the
Gods, shall know they are the unhappy issue of sinfull man?
It is an insolent part of reason to controvert the works of God,
or question the justice of his proceedings; Could humility teach
others, as it hath instructed me, to contemplate the infinite and
incomprehensible distance betwixt the Creator and the creature,
or did we seriously perpend that one Simile of Saint *Paul, Shall
the vessell say unto the Potter, why hast thou made me thus?* it would
prevent these arrogant disputes of reason, nor would wee argue
the definitive sentence of God, either to Heaven or Hell. Men
that live according to the right rule and law of reason, live but
in their owne kinde, as beasts doe in theirs; who justly obey
the prescript of their natures, and therefore cannot reasonably
demand a reward of their actions, as onely obeying the naturall
dictates of their reason. It will therefore, and must at last
appeare, that all salvation is through Christ; which verity I
feare these great examples of vertue must confirme, and make
it good, how the perfectest actions of earth have no title or
claime unto Heaven.

NOR truely doe I thinke the lives of these or of any other were Section 55
ever correspondent, or in all points conformable unto their
doctrines; it is evident that *Aristotle* transgressed the rule of his
owne Ethicks; the Stoicks that condemne passion, and command a man to laugh in *Phalaris* his Bull, could not endure
without a groane a fit of the stone or collick. The *Scepticks* that
affirmed they knew nothing, even in that opinion confuted
themselves, and thought they knew more than all the world
besides. *Diogenes* I hold to bee the most vaineglorious man of his
time, and more ambitious in refusing all honours, than *Alexander* in rejecting none. Vice and the Devill put a fallacie upon our
reasons, and provoking us too hastily to run from it, entangle
and profound us deeper in it. The Duke of *Venice,* that [yearly]
weds himselfe unto his Sea, by [casting therein] a ring of Gold,
I will not argue of prodigality, because it is a solemnity of good
use and consequence in the State. But the Philosopher that

PART I threw his money into the Sea to avoyd avarice, was a notorious prodigal. There is no road or ready way to vertue, it is not an easie point of art to disentangle our selves from this riddle, or web of sin: To perfect vertue, as to Religion, there is required a Panoplia or compleat armour, that whilst we lye at close ward against one vice we lye [not] open to the venue of another: And indeed wiser discretions that have the thred of reason to conduct them, offend without a pardon; whereas under[1] heads may stumble without dishonour. There goe so many circumstances to piece up one good action, that it is a lesson to be good, and wee are forced to be vertuous by the booke. Againe, the practice of men holds not an equall pace, yea, and often runnes counter to their Theory; we naturally know what is good, but naturally pursue what is evill: the Rhetoricke wherewith I perswade another cannot perswade my selfe: there is a depraved appetite in us, that will with patience heare the learned instructions of Reason; but yet performe no further than agrees to its owne irregular Humour. In briefe, we are all monsters, that is, a composition of man and beast, wherein we must endeavour to

* [Chiron, a Centaure.] be as the Poets fancy that wise man *Chiron,** that is, to have the Region of Man above that of Beast, and sense to sit but at the feete of reason. Lastly, I doe desire with God, that all, but yet affirme with men, that [very] few shall know salvation, that the bridge is narrow, the passage straite unto life; yet those who doe confine the Church of God, either to particular Nations, Churches, or Families, have made it far narrower than our Saviour ever meant it.

Section 56 THE vulgarity of those judgements that wrap the Church of God in *Strabo*'s cloake and restraine it unto Europe, seeme to mee as bad Geographers as *Alexander,* who thought hee had conquer'd all the world when hee [had] not subdued the halfe of any part thereof: For wee cannot deny the Church of God both in Asia and Africa, if we doe not forget the peregrinations of the Apostles, the death of their Martyrs, the sessions of many, and even in our reformed judgement lawfull councells, held in those parts in the minoritie and nonage of ours: nor must a few differences more remarkable in the eyes of man than

---

[1] *P has*: ruder.

perhaps in the judgement of God, excommunicate from heaven
one another, much lesse those Christians who are in a manner
all Martyrs, maintaining their faith in the noble way of persecution, and serving God in the fire, whereas we honour him but
in the Sunshine. 'Tis true we all hold there is a number of Elect
and many to be saved; yet take our opinions together, and from
the confusion thereof there will be no such thing as salvation,
nor shall any one be saved; for first the Church of *Rome* condemneth us, wee likewise them, the Sub-reformists and Sec-
taries sentence the Doctrine of our Church as damnable, the
Atomist, or Familist reprobates all these, and all these them
againe. Thus whilst the mercies of God doe promise us heaven,
our conceits and opinions exclude us from that place. There
must be therefore more than one Saint *Peter;* particular Churches
and Sects usurpe the gates of heaven, and turne the key against
each other; and thus we goe to heaven against each others wills,
conceits and opinions, and, with as much uncharity as ignorance, doe erre I feare in points, not onely of our own, but one
anothers salvation.[1]

I BELEEVE many are saved who to man seeme reprobated,
and many reprobated who in the opinion and sentence of man,
stand elected; there will appeare at the last day, strange, and
unexpected examples, both of his justice and his mercy, and
therefore to define either is folly in man, and insolency even in
the devils; those acute and subtill spirits, in all their sagacity,
can hardly divine who shall be saved; which if they could
prognosticate their labour were at an end, nor need they
compasse the earth, seeking whom they may devoure. Those
who upon a rigid application of the Law, sentence *Solomon*
unto damnation, condemne not onely him, but themselves, and
the whole world; for by the letter, and written Law[2] of God,
we are without exception in the state of death; but there is a
prerogative of God, and an arbitrary pleasure above the letter
of his owne Law, by which alone wee can pretend unto salvation, and through which *Solomon* might be as easily saved as
those who condemne him.

[1] *Section 56 is found only in 1643.*
[2] *Thus in PRJN. 1642, 1643 have* : word.

THE number of those who pretend unto salvation, and those infinite swarmes who thinke to passe through the eye of this Needle, have much amazed me. That name and compellation of *little Flocke*, doth not comfort but deject my devotion, especially when I reflect upon mine owne unworthinesse, wherein, according to my humble apprehension, I am below them all. I beleeve there shall never be an Anarchy in Heaven, but as there are Hierarchies amongst the Angels, so shall there be degrees of priority amongst the Saints. Yet is it (I protest) beyond my ambition to aspire unto the first rankes; my desires onely are, and I shall be happy therein, to be but the last man, and bring up the Rere in Heaven.

AGAINE, I am confident and fully perswaded, yet dare not take my oath of my salvation; I am as it were sure, and do beleeve, without all doubt, that there is such a city as *Constantinople;* yet for me to take my oath thereon, were a kinde of perjury, because I hold no infallible warrant from my owne sense, to confirme me in the certainty thereof. And truely, though many pretend an absolute certainty of their salvation, yet when an humble soule shall contemplate her owne unworthinesse, she shall meete with many doubts and suddainely finde how much[1] wee stand in need of the precept of Saint *Paul*, *Worke out your salvation with feare and trembling*. That which is the cause of my election, I hold to be the cause of my salvation, which was the mercy, and beneplacit of God, before I was, or the foundation of the world. *Before Abraham was, I am*, is the saying of Christ; yet is it true in some sense if I say it of my selfe, for I was not onely before my selfe, but *Adam*, that is, in the Idea of God, and the decree of that Synod held from all Eternity. And in this sense, I say, the world was before the Creation, and at an end before it had a beginning; and thus was I dead before I was alive; though my grave be *England*, my dying place was Paradise, and *Eve* miscarried of mee before she conceiv'd of *Cain*.

INSOLENT zeales that doe decry good workes and rely onely upon faith, take not away merits: for depending upon the

---

[1] *Thus in P, 1642. RJN, 1643 have*: little.

efficacy of their faith, they enforce the condition of God, and PART I
in a more sophisticall way doe seeme to challenge Heaven. It
was decreed by God, that onely those that lapt in the water
like dogges, should have the honour to destroy the *Midianites;*
yet could none of those justly challenge, or imagine hee deserved
that honour thereupon. I doe not deny, but that true faith,
and such as God requires, is not onely a marke or token, but
also a meanes of our Salvation; but where to finde this, is as
obscure to me, as my last end. And if our Saviour could object
unto his owne Disciples, & favourites, a faith, that to the
quantity of a graine of Mustard seed, is able to remove mountaines; surely that which wee boast of, is not any thing, or at
the most, but a remove from nothing. This is the Tenor of my
beleefe, wherein, though there be many things singular, and
to the humour of my irregular selfe, yet, if they square not with
maturer Judgements, I disclaime them, and doe no further
father them than the learned and best Judgements shall authorize
them.

F

RELIGIO MEDICI

THE SECOND PART

Now for that other Vertue of Charity, without which Faith is a meer notion, and of no existence, I have ever endeavoured to nourish the mercifull disposition, and humane inclination [which] I borrowed from my Parents, and [to] regulate it to the written and prescribed Lawes of Charity; and if I hold the true Anatomy of my selfe, I am delineated & naturally framed to such a piece of vertue: for I am of a constitution so generall, that it consorts and sympathizeth with all things; I have no antipathy, or rather Idio-syncrasie, in dyet, humour, ayre, any thing; I wonder not at the *French*, for their dishes of frogges, snailes, and toadstooles, nor at the Jewes for Locusts and Grasse-hoppers, but being amongst them, make them my common viands; and I finde they agree with my stomach as well as theirs; I could digest a Sallad gathered in a Church-yard, as well as in a Garden. I cannot start at the presence of a Serpent, Scorpion, Lizard, or Salamander; at the sight of a Toad, or Viper, I feel in me no desire to take up a stone to destroy them. I finde not in my selfe those common antipathies that I can discover in others: Those nationall repugnances doe not touch me, nor doe I behold with prejudice the *French, Italian, Spaniard,* or *Dutch;* but where I finde their actions in ballance with my Countreymens, I honour, love, and embrace them in the same degree; I was borne in the eighth Climate, but seeme to bee framed, and constellated unto all; I am no Plant that will not prosper out of a Garden. All places, all ayres make unto me one Countrey; I am in *England*, every where, and under any meridian; I have beene shipwrackt, yet am not enemy with the sea or winds; I can study, play, or sleepe in a tempest. In briefe, I am averse from nothing, [neither Plant, Animal, nor Spirit]; my conscience would give me the lie if I should say I

absolutely detest or hate any essence but the Devill, or so at PART II
least abhorre any thing but that wee might come to composition. If there be any among those common objects of hatred
[which I can safely say] I doe contemne and laugh at, it is that
great enemy of reason, vertue and religion, the multitude, that
numerous piece of monstrosity, which taken asunder seeme
men, and the reasonable creatures of God; but confused together, make but one great beast, & a monstrosity more prodigious than Hydra; it is no breach of Charity to call these
fooles; it is the stile all holy Writers have afforded them, set
down by *Solomon* in canonicall Scripture, and a point of our faith
to beleeve so. Neither in the name of multitude doe I onely
include the base and minor sort of people; there is a rabble even
amongst the Gentry, a sort of Plebeian heads, whose fancy
moves with the same wheele as these; men [even] in the same
Levell with Mechanickes, though their fortunes doe somewhat
guild their infirmities, and their purses compound for their
follies. But as in casting account, three or four men together
come short of one man placed by himself below them: So
neither are a troope of these ignorant Doradoes, of that true
esteeme and value, as many a forlorne person, whose condition
doth place him below their feet. Let us speake like Politicians;
there is a Nobility without Heraldry, a naturall dignity, whereby one man is ranked with another, another Filed before him,
according to the quality of his desert, and preheminence of his
good parts. Though the corruption of these times, and the byas
of present practice wheele another way, thus it was in the first
and primitive Commonwealths, and is yet in the integrity and
Cradle of well-ordered polities, till corruption getteth ground,
ruder desires labouring after that which wiser considerations
contemn, every one having a liberty to amasse & heape up
riches, and they a licence or faculty to doe or purchase any
thing.

THIS generall and indifferent temper of mine, doth more Section 2
neerely dispose mee to this noble vertue, [that with an easier
measure of grace I may obtaine it]. It is a happinesse to be borne
and framed unto vertue, and to grow up from the seeds of nature, rather than the inoculation and forced grafts of education;

PART II yet if we are directed only by our particular Natures, and regulate our inclinations by no higher rule than that of our reason, we are but Moralists; Divinity will still call us Heathens. Therfore this great worke of charity, must have other motives, ends, and impulsions: I give no almes to satisfie the hunger of my Brother, but to fulfill and accomplish the Will and Command of my God; I draw not my purse for his sake that demands it, but his that [hath] enjoyned it; I relieve no man upon the Rhetorick of his miseries, nor to content mine owne commiser-ating disposition, for this is still but morall charity, and an act that oweth more to passion than reason. Hee that relieves another upon the bare suggestion and bowels of pity, doth not this so much for his sake as for his own: for by compassion we make anothers misery our own, & so by relieving them, we relieve our selves also. It is an erroneous course to redresse other mens misfortunes upon the common considerations of mercifull natures, that it may bee one day our own case; for this is a sinister and politick kind of charity, wherby we seem to bespeak the pities of men in the like occasions, [buy out of God a faculty to be exempted from it][1]; and truly I have observed that those professed Eleemosynaries, though in a croud or multitude, doe yet direct and place their petitions on a few and selected persons; there is surely a Physiognomy, which those experi-enced and Master Mendicants observe, whereby they instantly discover a mercifull aspect, and will single out a face, wherein they spy the signatures and markes of mercy: for there are mystically in our faces certaine characters which carry in them the motto of our Soules, wherein he that cannot read A. B. C. may read our natures. I hold moreover that there is a Phyto-gnomy, or Physiognomy, not onely of men, but of Plants, and Vegetables; and in every one of them, some outward figures which hang as signes or bushes of their inward formes. The finger of God hath set an inscription upon all his workes, not graphicall or composed of Letters, but of their severall formes, constitutions, parts, and operations, which aptly joyned together make one word that doth expresse their natures. By these Letters God cals the Starres by their names, and by this Alphabet *Adam* assigned to every creature a name peculiar to its

[1] *This passage found only in P.*

Nature. Now there are besides these Characters in our faces,
certaine mysticall [lines and] figures in our hands, which I dare
not call meere dashes, strokes, *a la volee*, or at randome, because
delineated by a pencill, that never workes in vaine; and hereof
I take more particular notice, because I carry that in mine owne
hand, which I could never read of, or discover in another.
Aristotle, I confesse, in his acute, and singular booke of Physiognomy, hath made no mention of Chiromancy; yet I beleeve
the *Egyptians*, who were neerer addicted to those abstruse and
mysticall sciences, had a knowledge therein, to which those
vagabond and counterfeit *Egyptians* did after pretend, and
perhaps retained a few corrupted principles, which sometimes
might verifie their prognostickes.

It is the common wonder of all men, how among so many
millions of faces, there should be none alike; Now contrary,
I wonder as much how there should be any; he that shall consider how many thousand severall words have beene carelesly
and without study composed out of 24 Letters; withall how
many hundred lines there are to be drawn in the fabrick of one
man; shall easily finde that this variety is necessary: And it will
bee very hard that they should so concur as to make one portract
like another. Let a Painter carelesly limn out a Million of faces,
and you shall finde them all different; yea let him have his copy
before him, yet after all his art there will remaine a sensible
distinction; for the pattern or example of every thing is the
perfectest in that kind, whereof wee still come short, though
wee transcend or goe beyond it, because herein it is wide and
agrees not in all points unto its Copy. [I rather wonder how
almost all plants being of one colour, yet should bee all different
herein, and their severall kinds distinguished in one accident
of verte.]¹ Nor doth the similitude of creatures disparage the
variety of nature, nor any way confound the workes of God.
For even in things alike, there is diversitie, and those that doe
seeme to accord, doe manifestly disagree. And thus is Man like
God, for in the same things that wee resemble him, wee are
utterly different from him. There is never any thing so like
another, as in all points to concurre; there will ever some
reserved difference slip in, to prevent the Identity, without

¹ *This passage found only in P.*

PART II which two severall things would not be alike, but the same, which is impossible.

Section 3 BUT to returne from Philosophy to Charity, I hold not so narrow a conceit of this vertue, as to conceive that to give almes, is onely to be Charitable, or thinke a piece of Liberality can comprehend the Totall of Charity; Divinity hath wisely divided the acts thereof into many branches, and hath taught us in this narrow way, many pathes unto goodnesse; as many wayes as we may doe good, so many wayes we may bee Charitable; there are infirmities, not onely of body, but of soule, and fortunes, which doe require the mercifull hand of our abilities. I cannot contemn a man for ignorance but behold him with as much pity as I doe *Lazarus*. It is no greater Charity to cloath his body, than apparell the nakednesse of his Soule. It is an honourable object to see the reasons of other men weare our Liveries, and their borrowed understandings doe homage to the bounty of ours. It is the cheapest way of beneficence, and like the naturall charity of the Sunne illuminates another without obscuring it selfe. To be reserved and caitif in this part of goodnesse, is the sordidest piece of covetousnesse, and more contemptible than pecuniary avarice. To this (as calling my selfe a Scholler) I am obliged by the duty of my condition, I make not therefore my head a grave, but a treasure of knowledge; I intend no Monopoly, but a Community in learning; I study not for my owne sake onely, but for theirs that study not for themselves. I envy no man that knowes more than my selfe, but pity those that know less. I instruct no man as an exercise of my knowledge, or with intent rather to nourish and keepe it alive in mine owne head, than beget and propagate it in his; and in the midst of all my endeavours there is but one thought that dejects me, that my acquired parts must perish with my selfe, nor can bee Legacyed among my honoured Friends. I cannot fall out or contemne a man for an errour, or conceive why a difference in opinion should divide our affection: for controversies, disputes, and argumentations, both in Philosophy and in Divinity, if they meete with discreet and peaceable natures, doe not infringe the Lawes of Charity; in all disputes, so much as there is of passion, so much there is of

nothing to the purpose; for then reason like a bad hound spends PART II
upon a false sent, and forsakes the question first started. And
this is one reason why controversies are never determined, for
though they be amply proposed, they are scarce at all handled,
they doe so swell with unnecessary Digressions, and the
Parenthesis on the party, is often as large as the maine discourse
upon the Subject. The Foundations of Religion are already
established, and the principles of Salvation subscribed unto by
all; there remaine not many controversies worth a passion, and
yet never any disputed without, not onely in Divinity, but in
inferiour Arts: What a βατραχομυομαχία, and hot skirmish is
betwixt S. and T. in Lucian? How doe Grammarians hack and
slash for the Genitive case in *Iupiter?** [How many Synods have   * Whether
been assembled and angerly broke up again about a line in   *Jovis* or
Propria quæ Maribus?] How doe they break their owne pates to   *Jupiteris.*
save that of *Priscian? Si foret in terris, rideret Democritus.* Yea, even
amongst wiser militants, how many wounds have beene given,
and credits stained[1] for the poore victory of an opinion or
beggerly conquest of a distinction? Schollers are men of peace,
they beare no armes, but their tongues are sharper then *Actius** * [That cutt
his razor; their pens carry farther, and give a lowder report   a whetstone
than thunder; I had rather stand the shock of a Basilisco, than   in two.]
the fury of a mercilesse pen. It is not meere zeale to Learning, or
Devotion to the Muses, that wiser Princes Patron the Arts, and
carry an indulgent aspect unto Schollers; but a desire to have
their names eternized by the memory of their writings, and
a feare of the revengefull pen of succeeding ages: for these are
the men, that when they have played their parts, and had
their *exits,* must step out and give the morall of their Scenes,
and deliver unto Posterity an Inventory of their vertues and
vices. And surely there goes a great deale of conscience to
the compiling of an History; there is no reproach to the
scandall of a Story; It is such an Authenticke kinde of false-
hood that with authority belies our good names to all Nations
and Posteritie.

THERE is another offence unto Charity, which no Author   Section 4
hath ever written of, and [as] few take notice of, and that's the

---

[1]   *Thus in R JNW. P, 1643 has* : slaine.

PART II reproach, not of whole professions, mysteries and conditions, but of whole nations, wherein by opprobrious Epithets wee miscall each other, and by an uncharitable Logicke from a disposition in a few conclude a habit in all.

Le mutin Anglois, et le bravache Escossois;
Le bougre Italien, et le fol Francois;
Le poultron Romain, le larron de Gascongne,
L'Espagnol superbe, et l'Aleman yurongne.[1]

Saint *Paul* that cals the *Cretians* lyers, doth it but indirectly and upon quotation of their owne Poet. It is as bloody a thought in one way as *Neroes* was in another. For by a word wee wound a thousand, and at one blow assassine the honour of a Nation. It is as compleate a piece of madnesse to miscall and rave against the times, as thinke to recall men to reason by a fit of passion: *Democritus* that thought to laugh the times into goodnesse, seemes to mee as deeply Hypochondriack, as *Heraclitus* that bewailed them; it moves not my spleene to behold the multi-tude in their proper humours, that is, in their fits of folly and madnesse, as well understanding that Wisedome is not pro-phan'd unto the World, and 'tis the priviledge of a few to be vertuous. They that endeavour to abolish vice destroy also vertue, for contraries, though they destroy one another, are yet the life of one another. Thus vertue (abolish vice) is an Idea; againe the communitie of sinne doth not disparage goodnesse; for when vice gaines upon the major part, vertue, in whom it remaines, becomes more excellent, and being lost in some, multiplies its goodnesse in others which remaine untouched, and persists intire in the generall inundation. I can therefore behold vice without a Satyre, content onely with an admonition, or instructive reprehension; for Noble natures, and such as are capable of goodnesse, are railed into vice, but might as easily bee admonished into vertue; and we should be all so farre the Orators of goodnesse, as to protect her from the power of vice, and maintaine the cause of injured truth. No man can justly censure or condemne another, because indeed no man truly

---

[1] These lines are based on an imperfect memory of Sonnet lxviii of Joachim du Bellay's *Les Regrets* (*Œuvres poétiques*, Paris, 1927, pp. 104–5), as noted by H. G. Ward, *R.E.S.* (1929), v. 3 [Ed.]

knowes another. This I perceive in my selfe, for I am in the darke PART II
to all the world, and my nearest friends behold mee but in a
cloud; those that know mee but superficially, thinke lesse of
me than I doe of my selfe; those of my neere acquaintance thinke
more; God, who knowes me truly, knowes that I am nothing;
for hee onely beholds me, and all the world, who lookes not on
us through a derived ray, or a trajection of a sensible species, but
beholds the substance without the helpe of accidents, and the
formes of things, as wee their operations. Further, no man can
judge another, because no man knowes himselfe; for we censure
others but as they disagree from that humour which wee fancy
laudable in our selves, and commend others but for that wherein
they seeme to quadrate and consent with us. So that in conclusion, all is but that we all condemne, selfe-love. 'Tis the
generall complaint of these times, and perhaps of those past,
that charity growes cold; which I perceive most verified in
those which most doe manifest the fires and flames of zeale;
for it is a vertue that best agrees with coldest natures, and
such as are complexioned for humility: But how shall we expect
charity towards others, when we are uncharitable to our selves?
Charity begins at home, is the voyce of the world; yet is every
man his greatest enemy, and as it were, his owne executioner.
Non occides, is the Commandement of God, yet scarce observed
by any man; for I perceive every man is his owne *Atropos*, and
lends a hand to cut the thred of his owne dayes. *Cain* was not
therefore the first murtherer, but *Adam*, who brought in death;
whereof hee beheld the practice [onely] and example in his owne
sonne *Abel*, and saw that verified in the experience of another,
which faith could not perswade him in the Theory of himselfe.

THERE is, I thinke, no man that apprehends his owne miseries Section 5
lesse than my selfe, and no man that so neerely apprehends
anothers. I could lose an arme without a teare, and with few
groans, mee thinkes, be quartered into pieces; yet can I weepe
most seriously at a Play, and receive with a true passion, the
counterfeit griefes of those knowne and professed Impostors.
It is a barbarous part of inhumanity to adde unto an afflicted
parties misery, or endeavour to multiply in any man, a passion,
whose single nature is already above his patience; this was the

PART II greatest affliction of *Job*, and those oblique expostulations of his friends a deeper injury than the downe-right blowes of the Devill. It is not the teares of our owne eyes onely, but of our friends also, that doe exhaust the current of our sorrowes, which falling [asunder] into many streames, runs more peaceably [within its owne banke], and is contented with a narrower channel. It is an act within the power of charity, to translate a passion out of one breast into another, and to divide a sorrow almost out of it selfe; for an affliction like a dimension may be so divided, as if not indivisible, at least to become insensible. Now with my friend I desire not to share or participate, but to engrosse his sorrowes, that by making them mine owne, I may more easily discusse them; for in mine owne reason, and within my selfe I can command that, which I cannot entreate without my selfe, and within the circle of another. I have often thought those Noble paires and examples of friendship not so truely Histories of what had beene, as fictions of what should be; but I now perceive nothing therein, but possibilities, nor any thing in the Heroick examples of [*Nisus* and *Euryalus*], *Damon* and *Pythias*, *Achilles* and *Patroclus*, which mee thinkes upon some grounds I could not performe within the narrow compasse of my selfe. That a man should lay down his life for his friend, seemes strange to vulgar affections, and such as confine themselves within that worldly principle, Charity beginnes at home. For mine owne part I could never remember the relations that I hold unto my selfe, nor the respect that I owe unto mine owne nature, in the cause of God, my Country, and my Friends. Next to these three, I doe embrace my selfe; I confesse I doe not observe that order that the Schooles ordaine our affections, to love our Parents, Wives, Children, and then our Friends; for excepting the injunctions of Religion, I doe not finde in my selfe such a necessary and indissoluble Sympathy to all those of my bloud. I hope I doe not breake the fifth Commandement, if I conceive I may love my friend before the nearest of my bloud, even those to whom I owe the principles of life; I never yet cast a true affection on a Woman, but I have loved my friend as I do vertue, [and as I do] my soule, my God.[1] From

---

[1] *P only inserts here*: These individuall Sympathies are stronger and from a more powerfull hand then those specificall unions.

hence me thinkes I doe conceive how God loves man, what
happinesse there is in the love of God. Omitting all other there
are three most mysticall unions: Two natures in one person;
three persons in one nature; one soule in two bodies. For though
indeed they bee really divided, yet are they so united, as they
seeme but one, and make rather a duality then two distinct soules.

THERE are wonders in true affection; it is a body of *Ænig-*
maes, mysteries and riddles, wherein two so become one, as
they both become two; I love my friend before my selfe, and
yet me thinkes I do not love him enough; some few months
hence my multiplyed affection will make me beleeve I have not
loved him at all; when I am from him, I am dead till I bee with
him; when I am with him, I am not satisfied, but would still
be nearer him; united soules are not satisfied with embraces, but
desire each to be truely the other, which being impossible, their
desires are infinite, and must proceed without a possibility of
satisfaction. Another misery there is in affection: that whom we
truely love like our owne [selves], wee forget their lookes, nor
can our memory retaine the Idea of their faces; and it is no
wonder, for they are our selves, and affection makes their lookes
our owne. This noble affection fals not on vulgar and common
constitutions, but on such as are mark'd for vertue; he that
can love his friend with this noble ardour, will in a competent
degree affect all. Now, if wee can bring our affections to looke
beyond the body, and cast an eye upon the soule, wee have
found out the true object, not onely of friendship but charity;
and the greatest happinesse that wee can bequeath the soule, is
that wherein we all doe place our last felicity: Salvation, which
though it bee not in our power to bestow, it is in our charity,
and pious invocations to desire, if not procure, and further.
I cannot contentedly frame a Prayer for my particular selfe
without a catalogue of my friends, nor request a happinesse
wherein my sociable disposition doth not desire the fellowship
of my neighbour. I never heare the Toll of a passing Bell, though
in my mirth, [and at a Tavern], without my prayers and best
wishes for the departing spirit; I cannot goe to cure the body of
my Patient, but I forget my profession, and call unto God for his
soule; I cannot see one say his Prayers, but instead of imitating

PART II him, I fall into a supplication for him, who peradventure is no
more to mee than a common nature: and if God hath vouchsafed
an eare to my supplications, there are surely many happy that
never saw me, and enjoy the blessings of mine unknowne
devotions. To pray for enemies, that is, for their salvation, is
no harsh precept, but the practice of our daily and ordinary
devotions. I cannot beleeve the story of the Italian; our bad
wishes and malevolous[1] desires proceed no further than this
life; it is the Devill and the uncharitable votes of Hell, that
desire our misery in the world to come.

Section 7 TO doe no injury, nor take none, was a principle, which to
my former yeares, and impatient affections, seemed to containe
enough of morality; but my more setled yeares and Christian
constitution have fallen upon severer resolutions. I can hold
there is no such thing as injury; that if there be, there is no such
injury as revenge, and no such revenge as the contempt of an
injury; that to hate another, is to maligne himselfe, that the
truest way to love another, is to despise our selves. I were unjust
unto mine owne conscience, if I should say I am at variance with
any thing like my selfe; I finde there are many pieces in this
one fabricke of man; [and that] this frame is raised upon a masse
of Antipathies: I am one, mee thinkes, but as the world; wherein
notwithstanding there are a swarme of distinct essences, and in
them another world of contrarieties; wee carry private and
domesticke enemies within, publike and more hostile adversaries without. The Devill that did but buffet Saint *Paul,* playes
mee thinkes at sharpes with me: Let mee be nothing if within
the compasse of my selfe, I doe not find the battell of *Lepanto,*
passion against reason, reason against faith, faith against the
Devill, and my conscience against all. There is another man
within mee that's angry with mee, rebukes, commands, and
dastards mee. I have no conscience of Marble to resist the
hammer of more heavie offences, nor yet so soft and waxen, as
to take the impression of each single peccadillo or scape of
infirmity: I am of a strange beliefe, that it is as easie to be forgiven some sinnes, as to commit them. For my original sinne,
I hold it to be washed away in my Baptisme; for my actuall

[1] *Thus in* PRJN. *W, 1642, 1643 have:* uncharitable.

transgressions, I compute and reckon with God, but from my last repentance, Sacrament or generall absolution: And therefore am not terrified with the sinnes and madnesse of my youth. I thanke the goodnesse of God I have no sinnes that want a name; I am not singular in offences, my transgressions are Epidemicall, and from the common breath of our corruption. For there are certaine tempers of body, which matcht with an humorous depravity of mind, doe hatch and produce viciosities, whose newness and monstrosity of nature admits no name; this was the temper of that Lecher that carnald with a Statua, and the constitution of *Nero*[1] in his Spintrian recreations. For the heavens are not onely fruitfull in new and unheard of starres, the earth in plants and animals, but mens minds also in villany and vices; now the dulnesse of my reason, and the vulgarity of my disposition, never prompted my invention, nor sollicited my affection unto any of these; yet even those common and *quotidian* infirmities that so necessarily attend me, and doe seeme to bee my very nature, have so dejected me, so broken the estimation that I should have otherwise of my selfe, that I repute my selfe the abjectest piece of mortality; [that I detest mine owne nature, and in my retired imaginations cannot withhold my hands from violence on myselfe][2]; Divines prescribe a fit of sorrow to repentance; there goes indignation, anger, contempt, and hatred into mine, passions of a contrary nature, which neither seeme to sute with this action, nor my proper constitution. It is no breach of charity to our selves to be at variance with our vices, nor to abhorre that part of us, which is an enemy to the ground of charity, our God; wherein wee doe but imitate our great selves, the world, whose divided Antipathies and contrary faces doe yet carry a charitable regard unto the whole, by their particular discords preserving the common harmony, and keeping in fetters those powers whose rebellions, once Masters, might bee the ruine of all.

I THANKE God, amongst those millions of vices I doe inherit and hold from *Adam,* I have escaped one, and that a mortall enemy to charity, the first and father sin, not only of

[1] *The Emperor* Tiberius *is meant* [Ed.].
[2] *This passage in all MSS and* 1642.

man, but of the devil: Pride. A vice whose name is comprehended in a Monosyllable, but in its nature circumscribed not
with a world; I have escaped it in a condition that can hardly
avoid it: those petty acquisitions and reputed perfections that
advance and elevate the conceits of other men, adde no feathers
unto mine; I have seene a Grammarian towr,[1] and plume himselfe
over a single line in *Horace,* and shew more pride in the construction of one Ode, than the Author in the composure of the
whole book. For my owne part, besides the *Jargon* and *Patois*
of severall Provinces, I understand no less then six Languages;
yet I protest I have no higher conceit of my selfe than had our
Fathers before the confusion of *Babel,* when there was but one
Language in the world, and none to boast himselfe either
Linguist or Criticke. I have not onely seene severall Countries,
beheld the nature of their climes, the Chorography of their
Provinces, Topography of their Cities, but understand their
severall Lawes, Customes and Policies; yet cannot all this
perswade the dulnesse of my spirit unto such an opinion of my
self, as I behold in nimbler & conceited heads, that never looked
a degree beyond their nests. I know the names, and somewhat
more, of all the constellations in my Horizon, yet I have seene a
prating Mariner that could onely name the Poynters and the
North Starre, out-talke mee, and conceit himselfe a whole
Spheare above mee. I know most of the Plants of my Country,
and of those about mee; yet me thinkes I do not know so many
as when I did but know an hundred, and had scarcely ever
Simpled further than Cheap-side: for indeed heads of capacity,
and such as are not full with a handfull, or easie measure of
knowledg, thinke they know nothing, till they know all; which
being impossible, they fall upon the opinion of *Socrates,* and
onely know they know not any thing. I cannot thinke that
Homer pin'd away upon the riddle of the Fishermen,[2] or that
Aristotle, who understood the uncertainty of knowledge, and
so often confessed the reason of man too weake for the workes
of nature, did ever drowne himselfe upon the flux and reflux
of *Euripus:* wee doe but learne to day, what our better advanced
judgements will unteach us to morrow: and *Aristotle* doth but

[1] *1643 has:* toure; *altered to* towr *in 1656 and later eds.* [Ed.]
[2] *For a comment on this see* Pseudodoxia Epidemica, VII. 13, vol. ii, p. 52.

instruct us as *Plato* did him; that is, to confute himselfe. I have
runne through all sorts, yet finde no rest in any; though our
first studies & *junior* endeavors may stile us Peripateticks,
Stoicks, or Academicks, yet I perceive the wisest heads prove
at last, almost all Scepticks, and stand like *Janus* in the field
of knowledge. I have therefore one common and authentick
Philosophy I learned in the Schooles, whereby I discourse and
satisfie the reason of other men; another more reserved and
drawne from experience whereby I content mine owne. *Solomon*
that complained of ignorance in the height of knowledge, hath
not onely humbled my conceits, but discouraged my endeavours.
There is yet another conceit that hath sometimes made me
shut my bookes; which tels mee it is a vanity to waste our dayes
in the blind pursuit of knowledge; it is but attending a little
longer, and wee shall enjoy that by instinct and infusion which
we endeavour at here by labour and inquisition: it is better
to sit downe in a modest ignorance, & rest contented with
the naturall blessing of our owne reasons, then buy the uncertaine knowledge of this life, with sweat and vexation, which
death gives every foole gratis, and is an accessary of our glori-
fication.

I WAS never yet once married, and commend their resolutions
who never marry twice;[1] not that I disallow of second marriage;
as neither in all cases of Polygamy, which considering some
times and the unequall number of both sexes may bee also
necessary. The whole woman[2] was made for man, but the
twelfth part of man for woman: man is the whole world and the
breath of God, woman the rib [onely] and crooked piece of
man. I could be content that we might procreate like trees,
without conjunction, or that there were any way to perpetuate
the world without this triviall and vulgar way of coition;
It is the foolishest act a wise man commits in all his life, nor is
there any thing that will more deject his coold imagination,
when hee shall consider what an odde and unworthy piece of
folly hee hath committed; I speake not in prejudice, nor am [I]

---

[1] *The MSS and 1642 have*: I was never yet once and resolved never to be
married twice.
[2] *Thus in PRJN. W, 1642, 1643 have*: world.

PART II averse from that sweet sexe, but naturally amorous of all that is beautifull; I can looke a whole day with delight upon a handsome picture, though it be but of an Horse. It is my temper, & I like it the better, to affect all harmony; and sure there is musicke even in beauty, and the silent note which *Cupid* strikes, farre sweeter than the sound of an instrument. For there is a musicke where-ever there is a harmony, order or proportion; and thus farre we may maintain the musick of the spheares; for those well ordered motions, and regular paces, though they give no sound unto the eare, yet to the understanding they strike a note most full of harmony. Whosoever is harmonically composed delights in harmony; which makes me much distrust the symmetry of those heads which declaime against all Church musicke. For my selfe, not only from my obedience but my particular genius, I doe imbrace it; for even that vulgar and Taverne Musicke, which makes one man merry, another mad, strikes me into a deepe fit of devotion, and a profound contemplation of the first Composer; there is something in it of Divinity more than the eare discovers. It is an Hieroglyphicall and shadowed lesson of the whole world, and [the] Creatures of God; such a melody to the eare, as the whole world well understood, would afford the understanding. In briefe it is a sensible fit of that Harmony, which intellectually sounds in the eares of God: [it unties the ligaments of my frame, takes me to pieces, dilates me out of myself, and by degrees, mee thinkes, resolves me into Heaven].[1] I will not say with *Plato*, the Soule is an Harmony, but harmonicall, and hath its neerest sympathy unto musicke: thus some, whose temper of body agrees, and humours the constitution of their soules, are borne Poets, though indeed all are naturally inclined unto Rhythme. This★ made *Tacitus* in the very first line of his Story, fall upon a verse; and *Cicero*, the worst of Poets, but declayming★ for a Poet, fals in the very first sentence upon a perfect Hexameter.★ I feele not in me those sordid, and unchristian desires of my profession, I doe not secretly implore and wish for Plagues, rejoyce at Famines, revolve Ephemerides, and Almanacks, in expectation of malignant Aspects, fatall conjunctions, and Eclipses: I rejoyce not at unwholsome Springs, nor unseasonable Winters; my

★ *Urbem Romam in principio Reges habuere.*

★ *Pro Archia Poeta.*

★ *In qua me non inficior mediocriter esse.*

[1] *This passage is found in the MSS and 1642.*

Prayers go with the Husbandmans; I desire every thing in its
proper season, that neither men nor the times bee out of temper.
Let mee be sicke my selfe, if often times the malady of my patient
be not a disease unto me. I desire rather to cure his infirmities
than my owne necessities. Where I do him no good me thinkes
it is scarce honest gaine, though I confess 'tis but the worthy
salary of our well intended endeavours. I am not onely ashamed,
but heartily sorry, that besides death, there are diseases incurable; yet not for my own sake, or that they be beyond my
art, but for the general cause & sake of humanity, whose
common cause I apprehend as mine own: And to speak more
generally, those three Noble professions which al civil Common
wealths doe honour, are raised upon the fall of *Adam,* and are
not any exempt from their infirmities; there are not onely
diseases incurable in Physicke, but cases indissoluble in Lawe,
Vices incorrigible in Divinity: if general Councells may erre, I
doe not see why particular Courts should be infallible: their
perfectest rules are raised upon the erroneous reason of Man,
and the Lawes of one, doe but condemn the rules of another; as
Aristotle oft-times the opinions of his predecessours, because,
though agreeable to reason, yet were not consonant to his owne
rules, and the Logicke of his proper principles. Againe, to speake
nothing of the sinne against the Holy Ghost, whose cure not
onely, but whose nature is unknowne, I can cure the gout and
stone in some, sooner than Divinity, Pride, or Avarice in others.
I can cure vices by Physicke, when they remaine incurable by
Divinity, and shall obey my pils, when they contemne their
precepts. I boast nothing, but plainely say, we all labour against
our owne cure, for death is the cure of all diseases. There is no
Catholicon, or universall remedy I know but this, which thogh
nauseous to queasier stomachs, yet to prepared appetites is
Nectar and a pleasant potion of immortality.

FOR my conversation, it is like the Sunne's with all men;
and with a friendly aspect to good and bad. Me thinkes there is
no man bad, and the worst, best; that is, while they are kept
within the circle of those qualities, wherein they are good:
there is no mans minde of such discordant and jarring a temper
to which a tuneable disposition may not strike a harmony.

PART II   *Magnæ virtutes nec minora vitia* is the posie of the best natures,
and may bee inverted on the worst; there are in the most
depraved and venemous dispositions, certaine pieces that
remaine untoucht; which by an Antiperistasis become more
excellent, or by the excellency of their antipathies are able to
preserve themselves from the contagion of their enemy vices,
and persist entire beyond the generall corruption. For it is
also thus in nature. The greatest Balsames doe lie enveloped
in the bodies of [the] most powerfull Corrosives; I say moreover,
and I ground upon experience, that poysons containe within
themselves their owne Antidote, and that which preserves
them from the venom of themselves; without which they were
not deleterious to others onely, but to themselves also. But it
is the corruption that I feare within me, not the contagion of
commerce without me. 'Tis that unruly regiment within me
* [Adam,   that will destroy me, 'tis I that doe infect my selfe, the man*
whom I con- without a Navell yet lives in me; I feele that originall canker
ceive to want corrode and devoure me, and therefore *Defienda me Dios de mi*,[1]
a navill,   Lord deliver me from my selfe, is a part of my Letany, and the
because he
was not borne first voyce of my retired imaginations. There is no man alone,
of a woman.] because every man is a *Microcosme*, and carries the whole world
about him; *Nunquam minus solus quam cum solus,* though it bee
the Apophthegme of a wise man, is yet true in the mouth of a
foole; for indeed, though in a Wildernesse, a man is never alone,
not onely because hee is with himselfe, and his owne thoughts,
but because he is with the devill, who ever consorts with our
solitude, and is that unruly rebell that musters up those dis-
ordered motions, which accompany our sequestred imaginations: And to speake more narrowly, there is no such thing as
solitude, nor any thing that can be said to be alone, and by it
selfe, but God, who is his owne circle, and can subsist by himselfe; all others, besides their dissimilary and Heterogeneous
parts, which in a manner multiply their natures, cannot subsist
without the concourse of God, and the society of that hand
which doth uphold their natures. In briefe, there can be nothing

[1] 1643 has *Defenda me Dios de me.* As printed above it is the fourth line of a
quatrain in the second part of the *Epistolas Familiares* of Antonio de Guevara
(Valladolid, 1541), f. lxxix recto, as noted by Edward Bensly, *N. & Q.* (1922),
12 S xi. 347 [Ed.].

truely alone, and by its self, which is not truely one, and such is **PART II**
onely God: All others doe transcend an unity, and so by
consequence are many.

NOW for my life, it is a miracle of thirty yeares, which to relate, **Section 11**
were not a History, but a peece of Poetry, and would sound to
common eares like a fable; for the world, I count it not an Inne,
but an Hospitall, and a place, not to live, but to die in. The
world that I regard is my selfe, it is the Microcosme of mine
owne frame, that I cast mine eye on; for the other, I use it but
like my Globe, and turne it round sometimes for my recreation.
Men that look upon my outside, perusing onely my condition,
and fortunes, do erre in my altitude; for I am above *Atlas* his
shoulders, [and though I seeme on earth to stand, on tiptoe in
Heaven].[1] The earth is a point not onely in respect of the heavens
above us, but of that heavenly and celestiall part within us:
that masse of flesh that circumscribes me, limits not my mind:
that surface that tells the heavens it hath an end, cannot
perswade me I have any; I take my circle to be above three
hundred and sixty; though the number of the Arke do measure
my body, it comprehendeth not my minde: whilst I study to
finde how I am a Microcosme or little world, I finde my selfe
something more than the great. There is surely a peece of
Divinity in us, something that was before the Elements, and
owes no homage unto the Sun. Nature tels me I am the Image
of God as well as Scripture; he that understands not thus much,
hath not his introduction or first lesson, and is yet to begin the
Alphabet of man. Let me not injure the felicity of others, if I say
I am as happy as any. [I have that in me that can convert
poverty into riches, transforme adversity into prosperity. I am
more invulnerable than Achilles. Fortune hath not one place
to hit me].[2] *Ruat coelum, Fiat voluntas tua* salveth all; so that
whatsoever happens, it is but what our daily prayers desire. In
briefe, I am content, and what should providence adde more?
Surely this is it wee call Happinesse, and this doe I enjoy, with
this I am happy in a dreame, and as content to enjoy a happinesse
in a fancie as others in a more apparent truth and reality. There
is surely a neerer apprehension of any thing that delights us

[1] *This passage occurs in P only.*
[2] *This passage is found in the MSS and 1642.*

PART II in our dreames, than in our waked senses: [with this I can be a king without a crown, rich without a stiver; in Heaven though on earth; enjoy my friend and embrace him at a distance, when I cannot behold him];[1] without this I were unhappy, for my awaked judgement discontents me, ever whispering unto me, that I am from my friend; but my friendly dreames in the night requite me, and make me thinke I am within his armes. I thanke God for my happy dreames, as I doe for my good rest, for there is a satisfaction in them unto reasonable desires, and such as can be content with a fit of happinesse; and surely it is not a melancholy conceite to thinke we are all asleepe in this world, and that the conceits of this life are as meare dreames to those of the next, as the Phantasmes of the night, to the conceits of the day. There is an equall delusion in both, and the one doth but seeme to bee the embleme and picture of the other; we are somewhat more than our selves in our sleepes, and the slumber of the body seemes to bee but the waking of the soule. It is the ligation of sense, but the liberty of reason, and our waking conceptions doe not match the fancies of our sleepes. At my Nativity, my ascendant was the watery[2] signe of *Scorpius;* I was borne in the Planetary houre of *Saturne,* and I think I have a peece of that Leaden Planet in me. I am no way facetious, nor disposed for the mirth and galliardize of company; yet in one dreame I can compose a whole Comedy, behold the action, apprehend the jests, and laugh my selfe awake at the conceits thereof; were my memory as faithfull as my reason is then fruitfull, I would never study but in my dreames, and this time also would I chuse for my devotions; but our grosser memories have then so little hold of our abstracted understandings, that they forget the story, and can only relate to our awaked soules, a confused & broken tale of what hath passed. *Aristotle,* who hath written a singular tract of sleepe, hath not me thinkes throughly defined it, nor yet *Galen,* though hee seeme to have corrected it; for those *Noctambuloes* [or] night-walkers, though in their sleepe, doe yet enjoy the action of their senses; wee must therefore say that there is something in us that is not in the jurisdiction of

---

[1] *Thus in P, but also with variations in the other MSS and 1642.*

[2] *The MSS 1642 and 1643 have:* earthie, *or* earthly. *This is corrected in the* errata *of 1643.*

Morpheus; and that those abstracted and ecstaticke soules doe
walke about in their owne corps, as spirits in the bodies they
assume, wherein they seeme to heare, see and feele, though
indeed the organs are destitute of sense, and their natures of
those faculties that should informe them. Thus it is observed
that men sometimes upon the houre of their departure, doe
speake and reason above themselves. For then the soule
beginning to bee freed from the ligaments of the body, begins to
reason like her selfe, and to discourse in a straine above mortality.

WE tearme sleepe a death, and yet it is waking that kils us,
and destroyes those spirits which are the house of life. Tis
indeed a part of life that best expresseth death, for every man
truely lives so long as hee acts his nature, or someway makes
good the faculties of himselfe: *Themistocles* therefore that slew his
Souldier in his sleepe was a mercifull executioner; 'tis a kinde
of punishment the mildnesse of no lawes hath invented; I
wonder the fancy of *Lucan* and *Seneca* did not discover it. It is
that death by which we may be literally said to die daily, a
death which *Adam* died before his mortality; a death whereby
we live a middle and moderating point betweene life and death;
in fine, so like death, I dare not trust it without my prayers,
and an halfe adiew unto the world,[1] and take my farewell in a
Colloquy with God.

> *The night is come like to the day,*
> *Depart not thou great God away.*
> *Let not my sinnes, blacke as the night,*
> *Eclipse the lustre of thy light.*
> *Keepe still in my Horizon, for to me,*
> *The Sunne makes not the day, but thee.*
> *Thou whose nature cannot sleepe,*
> *On my temples centry keep;*
> *Guard me 'gainst those watchfull foes,*
> *Whose eyes are open while mine close.*
> *Let no dreames my head infest,*
> *But such as* Jacobs *temples blest.*

[1] *RJNW and 1642 add:* It is a fit time for devotion; I cannot therefore lay
me downe on my bed without an oration, and without taking my farewell in
a Colloquie with God.

While I doe rest, my soule advance,
Make my sleepe a holy trance:
That I may, my rest being wrought,
Awake into some holy thought.
And with as active vigour runne
My course, as doth the nimble Sunne.
Sleepe is a death, O make me try,
By sleeping what it is to die.
And [down] as gently lay my head
Upon my Grave, as now my bed.
How ere I rest, great God let me
Awake againe at last with thee.
And thus assur'd, behold I lie
Securely, whether to wake or die.
These are my drowsie dayes, in vaine
Now I doe wake to sleepe againe.
O come that houre, when I shall never
Sleepe [thus] againe, but wake for ever!

* [The name
of an extract
wherewith
wee use to
provoke
sleepe.]

This is the dormitive* I take to bedward; I need no other *Laudanum* than this to make me sleepe; after which I close mine eyes in security, content to take my leave of the Sunne, and sleepe unto the resurrection.

Section 13

THE method I should use in distributive justice, I often observe in commutative, and keepe a Geometricall proportion in both, whereby becomming equable to others, I become unjust to my selfe, and supererogate in that common principle, Doe unto others as thou wouldest be done unto thy selfe. I was not borne unto riches, nor is it I thinke my Starre to be wealthy; or if it were, the freedome of my minde, and frank.nesse of my disposition, were able to contradict and crosse my fates: for to me avarice seemes not so much a vice, as a deplorable piece of madnesse; to conceive our selves Urinals, or bee perswaded that wee are dead, is not so ridiculous, nor so many degrees beyond the power of Hellebore, as this. The opinions of theory and positions of men are not so voyd of reason as their practised conclusions: some have held that Snow is blacke, that the earth moves, that the soule is ayre, fire, water; but all this is Philosophy, and there is no *delirium*, if we doe but speculate the folly and indisputable dotage of avarice. To that subterraneous Idoll, and God of the earth, I doe confesse I am an Atheist; I cannot perswade my selfe to honour that which the world adores; whatsoever vertue its prepared substance may have within my body, it hath no influence nor operation without; I would not entertaine a base designe, or an action that should call mee villaine, for the Indies, and for this onely doe I love and honour my owne soule, and have mee thinkes, two armes too few to embrace my selfe. *Aristotle* is too severe, that will not allow us to be truely liberall without wealth, and the bountiful hand of fortune; if this be true, I must confesse I am charitable onely in my liberall intentions, and bountifull well-wishes. But if the example of the Mite bee not onely an act of wonder, but an example of the noblest charity, surely poore men may also build Hospitals, and the rich alone have not erected Cathedralls.[1] I have a private method which others observe not: I take the opportunity of my selfe to do good; I borrow occasion of charity from mine owne necessities, and supply the wants of others, when I am most in neede my selfe; [when I am reduced to the last tester, I love to divide it with the poore];[2] for it is an honest stratagem to take advantage of our selves, and so to husband the acts of vertue, that where they are defective in one circumstance, they may repay their want, and multiply their goodnesse in another. I have not *Peru* in my desires, but a competence, and abilitie to performe those good workes to which the Almighty hath inclined my nature. Hee is rich, who hath enough to bee charitable, and it is hard to bee so poore, that a noble minde may not finde a way to this piece of goodnesse. *Hee that gives to the poore lendeth to the Lord;* there is more Rhetorick in this one sentence than in a Library of Sermons, and indeed if these sentences were understood by the Reader, with the same Emphasis as they are delivered by the Author, wee needed not those Volumes of instructions, but might bee honest by an Epitome. Upon this motive onely I cannot behold a Begger without relieving his necessities with my purse, or his soule

---

[1] *The MSS and 1642 have instead*: I can justly boast I am as charitable as some who have built Hospitals, or erected Cathedrals.

[2] *This passage is found in the MSS and 1642.*

with my prayers; these scenicall and accidentall differences betweene us cannot make mee forget that common and untoucht part of us both; there is under these *Centoes* and miserable outsides, these mutilate and semi-bodies, a soule of the same alloy with our owne, whose Genealogy is God as well as ours, and in as faire a way unto salvation, as our selves. Statists that labour to contrive a Common-wealth without poverty,

* [The poore ye shall have alwaies with you.] take away the object of charity, not understanding only the Common-wealth of a Christian, but forgetting the prophecy of Christ.*

Section 14 NOW there is another part of charity, which is the Basis and Pillar of this, and that is the love of God, for whom wee love our neighbour: for this I thinke [is] charity, to love God for himselfe, and our neighbour for God. All that is truely amiable is God, or as it were a divided piece of him, that retaines a reflex or shadow of himselfe. Nor is it strange that wee should place [our] affection on that which is invisible; all that wee truely love is thus; what wee adore under [the] affection of our senses, deserves not the honour of so pure a title. Thus wee adore vertue, though to the eyes of sense shee bee invisible. Thus that part of our noble friends that wee love, is not that part that we embrace, but that insensible part that our armes cannot embrace. God being all goodnesse, can love nothing but himselfe; hee loves us but for that part which is as it were himselfe, and the traduction of his holy Spirit. Let us call to assize the love of our parents, the affection of our wives and children, and they are all dumb showes, and dreames, without reality, truth, or constancy; for first there is a strong bond of affection betweene us and our parents; yet how easily dissolved? We betake our selves to a woman, forgetting our mother in a wife, the wombe that bare us in that that shall [but] beare our image. This woman blessing us with children, our affection leaves the levell it held before and sinkes from our bed unto our issue and picture of [our] posterity, where affection holds no steady mansion. They growing up in yeares [either] desire our ends, or applying themselves to a woman, take a lawfull way to love another better than our selves. Thus I perceive a man may bee buried alive and behold his grave in his owne issue.

I CONCLUDE therefore and say, there is no happinesse PART II
Section 15
under (or as *Copernicus** will have it, above) the Sunne, nor any *[Who holds
the Sunne is
Crambe in that repeated veritie and burthen of all the wisedom the Sunne is
of *Solomon, All is vanitie and vexation of spirit;* there is no felicitie the center of
the World.]
in what the world adores. *Aristotle* whilst hee labours to refute
the Idea's of *Plato*, fals upon one himselfe: for his *summum bonum*,
is a *Chimæra*, and there is no such thing as his Felicity. That
wherein God himselfe is happy, the holy Angels are happy, in
whose defect the Devils are unhappy; that dare I call happinesse:
whatsoever conduceth unto this, may with an easie Metaphor
deserve that name; whatsoever else the world termes happines,
is to me a story out of *Pliny*, an apparition, or neat delusion,
wherin there is no more of happinesse than the name. Blesse
mee in this life but with the peace of my conscience, command
of my affections, the love of thy selfe and my dearest friend,[1]
and I shall be happy enough to pity *Cæsar*. These are O Lord
the humble desires of my most reasonable ambition and all I
dare call happinesse on earth: wherein I set no rule or limit to
thy hand or providence. Dispose of me according to the wisedome of thy pleasure. Thy will bee done, though in my owne
undoing.

FINIS

[1] *1642 and 1643 have*: friends. *P has*: the love of my dearest friend,
omitting: thyselfe and.

A LETTER
TO A FRIEND

A LETTER TO A FRIEND,
UPON OCCASION OF THE
DEATH OF HIS
INTIMATE FRIEND

GIVE me leave to wonder that News of this nature should have such heavy Wings, that you should hear so little concerning your dearest Friend, and that I must make that unwilling Repetition to tell you,

Ad portam rigidos calces extendit,

that he is Dead and Buried, and by this time no Puny among the mighty Nations of the Dead; for tho he left this World not very many days past, yet every hour you know largely addeth unto that dark Society; and considering the incessant Mortality of Mankind, you cannot conceive there dieth in the whole Earth so few as a thousand an hour.

Altho at this distance you had no early Account or Particular of his Death; yet your Affection may cease to wonder that you had not some secret Sense or Intimation thereof by Dreams, thoughtful Whisperings, Mercurisms, Airy Nuncio's, or sympathetical Insinuations, which many seem to have had at the Death of their dearest Friends: for since we find in that famous Story, that Spirits themselves were fain to tell their Fellows at a distance, that the great *Antonio* was dead; we have a sufficient Excuse for our Ignorance in such Particulars, and must rest content with the common Road, and *Appian* way of Knowledge by Information. Tho the uncertainty of the End of this World hath confounded all Humane Predictions; yet they who shall live to see the Sun and Moon darkned, and the Stars to fall from Heaven, will hardly be deceived in the Advent of the last Day; and therefore strange it is, that the common Fallacy of consumptive Persons, who feel not themselves dying, and therefore still hope to live, should also reach their Friends in perfect Health and Judgment. That you should be so little acquainted with *Plautus's* sick Complexion, or that almost an *Hippocratical* Face should not alarum you to higher fears, or rather despair of his Continuation in such an emaciated State, wherein medical Predictions fail not, as sometimes in acute Diseases, and wherein 'tis as dangerous to be sentenced by a Physician as a Judge.

Upon my first Visit I was bold to tell them who had not let fall all hopes of his Recovery, That in my sad Opinion he was not like to behold a Grashopper, much less to pluck another Fig; and in no long time after seemed to discover that odd mortal Symptom in him not mention'd by *Hippocrates*, that is, to lose his own Face and look like some of his near Relations; for he maintained not his proper Countenance, but looked like his Uncle, the Lines of whose Face lay deep and invisible in his healthful Visage before: for as from our beginning we run through variety of Looks, before we come to consistent and settled Faces; so before our End, by sick and languishing Alterations, we put on new Visages: and in our Retreat to Earth, may fall upon such Looks which from community of seminal Originals were before latent in us.

He was fruitlessly put in hope of advantage by change of Air, and imbibing the pure Aerial Nitre of these Parts; and therefore being so far spent, he quickly found *Sardinia* in *Tivoli*,* and the most healthful Air of little effect, where Death had set her Broad Arrow;* for he lived not unto the middle of *May*, and confirmed the Observation of *Hippocrates** of that mortal time of the Year when the Leaves of the Fig-tree resemble a Daw's Claw. He is happily seated who lives in Places whose Air, Earth, and Water, promote not the Infirmities of his weaker Parts, or is early removed into Regions that correct them. He that is tabidly inclined, were unwise to pass his days in *Portugal:* Cholical Persons will find little Comfort in *Austria* or *Vienna:* He that is Weak-legg'd must not be in Love with *Rome*, nor an infirm Head with *Venice* or *Paris*. Death hath not only particular Stars in Heaven, but malevolent Places on Earth, which single out our Infirmities, and strike at our weaker Parts; in which Concern, passager and migrant Birds have the great Advantages;

* *Cum mors venerit, in medio Tibure Sardinia est.*

* In the King's Forests they set the Figure of a broad Arrow upon Trees that are to be cut down.

* *Hippoc. Epidem.*

who are naturally constituted for distant Habitations, whom no Seas nor Places limit, but in their appointed Seasons will visit us from *Greenland* and Mount *Atlas*, and as some think, even from the *Antipodes*.*

Tho we could not have his Life, yet we missed not our desires in his soft Departure, which was scarce an Expiration; and his End not unlike his Beginning, when the salient Point scarce affords a sensible motion, and his Departure so like unto Sleep, that he scarce needed the civil Ceremony of closing his Eyes; contrary unto the common way wherein Death draws up, Sleep lets fall the Eye-lids. With what strift and pains we came into the World we know not; but 'tis commonly no easie matter to get out of it: yet if it could be made out, that such who have easie Nativities have commonly hard Deaths, and contrarily; his Departure was so easie, that we might justly suspect his Birth was of another nature, and that some *Juno* sat cross-legg'd at his Nativity.

Besides his soft Death, the incurable state of his Disease might somewhat extenuate your Sorrow, who know that Monsters but seldom happen, Miracles more rarely, in Physick.* *Angelus Victorius* gives a serious Account of a Consumptive, Hectical, Pthysical Woman, who was suddenly cured by the Intercession of *Ignatius*.* We read not of any in Scripture who in this case applied unto our Saviour, tho some may be contained in that large Expression, That *he went about Galilee healing all manner of Sickness, and all manner of Diseases*.* Amulets, Spells, Sigils and Incantations, practised in other Diseases, are seldom pretended in this; and we find no Sigil in the Archidoxis of *Paracelsus* to cure an extreme Consumption or *Marasmus*, which if other Diseases fail, will put a period unto long Livers, and at last make dust of all. And therefore the *Stoicks* could not but think that the firy Principle would wear out all the rest, and at last make an end of the World, which notwithstanding without such a lingring period the Creator may effect at his Pleasure: and to make an end of all things on Earth, and our Planetical System of the World, he need but put out the Sun.

I was not so curious to entitle the Stars unto any concern of his Death, yet could not but take notice that he died when the Moon was in motion from the Meridian; at which time, an old

* Bellonius *Avibus*.

* *Monstra contingunt in medicina.* Hippoc. Strange and rare Escapes there happen sometimes in Physick.

* *Angeli Victorii Consultationes.*

* Matth. iv. 23.

96 A LETTER TO A FRIEND

Italian long ago would persuade me, that the greatest part of Men died: but herein I confess I could never satisfie my Curiosity; altho from the time of Tides in Places upon or near the Sea, there may be considerable Deductions; and *Pliny** hath an odd and remarkable Passage concerning the Death of Men and Animals upon the Recess or Ebb of the Sea. However, certain it is he died in the dead and deep part of the Night, when *Nox* might be most apprehensibly said to be the Daughter of Chaos, the Mother of Sleep and Death, according to old Genealogy; and so went out of this World about that hour when our blessed Saviour entred it, and about what time many conceive he will return again unto it. *Cardan* hath a peculiar and no hard Observation from a Man's Hand, to know whether he was born in the day or night, which I confess holdeth in my own. And *Scaliger* to that purpose hath another from the tip of the Ear.* Most Men are begotten in the Night, most Animals in the Day; but whether more Persons have been born in the Night or the Day, were a Curiosity undecidable, tho more have perished by violent Deaths in the Day; yet in natural Dissolutions both Times may hold an Indifferency, at least but contingent Inequality. The whole course of Time runs out in the Nativity and Death of Things; which whether they happen by Succession or Coincidence, are best computed by the natural, not artificial Day.

That *Charles* the Fifth was Crowned upon the day of his Nativity, it being in his own power so to order it, makes no singular Animadversion; but that he should also take King *Francis* Prisoner upon that day, was an unexpected Coincidence, which made the same remarkable. *Antipater* who had an Anniversary Fever every Year upon his Birth day, needed no Astrological Revolution to know what day he should dye on. When the fixed Stars have made a Revolution unto the points from whence they first set out, some of the Ancients thought the World would have an end; which was a kind of dying upon the day of its Nativity. Now the Disease prevailing and swiftly advancing about the time of his Nativity, some were of Opinion, that he would leave the World on the day he entred into it: but this being a lingring Disease, and creeping softly on, nothing critical was found or expected, and he died not before fifteen

* *Aristoteles nullum animal nisi æstu recedente expirare affirmat: observatum id multum in Gallico Oceano & duntaxat in Homine compertum,* lib. 2 cap. 101.

* *Auris pars pendula Lobus dicitur, non omnibus ea pars est auribus; non enim iis qui noctu nati sunt, sed qui interdiu, maxima ex parte.* Com. in Aristot. de Animal. lib. I.

days after. Nothing is more common with Infants than to dye
on the day of their Nativity, to behold the worldly Hours and
but the Fractions thereof; and even to perish before their
Nativity in the hidden World of the Womb, and before their
good Angel is conceived to undertake them. But in Persons who
out-live many Years, and when there are no less than three
hundred sixty five days to determine their Lives in every Year;
that the first day should make the last, that the Tail of the
Snake should return into its Mouth precisely at that time, and
they should wind up upon the day of their Nativity,* is indeed   *According
a remarkable Coincidence, which tho Astrology hath taken   to the *Egyp-*
witty pains to salve, yet hath it been very wary in making Pre- *tian* Hiero-
dictions of it.   glyphick.

   In this consumptive Condition and remarkable Extenuation
he came to be almost half himself, and left a great part behind
him which he carried not to the Grave. And tho that Story of
Duke *John Ernestus Mansfield** be not so easily swallowed, that *[Knolles],
at his Death his Heart was found not to be so big as a Nut; yet *Turkish*
if the Bones of a good Sceleton weigh little more than twenty   History,
pounds, his Inwards and Flesh remaining could make no Bouff-   [ed. 1638,
age, but a light bit for the Grave. I never more lively beheld the p. 1471].
starved Characters of *Dante** in any living Face; an Aruspex   * In the Poet
might have read a Lecture upon him without Exenteration, his   *Dante* his
Flesh being so consumed that he might, in a manner, have   description.
discerned his Bowels without opening of him: so that to be   [*Purg.* c. xxiii.
carried *sextâ cervice* to the Grave, was but a civil unnecessity; 28].
and the Complements of the Coffin might out-weigh the Subject
of it.

   *Omnibonus Ferrarius** in mortal Dysenteries of Children looks * *De morbis*
for a Spot behind the Ear; in consumptive Diseases some eye   *Puerorum.*
the Complexion of Moals; *Cardan* eagerly views the Nails, some
the Lines of the Hand, the Thenar or Muscle of the Thumb;
some are so curious as to observe the depth of the Throat-pit,
how the proportion varieth of the Small of the Legs unto the
Calf, or the compass of the Neck unto the Circumference of the
Head: but all these, with many more, were so drowned in a
mortal Visage and last Face of *Hippocrates*, that a weak Physio- * *Morta*, the
gnomist might say at first eye, This was a Face of Earth, and that Deity of
*Morta** had set her Hard-Seal upon his Temples, easily perceiving Fate.

H

When Mens
Faces are
drawn with
resemblance
to some other
Animals, the
Italians call it,
to be drawn
in *Caricatura*.

★ *Ulmus de usu
barbæ humanæ.*

The Life of a
Man is
Three-score
and Ten.

His upper
and lower
Jaw being
solid, and
without
distinct rows
of Teeth.

★ See *Picotus de
Rheumatismo.*

★ Twice tell
over his
Teeth, never
live to three-
score Years.

what *Caricatura*★ Draughts Death makes upon pined Faces, and unto what an unknown degree a Man may live backward.

Tho the Beard be only made a distinction of Sex and sign of masculine Heat by *Ulmus*,★ yet the Precocity and early growth thereof in him, was not to be liked in reference unto long Life. *Lewis*, that virtuous but unfortunate King of *Hungary*, who lost his Life at the Battel of *Mohacz*, was said to be born without a Skin, to have bearded at Fifteen, and to have shewn some gray Hairs about Twenty; from whence the Diviners conjectured, that he would be spoiled of his Kingdom, and have but a short Life: But Hairs make fallible Predictions, and many Temples early gray have out-lived the Psalmist's Period.★ Hairs which have most amused me have not been in the Face or Head but on the Back, and not in Men but Children, as I long ago observed in that Endemial Distemper of little Children in *Languedock*, called the *Morgellons*, wherein they critically break out with harsh Hairs on their Backs, which takes off the unquiet Symptoms of the Disease, and delivers them from Coughs and Convulsions.

The *Egyptian* Mummies that I have seen, have had their Mouths open, and somewhat gaping, which affordeth a good opportunity to view and observe their Teeth, wherein 'tis not easie to find any wanting or decayed: and therefore in *Egypt*, where one Man practised but one Operation, or the Diseases but of single Parts, it must needs be a barren Profession to confine unto that of drawing of Teeth, and little better than to have been Tooth-drawer unto King *Pyrrhus*, who had but two in his Head.★ How the *Bannyans* of *India* maintain the Integrity of those Parts, I find not particularly observed; who notwithstanding have an Advantage of their Preservation by abstaining from all Flesh, and employing their Teeth in such Food unto which they may seem at first framed, from their Figure and Conformation: but sharp and corroding Rheums★ had so early mouldred those Rocks and hardest parts of his Fabrick, that a Man might well conceive that his Years were never like to double or twice tell over his Teeth.★ Corruption had dealt more severely with them, than sepulchral Fires and smart Flames with those of burnt Bodies of old; for in the burnt Fragments of Urns which I have enquired into, altho I seem to find few Incisors or Shearers, yet the Dog Teeth and Grinders do notably resist those Fires.

In the Years of his Childhood he had languished under the Disease of his Country, the Rickets; after which notwithstanding many I have seen become strong and active Men; but whether any have attained unto very great Years the Disease is scarce so old as to afford good Observation. Whether the Children of the *English* Plantations be subject unto the same Infirmity, may be worth the observing. Whether Lameness and Halting do still encrease among the Inhabitants of *Rovigno* in *Istria*, I know not; yet scarce twenty Years ago Monsieur *du Loyr* observed, that a third part of that People halted: but too certain it is, that the Rickets encreaseth among us; the Small-Pox grows more pernicious than the Great: the Kings Purse knows that the King's Evil grows more common. *Quartan* Agues are become no Strangers in *Ireland*; more common and mortal in *England:* and tho the Ancients gave that Disease very good Words,* yet now that Bell makes no strange sound which rings out for the Effects thereof.*

Some think there were few Consumptions in the Old World, when Men lived much upon Milk; and that the ancient Inhabitants of this Island were less troubled with Coughs when they went naked, and slept in Caves and Woods, than Men now in Chambers and Feather-beds. *Plato* will tell us, that there was no such Disease as a Catarrh in *Homer*'s time, and that it was but new in *Greece* in his Age. *Polydore Virgil* delivereth that Pleurisies were rare in *England*, who lived but in the days of *Henry* the Eighth. Some will allow no Diseases to be new, others think that many old ones are ceased; and that such which are esteemed new, will have but their time: However, the Mercy of God hath scattered the great heap of Diseases, and not loaded any one Country with all: some may be new in one Country which have been old in another. New Discoveries of the Earth discover new Diseases: for besides the common swarm, there are endemial and local Infirmities proper unto certain Regions, which in the whole Earth make no small number: and if *Asia*, *Africa*, and *America* should bring in their List, *Pandoras* Box would swell, and there must be a strange Pathology.

Most Men expected to find a consumed Kell, empty and

* Ἀσφαλέστα-τος καὶ ῥήϊστος *securissima & facillima,* Hippocrat.

* Pro febre quartana raro sonat campana.

bladder-like Guts, livid and marbled Lungs, and a withered *Pericardium* in this exuccous Corps: but some seemed too much to wonder that two Lobes of his Lungs adhered unto his side; for the like I had often found in Bodies of no suspected Consumptions or difficulty of Respiration. And the same more often happeneth in Men than other Animals; and some think, in Women than in Men: but the most remarkable I have met ★ So *A. J*¹. with, was in a Man,★ after a Cough of almost fifty Years, in whom all the Lobes adhered unto the Pleura, and each Lobe unto another; who having also been much troubled with the Gout, ★ *Cardan* in brake the Rule of *Cardan*,★ and died of the Stone in the Bladder. his *Encomium* *Aristotle* makes a Query, Why some Animals cough as Man, *Podagræ* reckoneth some not, as Oxen. If coughing be taken as it consisteth of a this among natural and voluntary motion, including Expectoration and the *Dona* spitting out, it may be as proper unto Man as bleeding at the *Podagræ*, that Nose; otherwise we find that *Vegetius* and Rural Writers have they are delivered not left so many Medicines in vain against the Coughs of thereby from Cattel; and Men who perish by Coughs dye the Death of Sheep, the Pthysis and Stone in Cats and Lyons: and tho Birds have no Midriff, yet we meet the Bladder. with divers Remedies in *Arrianus* against the Coughs of Hawks. And tho it might be thought, that all Animals who have Lungs do cough; yet in cetaceous Fishes, who have large and strong Lungs, the same is not observed; nor yet in oviparous Quadrupeds: and in the greatest thereof, the Crocodile, altho we read much of their Tears, we find nothing of that motion.

From the Thoughts of Sleep, when the Soul was conceived nearest unto Divinity, the Ancients erected an Art of Divination, wherein while they too widely expatiated in loose and ★ *Hippoc. de* inconsequent Conjectures, *Hippocrates*★ wisely considered Dreams *Insomniis* [§89, as they presaged Alterations in the Body, and so afforded hints t. vi, p. 652]. toward the preservation of Health, and prevention of Diseases; and therein was so serious as to advise Alteration of Diet, Exercise, Sweating, Bathing and Vomiting; and also so religious, as to order Prayers and Supplications unto respective Deities, in good Dreams unto *Sol, Jupiter cœlestis, Jupiter opulentus, Minerva, Mercurius,* and *Apollo;* in bad unto *Tellus* and the Heroes.

And therefore I could not but take notice how his Female Friends were irrationally curious so strictly to examine his

¹ See note on Sir Arthur Jenny, vol. iii, p. 301 of the *Collected Works*, 1964.

Dreams, and in this low state to hope for the Fantasms of
Health. He was now past the healthful Dreams of the Sun, Moon,
and Stars in their Clarity and proper Courses. 'Twas too late
to dream of Flying, of Limpid Fountains, smooth Waters, white
Vestments, and fruitful green Trees, which are the Visions of
healthful Sleeps, and at good distance from the Grave.

And they were also too deeply dejected that he should dream
of his dead Friends, inconsequently divining, that he would not
be long from them; for strange it was not that he should sometimes dream of the dead whose Thoughts run always upon
Death: beside, to dream of the dead, so they appear not in dark
Habits, and take nothing away from us, in *Hippocrates*★ his
Sense was of good signification: for we live by the dead, and
every thing is or must be so before it becomes our Nourishment. And *Cardan*, who dream'd that he discoursed with his
dead Father in the Moon, made thereof no mortal Interpretation: and even to dream that we are dead, was no condemnable
Fantasm in old *Oneirocriticism*, as having a signification of
Liberty, vacuity from Cares, exemption and freedom from
Troubles, unknown unto the dead.

★ *Hippoc. de
Insomniis* [§ 92,
t. vi, p. 658].

Some Dreams I confess may admit of easie and feminine
Exposition: he who dream'd that he could not see his right
Shoulder, might easily fear to lose the sight of his right Eye; he
that before a Journey dream'd that his Feet were cut off, had a
plain warning not to undertake his intended Journey. But why
to dream of Lettuce should presage some ensuing Disease, why
to eat Figs should signifie foolish Talk, why to eat Eggs great
Trouble, and to dream of Blindness should be so highly commended, according to the *Oneirocritical* Verses of *Astrampsychus*
and *Nicephorus*, I shall leave unto your Divination.

He was willing to quit the World alone and altogether,
leaving no Earnest behind him for Corruption or Aftergrave,
having small content in that common satisfaction to survive or
live in another, but amply satisfied that his Disease should dye
with himself, nor revive in a Posterity to puzzle Physick, and
make sad *Memento's* of their Parent hereditary. Leprosie awakes
not sometimes before Forty, the Gout and Stone often later;
but consumptive and tabid★ Roots sprout more early, and at the
fairest make seventeen Years of our Life doubtful before that

★ *Tabes maxime
contingunt ab
anno decimo
octavo ad tri-
gesimum quin-
tum*, Hippoc.

Age. They that enter the World with original Diseases as well as Sin, have not only common Mortality but sick Traductions to destroy them, make commonly short Courses, and live not at length but in Figures; so that a sound *Cæsarean* Nativity* may out-last a natural Birth, and a Knife may sometimes make way for a more lasting fruit than a Midwife; which makes so few Infants now able to endure the old Test of the River,* and many to have feeble Children who could scarce have been married at *Sparta*, and those provident States who studied strong and healthful Generations; which happen but contingently in mere *pecuniary* Matches, or Marriages made by the Candle, wherein notwithstanding there is little redress to be hoped from an Astrologer or a Lawyer, and a good discerning Physician were like to prove the most successful Counsellor.

> * A sound Child cut out of the Body of the Mother.
>
> * *Natos ad flumina primum deferimus sævoq; gelu duramus & undis.*

Julius Scaliger, who in a sleepless Fit of the Gout could make two hundred Verses in a Night, would have but five plain Words* upon his Tomb. And this serious Person, tho no *minor* Wit, left the Poetry of his Epitaph unto others; either unwilling to commend himself, or to be judged by a Distich, and perhaps considering how unhappy great Poets have been in versifying their own Epitaphs; wherein *Petrarcha, Dante,* and *Ariosto,* have so unhappily failed, that if their Tombs should out-last their Works, Posterity would find so little of *Apollo* on them, as to mistake them for Ciceronian Poets.

> * *Julii Cæsaris Scaligeri quod fuit.* Joseph Scaliger *in vita patris.*

In this deliberate and creeping progress unto the Grave, he was somewhat too young, and of too noble a mind, to fall upon that stupid Symptom observable in divers Persons near their Journeys end, and which may be reckoned among the mortal Symptoms of their last Disease; that is, to become more narrow minded, miserable and tenacious, unready to part with any thing when they are ready to part with all, and afraid to want when they have no time to spend; mean while Physicians, who know that many are mad but in a single depraved Imagination, and one prevalent Desipiency; and that beside and out of such single Deliriums a Man may meet with sober Actions and good Sense in *Bedlam;* cannot but smile to see the Heirs and concerned Relations, gratulating themselves in the sober departure of their Friends; and tho they behold such mad covetous Passages, content to think they dye in good Understanding, and in their sober Senses.

Avarice, which is not only Infidelity but Idolatry, either from covetous Progeny or questuary Education, had no Root in his Breast, who made good Works the Expression of his Faith, and was big with desires unto publick and lasting Charities; and surely where good Wishes and charitable Intentions exceed Abilities, Theorical Beneficency may be more than a Dream. They build not Castles in the Air who would build Churches on Earth; and tho they leave no such Structures here, may lay good Foundations in Heaven. In brief, his Life and Death were such, that I could not blame them who wished the like, and almost to have been himself; almost, I say; for tho we may wish the prosperous Appurtenances of others, or to be an other in his happy Accidents; yet so intrinsecal is every Man unto himself, that some doubt may be made, whether any would exchange his Being, or substantially become another Man.

He had wisely seen the World at home and abroad, and thereby observed under what variety Men are deluded in the pursuit of that which is not here to be found. And altho he had no Opinion of reputed Felicities below, and apprehended Men widely out in the estimate of such Happiness; yet his sober contempt of the World wrought no *Democritism* or *Cynicism*, no laughing or snarling at it, as well understanding there are not Felicities in this World to satisfie a serious Mind; and therefore to soften the stream of our Lives, we are fain to take in the reputed Contentations of this World, to unite with the Crowd in their Beatitudes, and to make our selves happy by Consortion, Opinion, or Co-existimation: for strictly to separate from received and customary Felicities, and to confine unto the rigor of Realities, were to contract the Consolation of our Beings unto too uncomfortable Circumscriptions.

Not to fear Death,* nor desire it, was short of his Resolution: to be dissolved, and be with Christ, was his dying ditty. He conceived his Thred long, in no long course of Years, and when he had scarce out-lived the second Life of *Lazarus;** esteeming it enough to approach the Years of his Saviour, who so ordered his own humane State, as not to be old upon Earth.

But to be content with Death may be better than to desire it: a miserable Life may make us wish for Death, but a virtuous one to rest in it; which is the Advantage of those resolved

* *Summum nec metuas diem nec optes.*

* Who upon some Accounts, and Tradition, is said to have lived 30 Years after he was raised by our Saviour. *Baronius.*

Christians, who looking on Death not only as the sting, but the period and end of Sin, the Horizon and Isthmus between this Life and a better, and the Death of this World but as a Nativity of another, do contentedly submit unto the common Necessity, and envy not *Enoch* or *Elias*.

Not to be content with Life is the unsatisfactory state of those which destroy themselves;* who being afraid to live, run blindly upon their own Death, which no Man fears by Experience: and the *Stoicks* had a notable Doctrine to take away the fear thereof; that is, In such Extremities to desire that which is not to be avoided, and wish what might be feared; and so made Evils voluntary, and to suit with their own Desires, which took off the terror of them.

But the ancient Martyrs were not encouraged by such Fallacies; who, tho they feared not Death were afraid to be their own Executioners; and therefore thought it more Wisdom to crucifie their Lusts than their Bodies, to circumcise than stab their Hearts, and to mortifie than kill themselves.

His willingness to leave this World about that Age when most Men think they may best enjoy it, tho paradoxical unto worldly Ears, was not strange unto mine, who have so often observed, that many, tho old, oft stick fast unto the World, and seem to be drawn like *Cacus*'s Oxen, backward with great strugling and reluctancy unto the Grave. The long habit of Living makes meer Men more hardly to part with Life, and all to be nothing, but what is to come. To live at the rate of the old World, when some could scarce remember themselves young, may afford no better digested Death than a more moderate period. Many would have thought it an Happiness to have had their lot of Life in some notable Conjunctures of Ages past; but the uncertainty of future Times hath tempted few to make a part in Ages to come. And surely, he that hath taken the true Altitude of Things, and rightly calculated the degenerate state of this Age, is not like to envy those that shall live in the next, much less three or four hundred Years hence, when no Man can comfortably imagine what Face this World will carry: and therefore since every Age makes a step unto the end of all things, and the Scripture affords so hard a Character of the last Times; quiet Minds will be content with their Generations, and rather bless Ages past than be ambitious of those to come.

* In the Speech of *Vulteius in Lucan*, animating his Souldiers in a great struggle to kill one another. *Decernite Lethum & metus omnis abest, cupias quodcunq; necesse est.* All fear is over, do but resolve to dye, and make your Desires meet Necessity.

Tho Age had set no Seal upon his Face, yet a dim Eye might clearly discover Fifty in his Actions; and therefore since Wisdom is the gray Hair, and an unspotted Life old Age;* altho his *Wisdom cap. Years came short, he might have been said to have held up iv. with longer Livers, and to have been *Solomon*'s Old Man. And surely if we deduct all those days of our Life which we might wish unlived, and which abate the comfort of those we now live; if we reckon up only those days which God hath accepted of our Lives, a Life of good Years will hardly be a span long: the Son in this sense may out-live the Father, and none be climaterically old. He that early arriveth unto the Parts and Prudence of Age, is happily old without the uncomfortable Attendants of it; and 'tis superfluous to live unto gray Hairs, when in a precocious Temper we anticipate the Virtues of them. In brief, he cannot be accounted young who out-liveth the old Man. He that hath early arrived unto the measure of a perfect Stature in Christ, hath already fulfilled the prime and longest Intention of his Being: and one day lived after the perfect Rule of Piety, is to be preferred before sinning Immortality.

Although he attained not unto the Years of his Predecessors, yet he wanted not those preserving Virtues which confirm the thread of weaker Constitutions. Cautelous Chastity and crafty Sobriety were far from him; those Jewels were Paragon, without Flaw, Hair, Ice, or Cloud in him: which affords me an hint to proceed in these good Wishes and few *Memento's* unto you.

Tread softly and circumspectly in this funambulous Track and narrow Path of Goodness: pursue Virtue virtuously; be sober and temperate, not to preserve your Body in a sufficiency to wanton Ends; not to spare your Purse; not to be free from the Infamy of common Transgressors that way, and thereby to ballance or palliate obscure and closer Vices; nor simply to enjoy Health: by all which you may leaven good Actions, and render Virtues disputable: but in one Word, that you may truly serve God; which every Sickness will tell you, you cannot well do without Health. The sick mans Sacrifice is but a lame Oblation. Pious Treasures laid up in healthful days, excuse the defect of sick Non-performances; without which we must needs look back with Anxiety upon the lost opportunities of Health; and may have cause rather to envy than pity the Ends of penitent

Malefactors, who go with clear parts unto the last Act of their Lives; and in the integrity of their Faculties return their Spirit unto God that gave it.

Consider whereabout thou art in *Cebes* his Table, or that old philosophical Pinax of the Life of Man; whether thou art still in the Road of Uncertainties; whether thou hast yet entred the narrow Gate, got up the Hill and asperous way which leadeth unto the House of Sanity, or taken that purifying Potion from the hand of sincere Erudition, which may send thee clear and pure a way unto a virtuous and happy Life.

In this virtuous Voyage let not disappointment cause Despondency, nor difficulty Despair: think not that you are sailing from *Lima* to *Manillia*, wherein thou may'st tye up the Rudder, and sleep before the Wind;* but expect rough Seas, Flaws, and contrary Blasts; and 'tis well if by many cross Tacks and Verings thou arrivest at thy Port. Sit not down in the popular Seats and common Level of Virtues, but endeavour to make them Heroical. Offer not only Peace-Offerings but Holocausts unto God. To serve him singly, to serve our selves, were too partial a piece of Piety, nor likely to place us in the highest Mansions of Glory.

* Through the Pacifick Sea, with a constant Gale from the East.

He that is chaste and continent, not to impair his Strength, or terrified by Contagion, will hardly be heroically virtuous. Adjourn not that Virtue unto those Years when *Cato* could lend out his Wife, and impotent Satyrs write Satyrs against Lust: but be chaste in thy flaming days, when *Alexander* dared not trust his Eyes upon the fair Daughters of *Darius*, and when so many Men think there is no other way but *Origen*'s.*

Who is said to have castrated himself.

Be charitable before Wealth makes thee covetous, and lose not the Glory of the Mite. If Riches increase, let thy Mind hold pace with them; and think it not enough to be liberal, but munificent. Tho a Cup of cold Water from some hand may not be without its ·Reward; yet stick not thou for Wine and Oyl for the Wounds of the distressed: and treat the Poor as our Saviour did the Multitude, to the Relicks of some Baskets.

Trust not to the Omnipotency of Gold, or say unto it, Thou art my Confidence: Kiss not thy Hand when thou beholdest that terrestrial Sun, nor bore thy Ear unto its Servitude. A Slave unto Mammon makes no Servant unto God: Covetousness cracks the Sinews of Faith, numbs the Apprehension of any thing above Sense, and only affected with the certainty of things present, makes a peradventure of Things to come; lives but unto one World, nor hopes but fears another; makes our own Death sweet unto others, bitter unto our selves; gives a dry Funeral, Scenical Mourning, and no wet Eyes at the Grave.

If Avarice be thy Vice, yet make it not thy Punishment: miserable Men commiserate not themselves, bowelless unto themselves, and merciless unto their own Bowels. Let the fruition of Things bless the possession of them, and take no satisfaction in dying but living rich: for since thy good Works, not thy Goods, will follow thee; since Riches are an Appurtenance of Life, and no dead Man is rich, to famish in Plenty, and live poorly to dye rich, were a multiplying improvement in Madness, and Use upon Use in Folly.

Persons lightly dip'd, not grain'd in generous Honesty, are but pale in Goodness, and faint hued in Sincerity: but be thou what thou virtuously art, and let not the Ocean wash away thy Tincture: stand magnetically upon that Axis where prudent Simplicity hath fix'd thee, and let no Temptation invert the Poles of thy Honesty: and that Vice may be uneasie, and even monstrous unto thee, let iterated good Acts, and long confirmed Habits, make Vertue natural, or a second Nature in thee. And since few or none prove eminently vertuous but from some advantageous Foundations in their Temper and natural Inclinations; study thy self betimes, and early find, what Nature bids thee to be, or tells thee what thou may'st be. They who thus timely descend into themselves, cultivating the good Seeds which Nature hath set in them, and improving their prevalent Inclinations to Perfection, become not Shrubs, but Cedars in their Generation; and to be in the form of the best of the Bad, or the worst of the Good, will be no satisfaction unto them.

Let not the Law of thy Country be the *non ultra* of thy Honesty, nor think that always good enough which the Law will make good. Narrow not the Law of Charity, Equity, Mercy; joyn Gospel Righteousness with Legal Right; be not a meer *Gamaliel* in the Faith; but let the Sermon in the Mount be thy *Targum* unto the Law of *Sinai*.

Make not the Consequences of Vertue the Ends thereof: be not beneficent for a Name or Cymbal of Applause, nor exact and punctual in Commerce, for the Advantages of Trust and Credit, which attend the Reputation of just and true Dealing; for such Rewards, tho unsought for, plain Virtue will bring with her, whom all Men honour, tho they pursue not. To have other bye ends in good Actions, sowers laudable Performances, which must have deeper Roots, Motions, and Instigations, to give them the Stamp of Vertues.

Tho humane Infirmity may betray thy heedless days into the popular ways of Extravagancy, yet let not thine own depravity, or the torrent of vicious Times, carry thee into desperate Enormities in Opinions, Manners, or Actions: if thou hast dip'd thy foot in the River, yet venture not over *Rubicon;* run not into Extremities from whence there is no Regression, nor be ever so closely shut up within the holds of Vice and Iniquity, as not to find some Escape by a Postern of Resipiscency.

Owe not thy Humility unto Humiliation by Adversity, but look humbly down in that State when others look upward upon thee: be patient in the Age of Pride and days of Will and Impatiency, when Men live but by Intervals of Reason, under the Sovereignty of Humor and Passion, when 'tis in the Power of every one to transform thee out of thy self, and put thee into the short Madness.* If you cannot imitate *Job,* yet come not short of *Socrates,* and those patient Pagans, who tired the Tongues of their Enemies, while they perceiv'd they spet their Malice at brazen Walls and Statues.

* Ira furor brevis est.

Let Age, not Envy, draw Wrinkles on thy Cheeks: be content to be envied, but envy not. Emulation may be plausible, and Indignation allowable; but admit no Treaty with that Passion which no Circumstance can make good. A Displacency at the good of others, because they enjoy it, altho we do not want it, is an absurd Depravity, sticking fast unto humane Nature from its primitive Corruption; which he that can well subdue, were a Christian of the first Magnitude, and for ought I know, may have one foot already in Heaven.

While thou so hotly disclaimst the Devil, be not guilty of Diabolism; fall not into one Name with that unclean Spirit, nor act his Nature whom thou so much abhorrest; that is, to accuse, calumniate, backbite, whisper, detract, or sinistrously interpret others; degenerous Depravities and narrow-minded Vices, not only below S. *Paul*'s noble Christian, but *Aristotle*'s true Gentleman.* Trust not with some, that the Epistle of S. *James* is Apocryphal, and so read with less fear that stabbing truth, that in company with this Vice thy Religion is in vain. *Moses* broke the Tables without breaking of the Law; but where Charity is broke the Law it self is shattered, which cannot be whole without Love, that is the fulfilling of it. Look humbly upon thy Virtues, and tho thou art rich in some, yet think thy self poor and naked without that crowning Grace, which thinketh no Evil, which envieth not, which beareth, believeth, hopeth, endureth all things. With these sure Graces, while busie Tongues are crying out for a drop of cold Water, Mutes may be in Happiness, and sing the *Trisagium** in Heaven.

* See *Arist.* *Ethicks* Chapt. of Magnanimity.

* Holy, Holy, Holy.

Let not the Sun in *Capricorn** go down upon thy Wrath, but write thy Wrongs in Water; draw the Curtain of Night upon Injuries; shut them up in the Tower of Oblivion,* and let them be as tho they had not been. Forgive thine Enemies totally, and without any Reserve of hope, that however, God will revenge thee.

* Even when the days are shortest.

* Alluding to the Tower of Oblivion mentioned by *Procopius*, which was the name of a Tower of Imprisonment among the *Persians:* whosoever was put therein, he was as it were buried alive, and it was Death for any but to name him.

Be substantially great in thy self, and more than thou appearest unto others; and let the World be deceived in thee, as they are in the Lights of Heaven. Hang early Plummets upon the Heels of Pride, and let Ambition have but an Epicycle or narrow Circuit in thee. Measure not thy self by thy Morning shadow, but by the Extent of thy Grave; and reckon thy self above the Earth by the Line thou must be contented with under it. Spread not into boundless Expansions either of Designs or Desires. Think not that Mankind liveth but for a few, and that the rest are born but to serve the Ambition of those, who make but Flies of Men, and Wildernesses of whole Nations. Swell not into Actions which embroil and confound the Earth; but be one of those violent ones which force the Kingdom of Heaven.* If thou must needs reign, be *Zeno*'s King, and enjoy that Empire which every Man gives himself. Certainly the iterated Injunctions of Christ unto Humility, Meekness, Patience, and that despised Train of Virtues, cannot but make pathetical Impressions upon those who have well considered the Affairs of all

* *Matthew* xi. [12].

Ages, wherein Pride, Ambition, and Vain-glory, have led up the worst of Actions, and whereunto Confusion, Tragedies, and Acts denying all Religion, do owe their Originals.

* Ovation a petty and minor kind of Triumph. Rest not in an Ovation,* but a Triumph over thy Passions; chain up the unruly Legion of thy Breast; behold thy Trophies within thee, not without thee: Lead thine own Captivity captive, and be *Cæsar* unto thy self.

Give no quarter unto those Vices which are of thine inward Family: and having a Root in thy Temper, plead a Right and Propriety in thee. Examine well thy complexional Inclinations. Raise early Batteries against those strong-holds built upon the Rock of Nature, and make this a great part of the Militia of thy Life. The politick Nature of Vice must be opposed by Policy, and therefore wiser Honesties Project and plot against Sin; wherein notwithstanding we are not to rest in Generals, or the trite Stratagems of Art: that may succeed with one Temper which may prove successless with another. There is no Community or Commonwealth of Virtue; every Man must study his own OEconomy, and erect these Rules unto the Figure of himself.

Lastly, If length of Days be thy Portion, make it not thy Expectation: reckon not upon long Life, but live always beyond thy Account. He that so often surviveth his Expectation, lives many Lives, and will hardly complain of the shortness of his Days. Time past is gone like a shadow; make Times to come, present; conceive that near which may be far off; approximate thy last Times by present Apprehensions of them: live like a Neighbour unto Death, and think there is but little to come. And since there is something in us that must still live on, joyn both Lives together; unite them in thy Thoughts and Actions, and live in one but for the other. He who thus ordereth the Purposes of this Life, will never be far from the next; and is in some manner already in it, by an happy Conformity, and close Apprehension of it.

FINIS

PUBLISHER'S NOTE

The text of *Hydriotaphia* is reprinted by permission, from the edition published by the Cambridge University Press, edited by John Carter.

En Sum quod digitis Quinque Levatur onus Propert:

HYDRIOTAPHIA
URNE-BURIAL

OR,
A BRIEF DISCOURSE
OF THE SEPULCHRALL URNES
LATELY FOUND IN
NORFOLK

TO MY

Worthy and Honoured Friend

THOMAS LE GROS

of *Crostwick* Esquire

WHEN the Funerall pyre was out, and the last valediction over, men took a lasting adieu of their interred Friends, little expecting the curiosity of future ages should comment upon their ashes, and having no old experience of the duration of their Reliques, held no opinion of such after considerations.

But who knows the fate of his bones, or how often he is to be buried? who hath the Oracle of his ashes, or whither they are to be scattered? The Reliques of many lie like the ruines of *Pompeys*,[a] in all parts of the earth; And when they arrive at your hands, these may seem to have wandred far, who in a direct[b] and *Meridian* Travell, have but few miles of known Earth between your self and the Pole.

That the bones of *Theseus* should be seen again in *Athens*,[c] was not beyond conjecture, and hopeful expectation; but that these should arise so opportunely to serve your self, was an hit of fate and honour beyond prediction.

We cannot but wish these Urnes might have the effect of Theatrical vessels, and great *Hippodrome* Urnes[d] in *Rome*; to resound the acclamations and honour due unto you. But these are sad and sepulchral Pitchers, which have no joyful voices; silently expressing old mortality, the ruines of forgotten times, and can only speak with life, how long in this corruptible frame, some parts may be uncorrupted; yet able to out-last bones long unborn, and noblest pyle[e] among us.

We present not these as any strange sight or spectacle unknown to your eyes, who have beheld the best of Urnes, and

a *Pompeios juvenes Asia, atque Europa, sed ipsum terra tegit Lybies.*

b Little directly, but Sea between your house and *Greenland.*

c Brought back by *Cimon.* Plutarch.

d The great Urnes in the *Hippodrome* at *Rome* conceived to resound the voices of people at their shows.

e Worthily possessed by that true Gentleman Sir *Horatio Townshend,* my honored Friend.

noblest variety of Ashes; Who are your self no slender master of Antiquities, and can daily command the view of so many Imperiall faces; Which raiseth your thoughts unto old things, and consideration of times before you, when even living men were Antiquities; when the living might exceed the dead, and to depart this world could not be properly said, to go unto the greater number.[f] And so run up your thoughts upon the ancient of dayes, the Antiquaries truest object, unto whom the eldest parcels are young, and earth it self an Infant; and without Ægyptian[g] account makes but small noise in thousands.

We were hinted by the occasion, not catched the opportunity to write of old things, or intrude upon the Antiquary. We are coldly drawn unto discourses of Antiquities, who have scarce time before us to comprehend new things, or make out learned Novelties. But seeing they arose as they lay, almost in silence among us, at least in short account suddenly passed over; we were very unwilling they should die again, and be buried twice among us.

Beside, to preserve the living, and make the dead to live, to keep men out of their Urnes, and discourse of humane fragments in them, is not impertinent unto our profession; whose study is life and death, who daily behold examples of mortality, and of all men least need artificial *memento's*, or coffins by our bed side, to minde us of our graves.

'Tis time to observe Occurrences, and let nothing remarkable escape us; The Supinity of elder dayes hath left so much in silence, or time hath so martyred the Records, that the most industrious heads[h] do finde no easie work to erect a new *Britannia*.

'Tis opportune to look back upon old times, and contemplate our Forefathers. Great examples grow thin, and to be fetched from the passed world. Simplicity flies away, and iniquity comes at long strides upon us. We have enough to do to make up our selves from present and passed times, and the whole stage of things scarce serveth for our instruction. A compleat peece of vertue must be made up from the *Centos* of all ages, as all the beauties of *Greece* could make but one handsome *Venus*.

When the bones of King *Arthur* were digged up,[i] the old Race might think, they beheld therein some Originals of themselves;

[f] *Abiit ad plures.*

[g] Which makes the world so many years old.

[h] Wherein Mr *Dugdale* hath excellently well endeavoured, and worthy to be countenanced by ingenuous and noble persons.

[i] In the time of *Henry* the second. *Cambden.*

Unto these of our Urnes none here can pretend relation, and can only behold the Reliques of those persons, who in their life giving the Law unto their predecessors, after long obscurity, now lye at their mercies. But remembring the early civility they brought upon these Countreys, and forgetting long passed mischiefs; We mercifully preserve their bones, and pisse not upon their ashes.

In the offer of these Antiquities we drive not at ancient Families, so long out-lasted by them; We are farre from erecting your worth upon the pillars of your Fore-fathers, whose merits you illustrate. We honour your old Virtues, conformable unto times before you, which are the Noblest Armoury. And having long experience of your friendly conversation, void of empty Formality, full of freedome, constant and Generous Honesty, I look upon you as a Gemme of the Old Rock,^k and must professe my self even to Urne and Ashes,

^k *Adamas de rupe veteri præstantissimus.*

Your ever faithfull Friend,

and Servant,

Norwich   *Thomas Browne.*

May 1

[1658]

HYDRIOTAPHIA

URNE-BURIALL

CHAPTER I

IN the deep discovery of the Subterranean world, a shallow part would satisfie some enquirers; who, if two or three yards were open about the surface, would not care to rake the bowels of *Potosi*,[a] and regions towards the Centre. Nature hath furnished one part of the Earth, and man another. The treasures of time lie high, in Urnes, Coynes, and Monuments, scarce below the roots of some vegetables. Time hath endlesse rarities, and shows of all varieties; which reveals old things in heaven, makes new discoveries in earth, and even earth it self a discovery. That great Antiquity *America* lay buried for thousands of years; and a large part of the earth is still in the Urne unto us.

a The rich mountain of *Peru.*

Though if *Adam* were made out of an extract of the Earth, all parts might challenge a restitution, yet few have returned their bones farre lower than they might receive them; not affecting the graves of Giants, under hilly and heavy coverings, but content with lesse than their owne depth, have wished their bones might lie soft, and the earth be light upon them; Even such as hope to rise again, would not be content with centrall interrment, or so desperately to place their reliques as to lie beyond discovery, and in no way to be seen again; which happy contrivance hath made communication with our forefathers, and left unto our view some parts, which they never beheld themselves.

Though earth hath engrossed the name yet water hath proved the smartest grave; which in forty dayes swallowed almost mankinde, and the living creation; Fishes not wholly escaping, except the Salt Ocean were handsomely contempered by admixture of the fresh Element.

Many have taken voluminous pains to determine the state of the soul upon disunion; but men have been most phantasticall in the singular contrivances of their corporall dissolution; whilest the sobrest Nations have rested in two wayes, of simple inhumation and burning.

That carnall interment or burying, was of the elder date, the old examples of *Abraham* and the Patriarchs are sufficient to illustrate; And were without competition, if it could be made out, that *Adam* was buried near *Damascus*, or Mount *Calvary*, according to some Tradition. God himself, that buried but one, was pleased to make choice of this way, collectible from Scripture-expression, and the hot contest between Satan and the Arch-Angel, about discovering the body of *Moses*. But the practice of Burning was also of great Antiquity, and of no slender extent. For (not to derive the same from *Hercules*) noble descriptions there are hereof in the Grecian Funerals of *Homer*, In the formall Obsequies of *Patroclus*, and *Achilles*; and somewhat elder in the *Theban* warre, and solemn combustion of *Meneceus*, and *Archemorus*, contemporary unto *Jair* the Eighth Judge of *Israel*. Confirmable also among the *Trojans*, from the Funerall Pyre of *Hector*, burnt before the gates of *Troy*, And the burning of *Penthisilea* the *Amazonean* *Queen*:[b] and long continuance of that practice, in the inward Countries of *Asia*; while as low as the Reign of *Julian*, we finde that the King of *Chionia*[c] burnt the body of his Son, and interred the ashes in a silver Urne.

The same practice extended also farre West,[d] and besides *Herulians*, *Getes*, and *Thracians*, was in use with most of the *Celtæ, Sarmatians, Germans, Gauls, Danes, Swedes, Norwegians;* not to omit some use thereof among *Carthaginians* and *Americans*: Of greater Antiquity among the *Romans* than most opinion, or *Pliny* seems to allow. For (beside the old Table Laws of burning[e] or burying within the City, of making the Funerall fire with plained wood, or quenching the fire with wine) *Manlius* the Consul burnt the body of his Son: *Numa* by speciall clause of his Will, was not burnt but buried; And *Remus* was solemnly burned, according to the description of *Ovid.*[f]

Cornelius Sylla was not the first whose body was burned in *Rome*, but of the *Cornelian* Family, which being indifferently, not frequently used before, from that time spread, and became the

b Q. Calaber lib. 1.

c Gumbrates King of *Chionia*, a countrey near *Persia*. Ammianus Marcellinus.

d Arnoldi Montani *not. in* Cæs. *Commentar.* L. Gyraldus. Kirkmannus.

e 12. *Tabul. part.* 1. *de jure sacro. Hominem mortuum in urbe ne sepelito, neve urito.* tom. 2. *Rogum ascia ne polito.* tom. 4. Item Vigeneri *Annotat. in Livium, &* Alex. ab Alex. *cum* Tirraquello. Roscinus *cum* Dempstero.

f *Ultima plorato subdita flamma rogo.* De Fast., *lib.* 4 *cum* Car. Neapol. anaptyxi.

prevalent practice. Not totally pursued in the highest runne of Cremation; For when even Crows were funerally burnt, *Poppæa* the Wife of *Nero* found a peculiar grave enterment. Now as all customes were founded upon some bottome of Reason, so there wanted not grounds for this; according to severall apprehensions of the most rationall dissolution. Some being of the opinion of *Thales*, that water was the originall of all things, thought it most equall to submit unto the principle of putrefaction, and conclude in a moist relentment. Others conceived it most natural to end in fire, as due unto the master principle in the composition, according to the doctrine of *Heraclitus*. And therefore heaped up large piles, more actively to waft them toward that Element, whereby they also declined a visible degeneration into worms, and left a lasting parcell of their composition.

Some apprehended a purifying virtue in fire, refining the grosser commixture, and firing out the Æthereall particles so deeply immersed in it. And such as by tradition or rationall conjecture held any hint of the finall pyre of all things; or that this Element at last must be too hard for all the rest; might conceive most naturally of the fiery dissolution. Others pretending no natural grounds, politickly declined the malice of enemies upon their buried bodies. Which consideration led *Sylla* unto this practise; who having thus served the body of *Marius*, could not but fear a retaliation upon his own, entertained after in the Civill wars, and revengeful contentions of *Rome*.

But as many Nations embraced, and many left it indifferent, so others too much affected, or strictly declined this practice. The *Indian Brachmans* seemed too great friends unto fire, who burnt themselves alive, and thought it the noblest way to end their dayes in fire; according to the expression of the Indian, burning himself at *Athens*,[g] in his last words upon the pyre unto the amazed spectators, *Thus I make my selfe Immortall.*

But the *Chaldeans*, the great Idolaters of fire, abhorred the burning of their carcasses, as a pollution of that Deity. The *Persian Magi* declined it upon the like scruple, and being only sollicitous about their bones, exposed their flesh to the prey of Birds and Dogges. And the *Persees* now in *India*, which expose their bodies unto Vultures, and endure not so much as *feretra*

[g] And therefore the Inscription of his Tomb was made accordingly. Nic. Damasc.

or Beers of Wood, the proper Fuell of fire, are led on with such
niceties. But whether the ancient *Germans* who burned their
dead, held any such fear to pollute their Deity of *Herthus*, or the
earth, we have no Authentick conjecture.

The Ægyptians were afraid of fire, not as a Deity, but a devouring Element, mercilesly consuming their bodies, and leaving
too little of them; and therefore by precious Embalments,
depositure in dry earths, or handsome inclosure in glasses, contrived the notablest wayes of integrall conservation. And from
such Ægyptian scruples imbibed by *Pythagoras*, it may be conjectured that *Numa* and the Pythagoricall Sect first waved the
fiery solution.

The *Scythians* who swore by winde and sword, that is, by life
and death, were so farre from burning their bodies, that they
declined all interrment, and made their graves in the ayr: And
the *Ichthyophagi* or fish-eating Nations about Ægypt, affected
the Sea for their grave: Thereby declining visible corruption,
and restoring the debt of their bodies. Whereas the old Heroes
in *Homer* dread nothing more than water or drowning; probably upon the old opinion of the fiery substance of the soul,
only extinguishable by that Element; And therefore the Poet
emphatically implieth the totall destruction in this kinde of
death, which happened to *Ajax Oileus*.[h]

The old *Balearians*[i] had a peculiar mode, for they used great
Urnes and much wood, but no fire in their burials, while they
bruised the flesh and bones of the dead, crowded them into
Urnes, and laid heapes of wood upon them. And the *Chinois*[k]
without cremation or urnall interrment of their bodies, make
use of trees and much burning, while they plant a Pine-tree by
their grave, and burn great numbers of printed draughts of
slaves and horses over it, civilly content with their companies
in effigie, which barbarous Nations exact unto reality.

Christians abhorred this way of obsequies, and though they
stickt not to give their bodies to be burnt in their lives, detested
that mode after death; affecting rather a depositure than absump-
tion, and properly submitting unto the sentence of God, to
return not unto ashes but unto dust againe, conformable unto
the practice of the Patriarchs, the interrment of our Saviour,
of *Peter*, *Paul*, and the ancient Martyrs. And so farre at last

[h] Which Magius reads ἐξαπόλωλε.

[i] Diodorus Siculus.

[k] Ramusius in *Navigat.*

declining promiscuous enterrment with Pagans, that some have
suffered Ecclesiastical censures,[1] for making no scruple thereof.

The *Musselman* beleevers will never admit this fiery resolution. For they hold a present trial from their black and white
Angels in the grave; which they must have made so hollow,
that they may rise upon their knees.

The Jewish Nation, though they entertained the old way of
inhumation, yet sometimes admitted this practice. For the men
of *Jabesh* burnt the body of *Saul*. And by no prohibited practice,
to avoid contagion or pollution, in time of pestilence, burnt the
bodies of their friends.[m] And when they burnt not their dead
bodies, yet sometimes used great burnings neare and about
them, deducible from the expressions concerning *Jehoram*,
Sedechias, and the sumptuous pyre of *Asa*: And were so little
averse from Pagan burning, that the Jews lamenting the death
of *Cæsar* their friend, and revenger on *Pompey*, frequented the
place where his body was burnt for many nights together.[n] And
as they raised noble Monuments and *Mausolæums* for their own
Nation,[o] so they were not scrupulous in erecting some for
others, according to the practice of *Daniel*, who left that lasting sepulchrall pyle in *Echbatana*, for the *Medean* and *Persian*
Kings.[p]

But even in times of subjection and hottest use, they conformed not unto the *Romane* practice of burning; whereby the
Prophecy was secured concerning the body of Christ, that it
should not see corruption, or a bone should not be broken; which
we beleeve was also providentially prevented, from the Souldiers spear and nails that past by the little bones both in his
hands and feet: Nor of ordinary contrivance, that it should not
corrupt on the Crosse, according to the Laws of *Romane* Crucifixion, or an hair of his head perish, though observable in Jewish
customes, to cut the hairs of Malefactors.

Nor in their long co-habitation with Ægyptians, crept into
a custome of their exact embalming, wherein deeply slashing
the muscles, and taking out the brains and entrails, they had
broken the subject of so entire a Resurrection, nor fully answered
the types of *Enoch*, *Eliah*, or *Jonah*, which yet to prevent or
restore, was of equall facility unto that rising power, able to
break the fasciations and bands of death, to get clear out of

1 Martialis
the Bishop,
Cyprian.

m Amos 6. 10.

n Sueton. *in
vita Jul. Cæs.*

o As that
magnificent
Monument
erected by
Simon.
1 Macc. 13.

p κατα-
σκεύασμα
θαυμασίως
πεποιημένον,
whereof a
Jewish Priest
had alwayes
the custody
unto *Josephus*
his dayes.
Jos. Lib. 10.
Antiq.

the Cere-cloth, and an hundred pounds of oyntment, and out of
the Sepulchre before the stone was rolled from it.

But though they embraced not this practice of burning, yet
entertained they many ceremonies agreeable unto *Greeke* and
Romane obsequies. And he that observeth their funerall Feasts,
their Lamentations at the grave, their musick, and weeping
mourners; how they closed the eyes of their friends, how they
washed, anointed, and kissed the dead; may easily conclude
these were not meere Pagan-Civilities. But whether that mourn-
full burthen, and treble calling out after *Absalom*,* had any
reference unto the last conclamation, and triple valediction,
used by other Nations, we hold but a wavering conjecture.

* *O Absolom,*
Absolom,
Absolom.
2 Sam. 18.

Civilians make sepulture but of the Law of Nations, others
doe naturally found it and discover it also in animals. They
that are so thick skinned as still to credit the story of the
Phœnix, may say something for animall burning: More serious
conjectures finde some examples of sepulture in Elephants,
Cranes, the Sepulchrall Cells of Pismires and practice of Bees;
which civill society carrieth out their dead, and hath exequies,
if not interrments.

CHAPTER II

THE Solemnities, Ceremonies, Rites of their Cremation
or enterrment, so solemnly delivered by Authours, we
shall not disparage our Reader to repeat. Only the last
and lasting part in their Urns, collected bones and Ashes, we
cannot wholly omit, or decline that Subject, which occasion
lately presented, in some discovered among us.

In a Field of old *Walsingham*, not many moneths past, were
digged up between fourty and fifty Urnes, deposited in a dry
and sandy soile, not a yard deep, nor farre from one another:
Not all strictly of one figure, but most answering these described: Some containing two pounds of bones, distinguishable
in skulls, ribs, jawes, thigh-bones, and teeth, with fresh impressions of their combustion. Besides the extraneous substances,

like peeces of small boxes, or combes handsomely wrought, handles of small brasse instruments, brazen nippers, and in one some kinde of *Opale*.[a]

[a] In one sent me by my worthy friend Dr *Thomas Witherley* of *Walsingham*.

Near the same plot of ground, for about six yards compasse were digged up coals and incinerated substances, which begat conjecture that this was the *Ustrina* or place of burning their bodies, or some sacrificing place unto the *Manes*, which was properly below the surface of the ground, as the *Aræ* and Altars unto the gods and *Heroes* above it.

That these were the Urnes of *Romanes* from the common custome and place where they were found, is no obscure conjecture, not farre from a *Romane* Garrison, and but five Miles from *Brancaster*, set down by ancient Record under the name of *Brannodunum*. And where the adjoyning Towne, containing seven Parishes, in no very different sound, but Saxon Termination, still retains the Name of *Burnham*, which being an early station, it is not improbable the neighbour parts were filled with habitations, either of *Romanes* themselves, or *Brittains Romanised*, which observed the *Romane* customes.

Nor is it improbable that the *Romanes* early possessed this Countrey; for though we meet not with such strict particulars of these parts, before the new Institution of *Constantine*, and military charge of the Count of the *Saxon* shore, and that about the *Saxon* Invasions, the *Dalmatian* Horsemen were in the Garrison of *Brancaster*: Yet in the time of *Claudius*, *Vespasian*, and *Severus*, we finde no lesse than three Legions dispersed through the Province of *Brittain*.★ And as high as the Reign of *Claudius* a great overthrow was given unto the *Iceni*, by the *Romane* Lieutenant *Ostorius*. Not long after the Countrey was so molested, that in hope of a better state, *Prasutagus* bequeathed his Kingdome unto *Nero* and his Daughters; and *Boadicea* his Queen fought the last decisive Battle with *Paulinus*. After which time and Conquest of *Agricola* the Lieutenant of *Vespasian*, probable it is they wholly possessed this Countrey, ordering it into Garrisons or Habitations, best suitable with their securities. And so some *Romane* Habitations, not improbable in these parts, as high as the time of *Vespasian*, where the *Saxons* after seated, in whose thin-fill'd Mappes we yet finde the Name of *Walsingham*. Now if the *Iceni* were but *Gammadims*, *Anconians*, or men that lived in

★ In Onuphrius.

an Angle wedge or Elbow of *Brittain*, according to the Originall Etymologie, this countrey will challenge the Emphaticall appellation, as most properly making the Elbow or Iken of *Icenia*.

That *Britain* was notably populous is undeniable, from that expression of *Cæsar*.[b] That the *Romans* themselves were early in no small Numbers, Seventy Thousand with their associats slain by *Boadicea*, affords a sure account. And though many *Roman* habitations are now unknowne, yet some by old works, Rampiers, Coynes, and Urnes doe testifie their Possessions. Some Urnes have been found at *Castor*, some also about *Southcreake*, and not many years past, no lesse than ten in a Field at *Buxton*,[c] not near any recorded Garison. Nor is it strange to finde *Romane* Coynes of Copper and Silver among us; of *Vespasian*, *Trajan*, *Adrian*, *Commodus*, *Antoninus*, *Severus*, &c. But the greater number of *Dioclesian*, *Constantine*, *Constans*, *Valens*, with many of *Victorinus*, *Posthumius*, *Tetricus*, and the thirty Tyrants in the Reigne of *Gallienus*; and some as high as *Adrianus* have been found about *Thetford*, or *Sitomagus*, mentioned in the itinerary of *Antoninus*, as the way from *Venta* or *Castor* unto *London*.[d] But the most frequent discovery is made at the two *Casters* by *Norwich* and *Yarmouth*,[e] at *Burghcastle* and *Brancaster*.[f]

Besides the *Norman*, *Saxon* and *Danish* peeces of *Cuthred*, *Canutus*, *William*, *Matilda*,[g] and others, som *Brittish* Coynes of gold have been dispersedly found; And no small number of silver peeces near[h] *Norwich*; with a rude head upon the obverse, and an ill formed horse on the reverse, with Inscriptions *Ic. Duro. T.* whether implying *Iceni*, *Durotriges*, *Tascia*, or *Trinobantes*, we leave to higher conjecture. Vulgar Chronology will have *Norwich* Castle as old as *Julius Cæsar*; but his distance from these parts, and its *Gothick* form of structure, abridgeth such Antiquity. The *British* Coyns afford conjecture of early habitation in these parts, though the City of *Norwich* arose from the

Sidenotes:

[b] *Hominum infinita multitudo est, creberrimaque ædificia fere Gallicis consimilia.* Cæs. de bello Gal. l. 5.

[c] In the ground of my worthy Friend *Rob. Jegon* Esq. wherein contained were preserved by the most worthy Sir William Paston, Bt.

[d] From *Castor* to *Thetford* the Romans accounted thirty-two miles, and from thence observed not our common road to *London*, but passed by *Combretonium ad Ansam, Canonium, Cæsaromagus*, &c. by *Bretenham, Coggeshall, Chelmeford, Burntwood,* &c.

[e] Most at *Caster* by *Yarmouth*, found in a place called *East-bloudy-burgh furlong*, belonging to Mr *Thomas Wood*, a person of civility, industry and knowledge in this way, who hath made observation of remarkable things about him, and from whom we have received divers Silver and Copper Coynes.

[f] Belonging to that Noble Gentleman, and true example of worth Sir *Ralph Hare* Baronet, my honoured Friend.

[g] A peece of *Maud* the Empresse said to be found in *Buckenham* Castle with this Inscription, *Elle n'a elle.*

[h] At *Thorpe.*

ruines of *Venta*, and though perhaps not without some habitation before, was enlarged, builded, and nominated by the
Saxons. In what bulk or populosity it stood in the old East-angle
Monarchy, tradition and history are silent. Considerable it was
in the *Danish* Eruptions, when *Sueno* burnt *Thetford* and *Norwich*,[i]   [i] *Brampton Abbas Jorvallensis.*
and *Ulfketel* the Governour thereof was able to make some
resistance, and after endeavoured to burn the *Danish* Navy.

How the *Romanes* left so many Coynes in Countreys of their
Conquests, seems of hard resolution, except we consider how
they buried them under ground, when upon barbarous invasions they were fain to desert their habitations in most part of
their Empire; and the strictnesse of their laws forbidding to
transfer them to any other uses; Wherein the *Spartans*[a] were   [a] Plut. *in Vita Lycurg.*
singular, who to make their Copper money uselesse, contem-
pered it with vinegar. That the *Brittains* left any, some wonder;
since their money was iron, and Iron rings before *Cæsar*; and
those of after stamp by permission, and but small in bulk and
bignesse. That so few of the *Saxons* remain, because overcome
by succeeding Conquerours upon the place, their Coynes by
degrees passed into other stamps, and the marks of after ages.

Than the time of these Urnes deposited, or precise Antiquity
of these Reliques, nothing of more uncertainty. For since the
Lieutenant of *Claudius* seems to have made the first progresse
into these parts, since *Boadicea* was overthrown by the Forces
of *Nero*, and *Agricola* put a full end to these Conquests; it is not
probable the Countrey was fully garrison'd or planted before;
and therefore however these Urnes might be of later date, not
likely of higher Antiquity.

And the succeeding Emperours desisted not from their Conquests in these and other parts; as testified by history and
medall inscription yet extant. The Province of *Brittain* is so
divided a distance from *Rome*, beholding the faces of many
Imperiall persons, and in large account no fewer than *Cæsar*,
Claudius, *Britannicus*, *Vespasian*, *Titus*, *Adrian*, *Severus*, *Commodus*,
Geta, and *Caracalla*.

A great obscurity herein, because no medall or Emperours
Coyne enclosed, which might denote the date of their enterr-
ments; observable in many Urnes, and found in those of *Spittle*   [b] Stowe's *Survey of London.*
Fields by *London*,[b] which contained the Coynes of *Claudius*,

Vespasian, Commodus, Antoninus, attended with Lacrymatories, Lamps, Bottles of Liquor, and other appurtenances of affectionate superstition, which in these rurall interrements were wanting.

Some uncertainty there is from the period or term of burning, or the cessation of that practise. *Macrobius* affirmeth it was disused in his dayes. But most agree, though without authentick record, that it ceased with the *Antonini.* Most safely to be understood, after the Reigne of those Emperours which assumed the name of *Antoninus,* extending unto *Heliogabalus.* Not strictly after *Marcus;* For about fifty years later we finde the magnificent burning, and consecration of *Severus;* and if we so fix this period or cessation, these Urnes will challenge above thirteen hundred years.

But whether this practise was onely then left by Emperours and great persons, or generally about *Rome,* and not in other Provinces, we hold no authentick account. For after *Tertullian,* in the dayes of *Minucius* it was obviously objected upon Christians, that they condemned the practise of burning.[c] And we finde a passage in *Sidonius,*[d] which asserteth that practise in *France* unto a lower account. And perhaps not fully disused till Christianity fully established, which gave the finall extinction to these sepulchrall Bonefires.

Whether they were the bones of men or women or children, no authentick decision from ancient custome in distinct places of buriall. Although not improbably conjectured, that the double Sepulture or burying place of *Abraham,** had in it such intension. But from exility of bones, thinnesse of skulls, smallnesse of teeth, ribbes, and thigh-bones; not improbable that many thereof were persons of *minor* age, or women. Confirmable also from things contained in them: In most were found substances resembling Combes, Plates like Boxes, fastened with Iron pins, and handsomely overwrought like the necks or Bridges of Musicall Instruments, long brasse plates overwrought like the handles of neat implements, brazen nippers to pull away hair, and in one a kinde of *Opale* yet maintaining a blewish colour.

Now that they accustomed to burn or bury with them things wherein they excelled, delighted, or which were dear unto them,

c *Execrantur rogos, & damnant ignium sepulturam.* Min. in Oct.

d Sidon. Apollinaris.

* *Det mihi speluncam duplicem.* Gen. 23.

either as farewells unto all pleasure, or vain apprehension that they might use them in the other world, is testified by all Antiquity. Observable from the Gemme or Berill Ring upon the finger of *Cynthia*, the Mistresse of *Propertius*, when after her Funerall Pyre her Ghost appeared unto him. And notably illustrated from the Contents of that *Romane* Urne preserved by Cardinall *Farnese*,[e] wherein besides great number of Gemmes with heads of Gods and Goddesses, were found an Ape of *Agath*, a Grashopper, an Elephant of Ambre, a Crystall Ball, three glasses, two Spoones, and six Nuts of Crystall. And beyond the content of Urnes, in the Monument of *Childerick* the first,[f] and fourth King from *Pharamond*, casually discovered three years past at *Tournay*, restoring unto the world much gold richly adorning his Sword, two hundred Rubies, many hundred Imperial Coyns, three hundred golden Bees, the bones and horseshoe of his horse enterred with him, according to the barbarous magnificence of those dayes in their sepulchral Obsequies. Although if we steer by the conjecture of many and Septuagint expression; some trace thereof may be found even with the ancient Hebrews, not only from the Sepulcrall treasure of *David*, but the circumcision knives which *Josuah* also buried.

   Some men considering the contents of these Urnes, lasting peeces and toyes included in them, and the custome of burning with many other Nations, might somewhat doubt whether all Urnes found among us were properly *Romane* Reliques, or some not belonging unto our *Brittish*, *Saxon*, or *Danish* Forefathers.

   In the form of Buriall among the ancient *Brittains*, the large Discourses of *Cæsar*, *Tacitus*, and *Strabo* are silent: For the discovery whereof, with other particulars, we much deplore the losse of that Letter which *Cicero* expected or received from his Brother *Quintus*, as a resolution of *Brittish* customes; or the account which might have been made by *Scribonius Largus*, the Physician accompanying the Emperour *Claudius*, who might have also discovered that frugall Bit of the Old *Brittains*,[g] which in the bignesse of a Bean could satisfie their thirst and hunger.

   But that the *Druids* and ruling Priests used to burn and bury, is expressed by *Pomponius*; That *Bellinus* the Brother of *Brennus* and King of *Brittains* was burnt, is acknowledged by *Polydorus*.* That they held that practise in *Gallia*, *Cæsar* expresly delivereth.

e *Vigeneri Annot. in* 4. Liv.

f Chifflet in *Anast. Childer.*

g *Dionis excerpta per Xiphilin. in Severo.*

* As also by Amandus Zierexensis in *Historia*, and Pineda in his *Universa historia*, Spanish.

Whether the *Brittains* (probably descended from them, of like Religion, Language and Manners) did not sometimes make use of burning; or whether at least such as were after civilized unto the *Romane* life and manners, conformed not unto this practise, we have not historicall assertion or deniall. But since from the account of *Tacitus* the *Romanes* early wrought so much civility upon the British stock, that they brought them to build Temples, to wear the Gowne, and study the *Romane* Laws and language, that they conformed also unto their religious rites and customes in burials, seems no improbable conjecture.

That burning the dead was used in *Sarmatia*, is affirmed by *Gaguinus*, that the *Sueons* and *Gothlanders* used to burne their Princes and great persons, is delivered by *Saxo* and *Olaus*; that this was the old *Germane* practise, is also asserted by *Tacitus*. And though we are bare in historicall particulars of such obsequies in this Island, or that the *Saxons*, *Jutes*, and *Angles* burnt their dead, yet came they from parts where 'twas of ancient practise; the *Germanes* using it, from whom they were descended. And even in *Jutland* and *Sleswick* in *Anglia Cymbrica*, Urnes with bones were found not many years before us.

But the *Danish* and Northern Nations have raised an *Æra* or point of compute from their Custome of burning their dead:[h] Some deriving it from *Unguinus*, some from *Frotho* the great; who ordained by Law, that Princes and Chief Commanders should be committed unto the fire, though the common sort had the common grave enterrment. So *Starkatterus* that old *Heroe* was burnt, and *Ringo* royally burnt the body of *Harald* the King slain by him.

What time this custome generally expired in that Nation, we discern no assured period; whether it ceased before Christianity, or upon their Conversion, by *Ansgarius* the Gaul in the time of *Ludovicus Pius* the Sonne of *Charles* the great, according to good computes; or whether it might not be used by some persons, while for a hundred and eighty years Paganisme and Christianity were promiscuously embraced among them, there is no assured conclusion. About which times the *Danes* were busie in *England*, and particularly infested this Countrey: Where many Castles and strong holds were built by them, or against them, and great number of names and Families still derived from them.

[h] Roisold, Brendetiide. Ild tyde.

But since this custome was probably disused before their Invasion or Conquest, and the *Romanes* confessedly practised the same, since their possession of this Island, the most assured account will fall upon the *Romanes*, or *Brittains Romanized*.

However, certain it is, that Urnes conceived of no *Romane* Originall, are often digged up both in *Norway*, and *Denmark*, handsomely described, and graphically represented by the Learned Physician *Wormius*,[i] And in some parts of *Denmark* in no ordinary number, as stands delivered by Authours exactly describing those Countreys.[k] And they contained not only bones, but many other substances in them, as Knives, peeces of Iron, Brasse and Wood, and one of *Norwaye* a brasse guilded Jewes-harp.

Nor were they confused or carelesse in disposing the noblest sort, while they placed large stones in circle about the Urnes, or bodies which they interred: Somewhat answerable unto the Monument of *Rollrich* stones in England,[l] or sepulcrall Monument probably erected by *Rollo*, who after conquered *Normandy*. Where 'tis not improbable somewhat might be discovered. Mean while to what Nation or person belonged that large Urne found at *Ashburie*,[m] containing mighty bones, and a Buckler; What those large Urnes found at little *Massingham*,[n] or why the *Anglesea* Urnes are placed with their mouths downward, remains yet undiscovered.

[i] *Olai Wormii monumenta & Antiquitat. Dan.*

[k] Adolphus Cyprius in *Annal. Sleswic., urnis adeo abundabat collis*; &c.

[l] In Oxfordshire. Cambden.

[m] In Cheshire, Twinus *de rebus Albionicis.*

[n] In Norfolk, Hollingshead.

CHAPTER III

PLAYSTERED and whited Sepulchres were anciently affected in cadaverous and corruptive Burials; And the rigid Jews were wont to garnish the Sepulchres of the righteous;[a] *Ulysses* in *Hecuba*[b] cared not how meanly he lived, so he might finde a noble Tomb after death. Great Persons affected great Monuments, And the fair and larger Urnes contained no vulgar ashes, which makes that disparity in those which time discovereth among us. The present Urnes were not of one capacity, the largest containing above a gallon, Some not

[a] Mat. 23.

[b] Euripides.

much above half that measure; nor all of one figure, wherein there is no strict conformity, in the same or different Countreys; Observable from those represented by *Casalius, Bosio,* and others, though all found in *Italy*: While many have handles, ears, and long necks, but most imitate a circular figure, in a sphericall and round composure; whether from any mystery, best duration or capacity, were but a conjecture. But the common form with necks was a proper figure, making our last bed like our first; nor much unlike the Urnes of our Nativity, while we lay in the nether part of the Earth,[c] and inward vault of our Microcosme. Many Urnes are red, these but of a black colour, somewhat smooth, and dully sounding, which begat some doubt, whether they were burnt, or only baked in Oven or Sunne: According to the ancient way, in many bricks, tiles, pots, and testaceous works; and as the word *testa* is properly to be taken, when occurring without addition: And chiefly intended by *Pliny,* when he commendeth bricks and tiles of two years old, and to make them in the spring. Nor only these concealed peeces, but the open magnificence of Antiquity, ran much in the Artifice of Clay. Hereof the house of *Mausolus* was built, thus old *Jupiter* stood in the Capitoll, and the *Statua* of *Hercules* made in the Reign of *Tarquinius Priscus,* was extant in *Plinies* dayes. And such as declined burning or Funerall Urnes, affected Coffins of Clay, according to the mode of *Pythagoras,* and way preferred by *Varro.* But the spirit of great ones was above these circumscriptions, affecting copper, silver, gold, and *Porphyrie* Urnes, wherein *Severus* lay, after a serious view and sentence on that which should contain him.[d] Some of these Urnes were thought to have been silvered over, from sparklings in several pots, with small Tinsell parcels; uncertain whether from the earth, or the first mixture in them.

    Among these Urnes we could obtain no good account of their coverings; Only one seemed arched over with some kinde of brickwork. Of those found at *Buxton* some were covered with flints, some in other parts with tiles, those at *Yarmouth Caster* were closed with *Romane* bricks. And some have proper earthen covers adapted and fitted to them. But in the *Homericall* Urne of *Patroclus,* whatever was the solid Tegument, we finde the immediate covering to be a purple peece of silk: And such as had no covers might have the earth closely pressed into them, after which disposure were probably some of these, wherein we found the bones and ashes half mortered unto the sand and sides of the Urne; and some long roots of Quich, or Dogs-grass wreathed about the bones.

No Lamps, included Liquors, Lachrymatories, or Tear-bottles attended these rurall Urnes, either as sacred unto the *Manes*, or passionate expressions of their. surviving friends. While with rich flames and hired tears they solemnized their Obsequies, and in the most lamented Monuments made one part of their Inscriptions.[e] Some finde sepulchrall Vessels containing liquors, which time hath incrassated into gellies. For beside these Lachrymatories, notable Lamps with Vessels of Oyles and Aromaticall Liquors attended noble Ossuaries. And some yet retaining a Vinosity[f] and spirit in them, which if any have tasted they have farre exceeded the Palats of Antiquity. Liquors not to be computed by years of annuall Magistrates, but by great conjunctions and the fatall periods of Kingdomes.[g] The draughts of Consulary date were but crude unto these, and *Opimian*[h] Wine but in the must unto them.

In sundry Graves and Sepulchres, we meet with Rings, Coynes, and Chalices; Ancient frugality was so severe, that they allowed no gold to attend the Corps, but only that which served to fasten their teeth.[i] Whether the *Opaline* stone in this Urne were burnt upon the finger of the dead, or cast into the fire by some affectionate friend, it will consist with either custome. But other incinerable substances were found so fresh, that they could feel no sindge from fire. These upon view were judged to be wood, but sinking in water and tried by the fire, we found them to be bone or Ivory. In their hardnesse and yellow colour they most resembled Box, which in old expressions found the Epithete[k] of Eternall, and perhaps in such conservatories might have passed uncorrupted.

That Bay-leaves were found green in the Tomb of S. *Humbert*,[l] after an hundred and fifty years, was looked upon as miraculous. Remarkable it was unto old Spectators, that the Cypresse of the Temple of *Diana* lasted so many hundred years: The wood of the Ark and Olive Rod of *Aaron* were older at the Captivity. But the Cypresse of the Ark of *Noah* was the greatest

e *Cum lacrymis posuere.*

f Lazius.

g About five hundred years. Plato.

h *Vinum opimianum annorum centum.* Petron.

i 12. *Tabul. l. xi de Jure Sacro. Neve aurum addito, ast quoi auro dentes vincti erunt, im cum illo sepelire & urere, se fraude esto.*

k Plin. l. xvi. Inter ξύλα ἀσαπῆ numerat Theophrastus.

l Surius.

vegetable Antiquity, if *Josephus* were not deceived by some fragments of it in his dayes. To omit the Moore-logs, and Firre-trees found under-ground in many parts of *England*; the undated ruines of windes, flouds or earthquakes; and which in *Flanders* still shew from what quarter they fell, as generally lying in a North-East position.[m]

But though we found not these peeces to be Wood, according to first apprehension, yet we missed not altogether of some woody substance; For the bones were not so clearly pickt, but some coals were found amongst them; A way to make wood perpetuall, and a fit associat for metall, whereon was laid the foundation of the great *Ephesian* Temple, and which were made the lasting tests of old boundaries and Landmarks; Whilest we look on these, we admire not Observations of Coals found fresh, after four hundred years.[n] In a long deserted habitation,[o] even Egge-shels have been found fresh, not tending to corruption.

In the Monument of King *Childerick*, the Iron Reliques were found all rusty and crumbling into peeces. But our little Iron pins which fastened the Ivory works, held well together, and lost not their Magneticall quality, though wanting a tenacious moisture for the firmer union of parts; although it be hardly drawn into fusion, yet that metall soon submitteth unto rust and dissolution. In the brazen peeces we admired not the duration but the freedome from rust and ill savour, upon the hardest attrition; but now exposed unto the piercing Atomes of ayre, in the space of a few moneths, they begin to spot and betray their green entrals. We conceive not these Urnes to have descended thus naked as they appear, or to have entred their graves without the old habit of flowers.[*] The Urne of *Philopœmen* was so laden with flowers and ribbons, that it afforded no sight of it self. The rigid *Lycurgus* allowed Olive and Myrtle. The *Athenians* might fairly except against the practise of *Democritus* to be buried up in honey; as fearing to embezzle a great commodity of their Countrey, and the best of that kinde in *Europe*. But *Plato* seemed too frugally politick, who allowed no larger Monument than would contain four Heroick Verses, and designed the most barren ground for sepulture: Though we cannot commend the goodnesse of that sepulchrall ground, which was set at no higher rate than the mean salary of *Judas*. Though the

[m] Gorop. Becanus *in Niloscopio.*

[n] Of Beringuccio *nella pyrotechnia.*

[o] At Elmeham.

[*] ὑδρία Plutarch.

earth had confounded the ashes of these Ossuaries, yet the bones
were so smartly burnt, that some thin plates of brasse were
found half melted among them; whereby we apprehend they
were not of the meanest carcasses, perfunctorily fired as sometimes in military, and commonly in pestilence, burnings; or
after the manner of abject corps, hudled forth and carelesly
burnt, without the Esquiline Port at *Rome*; which was an affront
contrived upon *Tiberius*, while they but half burnt his body,[a]
and in the Amphitheatre, according to the custome in notable
Malefactors; whereas *Nero* seemed not so much to feare his
death, as that his head should be cut off, and his body not
burnt entire.

   Some finding many fragments of sculs in these Urnes,
suspected a mixture of bones; In none we searched was there
cause of such conjecture, though sometimes they declined not
that practise; The ashes of *Domitian*[b] were mingled with those
of *Julia*, of *Achilles* with those of *Patroclus*: All Urnes contained
not single Ashes; Without confused burnings they affec-
tionately compounded their bones; passionately endeavouring
to continue their living Unions. And when distance of death
denied such conjunctions, unsatisfied affections conceived some
satisfaction to be neighbours in the grave, to lye Urne by Urne,
and touch but in their names. And many were so curious to
continue their living relations, that they contrived large, and
family Urnes, wherein the Ashes of their nearest friends and
kindred might successively be received,[c] at least some parcels
thereof, while their collaterall memorials lay in *minor* vessels
about them.

   Antiquity held too light thoughts from Objects of mortality,
while some drew provocatives of mirth from Anatomies,[d] and
Juglers shewed tricks with Skeletons. When Fidlers made not
so pleasant mirth as Fencers, and men could sit with quiet
stomacks while hanging was plaied before them.[e] Old considerations made few *memento*'s by sculs and bones upon their
monuments. In the Ægyptian Obelisks and Hieroglyphicall
figures it is not easie to meet with bones. The sepulchrall
Lamps speak nothing lesse than sepulture; and in their literall
draughts prove often obscene and antick peeces: Where we finde
D.M.[f] it is obvious to meet with sacrificing *patera*'s, and vessels

a Sueton. in
*vita Tib. Et in
Amphitheatro
semiustuland-
dum*, not.
Casaub.

b Sueton. in
vitâ Domitian.

c S. the most
learned and
worthy Mr
M. Casaubon
upon
Antoninus.

d *Sic erimus
cuncti*, &c.
*Ergo dum
vivimus
vivamus.*

e Ἀγχώνην
παίζειν. A
barbarous
pastime at
Feasts, when
men stood
upon a rolling
Globe, with
their necks in
a Rope
fastned
to a beame,
and a knife in
their hands,
ready to cut
it when the
stone was
rolled away,
wherein if
they failed
they lost their
lives tô the
laughter of
their
spectators.
Athenæus.

f *Diis manibus.*

of libation, upon old sepulchrall Monuments. In the Jewish
Hypogæum[g] and subterranean Cell at *Rome*, was little observable
beside the variety of Lamps, and frequent draughts of the holy
Candlestick. In authentick draughts of *Anthony* and *Jerome*, we
meet with thigh-bones and deaths heads; but the cemiteriall
Cels of ancient Christians and Martyrs, were filled with draughts
of Scripture Stories; not declining the flourishes of Cypresse,
Palmes, and Olive; and the mysticall Figures of Peacocks, Doves
and Cocks. But iterately affecting the pourtraits of *Enoch*,
Lazarus, *Jonas*, and the Vision of *Ezechiel*, as hopefull draughts,
and hinting imagery of the Resurrection; which is the life of
the grave, and sweetens our habitations in the Land of Moles
and Pismires.

Gentile Inscriptions precisely delivered the extent of mens
lives, seldome the manner of their deaths, which history it self
so often leaves obscure in the records of memorable persons.
There is scarce any Philosopher but dies twice or thrice in
Laertius; Nor almost any life without two or three deaths in
Plutarch; which makes the tragicall ends of noble persons more
favourably resented by compassionate Readers, who finde some
relief in the Election of such differences.

The certainty of death is attended with uncertainties, in
time, manner, places. The variety of Monuments hath often
obscured true graves: and *Cenotaphs* confounded Sepulchres.
For beside their reall Tombs, many have founded honorary and
empty Sepulchres. The variety of *Homers* Monuments made
him of various Countreys. *Euripides*[h] had his Tomb in *Attica*, but
his sepulture in *Macedonia*. And *Severus*[i] found his real Sepulchre
in *Rome*, but his empty grave in *Gallia*.

He that lay in a golden Urne[k] eminently above the Earth,
was not likely to finde the quiet of these bones. Many of these
Urnes were broke by a vulgar discoverer in hope of inclosed
treasure. The ashes of *Marcellus*[l] were lost above ground, upon
the like account. Where profit hath prompted, no age hath
wanted such miners. For which the most barbarous Expilators
found the most civill Rhetorick. Gold once out of the earth is
no more due unto it; What was unreasonably committed to the
ground is reasonably resumed from it: Let Monuments and rich
Fabricks, not Riches adorn mens ashes. The commerce of the

g Bosio.

h Pausan. *in Atticis.*
i Lamprid. in *vit. Alexand. Severi.*
k *Trajanus.* Dion.
l Plut. in *vit. Marcelli.* The Commission of the Gothish King Theodoric for finding out sepulchrall treasure. *Cassiodor. Var.* 1. 4.

living is not to be transferred unto the dead: It is no injustice to take that which none complains to lose, and no man is wronged where no man is possessor.

What virtue yet sleeps in this *terra damnata* and aged cinders, were petty magick to experiment; These crumbling reliques and long-fired particles superannuate such expectations: Bones, hairs, nails, and teeth of the dead, were the treasures of old Sorcerers. In vain we revive such practices; Present superstition too visibly perpetuates the folly of our Fore-fathers, wherein unto old Observation[a] this Island was so compleat, that it might have instructed *Persia.*

Plato's historian of the other world lies twelve dayes incorrupted, while his soul was viewing the large stations of the dead. How to keep the corps seven dayes from corruption by anointing and washing, without exenteration, were an hazardable peece of art, in our choisest practise. How they made distinct separation of bones and ashes from fiery admixture, hath found no historicall solution. Though they seemed to make a distinct collection, and overlooked not *Pyrrhus* his toe.[*] Some provision they might make by fictile Vessels, Coverings, Tiles, or flat stones, upon and about the body. And in the same Field, not farre from these Urnes, many stones were found under ground, as also by carefull separation of extraneous matter, composing and raking up the burnt bones with forks, observable in that notable Lamp of *Galvanus.*[b] *Marlianus,*[c] who had the sight of the *Vas Ustrinum,* or vessell wherein they burnt the dead, found in the Esquiline Field at *Rome,* might have afforded clearer solution. But their insatisfaction herein begat that remarkable invention in the Funerall Pyres of some Princes, by incombustible sheets made with a texture of *Asbestos,* incremable flax, or Salamanders wool, which preserved their bones and ashes incommixed.

How the bulk of a man should sink into so few pounds of bones and ashes, may seem strange unto any who considers not its constitution, and how slender a masse will remain upon an open and urging fire of the carnall composition. Even bones themselves reduced into ashes, do abate a notable proportion. And consisting much of a volatile salt, when that is fired out, make a light kind of cinders. Although their bulk be

a *Britannia hodie eam attonitè celebrat tantis ceremoniis, ut dedisse Persis videri possit.* Plin. I. 30.

* Which could not be burnt.

b To be seen in Licet. *de reconditis veterum lucernis.*

c *Topographia Romæ ex Marliano. Erat & vas ustrinum appellatum quod in eo cadavera comburerentur. Cap. de Campo Esquilino.*

disproportionable to their weight, when the heavy principle of Salt is fired out, and the Earth almost only remaineth; Observable in sallow, which makes more Ashes than Oake; and discovers the common fraud of selling Ashes by measure, and not by ponderation.

Some bones make best Skeletons,[a] some bodies quick and speediest ashes: Who would expect a quick flame from Hydropicall *Heraclitus?* The poysoned Souldier when his Belly brake, put out two pyres in *Plutarch.*[b] But in the plague of *Athens,*[c] one private pyre served two or three Intruders; and the *Saracens* burnt in large heaps, by the King of *Castile,*[d] shewed how little Fuell sufficeth. Though the Funerall pyre of *Patroclus* took up an hundred foot,[e] a peece of an old boat burnt *Pompey*; And if the burthen of *Isaac* were sufficient for an holocaust, a man may carry his owne pyre.

From animals are drawn good burning lights, and good medicines against burning;[f] Though the seminall humour seems of a contrary nature to fire, yet the body compleated proves a combustible lump, wherein fire findes flame even from bones, and some fuell almost from all parts. Though the Metropolis[g] of humidity seems least disposed unto it, which might render the sculls of these Urnes lesse burned than other bones. But all flies or sinks before fire almost in all bodies: When the common ligament is dissolved, the attenuable parts ascend, the rest subside in coal, calx or ashes.

To burn the bones of the King of *Edom*[h] for Lyme, seems no irrationall ferity; But to drink of the ashes of dead relations,[i] a passionate prodigality. He that hath the ashes of his friend, hath an everlasting treasure: where fire taketh leave, corruption slowly enters; In bones well burnt, fire makes a wall against it self; experimented in copels, and tests of metals, which consist of such ingredients. What the Sun compoundeth, fire analyseth, not transmuteth. That devouring agent leaves almost allwayes a morsell for the Earth, whereof all things are but a colonie; and which, if time permits, the mother Element will have in their primitive masse again.

He that looks for Urnes and old sepulchrall reliques, must not seek them in the ruines of Temples; where no Religion anciently placed them. These were found in a Field, according

a Old bones according to Lyserus.
Those of young persons not tall nor fat according to Columbus.
b In *vita Gracc.*
c Thucydides.
d Laurent. Valla.
e Ἑκατόμπεδον ἔνθα και ἔνθα. [Iliad. xxiii. 164]
f *Sperm. ranarum.* Alb. Ovor.
g The brain. Hippocrates.
h Amos. 2. 1.
i As Artemisia of her husband Mausolus.

to ancient custome, in noble or private buriall; the old practise of the *Canaanites*, the Family of *Abraham*, and the burying place of *Josua*, in the borders of his possessions; and also agreeable unto *Roman* practice to bury by high-wayes, whereby their Monuments were under eye: Memorials of themselves, and *memento's* of mortality unto living passengers; whom the Epitaphs of great ones were fain to beg to stay and look upon them. A language though sometimes used, not so proper in Church-Inscriptions.[a] The sensible Rhetorick of the dead, to exemplarity of good life, first admitted the bones of pious men and Martyrs within Church-wals; which in succeeding ages crept into promiscuous practise. While *Constantine* was peculiarly favoured to be admitted unto the Church Porch; and the first thus buried in *England* was in the dayes of *Cuthred*.

[a] Siste viator.

Christians dispute how their bodies should lye in the grave. In urnall enterrment they clearly escaped this Controversie: Though we decline the Religious consideration, yet in cemiteriall and narrower burying places, to avoid confusion and crosse position, a certain posture were to be admitted; Which even Pagan civility observed.[b] The *Persians* lay North and South, The *Megarians* and *Phœnicians* placed their heads to the East: The *Athenians*, some think, towards the West, which Christians still retain. And *Beda* will have it to be the posture of our Saviour. That he was crucified with his face towards the West, we will not contend with tradition and probable account; but we applaud not the hand of the Painter, in exalting his Crosse so high above those on either side; since hereof we finde no authentick account in history, and even the crosses found by *Helena* pretend no such distinction from longitude or dimension.

[b] Kirckmannus *de funer.*

To be gnaw'd out of our graves, to have our sculs made drinking-bowls, and our bones turned into Pipes, to delight and sport our Enemies, are Tragicall abominations, escaped in burning Burials.

Urnall enterrments, and burnt Reliques lye not in fear of worms, or to be an heritage for Serpents; In carnall sepulture, corruptions seem peculiar unto parts, and some speak of snakes out of the spinall marrow. But while we suppose common wormes in graves, 'tis not easie to finde any there; few in Church-yards above a foot deep, fewer or none in Churches, though in fresh decayed bodies. Teeth, bones, and hair, give the most lasting defiance to corruption. In an Hydropicall body ten years buried in a Church-yard, we met with a fat concretion, where the nitre of the Earth, and the salt and lixivious liquor of the body, had coagulated large lumps of fat, into the consistence of the hardest castle-soap; whereof part remaineth with us. After a battle with the *Persians* the *Roman* Corps decayed in few dayes, while the *Persian* bodies remained dry and uncorrupted. Bodies in the same ground do not uniformly dissolve, nor bones equally moulder; whereof in the opprobrious disease we expect no long duration. The body of the Marquesse of *Dorset* seemed sound and handsomely cereclothed, that after seventy eight years was found uncorrupted.[c] Common Tombs preserve not beyond powder: A firmer consistence and compage of parts might be expected from Arefaction, deep buriall or charcoal. The greatest Antiquities of mortall bodies may remain in petrified bones, whereof, though we take not in the pillar of *Lots* wife, or Metamorphosis of *Ortelius*,[d] some may be older than Pyramids, in the petrified Reliques of the generall inundation.* When *Alexander* opened the Tomb of *Cyrus*, the remaining bones discovered his proportion, whereof urnall fragments afford but a bad conjecture, and have this disadvantage of grave enterrments, that they leave us ignorant of most personall discoveries. For since bones afford not only rectitude and stability, but figure unto the body; It is no impossible Physiognomy to conjecture at fleshy appendencies; and after what shape the muscles and carnous parts might hang in their full consistences. A full spread *Cariola*† shews a well-shaped horse behinde, handsome formed sculls give some analogie of fleshy resemblance. A criticall view of bones makes a good distinction of sexes. Even colour is not beyond conjecture; since it is hard to be deceived in the distinction of *Negro's* sculls.‡ *Dantes*[e] Characters are to be found in sculls as well as faces. *Hercules* is

[c] Of Thomas, Marquesse of Dorset, whose body being buried 1530, was 1608 upon the cutting open of the Cerecloth found perfect and nothing corrupted, the flesh not hardened, but in colour, proportion, and softnesse like an ordinary corps newly to be interred. Burton's *descript. of Leicestershire.*

[d] In his Map of Russia.

*Wher in great numbers of men, oxen, and sheep were petrified.

† That part in the Skeleton of an Horse, which is made by the haunchbones.

‡ For their extraordinary thicknesse.

[e] The Poet Dante in his view of Purgatory, found gluttons so meagre, and extenuated, that he conceited them to have been in the Siege of Jerusalem, and that it was easie to have discovered *Homo* or *Omo* in their faces: M being made by the two lines of their cheeks, arching over the Eyebrows to the nose, and their sunk eyes making O O which makes up *Omo.*

Parean l'occhiaie anella senza gemme:
Che nel viso degli huomini legge huomo,
Ben'havria quivi conosciuto l'emme.

not onely known by his foot. Other parts make out their com-proportions, and inferences upon whole or parts. And since the dimensions of the head measure the whole body, and the figure thereof gives conjecture of the principall faculties; Physiognomy outlives our selves, and ends not in our graves.

Severe contemplators observing these lasting reliques, may think them good monuments of persons past, little advantage to future beings. And considering that power which subdueth all things unto it self, that can resume the scattered Atomes, or identifie out of any thing, conceive it superfluous to expect a resurrection out of Reliques. But the soul subsisting, other matter clothed with due accidents may salve the individuality: Yet the Saints we observe arose from graves and monuments, about the holy City. Some think the ancient Patriarchs so earnestly desired to lay their bones in *Canaan,* as hoping to make a part of that Resurrection, and though thirty miles from Mount *Calvary,* at least to lie in that Region, which should produce the first-fruits of the dead. And if according to learned conjecture, the bodies of men shall rise where their greatest Reliques remain, many are not like to erre in the Topography of their Resurrection, though their bones or bodies be after translated by Angels into the field of *Ezechiels* vision, or as some will order it, into the Valley of Judgement, or *Jehosaphat.*[f]

f *Tirin.* in Ezek.

CHAPTER IV

CHRISTIANS have handsomely glossed the deformity of death, by careful consideration of the body, and civil rites which take off brutall terminations. And though they conceived all reparable by a resurrection, cast not off all care of enterrment. For since the ashes of Sacrifices burnt upon the Altar of God, were carefully carried out by the Priests, and deposed in a clean field; since they acknowledged their bodies to be the lodging of Christ, and temples of the holy Ghost, they devolved not all upon the sufficiency of soul existence; and therefore with long services and full solemnities concluded their last Exequies, wherein to all distinctions the Greek devotion seems most pathetically ceremonious.[a]

Christian invention hath chiefly driven at Rites, which speak hopes of another life, and hints of a Resurrection. And if the ancient Gentiles held not the immortality of their better part, and some subsistence after death; in severall rites, customes, actions and expressions, they contradicted their own opinions: wherein *Democritus* went high, even to the thought of a resurrection,[b] as scoffingly recorded by *Pliny*. What can be more expresse than the expression of *Phocyllides*?[c] Or who would expect from *Lucretius*[d] a sentence of *Ecclesiastes*? Before *Plato* could speak, the soul had wings in *Homer*, which fell not, but flew out of the body into the mansions of the dead; who also observed that handsome distinction of *Demas* and *Soma*, for the body conjoyned to the soul and body separated from it. *Lucian* spoke much truth in jest, when he said, that part of *Hercules* which proceeded from *Alchmena* perished, that from *Jupiter* remained immortall. Thus *Socrates*[e] was content that his friends should bury his body, so they would not think they buried *Socrates*, and regarding only his immortall part, was indifferent to be burnt or buried. From such Considerations *Diogenes* might contemn Sepulture. And being satisfied that the soul could not perish, grow carelesse of corporall enterrment. The *Stoicks* who thought the souls of wise men had their habitation about the moon, might make slight account of subterraneous deposition; whereas the *Pythagorians* and transcorporating Philosophers, who were to be often buried, held great care of their enterrment. And the Platonicks rejected not a due care of the grave, though they put their ashes to unreasonable expectations, in their tedious term of return and long set revolution.

Men have lost their reason in nothing so much as their religion, wherein stones and clouts make Martyrs; and since the religion of one seems madnesse unto another, to afford an account or rationall of old Rites, requires no rigid Reader; That they kindled the pyre aversly, or turning their face from it, was an handsome Symbole of unwilling ministration; That they washed their bones with wine and milk, that the mother wrapt them in Linnen, and dryed them in her bosome, the first fostering part, and place of their nourishment; That they

a *Rituale Græcorum opera J. Goar, in officio exequiarum.*

b *Similis reviviscendi promissa a Democrito vanitas, qui non revixit ipse. Quæ malùm, ista dementia est; iterari vitam morte?* Plin. l. 7, c. 55.

c Καί τάχα δ' ἐκ γαίης ἐλπίζομεν ἐς φάος ἐλθεῖν λείψαν, ἀποιχωμένων, & deinceps.

d *Cedit enim retro de terra quod fuit ante. In terras*, &c. Lucret.

e Plato in *Phæd.*

opened their eyes towards heaven, before they kindled the fire, as the place of their hopes or originall, were no improper Ceremonies. Their last valediction[f] thrice uttered by the attendants was also very solemn, and somewhat answered by Christians, who thought it too little, if they threw not the earth thrice upon the enterred body. That in strewing their Tombs the *Romans* affected the Rose, the Greeks *Amaranthus* and myrtle; that the Funerall pyre consisted of sweet fuell, Cypresse, Firre, Larix, Yewe, and Trees perpetually verdant, lay silent expressions of their surviving hopes: Wherein Christians which deck their Coffins with Bays have found a more elegant Embleme. For that tree seeming dead, will restore it self from the root, and its dry and exuccous leaves resume their verdure again; which if we mistake not, we have also observed in furze. Whether the planting of yewe in Churchyards hold not its originall from ancient Funerall rites, or as an Embleme of Resurrection from its perpetual verdure, may also admit conjecture.

They made use of Musick to excite or quiet the affections of their friends, according to different harmonies. But the secret and symbolicall hint was the harmonical nature of the soul; which delivered from the body, went again to enjoy the primitive harmony of heaven, from whence it first descended; which according to its progresse traced by antiquity, came down by *Cancer*, and ascended by *Capricornus*.

They burnt not children before their teeth appeared, as apprehending their bodies too tender a morsell for fire, and that their gristly bones would scarce leave separable reliques after the pyrall combustion. That they kindled not fire in their houses for some dayes after, was a strict memoriall of the late afflicting fire. And mourning without hope, they had an happy fraud against excessive lamentation, by a common opinion that deep sorrows disturbed their ghosts.[a]

That they buried their dead on their backs, or in a supine position, seems agreeable unto profound sleep, and common posture of dying; contrary to the most naturall way of birth; nor like our pendulous posture, in the doubtfull state of the womb. *Diogenes* was singular, who preferred a prone situation in the grave, and some Christians[b] like neither, who decline the figure of rest, and make choice of an erect posture.

[f] *Vale, vale, vale, nos te ordine quo natura permittet sequemur.*

[a] *Tu manes ne læde meos.*

[b] Russians, &c.

That they carried them out of the world with their feet forward, not inconsonant unto reason: As contrary unto the native posture of man, and his production first into it. And also agreeable unto their opinions, while they bid adieu unto the world, not to look again upon it; whereas *Mahometans* who think to return to a delightfull life again, are carried forth with their heads forward, and looking toward their houses.

They closed their eyes as parts which first die or first discover the sad effects of death. But their iterated clamations to excitate their dying or dead friends, or revoke them unto life again, was a vanity of affection; as not presumably ignorant of the criticall tests of death, by apposition of feathers, glasses, and reflexion of figures, which dead eyes represent not; which however not strictly verifiable in fresh and warm *cadavers*, could hardly elude the test, in corps of four or five dayes.*

* At least by some difference from living eyes.

That they suck'd in the last breath of their expiring friends, was surely a practice of no medicall institution, but a loose opinion that the soul passed out that way, and a fondnesse of affection from some *Pythagoricall* foundation,[c] that the spirit of one body passed into another; which they wished might be their own.

c Francesco Perucci, *Pompe funebri.*

That they powred oyle upon the pyre, was a tolerable practise, while the intention rested in facilitating the accension; But to place good *Omens* in the quick and speedy burning, to sacrifice unto the windes for a dispatch in this office, was a low form of superstition.

The *Archimime* or *Jester* attending the Funerall train, and imitating the speeches, gesture, and manners of the deceased, was too light for such solemnities, contradicting their Funerall Orations, and dolefull rites of the grave.

That they buried a peece of money with them as a Fee of the *Elysian Ferry-man*, was a practise full of folly. But the ancient custome of placing coynes in considerable Urnes, and the present practise of burying medals in the Noble Foundations of *Europe*, are laudable wayes of historicall discoveries, in actions, persons, Chronologies; and posterity will applaud them.

We examine not the old Laws of Sepulture, exempting certain persons from buriall or burning. But hereby we apprehend that these were not the bones of persons Planet-struck or

burnt with fire from Heaven: No Reliques of Traitors to their
Countrey, Self-killers, or Sacrilegious Malefactors; Persons in
old apprehension unworthy of the *earth*; condemned unto the
Tartarus of Hell, and bottomlesse pit of *Pluto*, from whence there
was no redemption.

Nor were only many customes questionable in order to their
Obsequies, but also sundry practises, fictions, and conceptions,
discordant or obscure, of their state and future beings; whether
unto eight or ten bodies of men to adde one of a woman, as being
more inflammable, and unctuously constituted for the better
pyrall combustion, were any rationall practise: Or whether the
complaint of *Perianders* Wife be tolerable, that wanting her
Funerall burning she suffered intolerable cold in Hell, according
to the constitution of the infernall house of *Pluto*, wherein cold
makes a great part of their tortures; it cannot passe without
some question.

Why the Female Ghosts appear unto *Ulysses*, before the
Heroes and masculine spirits? Why the *Psyche* or soul of *Tiresias*
is of the masculine gender;* who being blinde on earth sees
more than all the rest in hell; Why the Funerall Suppers consisted of Egges, Beans, Smallage, and Lettuce, since the dead
are made to eat *Asphodels*† about the *Elyzian* medows? Why since
there is no Sacrifice acceptable, nor any propitiation for the
Covenant of the grave; men set up the Deity of *Morta*, and
fruitlessly adored Divinities without ears? it cannot escape some
doubt.

The dead seem all alive in the human *Hades* of *Homer*, yet
cannot well speak, prophesie, or know the living, except they
drink bloud, wherein is the life of man. And therefore the souls
of *Penelope's* Paramours conducted by *Mercury* chirped like bats,
and those which followed *Hercules* made a noise but like a flock
of birds.

The departed spirits know things past and to come, yet are
ignorant of things present. *Agamemnon* foretels what should
happen unto *Ulysses*, yet ignorantly enquires what is become
of his own Son. The Ghosts are afraid of swords in *Homer*, yet
Sybilla tels *Æneas* in *Virgil*, the thin habit of spirits was beyond
the force of weapons. The spirits put off their malice with their
bodies, and *Cæsar* and *Pompey* accord in Latine Hell, yet *Ajax* in

* In Homer,
ψυχὴ Θηβαίου
Τειρεσίαο
σκῆπτρον ἔχων.

† In Lucian.

Homer endures not a conference with *Ulysses*: And *Deiphobus*
appears all mangled in *Virgils* Ghosts, yet we meet with perfect
shadows among the wounded ghosts of *Homer*.

Since *Charon* in *Lucian* applauds his condition among the
dead, whether it be handsomely said of *Achilles,* that living
contemner of death, that he had rather be a Plowmans servant
than Emperour of the dead? How *Hercules* his soul is in hell, and
yet in heaven, and *Julius* his soul in a Starre, yet seen by *Æneas*
in hell, except the Ghosts were but Images and shadows of
the soul, received in higher mansions, according to the ancient
division of body, soul, and image or *simulachrum* of them both.
The particulars of future beings must needs be dark unto
ancient Theories, which Christian Philosophy yet determines
but in a Cloud of opinions. A Dialogue between two Infants
in the womb concerning the state of this world, might handsomely illustrate our ignorance of the next, whereof methinks
we yet discourse in *Platoes* denne, and are but *Embryon* Philosophers.

ᵃ *Del inferno,*
cant. 4.
Pythagoras escapes in the fabulous hell of *Dante,*[a] among that
swarm of Philosophers, wherein whilest we meet with *Plato*
and *Socrates, Cato* is to be found in no lower place than Purgatory.
Among all the set, *Epicurus* is most considerable, whom men
make honest without an *Elyzium,* who contemned life without
encouragement of immortality, and making nothing after death,
yet made nothing of the King of terrours.

Were the happinesse of the next world as closely apprehended as the felicities of this, it were a martyrdome to live;
and unto such as consider none hereafter, it must be more than
death to dye, which makes us amazed at those audacities,
that durst be nothing, and return into their *Chaos* again.
Certainly such spirits as could contemn death, when they
expected no better being after, would have scorned to live
had they known any. And therefore we applaud not the judgment of *Machiavel,* that Christianity makes men cowards, or
that with the confidence of but half dying, the despised virtues
of patience and humility have abased the spirits of men, which
Pagan principles exalted, but rather regulated the wildenesse
of audacities, in the attempts, grounds, and eternall sequels of
death; wherein men of the boldest spirits are often prodigiously

temerarious. Nor can we extenuate the valour of ancient Martyrs, who contemned death in the uncomfortable scene of their lives, and in their decrepit Martyrdomes did probably lose not many moneths of their dayes, or parted with life when it was scarce worth the living. For (beside that long time past holds no consideration unto a slender time to come) they had no small disadvantage from the constitution of old age, which naturally makes men fearfull; complexionally superannuated from the bold and couragious thoughts of youth and fervent years. But the contempt of death from corporall animosity promoteth not our felicity. They may sit in the *Orchestra*, and noblest Seats of Heaven, who have held up shaking hands in the fire, and humanly contended for glory.

Mean while *Epicurus* lyes deep in *Dante's* hell, wherein we meet with Tombs enclosing souls which denied their immortalities. But whether the virtuous heathen, who lived better than he spake, or erring in the principles of himself, yet lived above Philosophers of more specious Maximes, lye so deep as he is placed; at least so low as not to rise against Christians, who beleeving or knowing that truth, have lastingly denied it in their practise and conversation, were a quæry too sad to insist on.

But all or most apprehensions rested in Opinions of some future being, which ignorantly or coldly beleeved, begat those perverted conceptions, Ceremonies, Sayings, which Christians pity or laugh at. Happy are they, which live not in that disadvantage of time, when men could say little for futurity, but from reason. Whereby the noblest mindes fell often upon doubtfull deaths, and melancholly Dissolutions; With these hopes *Socrates* warmed his doubtfull spirits against that cold potion, and *Cato* before he durst give the fatall stroak spent part of the night in reading the immortality of *Plato*, thereby confirming his wavering hand unto the animosity of that attempt.

It is the heaviest stone that melancholy can throw at a man, to tell him he is at the end of his nature; or that there is no further state to come, unto which this seemes progressionall, and otherwise made in vaine; Without this accomplishment the naturall expectation and desire of such a state, were but a fallacy in nature; unsatisfied Considerators would quarrell the justice of their constitutions, and rest content that *Adam* had fallen lower, whereby by knowing no other Originall, and deeper ignorance of themselves, they might have enjoyed the happinesse of inferiour Creatures; who in tranquility possesse their Constitutions, as having not the apprehension to deplore their own natures. And being framed below the circumference of these hopes, or cognition of better being, the wisedom of God hath necessitated their Contentment: But the superiour ingredient and obscured part of our selves, whereto all present felicities afford no resting contentment, will be able at last to tell us we are more than our present selves; and evacuate such hopes in the fruition of their own accomplishments.

CHAPTER V

Now since these dead bones have already out-lasted the living ones of *Methuselah*, and in a yard under ground, and thin walls of clay, out-worn all the strong and specious buildings above it; and quietly rested under the drums and tramplings of three conquests; What Prince can promise such diuturnity unto his Reliques, or might not gladly say,

Sic ego componi versus in ossa velim.[a]

[a] Tibullus.

Time which antiquates Antiquities, and hath an art to make dust of all things, hath yet spared these *minor* Monuments. In vain we hope to be known by open and visible conservatories, when to be unknown was the means of their continuation and obscurity their protection: If they dyed by violent hands, and were thrust into their Urnes, these bones become considerable, and some old Philosophers would honour them,[b] whose souls they conceived most pure, which were thus snatched from their bodies; and to retain a stronger propension unto them: whereas they weariedly left a languishing corps, and with faint desires of re-union. If they fell by long and aged decay, yet wrapt up in the bundle of time, they fall into indistinction, and make but one blot with Infants. If we begin to die when we live, and

[b] *Oracula Chaldaica cum scholiis Pselli & Plethonis. βίη λιπόντων σῶμα ψυχαὶ καθαρώταται. Vi corpus reliquentium animæ urisimsæ.*

long life be but a prolongation of death, our life is a sad composition; We live with death, and die not in a moment. How many pulses made up the life of *Methuselah*, were work for *Archimedes*: Common Counters summe up the life of *Moses* his man.[c] Our dayes become considerable like petty sums by minute accumulations; where numerous fractions make up but small round numbers; and our dayes of a span long make not one little finger.[d]

If the nearnesse of our last necessity brought a nearer conformity unto it, there were a happinesse in hoary hairs, and no calamity in half senses. But the long habit of living indisposeth us for dying; When Avarice makes us the sport of death; When even *David* grew politickly cruell; and *Solomon* could hardly be said to be the wisest of men. But many are too early old, and before the date of age. Adversity stretcheth our dayes, misery makes *Alcmenas* nights,[e] and time hath no wings unto it. But the most tedious being is that which can unwish it self, content to be nothing, or never to have been, which was beyond the *male*-content of *Job*, who cursed not the day of his life, but his Nativity: Content to have so farre been, as to have a Title to future being; Although he had lived here but in an hidden state of life, and as it were an abortion.

What Song the *Syrens* sang, or what name *Achilles* assumed when he hid himself among women, though puzling Questions[f] are not beyond all conjecture. What time the persons of these Ossuaries entred the famous Nations of the dead,[g] and slept with Princes and Counsellours,[h] might admit a wide solution. But who were the proprietaries of these bones, or what bodies these ashes made up, were a question above Antiquarism. Not to be resolved by man, nor easily perhaps by spirits, except we consult the Provinciall Guardians, or tutellary Observators. Had they made as good provision for their names, as they have done for their Reliques, they had not so grosly erred in the art of perpetuation. But to subsist in bones, and be but Pyramidally extant, is a fallacy in duration. Vain ashes, which in the oblivion of names, persons, times, and sexes, have found unto themselves a fruitlesse continuation, and only arise unto late posterity, as Emblemes of mortall vanities; Antidotes against pride, vainglory, and madding vices. Pagan vain-glories which thought

[c] In the Psalme of Moses.

[d] According to the ancient Arithmetick of the hand wherein the little finger of the right hand contracted, signified an hundred. Pierius in Hieroglyph.

[e] One night as long as three.

[f] The puzling questions of Tiberius unto grammarians. Marcel. Donatus in Suet.

[g] κλυτὰ ἔθνεα νεκρῶν. Hom.

[h] Job.

the world might last for ever, had encouragement for ambition, and finding no *Atropos* unto the immortality of their Names, were never dampt with the necessity of oblivion. Even old ambitions had the advantage of ours, in the attempts of their vainglories, who acting early, and before the probable Meridian of time, have by this time found great accomplishment of their designes, whereby the ancient *Heroes* have already out-lasted their Monuments, and Mechanicall preservations. But in this latter Scene of time we cannot expect such Mummies unto our memories, when ambition may fear the Prophecy of *Elias*,[i] and *Charles* the fifth can never hope to live within two *Methusela's* of *Hector*.[k]

[i] That the world may last but six thousand years.

[k] Hector's fame lasting above two lives of Methuselah, before that famous Prince was extant.

And therefore restlesse inquietude for the diuturnity of our memories unto present considerations seems a vanity almost out of date, and superanuated peece of folly. We cannot hope to live so long in our names as some have done in their persons, one face of *Janus* holds no proportion unto the other. 'Tis too late to be ambitious. The great mutations of the world are acted, our time may be too short for our designes. To extend our memories by Monuments, whose death we dayly pray for, and whose duration we cannot hope, without injury to our expectations in the advent of the last day, were a contradiction to our beliefs. We whose generations are ordained in this setting part of time, are providentially taken off from such imaginations. And being necessitated to eye the remaining particle of futurity, are naturally constituted unto thoughts of the next world, and cannot excusably decline the consideration of that duration, which maketh Pyramids pillars of snow, and all that's past a moment.

[l] Θ The Character of death.

[m] Old ones being taken up, and other bodies laid under them.

[n] *Gruteri Inscriptiones Antiquæ.*

Circles and right lines limit and close all bodies, and the mortall right-lined circle[l] must conclude and shut up all. There is no antidote against the *Opium* of time, which temporally considereth all things; Our Fathers finde their graves in our short memories, and sadly tell us how we may be buried in our Survivors. Grave-stones tell truth scarce fourty years:[m] Generations passe while some trees stand, and old Families last not three Oaks. To be read by bare Inscriptions like many in *Gruter*,[n] to hope for Eternity by Ænigmaticall Epithetes, or first letters of our names, to be studied by Antiquaries, who

we were, and have new Names given us like many of the
Mummies,* are cold consolations unto the Students of perpetuity, even by everlasting Languages.

To be content that times to come should only know there
was such a man, not caring whether they knew more of him,
was a frigid ambition in *Cardan:*° disparaging his horoscopal
inclination and judgement of himself. Who cares to subsist like
Hippocrates Patients, or *Achilles* horses in *Homer,* under naked
nominations, without deserts and noble acts, which are the
balsame of our memories, the *Entelechia* and soul of our sub-
sistences? To be namelesse in worthy deeds exceeds an infamous
history. The *Canaanitish* woman lives more happily without a
name, than *Herodias* with one. And who had not rather have
been the good theef, than *Pilate?*

But the iniquity of oblivion blindely scattereth her poppy,
and deals with the memory of men without distinction to
merit of perpetuity. Who can but pity the founder of the
Pyramids? *Herostratus* lives that burnt the Temple of *Diana,*
he is almost lost that built it; Time hath spared the Epitaph
of *Adrians* horse, confounded that of himself. In vain we compute our felicities by the advantage of our good names, since
bad have equall durations; and *Thersites* is like to live as long as
Agamemnon. Who knows whether the best of men be known?
or whether there be not more remarkable persons forgot, than
any that stand remembred in the known account of time?
Without the favour of the everlasting Register the first man
had been as unknown as the last, and *Methuselahs* long life had
been his only Chronicle.

Oblivion is not to be hired: The greater part must be content
to be as though they had not been, to be found in the Register
of God, not in the record of man. Twenty seven Names make
up the first story,† and the recorded names ever since contain
not one living Century. The number of the dead long exceedeth
all that shall live. The night of time far surpasseth the day,
and who knows when was the Æquinox? Every houre addes
unto that current Arithmetique, which scarce stands one
moment. And since death must be the *Lucina* of life, and even
Pagans could doubt‡ whether thus to live, were to dye. Since
our longest Sunne sets at right descensions, and makes but

* Which men
show in
several
Countries,
giving them
what names
they please;
and unto
some the
names of the
old Ægyptian
Kings out of
Herodotus.

° *Cuperem
notum esse
quod sim, non
opto ut sciatur
qualis sim.*
Card. in *vita
propria.*

† Before the
flood.

‡ Euripides
[Polyidos].

winter arches, and therefore it cannot be long before we lie down in darknesse, and have our light in ashes.* Since the brother of death daily haunts us with dying *memento's*, and time that grows old it self, bids us hope no long duration: Diuturnity is a dream and folly of expectation.

* According to the custome of the Jewes, who place a lighted wax-candle in a pot of ashes by the corps. Leo [of Modena].

Darknesse and light divide the course of time, and oblivion shares with memory a great part even of our living beings; we slightly remember our felicities, and the smartest stroaks of affliction leave but short smart upon us. Sense endureth no extremities, and sorrows destroy us or themselves. To weep into stones are fables. Afflictions induce callosities, miseries are slippery, or fall like snow upon us, which notwithstanding is no unhappy stupidity. To be ignorant of evils to come, and forgetfull of evils past, is a mercifull provision in nature, whereby we digest the mixture of our few and evil dayes, and our delivered senses not relapsing into cutting remembrances, our sorrows are not kept raw by the edge of repetitions. A great part of Antiquity contented their hopes of subsistency with a transmigration of their souls. A good way to continue their memories, while having the advantage of plurall successions, they could not but act something remarkable in such variety of beings, and enjoying the fame of their passed selves, make accumulation of glory unto their last durations. Others rather than be lost in the uncomfortable night of nothing, were content to recede into the common being, and make one particle of the publick soul of all things, which was no more than to return into their unknown and divine Originall again. Ægyptian ingenuity was more unsatisfied, continuing their bodies in sweet consistences, to attend the return of their souls. But all was vanity, feeding the winde,[a] and folly. The Ægyptian Mummies, which *Cambyses* or time hath spared, avarice now consumeth. Mummie is become Merchandise, *Miszraim* cures wounds, and *Pharaoh* is sold for balsoms.

[a] *Omnia vanitas & pastio venti, νομὴ ἀνέμου, βόσκησις ut olim Aquila & Symmachus V. Drus. Eccles.*

In vain do individuals hope for Immortality, or any patent from oblivion, in preservations below the Moon: Men have been deceived even in their flatteries above the Sun, and studied conceits to perpetuate their names in heaven. The various Cosmography of that part hath already varied the names of contrived constellations; *Nimrod* is lost in *Orion*, and *Osyris* in the

Dogge-starre. While we look for incorruption in the heavens, we finde they are but like the Earth; Durable in their main bodies, alterable in their parts: whereof beside Comets and new Stars, perspectives begin to tell tales. And the spots that wander about the Sun, with *Phaetons* favour, would make clear conviction.

There is nothing strictly immortall, but immortality. Whatever hath no beginning may be confident of no end (all others have a dependent being, and within the reach of destruction) which is the peculiar of that necessary essence that cannot destroy it self; And the highest strain of omnipotency to be so powerfully constituted, as not to suffer even from the power of it self. But the sufficiency of Christian Immortality frustrates all earthly glory, and the quality of either state after death makes a folly of posthumous memory. God who only can destroy our souls, and hath assured our resurrection, either of our bodies or names hath directly promised no duration. Wherein there is so much of chance that the boldest Expectants have found unhappy frustration; and to hold long subsistence, seems but a scape in oblivion. But man is a Noble Animal, splendid in ashes, and pompous in the grave, solemnizing Nativities and Deaths with equall lustre, nor omitting Ceremonies of bravery, in the infamy of his nature.

Life is a pure flame, and we live by an invisible Sun within us. A small fire sufficeth for life, great flames seemed too little after death, while men vainly affected precious pyres, and to burn like *Sardanapalus*; but the wisdom of funerall Laws found the folly of prodigall blazes, and reduced undoing fires unto the rule of sober obsequies, wherein few could be so mean as not to provide wood, pitch, a mourner, and an Urne.*

Five languages secured not the Epitaph of *Gordianus*;† The man of God lives longer without a Tomb than any by one, invisibly interred by Angels, and adjudged to obscurity though not without some marks directing human discovery. *Enoch* and *Elias* without either tomb or buriall, in an anomalous state of being, are the great Examples of perpetuity in their long and living memory, in strict account being still on this side death, and having a late part yet to act upon this stage of earth. If in the decretory term of the world we shall not all dye but be

* According to the Epitaph of Rufus and Beronica in Gruterus. *... Nec ex Eorum bonis plus inventum est, quam Quod sufficeret ad emendam pyram, Et picem quibus corpora cremarentur, Et præfica conducta & olla empta.*

† In Greek, Latine, Hebrew, Ægyptian, Arabick, defaced by Licinius the Emperour.

changed, according to received translation, the last day will make but few graves; at least quick Resurrections will anticipate lasting Sepultures; Some Graves will be opened before they be quite closed, and *Lazarus* be no wonder. When many that feared to dye shall groane that they can dye but once, the dismall state is the second and living death; when life puts despair on the damned; when men shall wish the coverings of Mountaines, not of Monuments, and annihilation shall be courted.

While some have studied Monuments, others have studiously declined them: and some have been so vainly boisterous, that they durst not acknowledge their Graves; wherein[b] *Alaricus* seems most subtle, who had a River turned to hide his bones at the bottome. Even *Sylla* that thought himself safe in his Urne, could not prevent revenging tongues, and stones thrown at his Monument. Happy are they whom privacy makes innocent, who deal so with men in this world, that they are not afraid to meet them in the next, who when they dye, make no commotion among the dead, and are not toucht with that poeticall taunt of *Isaiah*.[c]

Pyramids, Arches, Obelisks, were but the irregularities of vainglory, and wilde enormities of ancient magnanimity. But the most magnanimous resolution rests in the Christian Religion, which trampleth upon pride, and sits on the neck of ambition, humbly pursuing that infallible perpetuity, unto which all others must diminish their diameters, and be poorly seen in Angles of contingency.[d]

Pious spirits who passed their dayes in raptures of futurity, made little more of this world than the world that was before it, while they lay obscure in the Chaos of pre-ordination, and night of their fore-beings. And if any have been so happy as truly to understand Christian annihilation, extasis, exolution, liquefaction, transformation, the kisse of the Spouse, gustation of God, and ingression into the divine shadow, they have already had an handsome anticipation of heaven; the glory of the world is surely over, and the earth in ashes unto them.

To subsist in lasting Monuments, to live in their productions, to exist in their names, and prædicament of *Chymera's*, was large satisfaction unto old expectations, and made one part of their

[b] Jornandes de rebus Geticis.

[c] Isa. 14.

[d] *Angulus contingentiæ*, the least of Angles.

Elyziums. But all this is nothing in the Metaphysicks of true belief. To live indeed is to be again our selves, which being not only an hope but an evidence in noble beleevers, 'Tis all one to lye in St *Innocents*^e Church-yard, as in the Sands of *Ægypt*: Ready to be any thing, in the extasie of being ever, and as content with six foot as the Moles of *Adrianus.*^f

e In Paris where bodies soon consume.

f A stately *Mausoleum* or sepulchral pyle built by Adrianus in Rome, where now standeth the Castle of St. Angelo.

Lucan

——*Tabesne cadavera solvat*
An rogus haud refert.——

HYDRIOTAPHIA

ADDITIONAL PASSAGE FROM A MS

WILKIN prints the following passage related to p. 168, l. 6 [Brit. Mus. Sloane MS 1848, f. 194]: 'Large are the treasures of oblivion, and heapes of things in a state next to nothing almost numberlesse; much more is buried in silence than is recorded, and the largest volumes are butt epitomes of what hath been. The account of time beganne with night, and darknesse still attendeth it. Some things never come to light; many have been delivered; butt more hath been swallowed in obscurity & the caverns of oblivion. How much is as it were *in vacuo*, and will never be cleered up, of those long living times when men could scarce remember themselves young; and men seeme to us not ancient butt antiquities; when they subsisted longer in their lives then wee can now hope to do in our memories; when men feared apoplexies & palsies after 7 or 8 hundred years; when living was so lasting that homicide might admitt of distinctive qualifications from the age of the person, & it might seeme a lesser offense to kill a man at 8 hundred then at fortie, and when life was so well worth the living that few or none would kill themselves.'

THE GARDEN OF CYRUS

OR,

THE QUINCUNCIALL, LOZENGE, OR
NET-WORK PLANTATIONS OF THE
ANCIENTS, ARTIFICIALLY,
NATURALLY, MYSTICALLY
CONSIDERED

TO MY
Worthy and Honored Friend
NICHOLAS BACON
of *Gillingham* Esquire

HAD I not observed that Purblinde men[a] have diſcoursed well of sight, and some without issue,[b] excellently of Generation; I that was never master of any considerable garden, had not attempted this Subject. But the Earth is the Garden of Nature, and each fruitfull Countrey a Paradise. *Dioscorides* made most of his Observations in his march about with *Antonius*; and *Theophrastus* raised his generalities chiefly from the field.

Beside we write no Herball, nor can this Volume deceive you, who have handled the massiest thereof:[c] who know that three Folio's[d] are yet too little, and how New Herbals fly from *America* upon us. From persevering Enquirers, and olde[e] in those singularities, we expect such Descriptions. Wherein *England*[f] is now so exact, that it yeelds not to other Countreys.

We pretend not to multiply vegetable divisions by Quincuncial and Reticulate plants; or erect a new Phytology. The Field of knowledge hath been so traced, it is hard to spring any thing new. Of old things we write something new, If truth may receive addition, or envy will have any thing new; since the Ancients knew the late Anatomicall discoveries, and *Hippocrates* the Circulation.

You have been so long out of trite learning, that 'tis hard to finde a subject proper for you; and if you have met with a Sheet upon this, we have missed our intention. In this multiplicity of writing, bye and barren Themes are best fitted for invention; Subjects so often discoursed confine the Imagination, and fix our conceptions unto the notions of fore-writers. Beside, such

[a] Plempius, Cabeus, &c.
[b] D. Harvey

[c] Besleri *Hortus Eystetensis.*
[d] Bauhini *Theatrum Botanicum, &c.*
[e] My worthy friend M. Goodier, an ancient and learned Botanist.
[f] As in London and divers parts, whereof we mention none, lest we seem to omit any.

Discourses allow excursions, and venially admit of collaterall truths, though at some distance from their principals. Wherein if we sometimes take wide liberty, we are not single, but erre by great example.[g]

[g] Hippocrates de superfœtatione, de dentitione.

He that will illustrate the excellency of this order, may easily fail upon so spruce a Subject, wherein we have not affrighted the common Reader with any other Diagramms than of it self; and have industriously declined illustrations from rare and unknown plants.

Your discerning judgement so well acquainted with that study, will expect herein no mathematicall truths, as well understanding how few generalities and *U finita's*[h] there are in nature. How *Scaliger* hath found exceptions in most Universals of *Aristotle* and *Theophrastus.* How Botanicall Maximes must have fair allowance, and are tolerably currant, if not intolerably over-ballanced by exceptions.

[h] Rules without exceptions.

You have wisely ordered your vegetable delights, beyond the reach of exception. The Turks who passt their dayes in Gardens here, will have Gardens also hereafter, and delighting in Flowers on earth, must have Lillies and Roses in Heaven. In Garden Delights 'tis not easie to hold a Mediocrity; that insinuating pleasure is seldome without some extremity. The Antients venially delighted in flourishing Gardens; Many were Florists that knew not the true use of a Flower; And in *Plinies* dayes none had directly treated of that Subject. Some commendably affected Plantations of venemous Vegetables, some confined their delights unto single plants, and *Cato* seemed to dote upon Cabbadge; While the Ingenuous delight of Tulipists stands saluted with hard language, even by their own Professors.[i]

[i] Tulipomania, *Narrencruiid*, Laurenburg, Pet. Hondius *in lib. Belg.*

That in this Garden Discourse we range into extraneous things, and many parts of Art and Nature, we follow herein the example of old and new Plantations, wherein noble spirits contented not themselves with Trees, but by the attendance of Aviaries, Fish Ponds, and all variety of Animals, they made their gardens the Epitome of the earth, and some resemblance of the secular shows of old.

That we conjoyn these parts of different Subjects, or that this should succeed the other; Your judgement will admit without impute of incongruity; Since the delightfull World comes after

death, and Paradise succeeds the Grave. Since the verdant state
of things is the Symbole of the Resurrection, and to flourish in
the state of Glory, we must first be sown in corruption. Beside
the ancient practise of Noble Persons, to conclude in Garden-
Graves, and Urnes themselves of old, to be wrapt up in flowers
and garlands.

Nullum sine venia placuisse eloquium, is more sensibly understood
by Writers than by Readers; nor well apprehended by either,
till works have hanged out like *Apelles* his Pictures; wherein
even common eyes will finde something for emendation.

To wish all Readers of your abilities, were unreasonably to
multiply the number of Scholars beyond the temper of these
times. But unto this ill-judging age, we charitably desire a
portion of your equity, judgement, candour, and ingenuity;
wherein you are so rich, as not to lose by diffusion. And being a
flourishing branch of that Noble Family,[k] unto which we owe so
much observance, you are not new set, but long rooted in such
perfection; whereof having had so lasting confirmation in your
worthy conversation, constant amity, and expression; and
knowing you a serious Student in the highest *arcana's* of Nature;
with much excuse we bring these low delights, and poor
maniples to your Treasure.

[k] Of the most worthy Sr. Edmund Bacon prime Baronet, my true and noble Friend.

Your affectionate Friend

and Servant,

Thomas Browne.

Norwich
May 1
[1658]

M

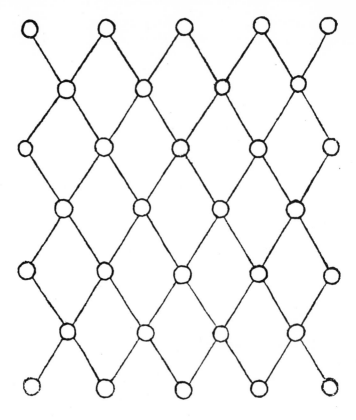

Quid Quincunce speciosius, qui, in
quam cunq; partem spectaueris,
rectus est. Quintilian;∥

THE GARDEN OF CYRUS

CHAPTER I

THAT *Vulcan* gave arrows unto *Apollo* and *Diana* the fourth day after their Nativities, according to Gentile Theology, may passe for no blinde apprehension of the Creation of the Sunne and Moon, in the work of the fourth day; When the diffused light contracted into Orbes, and shooting rayes, of those Luminaries. Plainer Descriptions there are from Pagan pens, of the creatures of the fourth day; While the divine Philosopher[a] unhappily omitteth the noblest part of the third; And *Ovid* (whom many conceive to have borrowed his description from *Moses*) coldly deserting the remarkable account of the text, in three words,[b] describeth this work of the third day; the vegetable creation, and first ornamentall Scene of nature; the primitive food of animals, and first story of Physick, in Dietetical conservation.

For though Physick may pleade high, from that medicall act of God, in casting so deep a sleep upon our first Parent; And Chirurgery[c] finde its whole art, in that one passage concerning the Rib of *Adam*, yet is there no rivality with Garden contrivance and Herbary. For if Paradise were planted the third day of the Creation, as wiser Divinity concludeth, the Nativity thereof was too early for Horoscopie; Gardens were before Gardiners, and but some hours after the earth.

Of deeper doubt is its Topography, and locall designation; yet being the primitive garden, and without much controversie[d] seated in the East, it is more than probable the first curiosity, and cultivation of plants, most flourished in those quarters. And since the Ark of *Noah* first toucht upon some mountains of *Armenia*, the planting art arose again in the East, and found its revolution not far from the place of its Nativity, about the Plains of those Regions. And if *Zoroaster* were either *Cham, Chus,*

a Plato in *Timæo.*

b *fronde tegi silvas.*

c διαίρεσις in opening the flesh; ἐξαίρεσις in taking out the rib; σύνθεσις in closing up the part again.

d For some there is from the ambiguity of the word *Mikedem* whether *ab oriente,* or *a principio.*

or *Mizraim,* they were early proficients therein, who left (as *Pliny* delivereth) a work of Agriculture.

However the account of the Pensill or hanging gardens of *Babylon,* if made by *Semiramis,* the third or fourth from *Nimrod,* is of no slender antiquity; which being not framed upon ordinary levell of ground, but raised upon pillars, admitting under-passages, we cannot accept as the first *Babylonian* Gardens; But a more eminent progress and advancement in that art, than any that went before it: Somewhat answering or hinting the old Opinion concerning Paradise it self, with many conceptions elevated above the plane of the Earth.

Nebuchodonosor whom some will have to be the famous *Syrian* King of *Diodorus,* beautifully repaired that City; and so magni-

^e Josephus. ficently built his hanging gardens,[e] that from succeeding Writers he had the honour of the first. From whence over-looking *Babylon,* and all the Region about it, he found no circumscription to the eye of his ambition; till over-delighted with the bravery of this Paradise, in his melancholy metamorphosis, he found the folly of that delight, and a proper punishment, in the contrary habitation, in wilde plantations and wandrings of the fields.

The *Persian* Gallants who destroyed this Monarchy, maintained their Botanicall bravery. Unto whom we owe the very name of Paradise: wherewith we meet not in Scripture before the time of *Solomon,* and conceived originally *Persian.* The word for that disputed Garden expressing in the Hebrew no more than a Field enclosed, which from the same Root is content to derive a garden and a Buckler.

Cyrus the elder, brought up in Woods and Mountains, when time and power enabled, pursued the dictate of his education, and brought the treasures of the field into rule and circumscription. So nobly beautifying the hanging Gardens of *Babylon,* that he was also thought to be the authour thereof.

Ahasuerus (whom many conceive to have been *Artaxerxes*

^f Sushan in Susiana. *Longimanus*) in the Countrey and City of Flowers,[f] and in an open Garden, entertained his Princes and people, while *Vasthi* more modestly treated the Ladies within the Palace thereof.

^g Plutarch in the *life of Artaxerxes.* But if (as some opinion)[g] King *Ahasuerus* were *Artaxerxes Mnemon,* that found a life and reign answerable unto his great

memory, our magnified *Cyrus* was his second Brother: who gave the occasion of that memorable work, and almost miraculous retrait of *Xenophon*. A person of high spirit and honour, naturally a King, though fatally prevented by the harmlesse chance of *post*-geniture: Not only a Lord of Gardens, but a manuall planter thereof: disposing his trees like his armies in regular ordination. So that while old *Laertas* hath found a name in *Homer* for pruning hedges, and clearing away thorns and bryars; while King *Attalus* lives for his poysonous plantations of *Aconites*, Henbane, Hellebore, and plants hardly admitted within the walls of Paradise; While many of the Ancients do poorly live in the single name of Vegetables; All stories do look upon *Cyrus*, as the splendid and regular planter.

According whereto *Xenophon*[h] describeth his gallant plantation at *Sardis*, thus rendred by *Strebæus*. *Arbores pari intervallo sitas, rectos ordines, & omnia perpulchrè in Quincuncem directa.*[i] Which we shall take for granted as being accordingly rendred by the most elegant of the *Latines*;[k] and by no made term, but in use before by *Varro*. That is the rows and orders so handsomly disposed; or five trees so set together, that a regular angularity, and through prospect, was left on every side. Owing this name not only unto the Quintuple number of Trees, but the figure declaring that number; which being doubled at the angle, makes up the Letter χ, that is the Emphaticall decussation, or fundamentall figure.

Now though in some ancient and modern practice the *area* or decussated plot, might be a perfect square, answerable to a *Tuscan Pedestall,* and the *Quinquernio* or Cinque-point of a dye; wherein by Diagonall lines the intersection was rectangular; accomodable unto Plantations of large growing Trees; and we must not deny our selves the advantage of this order; yet shall we chiefly insist upon that of *Curtius* and *Porta*,[l] in their brief description hereof. Wherein the *decussis* is made within a longilaterall square, with opposite angles, acute and obtuse at the intersection; and so upon progression making a *Rhombus* or Lozenge figuration, which seemeth very agreeable unto the Originall figure; Answerable whereunto we observe the decussated characters in many consulary Coynes, and even in those of *Constantine* and his Sons, which pretend their pattern in

[h] Xenophon in *Oeconomico.*

[i] καλὰ μὲν τὰ δένδρα δι᾽ ἴσου δὲ τὰ πεφυτευμένα, ὀρθοὶ δὲ οἱ στίχοι τῶν δένδρων, εὐγώνια δὲ πάντα καλῶς.

[k] Cicero in *Cat. Major.*

[l] Benedict. Curtius *de Hortis*. Bapt. Porta in *Villa.*

the Sky; the crucigerous Ensigne carried this figure, not trans-
versely or rectangularly intersected, but in a decussation, after
the form of an *Andrean* or *Burgundian* cross, which answereth
this description.

Where by the way we shall decline the old Theme, so traced
by antiquity, of crosses and crucifixion: Whereof some being
right, and of one single peece without transversion or transome,
do little advantage our subject. Nor shall we take in the mysticall
Tau, or the Crosse of our blessed Saviour, which having in some
descriptions an *Empedon* or crossing foot-stay, made not one
single transversion. And since the Learned *Lipsius* hath made
some doubt even of the Crosse of St *Andrew*, since some Mar-
tyrologicall Histories deliver his death by the generall Name of
a crosse, and *Hippolitus* will have him suffer by the sword; we
should have enough to make out the received Crosse of that
Martyr. Nor shall we urge the *labarum*, and famous Standard of
Constantine, or make further use thereof, than as the first Letters
in the Name of our Saviour Christ, in use among Christians
before the dayes of *Constantine*, to be observed in Sepulchral
Monuments[a] of Martyrs, in the Reign of *Adrian*, and *Antoninus*;
and to be found in the Antiquities of the Gentiles, before the
advent of Christ, as in the Medall of King *Ptolemy*, signed with
the same characters, and might be the beginning of some word
or name, which Antiquaries have not hit on.

We will not revive the mysterious crosses of *Ægypt*, with
circles on their heads, in the breast of *Serapis*, and the hands
of their Geniall spirits, not unlike the character of *Venus*, and
looked on by ancient Christians, with relation unto Christ.
Since however they first began, the Ægyptians thereby expressed the processe and motion of the spirit of the world,
and the diffusion thereof upon the Celestiall and Elementall
nature; implyed by a circle and right-lined intersection. A
secret in their Telesmes and magicall Characters among them.
Though he that considereth the plain crosse[b] upon the head
of the Owl in the Laterane Obelisk, or the crosse[c] erected upon
a picher diffusing streams of water into two basins, with sprink-
ling branches in them, and all described upon a two-footed
Altar, as in the Hieroglyphicks of the brasen Table of *Bembus*;
will hardly decline all thought of Christian signality in them.

[a] Of Marius, Alexander, *Roma Sotter-*
ranea.

[b] Wherein the lower part is somewhat longer, as defined by Upton *de*
studio militari, and *Johannes*
de Bado Aureo,
cum comment.
clariss. &
doctiss. Bissæi.

[c] Casal. *de*
Ritibus. Bosio
nella Trion-
fante croce.

We shall not call in the Hebrew *Tenupha*, or ceremony of their Oblations, waved by the Priest unto the four quarters of the world, after the form of a cross; as in the peace-offerings. And if it were clearly made out what is remarkably delivered from the Traditions of the Rabbins, that as the Oyle was powred coronally or circularly upon the head of Kings, so the High-Priest was anointed decussatively or in the form of a X; though it could not escape a typicall thought of Christ, from mysticall considerators; yet being the conceit is Hebrew, we should rather expect its verification from Analogy in that language, than to confine the same unto the unconcerned Letters of *Greece*, or make it out by the characters of *Cadmus* or *Palamedes*.

Of this Quincunciall Ordination the Ancients practised much, discoursed little; and the Moderns have nothing enlarged; which he that more nearly considereth, in the form of its square *Rhombus*, and decussation,[d] with the severall commodities, mysteries, parallelismes, and resemblances, both in Art and Nature, shall easily discern the elegancy of this order.

That this was in some wayes of practice in diverse and distant Nations, hints or deliveries there are from no slender Antiquity. In the hanging Gardens of *Babylon*, from *Abydenus*, *Eusebius*, and others, *Curtius* describeth this Rule of decussation. In the memorable Garden of *Alcinous*, anciently conceived an originall phancy, from Paradise, mention there is of well contrived order; For so hath *Didymus* and *Eustathius* expounded the emphatical word. *Diomedes* describing the Rurall possessions of his father, gives account in the same Language of Trees orderly planted. And *Ulysses* being a boy was promised by his Father fourty Figge-trees, and fifty rows of Vines producing all kinde of grapes.[e]

That the Eastern Inhabitants of *India* made use of such order, even in open Plantations, is deducible from *Theophrastus*; who describing the trees whereof they made their garments, plainly delivereth that they were planted κατ᾽ὄρχους, and in such order that at a distance men would mistake them for Vineyards. The same seems confirmed in *Greece* from a singular expression in *Aristotle*[f] concerning the order of Vines, delivered by a military term representing the orders of Souldiers, which also confirmeth the antiquity of this form yet used in vineall plantations.

d *Decussatio ipsa jucundum ac peramœnum conspectum præbuit.* Curt. Hortor. l. 6.

e ὄρχοι, στίχοι ἀμπέλων φυτῶν στίχος, ἡ κατὰ τάξιν, φυτεία. Phavorinus, Philoxenus.

f συστάδας ἀμπέλων. Polit. 7.

That the same was used in Latine plantations is plainly confirmed from the commending penne of *Varro*, *Quintilian*, and

g *Indulge ordinibus; nec secius omnis in unguem Arboribus positis secto via limite quadret. Georg.* 2.

handsome Description of *Virgil*.[g]

That the first Plantations not long after the Floud were disposed after this manner, the generality and antiquity of this order observed in Vineyards, and Wine plantations, affordeth some conjecture. And since from judicious enquiry, *Saturn* who divided the world between his three sonnes, who beareth a Sickle in his hand, who taught the plantations of Vines, the setting, grafting of trees, and the best part of Agriculture, is discovered to be *Noah*, whether this early dispersed Husbandry in Vineyards had not its Originall in that Patriarch, is no such Paralogicall doubt.

And if it were clear that this was used by *Noah* after the Floud, I could easily beleeve it was in use before it; Not willing to fix to such ancient inventions no higher originall than *Noah*; Nor readily conceiving those aged. *Heroes*, whose diet was vegetable, and only or chiefly consisted in the fruits of the earth, were much deficient in their splendid cultivations; or after the experience of fifteen hundred years, left much for future discovery in Botanicall Agriculture. Nor fully perswaded that Wine was the invention of *Noah*, that fermented Liquors, which often make themselves, so long escaped their Luxury or experience; that the first sinne of the new world was no sin of the old. That *Cain* and *Abel* were the first that offered Sacrifice; or because the Scripture is silent that *Adam* or *Isaac* offered none at all.

Whether *Abraham*, brought up in the first planting Countrey, observed not some rule hereof, when he planted a grove at *Beer-sheba*; or whether at least a like ordination were not in the Garden of *Solomon*, probability may contest. Answerably unto the wisdom of that eminent Botanologer, and orderly disposer of all his other works. Especially since this was one peece of Gallantry, wherein he pursued the specious part of felicity, according to his own description. I made me Gardens and Orchards, and planted Trees in them of all kindes of fruit. I made me Pools of water, to water therewith the wood that

h *Eccles.* 2.

bringeth forth Trees;[h] which was no ordinary plantation, if according to the *Targum*, or *Chaldee Paraphrase*, it contained all

kindes of Plants, and some fetched as far as *India*; And the extent
thereof were from the wall of *Jerusalem* unto the water of *Siloah*.

And if *Jordan* were but *Jaar Eden*, that is, the River of *Eden*,
Genesar but *Gansar* or the Prince of Gardens; and it could be
made out, that the Plain of *Jordan* were watered not compara-
tively, but causally, and because it was the Paradise of God, as
the Learned *Abramas*[i] hinteth, he was not far from the Prototype
and originall of Plantations. And since even in Paradise it self,
the tree of knowledge was placed in the middle of the Garden,
whatever was the ambient figure, there wanted not a centre
and rule of decussation. Whether the groves and sacred Plantations of Antiquity were not thus orderly placed, either by
quaternio's, or quintuple ordinations, may favourably be doubted.
For since they were so methodicall in the constitutions of their
temples, as to observe the due situation, aspect, manner, form,
and order in Architectonicall relations, whether they were not
as distinct in their groves and Plantations about them, in form
and *species* respectively unto their Deities, is not without probability of conjecture. And in their groves of the Sunne this
was a fit number, by multiplication to denote the dayes of
the year; and might Hieroglyphically speak as much, as the
mysticall *Statua* of *Janus*[k] in the Language of his fingers. And
since they were so criticall in the number of his horses, the
strings of his Harp, and rayes about his head, denoting the
orbes of heaven, the Seasons and Moneths of the Yeare; witty
Idolatry would hardly be flat in other appropriations.

i *Vet. Testa-
menti Pharus.*

k Which
King Numa
set up, with
his fingers so
disposed that
they numeric-
ally denoted
365. Pliny.

CHAPTER II

NOR was this only a form of practise in Plantations, but
found imitation from high Antiquity, in sundry artificiall contrivances and manuall operations. For to
omit the position of squared stones, *cuneatim* or *wedgwise* in the
Walls of *Roman* and *Gothick* buildings; and the *lithostrata* or
figured pavements of the ancients, which consisted not all of
square stones, but were divided into triquetrous segments,

honey-combs, and sexangular figures, according to *Vitruvius*; The squared stones and bricks in ancient fabricks were placed after this order. And two above or below conjoyned by a middle stone or *Plinthus*, observable in the ruines of *Forum Nervæ*, the *Mausoleum* of *Augustus*, the Pyramid of *Cestius*, and the sculpture draughts of the larger Pyramids of Ægypt. And therefore in the draughts of eminent fabricks, Painters do commonly imitate this order in the lines of their description.

In the Laureat draughts of sculpture and picture, the leaves and foliate works are commonly thus contrived, which is but in imitation of the *Pulvinaria*, and ancient pillow-work, observable in *Ionick* peeces, about columns, temples and altars. To omit many other analogies, in Architectonicall draughts, which art it self is founded upon fives,[a] as having its subject, and most gracefull peeces divided by this number.

The Triumphal Oval, and Civicall Crowns of Laurel, Oake, and Myrtle, when fully made, were pleated after this order. And to omit the crossed Crowns of Christian Princes; what figure that was which *Anastatius* described upon the head of *Leo* the third; or who first brought in the Arched Crown; That of Charles the great, (which seems the first remarkably closed Crown,) was framed after this manner;[b] with an intersection in the middle from the main crossing barres, and the interspaces unto the frontal circle, continued by handsome network-plates, much after this order. Whereon we shall not insist, because from greater Antiquity, and practice of consecration, we meet with the radiated, and starry Crown, upon the head of *Augustus*, and many succeeding Emperors. Since the Armenians and Parthians had a peculiar royall Capp; And the Grecians from *Alexander* another kinde of diadem. And even Diadems themselves were but fasciations, and handsome ligatures, about the heads of Princes; nor wholly omitted in the mitrall Crown, which common picture seems to set too upright and forward upon the head of *Aaron*: Worne sometimes singly,[c] or doubly by Princes, according to their Kingdomes; and no more to be expected from two Crowns at once, upon the head of *Ptolemy*. And so easily made out when historians tell us, some bound up wounds, some hanged themselves with diadems.

The beds of the antients were corded somewhat after this

[a] Of a structure five parts, *Fundamentum, parietes, aperturæ, Compartitio, tectum,* Leo. Alberti. Five columns, *Tuscan, Doric, Ionick Corinthian,* Compound. Five different intercolumniations, *Pycnostylos, diastylos, Systylos, Areostylos, Eustylos.* Vitruv.

[b] *Uti constat ex pergamena apud Chifflet*; in B.R. Bruxelli, & *Icon.* F. Stradæ.

[c] 1 Macc. 11.

fashion: That is not directly, as ours at present, but obliquely, from side to side, and after the manner of network; whereby they strengthened the spondæ or bedsides, and spent less cord in the work: as is demonstrated by *Blancanus.*[d]

And as they lay in crossed beds, so they sat upon seeming crosselegg'd seats: in which form the noblest thereof were framed: Observable in the triumphall seats, the *sella curulis,* or *Ædyle Chayres,* in the coyns of *Cestius, Sylla,* and *Julius.* That they sat also crosse legg'd many noble draughts declare; and in this figure the sitting gods and goddesses are drawn in medalls and medallions.* And beside this kinde of work in Retiarie and hanging textures, in embroderies, and eminent needle-works; the like is obvious unto every eye in glass-windows. Nor only in Glassie contrivances, but also in Lattice and Stone-work, conceived in the Temple of *Solomon;* wherein the windows are termed *fenestræ reticulatæ,* or lights framed like nets.[e] And agreeable unto the Greek expression concerning Christ in the Canticles,[f] looking through the nets, which ours hath rendered, he looketh forth at the windows, shewing him-selfe through the lattesse; that is, partly seen and unseen, according to the visible and invisible side of his nature. To omit the noble reticulate work, in the chapiters of the pillars of *Solomon,* with Lillies, and Pomegranats upon a network ground; and the *Craticula* or grate through which the ashes fell in the altar of burnt offerings.

That the networks and nets of antiquity were little different in the form from ours at present, is confirmable from the nets in the hands of the Retiarie gladiators, the proper combatants with the secutores. To omit the ancient Conopeion or gnatnet of the Ægyptians, the inventors of that Artifice: the rushey labyrinths of *Theocritus;* the nosegaynets, which hung from the head under the nostrils of Princes; and that uneasie meta-phor of *Reticulum Jecoris,** which some expound the lobe, we the caule above the liver. As for that famous network of *Vulcan,* which inclosed *Mars* and *Venus,* and caused that unextinguish-able laugh in heaven;[g] since the gods themselves could not discern it, we shall not prie into it; Although why *Vulcan* bound them, *Neptune* loosed them, and *Apollo* should first discover them, might afford no vulgar mythologie. Heralds have not omitted

[d] Aristot.
Mechan.
Quæst.

* The larger
sort of medals.

[e] δικτυωτά.

[f] Cant. 2.

* In
Leviticus.

[g] Ἄσβεστος
δ' ἄρ' ἐνῶρτο
γέλως. Hom.

this order or imitation thereof, whiles they Symbollically adorn their Scuchions with Mascles Fusils and Saltyrs, and while they disposed the figures of Ermins and vaired coats in this Quincùncial method.[h]

The same is not forgot by Lapidaries while they cut their gemms pyramidally, or by æquicrural triangles. Perspective picturers, in their Base, Horison, and lines of distances, cannot escape these Rhomboidall decussations. Sculptors in their strongest shadows, after this order do draw their double Haches. And the very *Americans* do naturally fall upon it, in their neat and curious textures, which is also observed in the elegant artifices of *Europe*. But this is no law unto the woof of the neat *Retiarie* Spider, which seems to weave without transversion, and by the union of right lines to make out a continued surface, which is beyond the common art of Textury, and may still nettle *Minerva*[a] the Goddesse of that mystery. And he that shall hatch the little seeds, either found in small webs, or white round Egges, carried under the bellies of some Spiders, and behold how at their first production in boxes, they will presently fill the same with their webbs, may observe the early and untaught finger of nature, and how they are natively provided with a stock, sufficient for such Texture.

The Rural charm against *Dodder, Tetter,* and strangling weeds, was contrived after this order, while they placed a chalked Tile at the four corners, and one in the middle of their fields, which though ridiculous in the intention, was rationall in the contrivance, and a good way to diffuse the magick through all parts of the *Area.*

Somewhat after this manner they ordered the little stones in the old game of *Pentalithismus,* or casting up five stones to catch them on the back of their hand. And with some resemblance hereof, the *Proci* or Prodigall Paramours disposed their men, when they played at *Penelope.*[b] For being themselves an hundred and eight, they set fifty four stones on either side, and one in the middle, which they called *Penelope,* which he that hit was master of the game.

In Chesse-boards and Tables we yet finde Pyramids and Squares, I wish we had their true and ancient description, farre

[h] *De armis Scaccatis masculatis, invectis, fuselatis, vide* Spelm., *Aspilog.*; & Upton *cum erudit.* Byssæo.

[a] As in the contention between Minerva and Arachne.

[b] In Eustathius his Comment upon Homer.

different from ours, or the *Chet mat*[1] of the *Persians*, which might
continue some elegant remarkables, as being an invention as
High as *Hermes* the Secretary of *Osyris*, figuring[c] the whole world,   [c] Plato.
the motion of the Planets, with Eclipses of Sunne and Moon.

   Physicians are not without the use of this decussation in several
operations, in ligatures and union of dissolved continuities.
Mechanicks make use hereof in forcipall Organs, and Instruments of Incision; wherein who can but magnifie the power of
decussation, inservient to contrary ends, solution and con-
solidation, union, and divisions, illustrable from *Aristotle* in the
old *Nucifragium* or Nut-cracker, and the Instruments of Evulsion, compression or incision; which consisting of two *Vectes* or
armes, converted towards each other, the innitency and stresse
being made upon the *hypomochlion* or fulciment in the decussation, the greater compression is made by the union of two
impulsors.

   The *Roman Batalia*[d] was ordered after this manner, whereof   [d] In the
as sufficiently known *Virgil* hath left but an hint, and obscure   disposure
intimation. For thus were the maniples and cohorts of the   of the Legions
                                                                  in the Wars of
Hastati, Principes and *Triarii* placed in their bodies, wherein   the Repub-
consisted the strength of the *Roman* battle. By this Ordination   like, before the
                                                                  division of
                                                                  the Legion
                                                                  into ten
                                                                  Cohorts by
                                                                  the Em-
                                                                  perours.
                                                                  Salmas. in his
                                                                  Epistle *à*
                                                                  Mounsieur de
                                                                  Peyresc, de Re
                                                                  militari Ro-
                                                                  manorum.

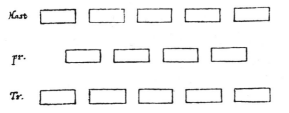

they readily fell into each other; the *Hastati* being pressed,
handsomely retired into the intervalls of the *principes*, these
into that of the *Triarii*, which making as it were a new body,
might joyntly renew the battle, wherein consisted the secret
of their successes. And therefore it was remarkably[e] singular   [e] Polybius;
in the battle of *Africa*, that *Scipio* fearing a rout from the   Appianus.
Elephants of the Enemy, left not the *Principes* in their alternate
distances, whereby the Elephants passing the vacuities of the

   [1] i.e. the Persian chess term, *shah mat*—the King is dead, 'Checkmate'
[Carter].

Hastati, might have run upon them, but drew his battle into right order, and leaving the passages bare, defeated the mischief intended by the Elephants. Out of this figure were made two remarkable forms of Battle, the *Cuneus* and *Forceps,* or the sheare and wedge battles, each made of half a *Rhombus,* and but differenced by position. The wedge invented to break or work into a body, the *forceps* to environ and defeat the power thereof, composed out of the selectest Souldiery and disposed into the form of an U, wherein receiving the wedge, it inclosed it on both sides. After this form the famous *Narses*[f] ordered his battle against the *Franks,* and by this figure the *Almans* were enclosed, and cut in peeces.

[f] Agathius;
Ammianus.

The *Rhombus* or Lozenge figure so visible in this order, was also a remarkable form of battle in the *Grecian* Cavalry,[g] observed by the *Thessalians,* and *Philip* King of *Macedon,* and frequently by the *Parthians,* As being most ready to turn every way, and best to be commanded, as having its ductors, or Commanders at each Angle.

[g] Ælian.
Tact.

The *Macedonian Phalanx* (a long time thought invincible) consisted of a long square. For though they might be sixteen in Rank and file, yet when they shut close, so that the sixt pike advanced before the first ranck, though the number might be square, the figure was oblong, answerable unto the Quincunciall quadrate of *Curtius.* According to this square, *Thucydides* delivers, the *Athenians* disposed their battle against the *Lacedemonians* brickwise,[h] and by the same word the Learned *Guellius* expoundeth the quadrate of *Virgil,*[i] after the form of a brick or tile.

[h] ἐν πλαισίῳ.
[i] Secto via
limite quadret.
Comment. in
Virgil.

And as the first station and position of trees, so was the first habitation of men, not in round Cities, as of later foundation; For the form of *Babylon* the first City was square, and so shall also be the last, according to the description of the holy City in the Apocalyps. The famous pillars of *Seth* before the floud, had also the like foundation, if they were but *antidiluvian* Obelisks,[*] and such as *Cham* and his *Ægyptian* race imitated after the Flood.

[*] Obelisks
being erected
upon a square
base.

But *Nineveh* which Authours acknowledge to have exceeded *Babylon,* was of a longilaterall figure, ninety[k] five Furlongs broad, and an hundred and fifty long, and so making about

[k] Diod. Sic.

sixty miles in circuit, which is the measure of three dayes journey, according unto military marches, or castrensiall mansions. So that if *Jonas* entred at the narrower side, he found enough for one dayes walk to attain the heart of the City, to make his Proclamation. And if we imagine a City extending from *Ware* to *London,* the expression will be moderate of six score thousand Infants, although we allow vacuities, fields, and intervals of habitation as there needs must be when the monument of *Ninus* took up no lesse than ten furlongs.

And, though none of the seven wonders, yet a noble peece of Antiquity, and made by a Copy exceeding all the rest, had its principall parts disposed after this manner, that is, the Labyrinth of *Crete,* built upon a long quadrate, containing five large squares, communicating by right inflections, terminating in the centre of the middle square, and lodging of the *Minotaur,* if we conform unto the description of the elegant medall thereof in *Agostino.*[1] And though in many accounts we reckon grosly by the square, yet is that very often to be accepted as a long sided quadrate, which was the figure of the Ark of the Covenant, the table of the Shew-bread, and the stone wherein the names of the twelve Tribes were engraved, that is, three in a row, naturally making a longilaterall Figure, the perfect quadrate being made by nine.

What figure the stones themselves maintained, tradition and Scripture are silent, yet Lapidaries in precious stones affect a Table or long square, and in such proportion, that the two laterall and also the three inferiour Tables are equall unto the superiour, and the angles of the laterall Tables contain and constitute the *hypothenusæ,* or broader sides subtending.

That the Tables of the Law were of this figure, general imitation and tradition hath confirmed; yet are we unwilling to load the shoulders of *Moses* with such massie stones, as some pictures lay upon them, since 'tis plainly delivered that he came down with them in his hand; since the word strictly taken implies no such massie hewing, but cutting, and fashioning of them into shape and surface; since some will have them Emeralds, and if they were made of the materials of Mount *Sina,* not improbable that they were marble: Since the words were not

[1] Antonio Agostino *delle medaglie.*

many, the letters short of seven hundred, and the Tables written on both sides required no such capacity.

The beds of the Ancients were different from ours at present, which are almost square, being framed ob-long, and about a double unto their breadth; not much unlike the *area*, or bed of this Quincuncial quadrate. The single beds of *Greece* were six foot,[m] and a little more in length, three in breadth; the Giant-like bed of *Og*, which had four cubits of bredth, nine and a half in length, varied not much from this proportion. The Funeral bed of King *Cheops*, in the greater Pyramid, which holds seven in length, and four foot in bredth, had no great difformity from this measure; And whatsoever were the bredth, the length could hardly be lesse, of the tyrannical bed of *Procrustes*, since in a shorter measure he had not been fitted with persons for his cruelty of extension. But the old sepulchral bed, or *Amazonian* Tomb[n] in the market-place of *Megara*, was in the form of a Lozenge; readily made out by the composure of the body. For the arms not lying fasciated or wrapt up after the *Grecian* manner, but in a middle distention, the including lines will strictly make out that figure.

m Aristot.
Mechan.

n Plut. in <i>vit.</i>
Thes.

CHAPTER III

NOW although this elegant ordination of vegetables hath found coincidence or imitation in sundry works of Art, yet is it not also destitute of naturall examples, and though overlooked by all, was elegantly observable in severall works of nature.

Could we satisfie our selves in the position of the lights above, or discover the wisedome of that order so invariably maintained in the fixed Stars of heaven; Could we have any light, why the stellary part of the first masse, separated into this order, that the Girdle of *Orion* should ever maintain its line, and the two Starres in *Charles's* Wain never leave pointing at the Pole-Starre, we might abate the *Pythagoricall* Musick of the Spheres, the sevenfold Pipe of *Pan*; and the strange Cryptography of *Gaffarell* in his Starrie Booke of Heaven.

But not to look so high as Heaven or the single Quincunx of the *Hyades* upon the head of *Taurus*, the Triangle and remarkable *Crusero* about the foot of the *Centaur*; observable rudiments there are hereof in subterraneous concretions, and bodies in the Earth; in the *Gypsum* or *Talcum Rhomboides*, in the Favaginites or honey-comb-stone, in the *Asteria* and *Astroites*, and in the crucigerous stone of S. *Iago* of *Gallicia*.

The same is observably effected in the *Julus*, *Catkins*, or pendulous excrescencies of severall Trees, of Wallnuts, Alders, and Hazels, which hanging all the Winter, and maintaining their Net-worke close, by the expansion thereof are the early foretellers of the Spring, discoverable also in long Pepper, and elegantly in the *Julus* of *Calamus Aromaticus*, so plentifully growing with us in the first palmes of Willowes, and in the Flowers of Sycamore, Petasites, Asphodelus, and *Blattaria*, before explication. After such order stand the flowery Branches in our best spread *Verbascum*, and the seeds about the spicous head or torch of *Tapsus Barbatus*, in as fair a regularity as the circular and wreathed order will admit, which advanceth one side of the square, and makes the same Rhomboidall.

In the squamous heads of *Scabious*, *Knapweed*, and the elegant *Jacea Pinea*, and in the Scaly composure of the *Oak-Rose*,[a] which some years most aboundeth. After this order hath Nature planted the Leaves in the Head of the common and prickled Artichoak; wherein the black and shining Flies do shelter themselves, when they retire from the purple Flower about it; The same is also found in the pricks, sockets, and impressions of the seeds, in the pulp or bottome thereof; wherein do elegantly stick the Fathers of their Mother.[b] To omit the Quincunciall Specks on the top of the Miscle-berry, especially that which grows upon the *Tilia* or Lime-Tree. And the remarkable disposure of those yellow fringes about the purple Pestill of *Aaron*, and elegant clusters of Dragons, so peculiarly secured by nature, with an *umbrella* or skreening Leaf about them.

The Spongy leaves of some Sea-wracks, Fucus, Oaks, in their several kindes, found about the shoar,[c] with ejectments of the Sea, are over-wrought with Net-work elegantly containing this order, which plainly declareth the naturality of this texture; And how the needle of nature delighteth to work, even in low and doubtful vegetations.

[a] *Capitula squammata Quercum,* Bauhini, Whereof though he saith, *perraro reperiuntur bis tantum invenimus,* yet we finde them commonly with us and in great numbers.

[b] *Anthol. Græc. inter Epigrammata.* γριφώδη ἔνδον ἐμῶν λαγόνων μητρὸς ἔχω πατέρα.

[c] Especially the *porus cervinus, Imperati, Sporosa,* or *Alga* πλατύκερως. Bauhini.

The *Arbustetum* or Thicket on the head of the Teazell, may be observed in this order. And he that considereth that fabrick so regularly palisadoed, and stemm'd with flowers of the royall colour; in the house of the solitary maggot,* may finde the Seraglio of *Solomon*, And contemplating the calicular shafts, and uncous disposure of their extremities, so accommodable unto the office of abstersion, not condemne as wholly improbable the conceit of those who accept it for the herbe *Borith*.[d] Where by the way, we could with much inquiry never discover any transfiguration, in this abstemious insect, although we have kept them long in their proper houses, and boxes. Where some wrapt up in their webbs, have lived upon their own bowels, from September unto July.

In such a grove doe walke the little creepers about the head of the burre. And such an order is observed in the aculeous prickly plantation, upon the heads of several common thistles, remarkably in the notable palisados about the flower of the milk-Thistle; and he that inquireth into the little bottome of the globe-thistle, may finde that gallant bush arise from a scalpe of like disposure.

The white umbrella or medicall bush of Elder, is an Epitome of this order: arising from five main stemms Quincuncially disposed, and tollerably maintained, in their subdivisions. To omit the lower observations in the seminal spike of Mercurie, weld, and Plantane.

Thus hath nature ranged the flowers of Santfoyne, and French honey suckle; and somewhat after this manner hath ordered the bush in *Jupiters* beard, or houseleek; which old superstition set on the tops of houses, as a defensative against lightening, and thunder. The like in Fenny Sengreen or the water Souldier;[e] which, though a militarie name from Greece, makes out the Roman order.

A like ordination there is in the favaginous Sockets, and Lozenge seeds of the noble flower of the Sunne. Wherein in Lozenge figured boxes nature shuts up the seeds, and balsame which is about them.

But the Firre and Pinetree from their fruits doe naturally dictate this position. The Rhomboidall protuberances in Pineapples maintaining this Quincuncial order unto each other, and

* There being a single Maggot found almost in every head.

[d] Jer. 2. 22.

[e] Stratiotes.

each Rhombus in it selfe. Thus are also disposed the triangular foliations, in the conicall fruit of the firre tree, orderly shadowing and protecting the winged seeds below them.

The like so often occurreth to the curiosity of observers, especially in spicated seeds and flowers, that we shall not need to take in the single Quincunx of Fuchsius in the grouth of the masle fearn, the seedie disposure of Gramen Ischemon, and the trunk or neat Reticulate work in the codde of the Sachell palme.

For even in very many round stalk plants, the leaves are set after a Quintuple ordination, the first leaf answering the fifth, in lateral disposition. Wherein the leaves successively rounding the stalke, in foure at the furthest the compass is absolved, and the fifth leafe or sprout returns to the position of the other fifth before it; as in accounting upward is often observable in furze, pellitorye, Ragweed, the sproutes of Oaks, and thorns upon pollards,[f] and very remarkably in the regular disposure of the rugged excrescencies in the yearly shoots of the Pine.

[f] Upon pollard Oaks and Thorns.

But in square stalked plants, the leaves stand respectively unto each other, either in crosse of decussation to those above or below them, arising at crosse positions; whereby they shadow not each other, and better resist the force of winds, which in a parallel situation, and upon square stalkes would more forcibly bear upon them.

And to omit, how leaves and sprouts which compasse not the stalk, are often set in a Rhomboides, and making long and short Diagonals, doe stand like the leggs of Quadrupeds when they goe: Nor to urge the thwart enclosure and furdling of flowers and blossomes before explication, as in the multiplyed leaves of Pionie; And the Chiasmus in five leaved flowers, while one lies wrapt about the staminous beards, the other foure obliquely shutting and closing upon each other; and how even flowers which consist of foure leaves stand not ordinarily in three and one, but two and two crossewise unto the Stylus; even the Autumnal budds, which awaite the returne of the sun, doe after the winter solstice multiply their calicular leaves, making little Rhombuses, and network figures, as in the Sycamore and Lilac.

The like is discoverable in the original production of plants, which first putting forth two leaves, those which succeed bear not over each other, but shoot obliquely or crossewise, untill the stalke appeareth; which sendeth not forth its first leaves without all order unto them; and he that from hence can discover in what position the two first leaves did arise, is no ordinary observator.

Where by the way, he that observeth the rudimental spring of seeds, shall finde strict rule, although not after this order. How little is required unto effectual generation, and in what diminutives the plastick principle lodgeth, is exemplified in seeds, wherein the greater mass affords so little comproduction. In Beanes the leaf and root sprout from the Germen, the main sides split, and lye by, and in some pull'd up near the time of blooming we have found the pulpous sides intire or little wasted. In Acorns the nebb dilating splitteth the two sides, which sometimes lye whole, when the Oak is sprouted two handfuls. In Lupins these pulpy sides do sometimes arise with the stalk in a resemblance of two fat leaves. Wheat and Rye will grow up, if after they have shot some tender Roots, the adhering pulp be taken from them. Beanes will prosper though a part be cut away, and so much set as sufficeth to contain and keep the Germen close. From this superfluous pulp, in unkindely and wet years, may arise that multiplicity of little insects, which infest the Roots and Sprouts of tender Graines and pulses.

In the little nebbe or fructifying principle, the motion is regular, and not transvertible, as to make that ever the leaf, which nature intendeth the root; observable from their conversion, until they attain their right position, if seeds be set inversedly.

In vain we expect the production of plants from different parts of the seed, from the same *corculum* or little original proceed both germinations; and in the power of this slender particle lye many Roots and sproutings, that though the same be pull'd away, the generative particle will renew them again, and proceed to a perfect plant; And malt may be observed to grow, though the Cummes be fallen from it.

The seminall nebbe hath a defined and single place, and not extended unto both extremes. And therefore many too vulgarly conceive that Barley and Oats grow at both ends; For they arise from one *punctilio* or generative nebbe, and the Speare sliding

under the husk, first appeareth nigh the toppe. But in Wheat
and Rye being bare the sprouts are seen together. If Barley
unhulled would grow, both would appear at once. But in this
and Oat-meal the nebbe is broken away, which makes them the
milder food, and lesse apt to raise fermentation in Decoctions.

Men taking notice of what is outwardly visible, conceive
a sensible priority in the Root. But as they begin from one
part, so they seem to start and set out upon one signall of
nature. In Beans yet soft, in Pease while they adhere unto
the Cod, the rudimentall Leafe and Root are discoverable.
In the Seeds of Rocket and Mustard, sprouting in Glasses of
water, when the one is manifest the other is also perceptible.
In muddy waters apt to breed *Duckweed*, and Periwinkles, if
the first and rudimentall stroaks of Duckweed be observed,
the Leaves and Root anticipate not each other. But in the
Date-stone the first sprout is neither root nor leaf distinctly,
but both together; For the Germination being to passe through
the narrow Navell and hole about the midst of the stone, the
generative germ is faine to enlengthen it self, and shooting
out about an inch, at that distance divideth into the ascending
and descending portion.

And though it be generally thought that Seeds will root at
that end, where they adhere to their Originals, and observable
it is that the nebbe sets most often next the stalk, as in Grains,
Pulses, and most small Seeds, yet is it hardly made out in
many greater plants. For in Acornes, Almonds, Pistachios,
Wallnuts, and accuminated shells, the germ puts forth at the
remotest part of the pulp. And therefore to set Seeds in that
posture, wherein the Leaf and Roots may shoot right without
contortion, or forced circumvolution, which might render them
strongly rooted, and straighter, were a Criticisme in Agriculture. And nature seems to have made some provision hereof
in many from their figure, that as they fall from the tree they
may lye in Positions agreeable to such advantages.

Beside the open and visible Testicles of plants, the seminall
powers lie in great part invisible, while the Sun findes polypody in stone-wals, the little stinging Nettle and nightshade
in barren sandy High-wayes, *Scurvy-grasse* in *Greeneland*, and
unknown plants in earth brought from remote Countries.

Beside the known longevity of some Trees, what is the most lasting herb, or seed, seems not easily determinable. Mandrakes upon known account have lived near an hundred yeares. Seeds found in Wilde-Fowls Gizards have sprouted in the earth. The Seeds of Marjorane and *Stramonium* carelessly kept, have grown after seven years. Even in Garden-plots long fallow, and digged up, the seeds of *Blattaria* and yellow henbane after twelve years burial have produced themselves again.

That bodies are first spirits *Paracelsus* could affirm, which in the maturation of Seeds and fruits, seems obscurely implied by *Aristotle*,[a] when he delivereth, that the spirituous parts are converted into water, and the water into earth, and attested by observation in the maturative progresse of Seeds, wherein at first may be discerned a flatuous distension of the husk, afterwards a thin liquor, which longer time digesteth into a pulp or kernell observable in Almonds and large Nuts. And some way answered in the progressionall perfection of animall semination, in its spermaticall maturation, from crude pubescency unto perfection. And even that seeds themselves in their rudimentall discoveries, appear in foliaceous surcles, or sprouts within their coverings, in a diaphanous gellie, before deeper incrassation, is also visibly verified in Cherries, Acorns, Plums.

[a] *In Met. cum* Cabeo.

From seminall considerations, either in reference unto one another, or distinction from animall production, the holy Scripture describeth the vegetable creation; And while it divideth plants but into Herb and Tree, though it seemeth to make but an accidental division, from magnitude, it tacitely containeth the naturall distinction of vegetables, observed by Herbarists, and comprehending the four kinds. For since the most naturall distinction is made from the production of leaf or stalk, and plants after the two first seminall leaves do either proceed to send forth more leaves, or a stalk, and the folious and stalky emission distinguisheth herbs and trees, in a large acception it comprizeth all vegetables; for the *frutex* and *suffrutex* are under the progression of trees, and stand Authentically differenced but from the accidents of the stalk.

The Æquivocall production of things under undiscerned principles, makes a large part of generation, though they seem to hold a wide univocacy in their set and certain Originals,

while almost every plant breeds its peculiar insect, most a
Butterfly, moth or fly, wherein the Oak seems to contain the
largest seminality, while the Julus,★ Oak-apple, pill, woolly tuft,
foraminous roundles upon the leaf, and grapes under ground
make a Fly with some difference. The great variety of Flyes
lyes in the variety of their originals, in the seeds of Caterpillars
or Cankers there lyeth not only a Butterfly or Moth, but if
they be sterill or untimely cast, their production is often a
Fly, which we have also observed from corrupted and mouldred
Egges, both of Hens and Fishes; To omit the generation of
Bees out of the bodies of dead Heifers, or what is strange yet
well attested, the production of Eeles in the backs of living
Cods and Perches.[b]

The exiguity and smallnesse of some seeds extending to
large productions is one of the magnalities of nature, somewhat illustrating the work of the Creation, and vast production
from nothing. The true seeds of Cypresse[c] and Rampions are
indistinguishable by old eyes. Of the seeds of Tobacco a
thousand make not one grain, The disputed seeds of Harts
tongue, and Maidenhair, require a greater number. From
such undiscernable seminalities arise spontaneous productions.
He that would discern the rudimentall stroak of a plant, may
behold it in the Originall of Duckweed, at the bignesse of a
pins point, from convenient water in glasses, wherein a watch-
full eye may also discover the puncticular Originals of Peri-
wincles and Gnats.

That seeds of some Plants are lesse than any animals, seems
of no clear decision; That the biggest of Vegetables exceedeth
the biggest of Animals, in full bulk, and all dimensions, admits
exception in the Whale, which in length and above ground
measure, will also contend with tall Oakes. That the richest
odour of plants surpasseth that of Animals may seem of some
doubt, since animall-musk seems to excell the vegetable, and
we find so noble a scent in the Tulip-Fly, and Goat-Beetle.[d]

Now whether seminall nebbes hold any sure proportion
unto seminall enclosures, why the form of the germe doth not
answer the figure of the enclosing pulp, why the nebbe is seated
upon the solid, and not the channeld side of the seed as in
grains, why since we often meet with two yolks in one shell,

★ These and
more to be
found upon
our Oaks;
not well
described by
any till the
Edition of
*Theatrum
Botanicum.*

[b] Schone-
veldus *de Pisc.*
[*Ichthyologia*]

[c] *Doctissim.*
Laurenburg.
Hort.

[d] The long
and tender
green *Capri-
cornus,* rarely
found; we
could never
meet with
but two.

and sometimes one Egge within another, we do not oftener meet with two nebbes in one distinct seed: why since the Egges of a Hen laid at one course do commonly out-weigh the bird, and some moths coming out of their cases, without assistance of food, will lay so many Egges as to out-weigh their bodies, trees rarely bear their fruit in that gravity or proportion: Whether in the germination of seeds according to *Hippocrates*, the lighter part ascendeth, and maketh the sprout, the heaviest tending downward frameth the root; Since we observe that the first shoot of seeds in water will sink or bow down at the upper and leafing end: Whether it be not more rational Epicurisme to contrive whole dishes out of the nebbes and spirited particles of plants, than from the Gallatures and treddles of Egges; since that part is found to hold no seminal share in Oval Generation, are quæries which might enlarge but must conclude this digression.

And though not in this order, yet how nature delighteth in this number, and what consent and coordination there is in the leaves and parts of flowers, it cannot escape our observation in no small number of plants. For the calicular or supporting and closing leaves do answer the number of the flowers, especially in such as exceed not the number of Swallows Egges;* as in Violets, Stichwort, Blossomes; and flowers of one leaf have often five divisions, answered by a like number of calicular leaves; as *Gentianella, Convolvulus,* Bell-flowers. In many the flowers, blades, or staminous shootes and leaves are all equally five, as in cockle, mullein and *Blattaria*; Wherein the flowers before explication are pentagonally wrappen up, with some resemblance of the *blatta* or moth from whence it hath its name: But the contrivance of nature is singular in the opening and shutting of Bindeweeds, performed by five inflexures, distinguishable by pyramidall figures, and also different colours.

* Which exceed not five.

The rose at first is thought to have been of five leaves, as it yet groweth wilde among us; but in the most luxuriant, the calicular leaves do still maintain that number. But nothing is more admired than the five Brethren of the Rose, and the strange disposure of the Appendices or Beards, in the calicular leaves thereof, which in despair of resolution is tolerably salved from this contrivance, best ordered and suited for the free closure of them before explication. For those two which are smooth, and of no beard, are contrived to lye undermost, as without prominent parts, and fit to be smoothly covered; the other two which are beset with Beards in either side, stand outward and uncovered, but the fifth or half-bearded leaf is covered on the bare side but on the open side stands free, and bearded like the other.

Besides a large number of leaves have five divisions, and may be circumscribed by a *Pentagon* or figure of five Angles, made by right lines from the extremity of their leaves, as in Maple, Vine, Figge-Tree: But five-leaved flowers are commonly disposed circularly about the *Stylus*; according to the higher Geometry of nature, dividing a circle by five *radii*, which concurre not to make Diameters, as in Quadrilaterall and sexangular Intersections.

Now the number of five is remarkable in every circle, not only as the first sphærical number, but the measure of sphærical motion. For sphærical bodies move by fives, and every globular figure placed upon a plane, in direct volutation, returns to the first point of contaction in the fifth touch, accounting by the Axes of the Diameters or Cardinall points of the four quarters thereof. And before it arriveth unto the same point again, it maketh five circles equall unto it self, in each progresse from those quarters absolving an equall circle.

By the same number doth nature divide the circle of the Sea-Starre, and in that order and number disposeth those elegant Semicircles, or dentall sockets and egges in the Sea Hedgehogge. And no mean Observations hereof there is in the Mathematicks of the neatest Retiary Spider, which concluding in fourty four Circles, from five Semidiameters beginneth that elegant texture.

And after this manner doth lay the foundation of the circular branches of the Oak, which being five-cornered, in the tender annual sprouts, and manifesting upon incision the signature of a Starre, is after made circular, and swel'd into a round body: Which practice of nature is become a point of art, and makes two Problemes in *Euclide*.[e] But the Bramble which sends forth   [e] *Elem. lib.* 4. shoots and prickles from its angles, maintains its pentagonall figure, and the unobserved signature of a handsome porch within it. To omit the five small buttons dividing the Circle of the Ivy-berry, and the five characters in the Winter stalk of the Walnut, with many other Observables, which cannot escape the eyes of signal discerners; Such as know where to finde *Ajax* his name in *Delphinium,* or *Aarons* Mitre in Henbane.

Quincuncial forms and ordinations are also observable in animal figurations. For to omit the hioides or throat-bone of animals, the *furcula* or *merry-thought* in birds, which supporteth the *scapulæ,* affording a passage for the windepipe and the gullet, the wings of Flyes, and disposure of their legges in their first formation from maggots, and the position of their horns, wings and legges, in their *Aurelian* cases and swadling clouts: The back of the *Cimex Arboreus,* found often upon Trees and lesser plants, doth elegantly discover the *Burgundian* decussation; And the like is observable in the belly of the *Notonecton,* or water-Beetle, which swimmeth on its back, and the handsome Rhombusses of the Sea-poult, or Weazell,[1] on either side the Spine.

The sexangular Cels in the Honeycombs of Bees are disposed after this order. Much there is not of wonder in the confused Houses of Pismires, though much in their busie life and actions; more in the edificial Palaces of Bees and Monarchical spirits; who make their combs six-corner'd, declining a circle, whereof many stand not close together, and compleatly fill the *area* of the place; But rather affecting a six-sided figure, whereby every cell affords a common side unto six more, and also a fit receptacle for the Bee it self, which gathering into a Cylindrical Figure, aptly enters its sexangular house, more nearly approaching a circular Figure, than either doth the Square or Triangle. And the Combes themselves so regularly contrived, that their mutual intersections make three Lozenges at the bottome of every Cell; which severally regarded make three Rows of neat Rhomboidall Figures, connected at the angles, and so continue three several chains throughout the whole comb.

As for the *Favago* found commonly on the sea shoar, though named from an honey-comb, it but rudely makes out the resemblance, and better agrees with the round Cels of humble Bees. He that would exactly discern the shop of a Bees mouth, needs observing eyes, and good augmenting glasses; wherein is discoverable one of the neatest peeces in nature; and must

[1] i.e the *mustela marina* or rockling fish.

have a more piercing eye than mine, who findes out the shape of Buls heads in the guts of Drones pressed out behinde, according to the experiment of *Gomesius*;[f] wherein notwith- standing there seemeth somewhat which might incline a pliant fancy to credulity of similitude.

[f] Gom. *de Sale.*

A resemblance hereof there is in the orderly and rarely disposed Cels, made by Flyes and Insects, which we have often found fastened about small sprigs, and in those cottonary and woolly pillows, which sometimes we meet with fastened unto Leaves, there is included an elegant Net-work Texture, out of which come many small Flies. And some resemblance there is of this order in the Egges of some Butterflies and moths, as they stick upon leaves, and other substances; which being dropped from behinde, nor directed by the eye, do neatly declare how nature Geometrizeth, and observeth order in all things.

A like correspondency in figure is found in the skins and outward teguments of animals, whereof a regardable part are beautiful by this texture. As the backs of several Snakes and Serpents, elegantly remarkable in the *Aspis*, and the Dartsnake, in the Chiasmus and larger decussations upon the back of the Rattlesnake, and in the close and finer texture of the *Mater formicarum*, or snake that delights in Anthils; whereby upon approach of outward injuries, they can raise a thicker Phalanx on their backs, and handsomely contrive themselves into all kindes of flexures: Whereas their bellies are commonly covered with smooth semicircular divisions, as best accommodable unto their quick and gliding motion.

This way is followed by nature in the peculiar and remarkable tayl of the Bever, wherein the scaly particles are disposed somewhat after this order, which is the plainest resolution of the wonder of *Bellonius*, while he saith, with incredible Artifice hath Nature framed the tayl or Oar of the Bever: where by the way we cannot but wish a model of their houses, so much extolled by some Describers: wherein since they are so bold as to venture upon three stages, we might examine their Artifice in the contignations, the rule and order in the compartitions; or whether that magnified structure be any more than a rude rectangular pyle or meer hovell-building.

Thus works the hand of nature in the feathery plantation

g Elegantly
conspicuous
on the inside
of the
stripped
skins of
Dive-Fowl, of
the Cor-
morant
Goshonder,
Weasell,
Loon, &c.

about birds. Observable in the skins of the breast,[g] legs and Pinions of Turkies, Geese, and Ducks, and the Oars or finny feet of Water-Fowl: And such a naturall Net is the scaly covering of Fishes, of Mullets, Carps, Tenches, &c. even in such as are excoriable and consist of smaller scales, as Bretts, Soals, and Flounders. The like Reticulate grain is observable in some *Russia* Leather. To omit the ruder Figures of the ostracion, the triangular or cunny fish, or the pricks of the Sea-Porcupine.

The same is also observable in some part of the skin of man, in habits of neat texture, and therefore not unaptly compared unto a Net: We shall not affirm that from such grounds the Ægyptian Embalmers imitated this texture, yet in their linnen folds the same is still observable among their neatest Mummies, in the figures of *Isis* and *Osyris,* and the Tutelary spirits in the Bembine Table. Nor is it to be overlooked how *Orus,* the Hieroglyphick of the world, is described in a Network covering, from the shoulder to the foot. And (not to enlarge upon the cruciated character of *Trismegistus,* or handed crosses,* so often occurring in the Needles of *Pharaoh,* and Obelisks of Antiquity) the *Statuæ Isiacæ,* Teraphims, and little Idols, found about the Mummies, do make a decussation or *Jacobs* Crosse with their armes, like that on the head of *Ephraim* and *Manasses,* and this *decussis* is also graphically described between them.

* *Cruces
ansatæ,* being
held by a
finger in the
circle.

This Reticulate or Net-work was also considerable in the inward parts of man, not only from the first *subtegmen* or warp of his formation, but in the netty *fibres* of the veins and vessels of life; wherein according to common Anatomy the right and transverse *fibres* are decussated by the oblique *fibres*; and so must frame a Reticulate and Quincunciall Figure by their Obliquations, Emphatically extending that Elegant expression of Scripture: Thou hast curiously embroydered me, thou hast wrought me up after the finest way of texture, and as it were with a Needle.

Nor is the same observable only in some parts, but in the whole body of man, which upon the extension of arms and legges, doth make out a square, whose intersection is at the genitals. To omit the phantastical Quincunx, in *Plato,* of the first Hermaphrodite or double man, united at the Loynes, which *Jupiter* after divided.

A rudimentall resemblance hereof there is in the cruciated and rugged folds of the *Reticulum,* or Net-like Ventricle of ruminating horned animals, which is the second in order, and culinarily called the Honey-comb. For many divisions there are in the stomack of severall animals; what number they maintain in the *Scarus* and ruminating Fish, common description or our own experiment hath made no discovery. But in the Ventricle of *Porpuses* there are three divisions. In many Birds a crop, Gizard, and little receptacle before it; but in Cornigerous animals, which chew the cudd, there are no less than four* of distinct position and office.

The *Reticulum* by these crossed cels makes a further digestion, in the dry and exuccous part of the Aliment received from the first Ventricle. For at the bottome of the gullet there is a double Orifice; What is first received at the mouth descendeth into the first and greater stomack, from whence it is returned into the mouth again; and after a fuller mastication, and salivous mixture, what part thereof descendeth again, in a moist and succulent body, it slides down the softer and more permeable Orifice, into the Omasus or third stomack; and from thence conveyed into the fourth, receives its last digestion. The other dry and exuccous part after rumination by the larger and stronger orifice beareth into the first stomack, from thence into the *Reticulum,* and so progressively into the other divisions. And therefore in Calves newly calved, there is little or no use of the two first Ventricles, for the milk and liquid aliment slippeth down the softer Orifice, into the third stomack; where making little or no stay, it passeth into the fourth, the seat of the *Coagulum,* or Runnet, or that division of stomack which seems to bear the name of the whole, in the Greek translation of the Priests Fee, in the Sacrifice of Peace-offerings.

As for those Rhomboidal Figures made by the Cartilagineous parts of the Wezon, in the Lungs of great Fishes, and other animals, as *Rondeletius* discovered, we have not found them so to answer our figure as to be drawn into illustration; Something we expected in the more discernable texture of the lungs of frogs, which notwithstanding being but two curious bladders

* Μεγάλη κοιλία, κεκρύφαλος, ἐχῖνος, ἤνυστρον. Arist. Magnus venter, Reticulum, omasus, abomasus. Gaza.

not weighing above a grain, we found interwoven with veins not observing any just order. More orderly situated are those cretaceous and chalky concretions found sometimes in the bignesse of a small fech on either side their spine; which being not agreeable unto our order, nor yet observed by any, we shall not here discourse on.

But had we found a better account and tolerable Anatomy of that prominent jowle of the *Sperma Ceti* Whale,[a] than ques- tuary operation, or the stench of the last cast upon our shoar, permitted, we might have perhaps discovered some handsome order in those Net-like creases and sockets, made like honey- combs, containing that medicall matter.

[a] 1652, de-
scribed in our
Pseudo.
Epidem.
Edit. 3.
[Bk. III, ch.
26]

Lastly, The incession of locall motion of animals is made with analogy unto this figure, by decussative diametrals, Quin- cunciall Lines and angles. For to omit the enquiry how Butter- flies and breezes move their four wings, how birds and fishes in ayre and water move by joynt stroaks of opposite wings and Finnes, and how salient animals in jumping forward seem to arise and fall upon a square base; As the station of most Quad- rupeds is made upon a long square, so in their motion they make a Rhomboides; their common progression being performed Diametrally, by decussation and crosse advancement of their legges, which not observed begot that remarkable absurdity in the position of the legges of *Castors* horse in the Capitol. The Snake which moveth circularly makes his spires in like order, the convex and concave spirals answering each other at alternate distances; In the motion of man the armes and legges observe this thwarting position, but the legges alone do move Quin- cuncially by single angles with some resemblance of a V measured by successive advancement from each foot, and the angle of indenture great or lesse, according to the extent or brevity of the stride.

Studious Observators may discover more analogies in the orderly book of nature, and cannot escape the Elegancy of her hand in other correspondencies. The Figures of nails and crucifying appurtenances, are but precariously made out in the *Granadilla* or flower of Christs passion: And we despair to behold in these parts that handsome draught of crucifixion in the fruit of the *Barbado* Pine. The seminal Spike of *Phalaris*, or

great shaking grasse, more nearly answers the tayl of a Rattle-
Snake than many resemblances in *Porta*: And if the man *Orchis*[b]
of *Columna* be well made out, it excelleth all analogies. In young
Wallnuts cut athwart, it is not hard to apprehend strange
characters; and in those of somewhat elder growth, handsome
ornamental draughts about a plain crosse. In the root of *Osmond*
or Water fern, every eye may discern the form of a Half Moon,
Rain-bow, or half the character of Pisces. Some finde Hebrew,
Arabick, Greek, and Latine Characters in Plants; In a common
one among us we seem to reade *Aiaia, Viviu, Lilil*.

Right lines and circles make out the bulk of plants; In the
parts thereof we finde Helicall or spirall roundles, voluta's,
conicall Sections, circular Pyramids, and frustums of *Archimedes*; And cannot overlook the orderly hand of nature, in the
alternate succession of the flat and narrower sides in the tender
shoots of the Ashe, or the regular inequality of bignesse in the
five-leaved flowers of Henbane, and something like in the
calicular leaves of *Tutson*. How the spots of *Persicaria* do manifest
themselves between the sixt and tenth ribbe. How the triangular
capp in the stemme or *stylus* of Tuleps doth constantly point at
three outward leaves. That spicated flowers do open first at the
stalk.★ That white flowers have yellow thrums or knops. That
the nebbe of Beans and Pease do all look downward, and so
presse not upon each other; And how the seeds of many pappous
or downy flowers lockt up in sockets, after a gomphosis or
mortis-articulation, diffuse themselves circularly into branches
of rare order, observable in *Tragopogon* or Goats-beard, conformable to the Spiders web, and the *Radii* in like manner
telarely inter-woven.

And how in animall natures, even colours hold correspondencies, and mutuall correlations. That the colour of the Cater-
pillar will shew again in the Butterfly, with some latitude is
allowable. Though the regular spots in their wings seem but a
mealie adhesion, and such as may be wiped away, yet since they
come in this variety out of their cases, there must be regular
pores in those parts and membranes, defining such Exudations.

That *Augustus*[c] had native notes on his body and belly,
after the order and number in the Starres of *Charles wayne*, will
not seem strange unto astral Physiognomy, which accordingly

b *Orchis An-
thropophora,*
Fabii
Columnæ.

★ Below.

c Suet. in *vit.*
Aug.

considereth moles in the body of man, or Physicall Observators, who from the position of moles in the face, reduce them to rule and correspondency in other parts. Whether after the like method medicall conjecture may not be raised, upon parts inwardly affected; since parts about the lips are the critical seats of Pustules discharged in Agues; And scrophulous tumours about the neck do so often speak the like about the Mesentery, may also be considered.

* To be observed in white young Lambs, which afterward vanisheth.

The russet neck in young Lambs* seems but adventitious, and may owe its tincture to some contaction in the womb; But that if sheep have any black or deep russet in their faces, they want not the same about their legges and feet; That black Hounds have mealy mouths and feet; That black Cows which have any white in their tayls, should not misse of some in their bellies; and if all white in their bodies, yet if black-mouth'd, their ears and feet maintain the same colour, are correspondent tinctures not ordinarily failing in nature, which easily unites the accidents of extremities, since in some generations she transmutes the parts themselves, while in the *Aurelian Metamorphosis* the head of the canker becomes the Tayl of the Butterfly. Which is in some way not beyond the contrivance of Art, in submersions and Inlays, inverting the extremes of the plant, and fetching the root from the top, and also imitated in handsome columnary work, in the inversion of the extremes; wherein the Capitel, and the Base, hold such near correspondency.

In the motive parts of animals may be discovered mutuall proportions; not only in those of Quadrupeds, but in the thighbone, legge, foot-bone, and claws of Birds. The legs of Spiders are made after a sesqui-tertian proportion, and the long legs of some locusts, double unto some others. But the internodial parts of Vegetables, or spaces between the joints are contrived with more uncertainty; though the joints themselves in many plants maintain a regular number.

In vegetable composure, the unition of prominent parts seems most to answer the *Apophyses* or processes of Animall bones, whereof they are the produced parts or prominent explantations. And though in the parts of plants which are not ordained for motion, we do not expect correspondent Articulations; yet in the setting on of some flowers, and seeds in their sockets, and the lineal commissure of the pulpe of severall seeds, may be observed some shadow of the Harmony; some show of the Gomphosis or *mortis*-articulation.

As for the Diarthrosis or motive Articulation, there is expected little Analogy, though long-stalked leaves doe move by long lines, and have observable motions, yet are they made by outward impulsion, like the motion of pendulous bodies, while the parts themselves are united by some kinde of *symphysis* unto the stock.

But standing vegetables, void of motive-Articulations, are not without many motions. For beside the motion of vegetation upward, and of radiation unto all quarters, that of contraction, dilatation, inclination, and contortion, is discoverable in many plants. To omit the rose of *Jericho*, the ear of Rye, which moves with change of weather, and the Magical spit, made of no rare plants, which windes before the fire, and rosts the bird without turning.

Even Animals near the Classis of plants, seem to have the most restlesse motions. The Summer-worm of Ponds and plashes makes a long waving motion; the hair-worm seldome lies still. He that would behold a very anomalous motion, may observe it in the Tortile and tiring stroakes of Gnat-worms.[d]

d Found often in some form of red maggot in the standing waters of Cisterns in the summer.

CHAPTER IV

As for the delights, commodities, mysteries, with other concernments of this order, we are unwilling to fly them over, in the short deliveries of *Virgil*, *Varro*, or others, and shall therefore enlarge with additionall ampliations.

By this position they had a just proportion of Earth, to supply an equality of nourishment. The distance being ordered, thick or thin, according to the magnitude or vigorous attraction of the plant, the goodnesse, leannesse, or propriety of the soyle; and therefore the rule of *Solon*, concerning the territory of *Athens*, not extendible unto all; allowing the distance of six foot unto common Trees, and nine for the Figge and Olive.

They had a due diffusion of their roots on all or both sides, whereby they maintained some proportion to their height, in Trees of large radication. For that they strictly make good their profundeur or depth unto their height, according to common conceit, and that expression of *Virgil*,[a] though confirmable from the plane Tree in *Pliny*, and some few examples, is not to be expected from the generallitie of Trees almost in any kinde, either of side-spreading, or tap-roots: Except we measure them by lateral and opposite diffusions; nor commonly to be found in *minor* or hearby plants; If we except Sea-holly, Liquorish, Sea-rush, and some others.

They had a commodious radiation in their growth; and a due expansion of their branches, for shadow or delight. For trees thickly planted do runne up in height and branch with no expansion, shooting unequally or short, and thinne upon the neighbouring side. And therefore Trees are inwardly bare, and spring and leaf from the outward and Sunny side of their branches.

Whereby they also avoided the perill of συνολεθρία or one tree perishing with another, as it happeneth ofttimes from the sick *effluviums* or entanglements of the roots, falling foul with each other. Observable in Elmes set in hedges, where if one dieth the neighbouring Tree prospereth not long after.

In this situation divided into many intervals and open unto six passages, they had the advantage of a fair perflation from windes, brushing and cleansing their surfaces, relaxing and closing their pores unto due perspiration. For that they afford large *effluviums* perceptible from odours, diffused at great distances, is observable from Onyons out of the earth; which though dry, and kept until the spring, as they shoot forth large and many leaves, do notably abate of their weight. And mint growing in glasses of water, until it arriveth unto the weight of an ounce, in a shady place, will sometimes exhaust a pound of water.

And as they send forth much, so may they receive somewhat in: For beside the common way and road of reception by the root, there may be a refection and imbibition from without; For gentle showrs refresh plants, though they enter not their roots; And the good and bad *effluviums* of Vegetables promote or debilitate each other. So *Epithymum* and *Dodder*, rootlesse and out of the ground, maintain themselves upon Thyme, Savory, and plants, whereon they hang. And *Ivy* divided from the root, we have observed to live some years, by the cirrous parts commonly conceived but as tenacles and holdfasts unto it. The stalks of mint cropt from the root stripped from the leaves, and set in *glasses* with the root end upward & out of the water, we have observed to send forth sprouts and leaves without the aid of roots, and *scordium* to grow in like manner, the leaves set downward in water. To omit several Sea-plants, which grow on single roots from stones, although in very many there are side-shoots and *fibres*, beside the fastening root.

By this open position they were fairly exposed unto the rayes of Moon and Sunne, so considerable in the growth of Vegetables. For though Poplars, Willows, and several Trees be made to grow about the brinks of *Acharon*, and dark habitations of the dead; Though some plants are content to grow in obscure Wells; wherein also old Elme pumps afford sometimes long bushy sprouts, not observable in any above-ground: And large fields of Vegetables are able to maintain their verdure at the bottome and shady part of the Sea; yet the greatest number are not content without the actual rayes of the Sunne, but bend, incline, and follow them; As large lists of solisequious and Sun-following plants. And some observe the method of its motion in their owne growth and conversion, twining towards the West by the South, as Bryony, Hops, Woodbine, and several kindes of Bindeweed; which we shall more admire, when any can tell us, they observe another motion, and Twist by the North at the *Antipodes*. The same plants rooted against an erect North-wall full of holes, will finde a way through them to look upon the Sunne. And in tender plants from mustard seed, sown in the winter, and in a pot of earth placed inwardly in a chamber against a South-window, the tender stalks of two leaves arose not erect, but bending towards the window, nor looking much higher than the Meridian Sun. And if the pot were turned they would work themselves into their former declinations, making their conversion by the East. That the Leaves of the Olive and some other Trees solstitially turn, and precisely tell us, when the Sun is entred *Cancer*, is scarce expectable in any Climate; and

Theophrastus warily observes it; Yet somewhat thereof is observable in our own, in the leaves of Willows and Sallows, some weeks after the Solstice. But the great *Convolvulus* or white-flower'd *Bindweed* observes both motions of the Sunne: while the flower twists Æquinoctionally from the left hand to the right, according to the daily revolution, The stalk twineth ecliptically from the right to the left, according to the annual conversion.*

★ Flectit ad Aquilonem, et declinat ad Austrum, is Solon's description of the motion of the Sunne [MS Sloane 1847, f. 195 v.]

Some commend the exposure of these orders unto the Western gales, as the most generative and fructifying breath of heaven. But we applaud the Husbandry of *Solomon*, whereto agreeth the doctrine of *Theophrastus*: Arise O North-winde, and blow thou South upon my garden, that the spices thereof may flow out; for the North-winde closing the pores, and shutting up the *effluviums,* when the South doth after open and relax them, the Aromatical gummes do drop, and sweet odours fly actively from them. And if his garden had the same situation, which mapps and charts afford it, on the East side of *Jerusalem,* and having the wall on the West; these were the winds unto which it was well exposed.

By this way of plantation they encreased the number of their trees, which they lost in *Quaternio's,* and square-orders, which is a commodity insisted on by *Varro,* and one great intent of nature, in this position of flowers and seeds in the elegant formation of plants, and the former Rules observed in naturall and artificiall Figurations.

Whether in this order and one Tree in some measure breaking the cold and pinching gusts of windes from the other, trees will not better maintain their inward circles, and either escape or moderate their excentricities, may also be considered. For the circles in Trees are naturally concentricall, parallell unto the bark, and unto each other, till frost and piercing windes contract and close them on the weather-side, the opposite semicircle widely enlarging, and at a comely distance, which hindreth oft-times the beauty and roundnesse of Trees and makes the Timber lesse serviceable; whiles the ascending juyce not readily passing, settles in knots and inequalities. And therefore it is no new course of Agriculture, to observe the native position of Trees according to North and South in their transplantations.

The same is also observable underground in the circinations
and sphærical rounds of Onyons, wherein the circles of the
Orbes are ofttimes larger, and the meridionall lines stand wider
upon one side than the other. And where the largenesse will
make up the number of planetical Orbes, that of *Luna* and the
lower planets excede the dimensions of *Saturne* and the higher:
Whether the like be not verified in the Circles of the large roots
of Briony and Mandrakes, or why in the knotts of Deale or Firre
the Circles are often eccentricall, although not in a plane, but
vertical and right position, deserves a further enquiry.

Whether there be not some irregularity of roundnesse in
most plants according to their position? Whether some small
compression of pores be not perceptible in parts which stand
against the current of waters, as in Reeds, Bullrushes, and other
vegetables toward the streaming quarter, may also be observed;
and therefore such as are long and weak are commonly contrived into a roundnesse of figure, whereby the water presseth
lesse, and slippeth more smoothly from them, and even in flags
of flat-figured leaves, the greater part obvert their sharper sides
unto the current in ditches.

But whether plants which float upon the surface of the water
be for the most part of cooling qualities, those which shoot
above it of heating vertues, and why? whether *Sargasso* for many
miles floating upon the Western Ocean, or Sea-lettuce, and
Phasganium at the bottome of our Seas, make good the like
qualities? Why Fenny waters afford the hottest and sweetest
plants, as Calamus, Cyperus, and Crowfoot, and mudd cast out
of ditches most naturally produceth Arsmart? Why plants so
greedy of water so little regard oyl? Why since many seeds
contain much oyle within them, they endure it not well
without, either in their growth or production? Why since Seeds
shoot commonly under ground, and out of the ayre, those which
are let fall in shallow glasses, upon the surface of the water, will
sooner sprout than those at the bottome? And if the water be
covered with oyle, those at the bottome will hardly sprout at
all, we have not room to conjecture.

Whether Ivy would not lesse offend the Trees in this clean
ordination, and well kept paths, might perhaps deserve the
question. But this were a quæry only unto some habitations,

and little concerning *Cyrus* or the Babylonian territory; wherein by no industry *Harpalus* could make Ivy grow: And *Alexander* hardly found it about those parts to imitate the pomp of *Bacchus.* And though in these Northern Regions we are too much acquainted with one Ivy, we know too little of another, whereby we apprehend not the expressions of Antiquity, the Splenetick medicine of *Galen,*[a] and the Emphasis of the Poet, in the beauty of the white Ivy.[b]

[a] Galen *de med. secundum loc.*

[b] *Hedera formosior alba.*

The like concerning the growth of Misseltoe, which dependeth not only of the *species,* or kinde of Tree, but much also of the Soil. And therefore common in some places, not readily found in others, frequent in *France,* not so common in *Spain,* and scarce at all in the Territory of *Ferrara:* Nor easily to be found where it is most required upon Oaks, lesse on Trees continually verdant. Although in some places the Olive escapeth it not, requiting its detriment in the delightfull view of its red Berries; as *Clusius* observed in *Spain,* and *Bellonius* about *Hierusalem.* But this Parasiticall plant suffers nothing to grow upon it, by any way of art; nor could we ever make it grow where nature had not planted it; as we have in vain attempted by inocculation and incision, upon its native or forreign stock. And though there seem nothing improbable in the seed, it hath not succeeded by sation in any manner of ground, wherein we had no reason to despair, since we reade of vegetable horns, and how Rams horns will root about *Goa.*[c]

[c] Linschoten.

But besides these rurall commodities, it cannot be meanly delectable in the variety of Figures, which these orders, open and closed, do make. Whilest every inclosure makes a *Rhombus,* the figures obliquely taken a Rhomboides, the intervals bounded with parallell lines, and each intersection built upon a square, affording two Triangles or Pyramids vertically conjoyned; which in the strict Quincunciall order doe oppositely make acute and blunt Angles.

And though therein we meet not with right angles, yet every Rhombus containing four Angles equall unto four right, it virtually contains four right. Nor is this strange unto such as observe the naturall lines of Trees, and parts disposed in them. For neither in the root doth nature affect this angle, which shooting downward for the stability of the plant, doth best effect the same by Figures of Inclination; Nor in the Branches and stalky leaves, which grow most at acute angles; as declining from their head the root, and diminishing their Angles with their altitude: Verified also in lesser Plants, whereby they better support themselves, and bear not so heavily upon the stalk: So that while near the root they often make an Angle of seventy parts, the sprouts near the top will often come short of thirty. Even in the nerves and master veins of the leaves the acute angle ruleth; the obtuse but seldome found, and in the backward part of the leaf, reflecting and arching about the stalk. But why ofttimes one side of the leaf is unequall unto the other, as in Hazell and Oaks, why on either side the master vein the lesser and derivative channels stand not directly opposite, nor at equall angles, respectively unto the adverse side, but those of one part do often exceed the other, as the Wallnut and many more, deserves another enquiry.

Now if for this order we affect coniferous and tapering trees, particularly the Cypresse, which grows in a conicall figure; we have found a Tree not only of great Ornament, but in its Essentials of affinity unto this order. A solid Rhombus being made by the conversion of two Equicrurall Cones, as *Archimedes* hath defined. And these were the common Trees about *Babylon*, and the East, whereof the Ark was made; and *Alexander* found no Trees so accomodable to build his Navy; And this we rather think to be the Tree mentioned in the Canticles, which stricter Botanology will hardly allow to be Camphire.

And if delight or ornamentall view invite a comely disposure by circular amputations, as is elegantly performed in Hawthorns; then will they answer the figures made by the conversion of a Rhombus, which maketh two concentricall Circles; the greater circumference being made by the lesser angles, the lesser by the greater.

The Cylindrical figure of Trees is virtually contained and latent in this order. A Cylinder or long round being made by the conversion or turning of a Parallelogram, and most handsomely by a long square, which makes an equall, strong, and lasting figure in Trees, agreeable unto the body and motive parts of animals, the greatest number of Plants, and almost all roots, though their stalks be angular, and of many corners, which seem not to follow the figure of their Seeds; Since many angular Seeds send forth round stalks, and sphæricall seeds arise from angular spindles, and many rather conform unto their Roots, as the round stalks of bulbous Roots, and in tuberous Roots stemmes of like figure. But why since the largest number of Plants maintain a circular Figure, there are so few with teretous or long round leaves; why coniferous Trees are tenuifolious or narrow-leafed, why Plants of few or no joynts have commonly round stalks, why the greatest number of hollow stalks are round stalks; or why in this variety of angular stalks the quadrangular most exceedeth, were too long a speculation; Mean while obvious experience may finde, that in Plants of divided leaves above, nature often beginneth circularly in the two first leaves below, while in the singular plant of Ivy she exerciseth a contrary Geometry, and beginning with angular leaves below, rounds them in the upper branches.

Nor can the rows in this order want delight, as carrying an aspect answerable unto the *dipteros hypœthros*, or double order of columns open above; the opposite ranks of Trees standing like pillars in the *Cavedia* of the Courts of famous buildings, and the *Portico's* of the *Templa subdialia* of old; Somewhat imitating the *Peristylia* or Cloyster buildings, and the *Exedræ* of the Ancients, wherein men discoursed, walked and exercised; For that they derived the rule of Columnes from Trees, especially in their proportionall diminutions, is illustrated by *Vitruvius* from the shafts of Firre and Pine. And though the interarborations do imitate the *Areostylos,* or thin order, not strictly answering the proportion of intercolumniations; yet in many Trees they will not exceed the intermission of the Columnes in the Court of the Tabernacle; which being an hundred cubits long, and made up by twenty pillars, will afford no less than intervals of five cubits.

Beside, in this kinde of aspect the sight being not diffused but circumscribed between long parallels and the ἐπισκιασμός and adumbration from the branches, it frameth a penthouse over the eye, and maketh a quiet vision: And therefore in diffused and open aspects, men hollow their hand above their eye, and make an artificiall brow, whereby they direct the dispersed rayes of sight, and by this shade preserve a moderate light in the chamber of the eye; keeping the *pupilla* plump and fair, and not contracted or shrunk as in light and vagrant vision.

And therefore providence hath arched and paved the great house of the world, with colours of mediocrity, that is, blew and green, above and below the sight, moderately terminating the *acies* of the eye. For most plants, though green above-ground, maintain their Originall white below it, according to the candour of their seminall pulp, and the rudimental leaves do first appear in that colour; observable in Seeds sprouting in water upon their first foliation. Green seeming to be the first supervenient, or above-ground complexion of Vegetables, separable in many upon ligature or inhumation, as Succory, Endive, Artichoaks, and which is also lost upon fading in the Autumn.

And this is also agreeable unto water it self, the alimental vehicle of plants, which first altereth into this colour; And containing many vegetable seminalities, revealeth their Seeds by greennesse; and therefore soonest expected in rain or standing water, not easily found in distilled or water strongly boiled; wherein the Seeds are extinguished by fire and decoction, and therefore last long and pure without such alteration, affording neither uliginous coats, gnatworms, Acari, hairworms, like crude and common water; And therefore most fit for wholsome beverage, and with malt makes Ale and Beer without boyling. What large water-drinkers some Plants are, the Canary-Tree and Birches in some Northern Countries, drenching the Fields about them do sufficiently demonstrate. How water it self is able to maintain the growth of Vegetables, and without extinction of their generative or medicall vertues; Beside the experiment of *Helmonts* tree, we have found in some which have lived six years in glasses. The seeds of Scurvy-grasse growing in waterpots have been fruitfull in the Land; and *Asarum* after a years space, and once casting its leaves in water, in the second leaves hath handsomely performed its vomiting operation.

Nor are only dark and green colors, but shades and shadows contrived through the great Volume of nature, and trees ordained not only to protect and shadow others, but by their shades and shadowing parts, to preserve and cherish themselves. The whole radiation or branchings shadowing the stock and the root, the leaves, the branches and fruit, too much exposed to the windes and scorching Sunne. The calicular leaves inclose the tender flowers, and the flowers themselves lye wrapt about the seeds, in their rudiment and first formations, which being advanced the flowers fall away; and are therefore contrived in variety of figures, best satisfying the intention; Handsomely observable in hooded and gaping flowers, and the Butterfly bloomes of leguminous plants, the lower leaf closely involving the rudimental Cod, and the alary or wingy divisions embracing or hanging over it.

But Seeds themselves do lie in perpetual shades, either under the leaf, or shut up in coverings; And such as lye barest, have their husks, skins, and pulps about them, wherein the nebbe and generative particle lyeth moist and secured from the injury of Ayre and Sunne. Darknesse and light hold interchangeable dominions, and alternately rule the seminal state of things. Light unto *Pluto*[a] is darknesse unto *Jupiter*. Legions of seminall *Idæa's* lye in their second Chaos and *Orcus* of *Hipocrates*; till putting on the habits of their forms, they shew themselves upon the stage of the world, and open dominion of Jove. They that held the Stars of heaven were but rayes and flashing glimpses of the Empyreall light, through holes and perforations of the upper heaven, took of the natural shadows of stars,[b] while according to better discovery the poor Inhabitants of the Moone have but a polary life, and must passe half their dayes in the shadow of that Luminary.

Light that makes things seen, makes some things invisible: were it nor for darknesse and the shadow of the earth, the noblest part of the Creation had remained unseen, and the Stars in heaven as invisible as on the fourth day, when they were created above the Horizon, with the Sun, or there was not an eye to behold them. The greatest mystery of Religion is expressed by adumbration, and in the noblest part of Jewish Types, we finde the Cherubims shadowing the Mercy-seat: Life it self is but the shadow of death, and souls departed but the shadows of the living: All things fall under this name. The Sunne it self is but the dark *simulachrum*, and light but the shadow of God.

Lastly, It is no wonder that this Quincunciall order was first

---

[a] *Lux Orco, tenebræ Jovi, tenebræ Orco, lux Jovi.* Hippocr. *de diæta.*

[b] J. Hevelii *Selenographia.*

and still affected as gratefull unto the Eye: For all things are seen Quincuncially; For at the eye the Pyramidal rayes from the object, receive a decussation, and so strike a second base upon the *Retina* or hinder coat, the proper organ of Vision; wherein the pictures from objects are represented, answerable to the paper, or wall in the dark chamber; after the decussation of the rayes at the hole of the hornycoat, and their refraction upon the Christalline humour, answering the *foramen* of the window, and the *convex* or burning-glasses, which refract the rayes that enter it. And if ancient Anatomy would hold, a like disposure there was of the optick or visual nerves in the brain, wherein Antiquity conceived a concurrence by decussation. And this not only observable in the Laws of direct Vision, but in some part also verified in the reflected rayes of sight. For making the angle of incidence equal to that of reflexion, the visual raye returneth Quincuncially, and after the form of a V, and the line of reflexion being continued unto the place of vision, there ariseth a semi-decussation, which makes the object seen in a perpendicular unto it self, and as farre below the reflectent, as it is from it above; observable in the Sun and Moon beheld in water.

And this is also the law of reflexion in moved bodies and sounds, which though nor made by decussation, observe the rule of equality between incidence and reflexion; whereby whispering places are framed by Ellipticall arches laid sidewise; where the voice being delivered at the *focus* of one extremity, observing an equality unto the angle of incidence, it will reflect unto the *focus* of the other end, and so escape the ears of the standers in the middle.

A like rule is observed in the reflection of the vocall and sonorous line in Ecchoes, which cannot therefore be heard in all stations. But happening in woody plantations, by waters, and able to return some words, if reacht by a pleasant and well-dividing voice, there may be heard the softest notes in nature.

And this not only verified in the way of sence, but in animall and intellectuall receptions. Things entring upon the intellect by a Pyramid from without, and thence into the memory by another from within, the common decussation being in the understanding as is delivered by *Bovillus*.[c] Whether the

[c] Car. Bovillus *de intellectu.*

intellectual and phantastical lines be not thus rightly disposed, but magnified, diminished, distorted, and ill placed in the Mathematicks of some brains, whereby they have irregular apprehensions of things, perverted notions, conceptions, and incurable hallucinations, were no unpleasant speculation.

And if Ægyptian Philosophy may obtain, the scale of influences was thus disposed, and the geniall spirits of both worlds do trace their way in ascending and descending Pyramids, mystically apprehended in the Letter X, and the open Bill and stradling Legges of a Stork, which was imitated by that Character.

Of this Figure *Plato* made choice to illustrate the motion of the soul, both of the world and man; while he delivereth that God divided the whole conjunction length-wise, according to the figure of a Greek χ, and then turning it about reflected it into a circle; By the circle implying the uniform motion of the first Orb, and by the right lines, the planetical and various motions within it. And this also with application unto the soul of man, which hath a double aspect, one right, whereby it beholdeth the body, and objects without; another circular and reciprocal, whereby it beholdeth it self. The circle declaring the motion of the indivisible soul, simple, according to the divinity of its nature, and returning into it self; the right lines respecting the motion pertaining unto sense, and vegetation, and the central decussation, the wondrous connexion of the severall faculties conjointly in one substance. And so conjoyned the unity and duality of the soul, and made out the three substances so much considered by him; That is, the indivisible or divine, the divisible or corporeal, and that third, which was the *Systasis* or harmony of those two, in the mystical decussation.

And if that were clearly made out which *Justin Martyr* took for granted, this figure hath had the honour to characterize and notifie our blessed Saviour, as he delivereth in that borrowed expression from *Plato*; *Decussavit eum in universo*,* the hint whereof he would have *Plato* derive from the figure of the brazen Serpent, and to have mistaken the Letter X for T, whereas it is not improbable, he learned these and other mystical expressions in his Learned Observations of Ægypt, where he might obviously behold the Mercurial characters, the handed crosses,

* ἐχίασεν αὐτὸν ἐν τῷ παντί.

and other mysteries not thoroughly understood in the sacred Letter X, which being derivative from the Stork, one of the ten sacred animals, might be originally Ægyptian, and brought into *Greece* by *Cadmus* of that Countrey.

CHAPTER V

TO enlarge this contemplation unto all the mysteries and secrets, accomodable unto this number, were inexcusable Pythagorisme, yet cannot omit the ancient conceit of five surnamed the number of justice;[a] as justly dividing between the digits, and hanging in the centre of Nine,[b] described by square numeration, which angularly divided will make the decussated number; and so agreeable unto the Quincunciall Ordination, and rowes divided by Equality, and just *decorum*, in the whole com-plantation; And might be the Originall of that common game among us, wherein the fifth place is Soveraigne, and carrieth the chief intention. The Ancients wisely instructing youth, even in their recreations unto virtue, that is, early to drive at the middle point and Central Seat of justice.

Nor can we omit how agreeable unto this number an handsome division is made in Trees and Plants, since *Plutarch* and the Ancients have named it the Divisive Number, justly dividing the Entities of the world, many remarkable things in it, and also comprehending the generall division of Vegetables.[c] And he that considers how most blossomes of Trees, and greatest number of Flowers, consist of five leaves; and therein doth rest the setled rule of nature; So that in those which exceed there is often found, or easily made a variety; may readily discover how nature rests in this number, which is indeed the first rest and pause of numeration in the fingers, the naturall Organs thereof. Nor in the division of the feet of perfect animals doth nature exceed this account. And even in the joints of feet, which in birds are most multiplied, surpasseth not this number; So progressionally making them out in many,* that from five in the fore-claw she descendeth unto

a δίκη.

b ...
  ...
  ...

c Δένδρον, θάμνος, φρύγανον, πόα, *Arbor, frutex, suffrutex, herba,* and that fifth which comprehendeth the *fungi* and *tubera,* whether to be named Ἄσχιον or γυμνόν, comprehending also *conferva marina salsa,* and Sea-cords of so many yards length.

* As Herns, Bitterns, and long-claw'd Fowls.

two in the hindemost; And so in fower feet makes up the number of joynts, in the five fingers or toes of man.

Not to omit the Quintuple Section of a Cone,[d] of handsome practise in Ornamentall Garden-plots, and in some way discoverable in so many works of Nature; In the leaves, fruits, and seeds of Vegetables, and scales of some Fishes, so much considerable in glasses, and the optick doctrine; wherein the learned may consider the Crystalline humour of the eye in the cuttle fish and *Loligo*.

He that forgets not how Antiquity named this the Conjugall or wedding number, and made it the Embleme of the most remarkable conjunction, will conceive it duely appliable unto this handsome Oeconomy, and vegetable combination; May hence apprehend the allegoricall sense of the obscure expression of *Hesiod*,[e] and afford no improbable reason why *Plato* admitted his Nuptiall guests by fives, in the kindred of the married couple.[f]

And though a sharper mystery might be implied in the Number of the five wise and foolish Virgins, which were to meet the Bridegroom, yet was the same agreeable unto the Conjugall Number, which ancient Numerists made out by two and three, the first parity and imparity, the active and passive digits, the materiall and formall principles in generative Societies. And not discordant even from the customes of the *Romans*, who admitted but five Torches in their Nuptiall solemnities.[g] Whether there were any mystery or not implied, the most generative animals were created on this day, and had accordingly the largest benediction: And under a Quintuple consideration, wanton Antiquity considered the Circumstances of generation, while by this number of five they naturally divided the Nectar of the fifth Planet.[*]

The same number in the Hebrew mysteries and Cabalistical accounts was the character of Generation;[h] declared by the Letter *He*, the fifth in their Alphabet; According to that Cabalisticall *Dogma*: If *Abram* had not had this Letter added unto his Name he had remained fruitlesse, and without the power of generation: Not onely because hereby the number of his Name attained two hundred fourty eight, the number of the affirmative precepts, but because as in created natures there is

[d] *Elleipsis, parabola, Hyperbole, Circulus, Triangulum.*

[e] πέμπτας, *id est, nuptias multas.* Rhodig.

[f] Plato *de leg.* 6.

[g] Plutarch *problem. Rom. I.*

[*] *Oscula quae Venus Quinta parte sui Nectaris imbuit.*

[h] Archang. *dog. Cabal.*

a male and female, so in divine and intelligent productions, the mother of Life and Fountain of souls in Cabalisticall Technology is called *Binah*; whose Seal and Character was *He*. So that being sterill before, he received the power of generation from that measure and mansion in the Archetype; and was made conformable unto *Binah*. And upon such involved considerations, the ten of *Sarai* was exchanged into five.[1] If any shall look upon this as a stable number, and fitly appropriable unto Trees, as Bodies of Rest and Station, he hath herein a great Foundation in nature, who observing much variety in legges and motive Organs of Animals, as two, four, six, eight, twelve, fourteen, and more, hath passed over five and ten, and assigned them unto none.* And for the stability of this Number, he shall not want the sphericity of its nature, which multiplied in it self, will return into its own denomination, and bring up the reare of the account. Which is also one of the Numbers that makes up the mysticall Name of God, which consisting of Letters denoting all the sphæricall Numbers, ten, five, and six; Emphatically sets forth the Notion of *Trismegistus*, and that intelligible Sphere which is the Nature of God.

[1] *Jod* into *He*.

* Or very few, as the *Phalangium monstrosum Brasilianum*, Clusii & Jo. de Læt. *Cur. poster. Americæ Descript.*, if perfectly described.

Many Expressions by this Number occurre in Holy Scripture, perhaps unjustly laden with mysticall Expositions, and little concerning our order. That the Israelites were forbidden to eat the fruit of their new planted Trees before the fifth yeare, was very agreeable unto the naturall Rules of Husbandry: Fruits being unwholsome and lash before the fourth or fifth Yeare. In the second day or Feminine part of five, there was added no approbation. For in the third or masculine day, the same is twice repeated; and a double benediction inclosed both Creations, whereof the one in some part was but an accomplishment of the other. That the Trespasser was to pay a fifth part above the head or principall, makes no secret in this Number, and implied no more than one part above the principall; which being considered in four parts, the additionall forfeit must bear the Name of a fift. The five golden mice had plainly their determination from the number of the Princes; That five should put to flight an hundred might have nothing mystically implyed; considering a rank of Souldiers could scarce consist of a lesser number. Saint *Paul* had rather speak five words in a known than ten thousand in an unknowne tongue: That is as little as could well be spoken. A simple proposition consisting of three words and a complexed one not ordinarily short of five.

More considerable there are in this mysticall account, which we must not insist on. And therefore why the radicall Letters in the Pentateuch should equall the number of the Souldiery of the Tribes; Why our Saviour in the Wildernesse fed five thousand persons with five Barley Loaves, and again but four thousand with no lesse than seven of Wheat? Why *Joseph* designed five changes of Rayment unto *Benjamin*? and *David* took just five pibbles out of the Brook against the Pagan Champion? We leave it unto Arithmeticall Divinity, and Theologicall explanation.

Yet if any delight in new Problemes, or think it worth the enquiry, whether the Criticall Physician hath rightly hit the nominall notation of Quinque;[k] Why the Ancients mixed five or three but not four parts of water unto their Wine: And *Hippocrates* observed a fifth proportion in the mixture of water with milk, as in *Dysenteries* and bloudy fluxes. Under what abstruse foundation Astrologers do Figure the good or bad Fate from our Children, in good Fortune,[l] or the fifth house of their Celestiall Schemes. Whether the Ægyptians described a Starr by a Figure of five points, with reference unto the five Capitall aspects,[m] whereby they transmit their Influences, or abstruser Considerations? Why the Cabalisticall Doctors, who conceive the whole *Sephiroth* or divine emanations to have guided the ten-stringed Harp of *David*, whereby he pacified the evil spirit of *Saul*, in strict numeration doe begin with the Perihypate Meson, or si fa ut, and so place the Tiphereth answering C sol fa ut, upon the fifth string: Or whether this number be oftner applied unto bad things and ends than good in holy Scripture, and why? He may meet with abstrusities of no ready resolution.

If any shall question the rationality of that Magick, in the cure of the blind man by *Serapis*, commanded to place five fingers on his Altar, and then his hand on his Eyes? Why since the whole Comœdy is primarily and naturally comprised in four parts,[n] and Antiquity permitted not so many persons to speak in one Scene, yet would not comprehend the same in

k τέσσαρα ἕν τε, four and one or five. Scalig.

l 'Αγαθὴ τύχη, or *bona fortuna*, the name of the fifth house.

m Conjunct, opposite, sextile, trigonal, tetragonal.

n Πρότασις, ἐπίτασις, κατάστασις, καταστροφή.

more or lesse than five acts? Why amongst Sea-starres nature chiefly delighteth in five points? And since there are found some of no fewer than twelve, and some of seven, and nine, there are few or none discovered of six or eight? If any shall enquire why the Flowers of *Rue* properly consisting of four Leaves, The first and third Flower have five? Why since many Flowers have one leaf or none,° as *Scaliger* will have it, diverse three, and the greatest number consist of five divided from their bottomes; there are yet so few of two: or why nature generally beginning or setting out with two opposite leaves at the Root, doth so seldome conclude with that order and number at the Flower? he shall not passe his hours in vulgar speculations.

If any shall further quæry why magneticall Philosophy excludeth decussations, and needles transversly placed do naturally distract their verticities? Why Geomancers do imitate the Quintuple Figure, in their Mother Characters of Acquisition and Amission, *&c.* somewhat answering the Figures in the Lady or speckled Beetle? With what Equity, Chiromanticall conjecturers decry these decussations in the Lines and Mounts of the hand? What that decussated Figure intendeth in the medall of *Alexander* the Great? Why the Goddesses sit commonly crosse-legged in ancient draughts, Since *Juno* is described in the same as a veneficial posture to hinder the birth of *Hercules*? If any shall doubt why at the Amphidromicall Feasts, on the fifth day after the Childe was born presents were sent from friends, of *Polipusses,* and Cuttle-fishes? Why five must be only left in that Symbolicall mutiny among the men of *Cadmus*? Why *Proteus* in *Homer* the Symbole of the first matter, before he setled himself in the midst of his Sea-monsters, doth place them out by fives? Why the fifth years Oxe was acceptable Sacrifice unto *Jupiter*? Or why the Noble *Antoninus* in some sence doth call the soul it self a Rhombus? He shall not fall on trite or triviall disquisitions. And these we invent and propose unto acuter enquirers, nauseating crambe verities and questions over-queried. Flat and flexible truths are beat out by every hammer; But *Vulcan* and his whole forge sweat to work out *Achilles* his armour. A large field is yet left unto sharper discerners to enlarge upon this order, to search out the *quaternio's* and figured draughts of this nature, and moderating the study of names, and meet

° *Unifolium, nullifolium.*

nomenclature of plants, to erect generalities, disclose unobserved proprieties, not only in the vegetable shop, but the whole volume of nature; affording delightful Truths, confirmable by sense and ocular Observation, which seems to me the surest path, to trace the Labyrinth of Truth. For though discursive enquiry and rationall conjecture may leave handsome gashes and flesh-wounds; yet without conjunction of this, expect no mortal or dispatching blows unto errour.

But the Quincunx[a] of Heaven runs low, and 'tis time to close the five ports of knowledge; We are unwilling to spin out our awaking thoughts into the phantasmes of sleep, which too often continueth præcogitations; making Cables of Cobwebbes and Wildernesses of handsome Groves. Beside, *Hippocrates*[b] hath spoke so little, and the Oneirocriticall Masters[c] have left such frigid Interpretations from plants, that there is little encouragement to dream of Paradise it self. Nor will the sweetest delight of Gardens afford much comfort in sleep; wherein the dulnesse of that sense shakes hands with delectable odours; and though in the Bed of *Cleopatra*,[d] can hardly with any delight raise up the ghost of a Rose.

Night which Pagan Theology could make the daughter of *Chaos*, affords no advantage to the description of order: Although no lower than that Masse can we derive its Genealogy. All things began in order, so shall they end, and so shall they begin again; according to the ordainer of order and mysticall Mathematicks of the City of Heaven.

Though *Somnus* in *Homer* be sent to rowse up *Agamemnon*, I finde no such effects in the drowsy approaches of sleep. To keep our eyes open longer were but to act our *Antipodes*. The Huntsmen are up in *America*, and they are already past their first sleep in *Persia*. But who can be drowsie at that howr which freed us from everlasting sleep? or have slumbring thoughts at that time, when sleep it self must end, and as some conjecture all shall awake again?

FINIS

a Hyades near the Horizon about midnight at that time.

b *De Insomniis.*

c Artemidorus & Apomazar.

d Strewed with Roses.

CHRISTIAN MORALS

CHRISTIAN MORALS

PART II

PUNISH not thy self with Pleasure; Glut not thy sense with palative Delights; nor revenge the contempt of Temperance by the penalty of Satiety. Were there an Age of delight or any pleasure durable, who would not honour Volupia? but the Race of Delight is short, and Pleasures have mutable faces. The pleasures of one age are not pleasures in another, and their Lives fall short of our own. Even in our sensual days the strength of delight is in its seldomness or rarity, and sting in its satiety: Mediocrity is its Life, and immoderacy its Confusion. The Luxurious Emperors of old inconsiderately satiated themselves with the Dainties of Sea and Land, till, wearied through all varieties, their refections became a study unto them, and they were fain to feed by Invention: Novices in true Epicurism! which by mediocrity, paucity, quick and healthful Appetite, makes delights smartly acceptable; whereby Epicurus himself found Jupiter's brain* in a piece of Cytheridian Cheese, and the Tongues of Nightingals in a dish of Onyons. Hereby healthful and temperate poverty hath the start of nauseating Luxury; unto whose clear and naked appetite every meal is a feast, and in one single dish the first course of Metellus;* who are cheaply hungry, and never loose their hunger, or advantage of a craving appetite, because obvious food contents it; while Nero* half famish'd could not feed upon a piece of Bread, and lingring after his snowed water, hardly got down an ordinary cup of *Calda*.† By such circumscriptions of pleasure the contemned Philosophers reserved unto themselves the secret of Delight, which the *Helluo*'s of those days lost in their exorbitances. In vain we study Delight: it is at the command of every sober Mind, and in every sense born with us; but Nature, who teacheth us the rule of pleasure, instructeth also in the bounds

marginal notes:

* *Cerebrum Jovis*, for a Delicious bit.

* Metellus his riotous Pontifical Supper, the great variety whereat is to be seen in Macrobius.

* Nero in his flight. *Sueton.*

† *Caldæ gelidæque Minister.*

PART II thereof, and where its line expireth. And therefore Temperate Minds, not pressing their pleasures until the sting appeareth, enjoy their contentations contentedly and without regret, and so escape the folly of excess, to be pleased unto displacency.

Section 2 BRING candid Eyes unto the perusal of men's works, and let not Zoilism or Detraction blast well-intended labours. He that endureth no faults in men's writings must only read his own, wherein for the most part all appeareth White. Quotation mistakes, inadvertency, expedition, and human Lapses, may make not only Moles but Warts in Learned Authors, who notwithstanding, being judged by the capital matter, admit not of disparagement. I should unwillingly affirm that Cicero was but slightly versed in Homer, because in his Work *De Gloria* he ascribed those verses unto Ajax, which were delivered by Hector. What if Plautus in the account of Hercules mistaketh nativity for conception? Who would have mean thoughts of Apollinaris Sidonius, who seems to mistake the River Tigris for Euphrates; and, though a good Historian and learned Bishop of Auvergne, had the misfortune to be out in the Story of David, making mention of him when the Ark was sent back by the Philistins upon a Cart; which was before his time? Though I have no great opinion of Machiavel's Learning, yet I shall not presently say, that he was but a Novice in Roman History, because he was mistaken in placing Commodus after the Emperour Severus. Capital Truths are to be narrowly eyed, collateral Lapses and circumstantial deliveries not to be too strictly sifted. And if the substantial subject be well forged out, we need not examine the sparks which irregularly fly from it.

Section 3 LET well-weighed Considerations, not stiff and peremptory Assumptions, guide thy discourses, Pen and Actions. To begin or continue our works like Trismegistus of old, *Verum, certè verum, atque verissimum est,** would sound arrogantly unto present Ears in this strict enquiring Age, wherein, for the most part, *Probably,* and *Perhaps,* will hardly serve to mollify the Spirit of captious Contradictors. If Cardan saith that a Parrot is a beautiful Bird, Scaliger will set his Wits o' work to prove it a deformed Animal. The Compage of all Physical Truths is not so closely

* *In Tabula Smaragdina.*

jointed, but opposition may find intrusion, nor always so closely maintained, as not to suffer attrition. Many Positions seem quodlibetically constituted, and like a Delphian Blade will cut on both sides. Some Truths seem almost Falshoods, and some Falshoods almost Truths; wherein Falshood and Truth seem almost æquilibriously stated, and but a few grains of distinction to bear down the ballance. Some have digged deep, yet glanced by the Royal Vein; and a Man may come unto the *Pericardium*, but not the Heart of Truth. Besides, many things are known, as some are seen, that is by Parallaxis, or at some distance from their true and proper beings, the superficial regard of things having a different aspect from their true and central Natures. And this moves sober Pens unto suspensory and timorous assertions, nor presently to obtrude them as Sibyl's leaves, which after considerations may find to be but folious apparences, and not the central and vital interiours of Truth.

VALUE the Judicious, and let not mere acquests in minor parts of Learning gain thy preexistimation. 'Tis an unjust way of compute to magnify a weak Head for some Latin abilities, and to undervalue a solid Judgment, because he knows not the genealogy of Hector. When that notable King of France* would have his Son to know but one sentence in Latin, had it been a good one, perhaps it had been enough. Natural parts and good Judgments rule the World. States are not governed by Ergotisms. Many have Ruled well who could not perhaps define a Commonwealth, and they who understand not the Globe of the Earth command a great part of it. Where natural Logick prevails not, Artificial too often faileth. Where Nature fills the Sails, the Vessel goes smoothly on, and when Judgment is the Pilot, the Ensurance need not be high. When Industry builds upon Nature, we may expect Pyramids: where that foundation is wanting, the structure must be low. They do most by Books, who could do much without them, and he that chiefly ows himself unto himself is the substantial Man.

* Lewis the Eleventh. *Qui nescit dissimulare nescit Regnare.*

LET thy Studies be free as thy Thoughts and Contemplations, but fly not only upon the wings of Imagination; Joyn Sense unto Reason, and Experiment unto Speculation, and so give life unto

PART II Embryon Truths, and Verities yet in their Chaos. There is nothing more acceptable unto the Ingenious World, than this noble Eluctation of Truth; wherein, against the tenacity of Prejudice and Prescription, this Century now prevaileth. What Libraries of new Volumes aftertimes will behold, and in what a new World of Knowledge the eyes of our Posterity may be happy, a few Ages may joyfully declare; and is but a cold thought unto those who cannot hope to behold this Exantlation of Truth, or that obscured Virgin half out of the Pit. Which might make some content with a commutation of the time of their lives, and to commend the Fancy of the Pythagorean metempsychosis; whereby they might hope to enjoy this happiness in their third or fourth selves, and behold that in Pythagoras, which they now

Ipse ego, but foresee in Euphorbus. The World, which took but six days
nam memini, to make, is like to take six thousand to make out: mean while
Trojani in
tempore belli old Truths voted down begin to resume their places, and new
Panthoides Eu- ones arise upon us; wherein there is no comfort in the happiness
phorbus eram.
[Ovid, Metam. of Tully's Elizium,† or any satisfaction from the Ghosts of the
xv. 160.] Ancients, who knew so little of what is now well known. Men
† Who com- disparage not Antiquity, who prudently exalt new Enquiries,
forted him-
self that he and make not them the Judges of Truth, who were but fellow
should there Enquirers of it. Who can but magnify the Endeavors of Aristotle,
converse with
the old and the noble start which Learning had under him; or less than
Philosophers. pitty the slender progression made upon such advantages,
while many Centuries were lost in repetitions and transcriptions sealing up the Book of Knowledge? And therefore, rather than to swell the leaves of Learning by fruitless Repetitions, to sing the same Song in all Ages, nor adventure at Essays beyond the attempt of others, many would be content that some would write like Helmont or Paracelsus; and be willing to endure the monstrosity of some opinions, for divers singular notions requiting such aberrations.

Section 6 DESPISE not the obliquities of younger ways, nor despair of better things whereof there is yet no prospect. Who would imagine that Diogenes, who in his younger days was a falsifier of Money, should in the aftercourse of his Life be so great a contemner of Metal? Some Negros, who believe the Resurrection,
Mandelslo. think that they shall rise white. Even in this life Regeneration

may imitate Resurrection, our black and vitious tinctures PART II
may wear off, and goodness cloath us with candour. Good
Admonitions Knock not always in vain. There will be signal
Examples of God's mercy, and the Angels must not want their
charitable Rejoyces for the conversion of lost Sinners. Figures
of most Angles do nearest approach unto Circles, which have
no Angles at all. Some may be near unto goodness, who are conceived far from it, and many things happen, not likely to ensue
from any promises of Antecedencies. Culpable beginnings have
found commendable conclusions, and infamous courses pious
retractations. Detestable Sinners have proved exemplary Con-
verts on Earth, and may be glorious in the Apartment of Mary
Magdalen in Heaven. Men are not the same through all divisions of their Ages. Time, Experience, self-Reflexions, and God's
mercies, make in some well-temper'd minds a kind of translation before Death, and Men to differ from themselves as well
as from other Persons. Hereof the old World afforded many
Examples to the infamy of latter Ages, wherein Men too often
live by the rule of their inclinations; so that, without any
Astral prediction, *the first day gives the last.** Men are commonly   * *Primusque*
as they were; or rather, as bad dispositions run into worser   *dies dedit*
habits, the Evening doth not crown, but sowerly conclude the   *extremum.*
Day.

IF the Almighty will not spare us according to his merciful Section 7
capitulation at Sodom, if his Goodness please not to pass over a
great deal of Bad for a small pittance of Good, or to look upon
us in the Lump; there is slender hope for Mercy, or sound presumption of fulfilling half his Will, either in Persons or Nations:
they who excel in some Virtues being so often defective in
others; few Men driving at the extent and amplitude of Goodness, but computing themselves by their best parts, and others
by their worst, are content to rest in those Virtues which
others commonly want. Which makes this speckled Face of
Honesty in the World; and which was the imperfection of the
old Philosophers and great pretenders unto Virtue, who, well
declining the gaping Vices of Intemperance, Incontinency,
Violence and Oppression, were yet blindly peccant in iniquities
of closer faces, were envious, malicious, contemners, scoffers,

PART II censurers, and stufft with Vizard Vices, no less depraving the Ethereal particle and diviner portion of Man. For Envy, Malice, Hatred are the qualities of Satan, close and dark like himself; and where such brands smoak, the Soul cannot be White. Vice may be had at all prices; expensive and costly iniquities, which make the noise, cannot be every Man's sins; but the soul may be foully inquinated at a very low rate, and a Man may be cheaply vitious, to the perdition of himself.

Section 8 OPINION rides upon the neck of Reason, and Men are Happy, Wise, or Learned, according as that Empress shall set them down in the Register of Reputation. However, weigh not thy self in the scales of thy own opinion, but let the Judgment of the Judicious be the Standard of thy Merit. Self-estimation is a flatterer too readily intitling us unto Knowledge and Abilities, which others sollicitously labour after, and doubtfully think they attain. Surely such confident tempers do pass their days in best tranquility, who, resting in the opinion of their own abilities, are happily gull'd by such contentation; wherein Pride, Self-conceit, Confidence and Opiniatry will hardly suffer any to complain of imperfection. To think themselves in the right, or all that right, or only that, which they do or think, is a fallacy of high content; though others laugh in their sleeves, and look upon them as in a deluded state of Judgment; wherein, notwithstanding, 'twere but a civil piece of complacency to suffer them to sleep who would not wake, to let them rest in their securities, nor by dissent or opposition to stagger their contentments.

Section 9 SINCE the Brow speaks often true, since Eyes and Noses have Tongues, and the countenance proclaims the Heart and inclinations; let observation so far instruct thee in Physiognomical lines, as to be some Rule for thy distinction, and Guide for thy affection unto such as look most like Men. Mankind, methinks, is comprehended in a few Faces, if we exclude all Visages which any way participate of Symmetries and Schemes of Look common unto other Animals. For as though Man were the extract of the World, in whom all were *in coagulato*, which in their forms were *in soluto* and at Extension; we often observe that Men do most act those Creatures, whose constitution, parts and complexion do most predominate in their mixtures. This is a cornerstone in Physiognomy, and holds some Truth not only in particular Persons but also in whole Nations. There are therefore Provincial Faces, National Lips and Noses, which testify not only the Natures of those Countries, but of those which have them elsewhere. Thus we may make England the whole Earth, dividing it not only into Europe, Asia, Africa, but the particular Regions thereof, and may in some latitude affirm, that there are Ægyptians, Scythians, Indians among us; who though born in England, yet carry the Faces and Air of those Countries, and are also agreeable and correspondent unto their Natures. Faces look uniformly unto our Eyes: How they appear unto some Animals of a more piercing or differing sight, who are able to discover the inequalities, rubbs and hairiness of the Skin, is not without good doubt; and therefore in reference unto Man, Cupid is said to be blind. Affection should not be too sharp-Eyed, and Love is not to be made by magnifying Glasses. If things were seen as they truly are, the beauty of bodies would be much abridged; and therefore the wise Contriver hath drawn the pictures and outsides of things softly and amiably unto the natural Edge of our Eyes, not leaving them able to discover those uncomely asperities, which make Oyster-shells in good Faces, and Hedghoggs even in Venus's moles.

COURT not Felicity too far, and weary not the favorable hand of Fortune. Glorious actions have their times, extent and *non ultra*'s. To put no end unto Attempts were to make prescription of Successes, and to bespeak unhappiness at the last. For the Line of our Lives is drawn with white and black vicissitudes, wherein the extremes hold seldom one complexion. That Pompey should obtain the sirname of Great at twenty-five years, that Men in their young and active days should be fortunate and perform notable things, is no observation of deep wonder, they having the strength of their fates before them, nor yet acted their parts in the World, for which they were brought into it: whereas Men of years, matured for counsels and designs, seem to be beyond the vigour of their active fortunes, and high exploits of life, providentially ordained unto Ages best agreeable

PART II unto them. And therefore many brave men, finding their fortune grow faint, and feeling its declination, have timely withdrawn themselves from great attempts, and so escaped the ends of mighty Men, disproportionable to their beginnings. But magnanimous Thoughts have so dimmed the Eyes of many, that, forgetting the very essence of Fortune, and the vicissitude of good and evil, they apprehend no bottom in felicity; and so have been still tempted on unto mighty Actions, reserved for their destructions. For Fortune lays the Plot of our Adversities in the foundation of our Felicities, blessing us in the first quadrate, to blast us more sharply in the last. And since in the highest felicities there lieth a capacity of the lowest miseries, she hath this advantage from our happiness to make us truly miserable: for to become acutely miserable we are to be first happy. Affliction smarts most in the most happy state, as having somewhat in it of Belisarius at Begger's bush, or Bajazet in the grate. And this the fallen Angels severely understand, who, having acted their first part in Heaven, are made sharply miserable by transition, and more afflictively feel the contrary state of Hell.

Section 11 CARRY no careless Eye upon the unexpected scenes of things; but ponder the acts of Providence in the publick ends of great and notable Men, set out unto the view of all for no common *memorandums*. The Tragical Exits and unexpected periods of some eminent Persons cannot but amuse considerate Observators; wherein notwithstanding most Men seem to see by extramission, without reception or self-reflexion, and conceive themselves unconcerned by the fallacy of their own Exemption: whereas the Mercy of God hath singled out but few to be the signals of his Justice, leaving the generality of Mankind to the pædagogy of Example. But the inadvertency of our Natures not well apprehending this favorable method and merciful decimation, and that he sheweth in some what others also deserve; they entertain no sense of his Hand beyond the stroak of themselves. Whereupon the whole becomes necessarily punished, and the contracted Hand of God extended unto universal Judgments; from whence nevertheless the stupidity of our tempers receives but faint impressions, and in the most Tragical

state of times holds but starts of good motions. So that to
continue us in goodness there must be iterated returns of
misery, and a circulation in afflictions is necessary. And since we
cannot be wise by warnings, since Plagues are insignificant,
except we be personally plagued, since also we cannot be
punish'd unto Amendment by proxy or commutation, nor by
vicinity, but contaction; there is an unhappy necessity that we
must smart in our own Skins, and the provoked arm of the
Almighty must fall upon our selves. The capital sufferings of
others are rather our monitions than acquitments. There is but
one who dyed salvifically for us, and able to say unto Death,
Hitherto shalt thou go, and no farther; only one enlivening Death,
which makes Gardens of Graves, and that which was sowed in
Corruption to arise and flourish in Glory: when Death it self
shall dye, and living shall have no Period, when the damned
shall mourn at the funeral of Death, when Life not Death shall
be the wages of sin, when the second Death shall prove a
miserable Life, and destruction shall be courted.

ALTHOUGH their Thoughts may seem too severe, who
think that few ill-natur'd Men go to Heaven; yet it may be
acknowledged that good-natur'd Persons are best founded for
that place; who enter the World with good Dispositions and
natural Graces, more ready to be advanced by impressions from
above, and christianized unto pieties; who carry about them
plain and down-right dealing Minds, Humility, Mercy, Charity,
and Virtues acceptable unto God and Man. But whatever
success they may have as to Heaven, they are the acceptable
Men on Earth, and *happy is he who hath his quiver full of them* for
his Friends. These are not the Dens wherein Falshood lurks,
and Hypocrisy hides its Head, wherein Frowardness makes its
Nest, or where Malice, Hard-heartedness and Oppression love
to dwell; not those by whom the Poor get little, and the
Rich some times loose all; Men not of retracted Looks, but who
carry their Hearts in their Faces, and need not to be look'd upon
with perspectives; not sordidly or mischievously ingrateful;
who cannot learn to ride upon the neck of the afflicted, nor load
the heavy laden, but who keep the Temple of Janus shut by
peaceable and quiet tempers; who make not only the best

PART II　Friends, but the best Enemies, as easier to forgive than offend, and ready to pass by the second offence before they avenge the first; who make natural Royalists, obedient Subjects, kind and merciful Princes, verified in our own, one of the best-natur'd Kings of this Throne. Of the old Roman Emperours the best were the best-natur'd; though they made but a small number, and might be writ in a Ring. Many of the rest were as bad Men as Princes; Humorists rather than of good humors, and of good natural parts rather than of good natures; which did but arm their bad inclinations, and make them wittily wicked.

Section 13　WITH what shift and pains we come into the World we remember not; but 'tis commonly found no easy matter to get out of it. Many have studied to exasperate the ways of Death, but fewer hours have been spent to soften that necessity. That the smoothest way unto the grave is made by bleeding, as common opinion presumeth, beside the sick and fainting Languors which accompany that effusion, the experiment in Lucan and Seneca will make us doubt; under which the noble Stoick so deeply laboured, that, to conceal his affliction, he was fain to retire from the sight of his Wife, and not ashamed to implore the merciful hand of his Physician to shorten his misery therein. Ovid,* the old Heroes, and the Stoicks, who were so afraid of drowning, as dreading thereby the extinction of their Soul, which they conceived to be a Fire, stood probably in fear of an easier way of Death; wherein the Water, entring the possessions of Air, makes a temperate suffocation, and kills as it were without a Fever. Surely many, who have had the Spirit to destroy themselves, have not been ingenious in the contrivance thereof. 'Twas a dull way practised by Themistocles† to overwhelm himself with Bulls-blood, who, being an Athenian, might have held an easier Theory of Death from the state potion of his Country; from which Socrates in Plato seemed not to suffer much more than from the fit of an Ague. Cato is much to be pitied, who mangled himself with poyniards; and Hannibal seems more subtle, who carried his delivery, not in the point but the pummel* of his Sword.

　　　The Egyptians were merciful contrivers, who destroyed their malefactors by Asps, charming their senses into an invincible

* Demito naufragium, mors mihi munus erit. [Trist. i. 2, 52.]

† Plutarch [cap. 31].

* Pummel, wherein he is said to have carried something, whereby upon a struggle or despair he might deliver himself from all misfortunes.

sleep, and killing as it were with Hermes his Rod. The Turkish PART II
Emperour,* odious for other Cruelty, was herein a remarkable
Master of Mercy, killing his Favorite in his sleep, and sending
him from the shade into the house of darkness. He who had
been thus destroyed would hardly have bled at the presence
of his destroyer; when Men are already dead by metaphor, and
pass but from one sleep unto another, wanting herein the
eminent part of severity, to feel themselves to dye, and escaping
the sharpest attendant of Death, the lively apprehension thereof. But to learn to dye is better than to study the ways of dying.
Death will find some ways to unty or cut the most Gordian
Knots of Life, and make men's miseries as mortal as themselves:
whereas evil Spirits, as undying Substances, are unseparable
from their calamities; and therefore they everlastingly struggle
under their *Angustia*'s, and bound up with immortality can
never get out of themselves.

* Solyman.
[Knolles]
*Turkish
History.*

TO THE READER

WOULD Truth dispense, we could be content, with Plato, that knowledge were but remembrance; that intellectual acquisition were but reminiscential evocation, and new Impressions but the colourishing of old stamps which stood pale in the soul before. For what is worse, knowledge is made by oblivion, and to purchase a clear and warrantable body of Truth, we must forget and part with much we know. Our tender Enquiries taking up Learning at large, and together with true and assured notions, receiving many, wherein our reviewing judgments do find no satisfaction. And therefore in this *Encyclopædie* and round of Knowledge, like the great and exemplary Wheels of Heaven, we must observe two Circles: that while we are daily carried about, and whirled on by the swing and rapt of the one, we may maintain a natural and proper course, in the slow and sober wheel of the other. And this we shall more readily perform, if we timely survey our knowledge, impartially singling out those encroachments, which junior compliance and popular credulity hath admitted. Whereof at present we have endeavoured a long and serious *Adviso*, proposing not only a large and copious List, but from experience and reason attempting their decisions.

And first we crave exceeding pardon in the audacity of the Attempt, humbly acknowledging a work of such concernment unto truth, and difficulty in itself, did well deserve the conjunction of many heads. And surely more advantageous had it been unto Truth, to have fallen into the endeavours of some co-operating advancers, that might have performed it to the life, and added authority thereto; which the privacy of our condition, and unequal abilities cannot expect. Whereby notwithstanding we have not been diverted; nor have our solitary attempts been so discouraged, as to dispair the favourable look of Learning upon our single and unsupported endeavours.

Nor have we let fall our Pen upon discouragement of Contradiction, Unbelief and Difficulty of disswasion from radicated
beliefs, and points of high prescription, although we are very
sensible, how hardly teaching years do learn, what roots old
age contracteth unto errors, and how such as are but acorns in
our younger brows, grow Oaks in our elder heads, and become
inflexible unto the powerfullest arms of reason. Although we
have also beheld, what cold requitals others have found in their
several redemptions of Truth; and how their ingenuous Enquiries have been dismissed with censure, and obloquie of
singularities.

Some consideration we hope from the course of our Profession,
which though it leadeth us into many truths that pass undiscerned by others, yet doth it disturb their Communications,
and much interrupt the office of our Pens in their well intended
Transmissions. And therefore surely in this work attempts will
exceed performances; it being composed by snatches of time, as
Inspection medical vacations, and the fruitless importunity of Uroscopy
of Urines. would permit us. And therefore also, perhaps it hath not found
that regular and constant stile, those infallible experiments and
those assured determinations, which the subject sometime
requireth, and might be expected from others, whose quiet
doors and unmolested hours afford no such distractions.
Although whoever shall indifferently perpend the exceeding
difficulty, which either the obscurity of the subject, or un-
avoidable paradoxology must often put upon the Attemptor,
he will easily discern, a work of this nature is not to be performed upon one legg; and should smel of oyl, if duly and
deservedly handled.

Our first intentions considering the common interest of
Truth, resolved to propose it unto the Latine republique and
equal Judges of Europe, but owing in the first place this service
unto our Country, and therein especially unto its ingenuous
Gentry, we have declared our self in a language best conceived.
Although I confess the quality of the Subject will sometimes
carry us into expressions beyond meer English apprehensions.
And indeed, if elegancy still proceedeth, and English Pens
maintain that stream we have of late observed to flow from
many, we shall within few years be fain to learn Latine to

understand English, and a work will prove of equal facility in
either. Nor have we addressed our Pen or Stile unto the people
(whom Books do not redress, and are this way incapable of reduction), but unto the knowing and leading part of Learning.
As well understanding (at least probably hoping) except they be
watered from higher regions and fructifying meteors of Knowledge, these weeds must lose their alimental sap and wither of
themselves. Whose conserving influence, could our endeavours
prevent, we should trust the rest unto the sythe of Time, and
hopefull dominion of Truth.

We hope it will not be unconsidered, that we find no open
tract, or constant manuduction in this Labyrinth; but are oft-
times fain to wander in the America and untravelled parts of
Truth. For though not many years past, Dr. Primrose hath made
a learned Discourse of vulgar Errors in Physick, yet have we discussed but two or three thereof. Scipio Mercurii hath also left
an excellent tract in Italian, concerning popular Errors; but
confining himself only unto those in Physick, he hath little
conduced unto the generality of our doctrine. Laurentius Jou-
bertus by the same Title led our expectation into thoughts of
great relief; whereby notwithstanding we reaped no advantage,
it answering scarce at all the promise of the inscription. Nor
perhaps (if it were yet extant) should we find any farther
Assistance from that ancient piece of Andreas, pretending the   περὶ τῶν ψευ-
same Title. And therefore we are often constrained to stand   δῶς πεπισ-
alone against the strength of opinion, and to meet the Goliah   τευμένων,
and Giant of Authority with contemptible pibbles, and feeble   Athenæi
arguments, drawn from the scrip and slender stock of our selves. *lib.* 7.
Nor have we indeed scarce named any Author whose Name we
do not honour; and if detraction could invite us, discretion
surely would contain us from any derogatory intention, where
highest Pens and friendliest eloquence must fail in commendation.

And therefore also we cannot but hope the equitable considerations, and candour of reasonable minds. We cannot expect
the frown of Theology herein; nor can they which behold the
present state of things, and controversie of points so long
received in Divinity, condemn our sober Enquiries in the doubtfull appertinances of Arts, and Receptaries of Philosophy.
Surely Philologers and Critical Discoursers, who look beyond

the shell and obvious exteriours of things, will not be angry with our narrower explorations. And we cannot doubt, our Brothers in Physick (whose knowledge in Naturals will lead them into a nearer apprehension of many things delivered) will friendly accept, if not countenance our endeavours. Nor can we conceive it may be unwelcome unto those honoured Worthies, who endeavour the advancement of Learning: as being likely to find a clearer progression, when so many rubs are levelled, and many untruths taken off, which passing as principles with common beliefs, disturb the tranquility of Axioms, which otherwise might be raised. And wise men cannot but know, that arts and learning want this expurgation: and if the course of truth be permitted unto its self, like that of time and uncorrected computations, it cannot escape many errors, which duration still enlargeth.

Lastly, we are not Magisterial in opinions, nor have we Dictator-like obtruded our conceptions; but in the humility of Ènquiries or disquisitions, have only proposed them unto more ocular discerners. And therefore opinions are free, and open it is for any to think or declare the contrary. And we shall so far encourage contradiction, as to promise no disturbance, or re-oppose any Pen, that shall Fallaciously or captiously[1] refute us; that shall only lay hold of our lapses, single out Digressions, Corollaries, or Ornamental conceptions, to evidence his own in as indifferent truths. And shall only take notice of such, whose experimental and judicious knowledge shall solemnly look upon it; not only to destroy of ours, but to establish of his own; not to traduce or extenuate, but to explain and dilucidate, to add and ampliate, according to the laudable custom of the Ancients in their sober promotions of Learning. Unto whom notwithstanding, we shall not contentiously rejoin, or only to justifie our own, but to applaud or confirm his maturer assertions; and shall confer what is in us unto his name and honour; Ready to be swallowed in any worthy enlarger: as having acquired our end, if any way, or under any name we may obtain a work, so much desired, and yet desiderated[2] of Truth.

THOMAS BROWNE

PSEUDODOXIA EPIDEMICA

THE FIRST BOOK
OR GENERAL PART

CHAP. I

Of the Causes of Common Errors

THE First and Father-cause of common Error, is, The common infirmity of Human Nature; of whose deceptible condition, although perhaps there should not need any other eviction, than the frequent Errors we shall our selves commit, even in the express declarement hereof: yet shall we illustrate the same from more infallible constitutions, and persons presumed as far from us in condition, as time, that is, our first and ingenerated forefathers. From whom as we derive our Being, and the several wounds of constitution, so may we in some manner excuse our infirmities in the depravity of those parts, whose Traductions were pure in them, and their Originals but once removed from God. Who notwithstanding (if posterity may take leave to judg of the fact, as they are assured to suffer in the punishment) were grosly deceived, in their perfection; and so weakly deluded in the clarity of their understanding, that it hath left no small obscurity in ours, How error should gain upon them.

For first, They were deceived by Satan; and that not in an invisible insinuation, but an open and discoverable apparition, that is, in the form of a Serpent; whereby although there were many occasions of suspition, and such as could not easily escape a weaker circumspection, yet did the unwary apprehension of Eve take no advantage thereof. It hath therefore seemed strange unto some, she should be deluded by a Serpent, or subject her reason to a beast, which God had subjected unto hers. It hath

BOOK I
Chapter I
The Introduction.

Matter of great dispute, how our first parents could be so deceived.

empuzzled the enquiries of others to apprehend, and enforced them unto strange conceptions, to make out, how without fear or doubt she could discourse with such a creature, or hear a Serpent speak, without suspition of Imposture. The wits of others have been so bold, as to accuse her simplicity, in receiving his Temptation so coldly; and when such specious effects of the Fruit were Promised, as to make them like God, not to desire, at least not to wonder he pursued not that benefit himself. And had it been their own case, would perhaps have replied: If the tast of this Fruit maketh the eaters like Gods, why remainest thou a Beast? If it maketh us but like Gods, we are so already. If thereby our eyes shall be opened hereafter, they are at present quick enough, to discover thy deceit; and we desire them no opener, to behold our own shame. If to know good and evil be our advantage, although we have Free-will unto both, we desire to perform but one; We know 'tis good to obey the commandment of God, but evil if we transgress it.

They were deceived by one another, and in the greatest disadvantage of Delusion, that is, the stronger by the weaker: For Eve presented the Fruit, and Adam received it from her. Thus the Serpent was cunning enough, to begin the deceit in the weaker, and the weaker of strength, sufficient to consummate the fraud in the stronger. Art and fallacy was used unto her; a naked offer proved sufficient unto him: So his superstruction was his Ruine, and the fertility of his Sleep an issue of Death unto him. And although the condition of Sex, and posteriority of Cremation, might somewhat extenuate the Error of the Woman: Yet was it very strange and inexcusable in the Man; especially, if as some affirm, he was the wisest of all men since; or if, as others have conceived, he was not ignorant of the Fall of the Angels, and had thereby Example and punishment to deterr him.

Adam
supposed by
some to have
been the
wisest man
that ever was.
Adam & Eve
how they fell.

They were deceived from themselves, and their own apprehensions; for Eve either mistook, or traduced the commandment of God: *Of every Tree of the Garden thou mayest freely eat, but of the Tree of knowledg of good and evil thou shalt not eat: for in the day thou eatest thereof, thou shalt surely die.* Now Eve upon the question of the Serpent, returned the Precept in different terms: *You shall not eat of it, neither shall you touch it, lest perhaps you die.* In which delivery, there were no less than two mistakes, or rather additional mendacities; for the Commandment forbad not the touch of the Fruit; and positively said, Ye shall surely die: but she extenuating, replied, *ne fortè moriamini*, lest perhaps ye die. For so in the vulgar translation it runneth, and so it is expressed in the *Thargum* or Paraphrase of Jonathan. And therefore although it be said, and that very truely, that the Devil was a lyer from the beginning, yet was the Woman herein the first express beginner: and falsified twice, before the reply of Satan. And therefore also, to speak strictly, the sin of the Fruit was not the first Offence: They first transgressed the Rule of their own Reason; and after the Commandment of God.

They were deceived through the Conduct of their Senses, and by Temptations from the Object it self; whereby although their intellectuals had not failed in the Theory of truth, yet did the inservient and brutal Faculties controll the suggestion of Reason: Pleasure and Profit already overswaying the instructions of Honesty, and Sensuality perturbing the reasonable commands of Vertue. For so it is delivered in the Text: That *when the Woman saw, that the Tree was good for food, and that it was pleasant unto the eye, and a Tree to be desired to make one wise, she took of the fruit thereof and did eat.* Now hereby it appeareth, that Eve, before the Fall, was by the same and beaten way of allurements inveigled, whereby her posterity hath been deluded ever since; that is, those three delivered by St. John, The lust of the flesh, the lust of the eye, and the pride of life: Wherein indeed they seemed as weakly to fail, as their debilitated posterity, ever after. Whereof notwithstanding, some in their imperfection, have resisted more powerful temptations; and in many moralities condemned the facility of their seductions.

Again, they might, for ought we know, be still deceived in the unbelief of their Mortality, even after they had eat of the Fruit: For, Eve observing no immediate execution of the Curse, she delivered the Fruit unto Adam: who, after the tast thereof, perceiving himself still to live, might yet remain in doubt, whether he had incurred Death; which perhaps he did not indubitably believe, until he was after convicted in the visible example of Abel. For he that would not believe the Menace of God at first, it may be doubted whether, before an ocular

Adam whence (probably) induced to eat.

example, he believed the Curse at last. And therefore they are not without all reason, who have disputed the Fact of Cain: that is, although he purposed to do mischief, whether he intended to kill his Brother; or designed that, whereof he had not beheld an example in his own kind. There might be somewhat in it, that he would not have done, or desired undone, when he brake forth as desperately, as before he had done uncivilly, *My iniquity is greater than can be forgiven me.*

Some nicities I confess there are which extenuate, but many more that aggravate this Delusion; which exceeding the bounds of this Discourse, and perhaps our Satisfaction, we shall at present pass over. And therefore whether the Sin of our First Parents were the greatest of any since; whether the transgression of Eve seducing, did not exceed that of Adam seduced; or whether the resistibility of His Reason, did not equivalence the facility of her Seduction; we shall refer it to the Schoolman; Whether there was not in Eve as great injustice in deceiving her husband, as imprudence in being deceived her self; especially, if foretasting the Fruit, her eyes were opened before his, and she knew the effect of it, before he tasted of it; we leave it unto the Moralist. Whether the whole relation be not Allegoricall, that is, whether the temptation of the Man by the Woman, be not the seduction of the rational and higher parts by the inferiour and feminine faculties: or whether the Tree in the midst of the Garden, were not that part in the Center of the body, in which was afterward the appointment of Circumcision

The Thalmudist's
Allegories
upon the
History of
Adam and
Eve's Fall.
in Males, we leave it unto the Thalmudist. Whether there were any Policy in the Devil to tempt them before the Conjunction, or whether the Issue before tentation, might in justice have suffered with those after, we leave it unto the Lawyer. Whether Adam foreknew the advent of Christ, or the reparation of his Error by his Saviour; how the execution of the Curse should have been ordered, if, after Eve had eaten, Adam had yet refused. Whether if they had tasted the Tree of life, before that of Good and Evil, they had yet suffered the curse of Mortality: or whether the efficacy of the one had not over-powred the penalty of the other, we leave it unto GOD. For he alone can truly determine these, and all things else; Who as he hath proposed the World unto our disputation, so hath he reserved

many things unto his own resolution; whose determination we
cannot hope from flesh, but must with reverence suspend unto
that great Day, whose justice shall either condemn our curiosities, or resolve our disquisitions.

   Lastly, Man was not only deceivable in his Integrity, but the
Angels of light in all their Clarity. He that said, He would be
like the highest, did Erre, if in some way he conceived himself
so already; but in attempting so high an effect from himself, he
mis-understood the nature of God, and held a false apprehension of his own; whereby vainly attempting not only insolencies,
but impossibilities, he deceived himself as low as Hell. In brief,
there is nothing infallible but GOD, who cannot possibly Erre.
For things are really true as they correspond unto His conception; and have so much verity as they hold of conformity unto
that Intellect, in whose Idea they had their first determinations.
And therefore being the Rule, he cannot be Irregular; nor,
being Truth it self, conceaveably admit the impossible society of
Error.

CHAP. II

A further Illustration of the same

B EING thus deluded before the Fall, it is no wonder if
   their conceptions were deceitful, and could scarce speak
   without an Error after. For, what is very remarkable (and
no man that I know hath yet observed) in the relations of
Scripture before the Flood, there is but one speech delivered by
Man, wherein there is not an erroneous conception; and, strictly
examined, most hainously injurious unto truth. The pen of
Moses is brief in the account before the Flood, and the speeches
recorded are but six. The first is that of Adam, when upon the
expostulation of God, he replied: *I heard thy voice in the Garden,
and because I was naked I hid my self.* In which reply, there was
included a very gross Mistake, and, if with pertinacity maintained, a high and capital Error. For thinking by this retirement
to obscure himself from God, he infringed the omnisciency and
essential Ubiquity of his Maker. Who as he created all things,

so is he beyond and in them all, not only in power, as under his subjection, or in his presence, as being in his cognition; but in his very Essence, as being the soul of their causalities, and the essential cause of their existencies. Certainly, his posterity at this distance and after so perpetuated an impairment, cannot but condemn the poverty of his conception, that thought to obscure himself from his Creator in the shade of the Garden, who had beheld him before in the darkness of his Chaos, and the great obscurity of Nothing; that thought to fly from God, which could not fly himself; or imagined that one tree should conceal his nakedness from God's eye, as another had revealed it unto his own. Those tormented Spirits that wish the mountains to cover them, have fallen upon desires of minor absurdity, and chosen ways of less improbable concealment. Though this be also as ridiculous unto reason, as fruitless unto their desires; for he that laid the foundations of the Earth, cannot be excluded the secrecy of the Mountains; nor can there any thing escape the perspicacity of those eyes which were before light, and in whose opticks there is no opacity. This is the consolation of all good men, unto whom his Ubiquity affordeth continual comfort and security: And this is the affliction of Hell, unto whom it affordeth despair, and remediless calamity. For those restless Spirits that fly the face of the Almighty, being deprived the fruition of his eye, would also avoid the extent of his hand; which being impossible, their sufferings are desperate, and their afflictions without evasion; until they can get out of Trismegistus his Circle, that is, to extend their wings above the Universe, and pitch beyond Ubiquity.

The Second is that speech of Adam unto God: *The woman whom thou gavest me to be with me, she gave me of the Tree, and I did eat.* This indeed was an unsatisfactory reply, and therein was involved a very impious Error, as implying God the Author of sin, and accusing his Maker of his transgression. As if he had said, If thou hadst not given me a woman, I had not been deceived: Thou promisedst to make her a help, but she hath proved destruction unto me: Had I remained alone, I had not sinned; but thou gavest me a Consort, and so I became seduced. This was a bold and open accusation of God, making the fountain of good, the contriver of evil, and the forbidder of the crime

an abettor of the fact prohibited. Surely, his mercy was great
that did not revenge the impeachment of his justice; And his
goodness to be admired, that it refuted not his argument in the
punishment of his excusation, and only pursued the first transgression without a penalty of this the second.

The third was that of Eve: *The Serpent beguiled me, and I did eat.*
In which reply, there was not only a very feeble excuse, but an
erroneous translating her own offence upon another; Extenuating her sin from that which was an aggravation, that is, to
excuse the Fact at all, much more upon the suggestion of a
beast, which was before in the strictest terms prohibited by her
God. For although we now do hope the mercies of God will
consider our degenerated integrities unto some minoration of
our offences; yet had not the sincerity of our first parents so
colourable expectations, unto whom the commandment was
but single, and their integrities best able to resist the motions
of its transgression. And therefore so heinous conceptions have
risen hereof, that some have seemed more angry there-with,
than God himself: Being so exasperated with the offence, as
to call in question their salvation, and to dispute the eternal
punishment of their Maker. Assuredly with better reason may
posterity accuse them than they the Serpent or one another;
and the displeasure of the Pelagians must needs be irreconcil-
able, who peremptorily maintaining they can fulfil the whole
Law, will insatisfactorily condemn the non-observation of one.

The fourth, was that speech of Cain upon the demand of
God, *Where is thy brother?* and he said, *I know not.* In which
Negation, beside the open impudence, there was implied a
notable Error; for returning a lie unto his Maker, and presum-
ing in this manner to put off the Searcher of hearts, he denied
the omnisciency of God, whereunto there is nothing conceal-
able. The answer of Satan in the case of Job, had more of truth,
wisdom, and Reverence than this: *Whence comest thou Satan?* and
he said, *From compassing of the Earth.* For though an enemy of
God, and hater of all Truth, his wisdom will hardly permit him
to falsifie with the All-mighty. For well understanding the The Devill
knew not our
Saviour to be
God when he
tempted him.
Omniscience of his nature, he is not so ready to deceive himself,
as to falsifie unto him whose cognition is no way deludable.
And therefore when in the tentation of Christ he played upon

the fallacy, and thought to deceive the Author of Truth, the Method of this proceeding arose from the uncertainty of his Divinity; whereof had he remained assured, he had continued silent; nor would his discretion attempt so unsucceedable a temptation. And so again at the last day, when our offences shall be drawn into accompt, the subtilty of that Inquisitor shall not present unto God a bundle of calumnies or confutable accusations, but will discreetly offer up unto his Omnisciency, a true and undeniable list of our transgressions.

The fifth is another reply of Cain upon the denouncement of his curse, *My iniquity is greater then can be forgiven:* For so it is expressed in some Translations. The assertion was not only desperate, but the conceit erroneous, overthrowing that glorious Attribute of God, his Mercy, and conceiving the sin of murder unpardonable. Which, how great soever, is not above the repentance of man, but far below the mercies of God, and was (as some conceive) expiated in that punishment he suffered temporally for it. There are but two examples of this error in holy Scripture, and they both for Murder, and both as it were of the same person; for Christ was mystically slain in Abel, and therefore Cain had some influence on his death as well as Judas; but the sin had a different effect on Cain, from that it had on Judas, and most that since have fallen into it. For they like Judas desire death, and not infrequently pursue it: Cain on the contrary grew afraid thereof, and obtained a securement from it. Assuredly, if his dispair continued, there was punishment enough in life, and Justice sufficient in the mercy of his protection. For the life of the desperate equalls the anxieties of death; who in uncessant inquietudes but act the life of the damned, and anticipate the desolations of Hell. 'Tis indeed a sin in man, but a punishment only in Devils, who offend not God but afflict themselves, in the appointed despair of his mercies. And as to be without hope is the affliction of the damned, so is it the happiness of the blessed; who having all their expectations present, are not distracted with futurities: So is it also their felicity to have no Faith; for enjoying the beatifical vision, there is nothing unto them inevident; and in the fruition of the object of Faith, they have received the full evacuation of it.

The last speech was that of Lamech, *I have slain a man to my*

wound, and a young man to my hurt: If Cain be avenged seven fold,
truly Lamech seventy and seven fold. Now herein there seems to be
a very erroneous Illation: from the Indulgence of God unto
Cain, concluding an immunity unto himself; that is, a regular
protection from a single example, and an exemption from
punishment in a fact that naturally deserved it. The Error of
this offender was contrary to that of Cain, whom the Rabbins Cain, as the
Rabbins think
was the man
slain by
Lamech,
Gen. 4. 23.
conceive that Lamech at this time killed. He despaired in God's
mercy in the same Fact, where this presumed of it; he by a
decollation of all hope annihilated his mercy, this by an im-
moderancy thereof destroyed his Justice. Though the sin were
less, the Error was as great; For as it is untrue, that his mercy
will not forgive offenders, or his benignity co-operate to their
conversions; So is it also of no less falsity to affirm His justice
will not exact account of sinners, or punish such as continue in
their transgressions.

Thus may we perceive, how weakly our Fathers did Erre
before the Floud, how continually and upon common discourse
they fell upon Errors after; it is therefore no wonder we have
been erroneous ever since. And being now at greatest distance
from the beginning of Error, are almost lost in its dissemination,
whose waies are boundless, and confess no circumscription.

CHAP. III

*Of the second cause of Popular Errors, the erroneous
disposition of the People*

HAVING thus declared the fallible nature of Man even Chapter 3
from his first production, we have beheld the general
cause of Error. But as for popular Errors, they are
more neerly founded upon an erroneous inclination of the
people; as being the most deceptable part of Mankind and ready
with open armes to receive the encroachments of Error. Which
condition of theirs although deducible from many Grounds, yet
shall we evidence it but from a few, and such as most neerly and
undeniably declare their natures.

affect. But the wisdom of our Saviour, and the simplicity of his truth proceeded another way; defying the popular provisions of happiness from sensible expectations; placing his felicity in things removed from sense, and the intellectual enjoyment of God. And therefore the doctrine of the one was never affraid of Universities, or endeavoured the banishment of learning, like the other. And though Galen doth sometimes nibble at Moses, *Iulian.* and, beside the Apostate Christian, some Heathens have questioned his Philosophical part, or treaty of the Creation: Yet is there surely no reasonable Pagan, that will not admire the rational and well grounded precepts of Christ; whose life, as it was conformable unto His Doctrine, so was that unto the highest rules of Reason; and must therefore flourish in the advancement of learning, and the perfection of parts best able to comprehend it.

Again, Their individual imperfections being great, they are moreover enlarged by their aggregation; and being erroneous in their single numbers, once hudled together, they will be Error it self. For being a confusion of knaves and fools, and a farraginous concurrence of all conditions, tempers, sexes, and ages; it is but natural if their determinations be monstrous, and many waies inconsistent with Truth. And therefore wise men have alwaies applauded their own judgment, in the contradiction of that of the People; and their soberest adversaries, have ever afforded them the stile of fools and mad men; and, to speak impartially, their actions have *Non sani esse* made good these Epithets. Had Orestes been Judg, he would *hominis, non* not have acquitted that Lystrian rabble of madness, who, upon *sanus juret* *Orestes.* a visible miracle, falling into so high a conceit of Paul and Barnabas, that they termed the one Jupiter, the other Mercurius; that they brought Oxen and Garlands, and were hardly restrained from sacrificing unto them; did notwithstanding suddenly after fall upon Paul, and having stoned him drew him for dead out of the City. It might have hazzarded the sides of Democritus, had he been present at that tumult of Demetrius; when the people flocking together in great numbers, some crying one thing, and some another, and the assembly was confused, and the most part knew not wherefore they were come together; notwithstanding, all with one voice for the space of

two hours cried out, Great is Diana of the Ephesians. It had
overcome the patience of Job, as it did the meekness of Moses,
and would surely have mastered any, but the longanimity, and
lasting sufferance of God; had they beheld the Mutiny in the
wilderness, when, after ten great Miracles in Egypt, and some
in the same place, they melted down their stoln ear-rings into
a Calf, and monstrously cryed out, *These are thy Gods, O Israel,*
that brought thee out of the land of Egypt. It much accuseth the
impatience of Peter, who could not endure the staves of the
multitude, and is the greatest example of lenity in our Saviour,
when he desired of God forgiveness unto those, who having
one day brought him into the City in triumph, did presently
after, act all dishonour upon him, and nothing could be heard
but, *Crucifige,* in their Courts. Certainly he that considereth
these things in God's peculiar people, will easily discern how
little of truth there is in the waies of the Multitude; and though
sometimes they are flattered with that Aphorism, will hardly
believe, The voice of the people to be the voice of God.

Lastly, being thus divided from truth in themselves, they are
yet farther removed by advenient deception. For true it is (and
I hope I shall not offend their vulgarities) if I say, they are daily
mocked into Error by subtler devisors, and have been expressly
deluded by all professions and ages. Thus the Priests of Elder
time, have put upon them many incredible conceits, not only
deluding their apprehensions with Ariolation, South saying,
and such oblick Idolatries, but winning their credulities unto
the literal and down-right adorement of Cats, Lizzards, and
Beetles. And thus also in some Christian Churches, wherein is
presumed an irreprovable truth, if all be true that is suspected,
or half what is related; there have not wanted many strange
deceptions, and some thereof are still confessed by the name of
Pious Frauds. Thus Theudas an Impostor was able to lead away
Four thousand into the Wilderness, and the delusions of
Mahomet almost the fourth part of Mankind. Thus all Heresies,
how gross soever, have found a welcome with the people. For
thus, many of the Jews were wrought into belief that Herod was
the Messias; and David George of Leyden, and Arden, were not
without a party amongst the people, who maintained the same
opinion of themselves almost in our days.

Physitians (many at least that make profession thereof) beside divers less discoverable wayes of fraud, have made them believe, there is the book of fate, or the power of Aaron's brest plate, in

Urins. And therefore hereunto they have recourse, as unto the Oracle of life, the great determinator of Virginity, Conception, Fertility, and the Inscrutable infirmities of the whole Body. For as though there were a seminality in Urine, or that, like the Seed, it carried with it the Idea of every part, they foolishly conceive, we visibly behold therein the Anatomy of every particle, and can thereby indigitate their Diseases: And running into any demands, expect from us a sudden resolution in things, whereon the Devil of Delphos would demurr; and we know hath taken respite of some dayes to answer easier questions.

Places in
Venice and
Paris, where
Mountebanks
play their
pranks.

Saltimbancoes, Quacksalvers, and Charlatans, deceive them in lower degrees. Were Esop alive, the Piazza and Pont-Neuf could not but speak their fallacies; mean while there are too many, whose cries cannot conceal their mischief. For their Impostures are full of cruelty, and worse than any other; deluding not only unto pecuniary defraudations, but the irreparable deceit of death.

Astrologers, which pretend to be of Cabala with the Starrs (such I mean as abuse that worthy Enquiry) have not been wanting in their deceptions; who having won their belief unto principles whereof they make great doubt themselves, have made them believe that arbitrary events below, have necessary causes above; whereupon their credulities assent unto any Prognosticks, and daily swallow the Predictions of men, which, considering the independency of their causes, and contigency in their Events, are only in the prescience of God.

Fortune-tellers, Juglers, Geomancers, and the like incantatory Impostors, though commonly men of Inferiour rank, and from whom without Illumination they can expect no more than from themselves, do daily and professedly delude them. Unto whom (what is deplorable in Men and Christians) too many applying themselves, betwixt jest and earnest, betray the cause of Truth, and sensibly make up the legionary body of Error.

Statists and Politicians, unto whom *Ragione di Stato* is the first Considerable, as though it were their business to deceive the people, as a Maxim, do hold, that truth is to be concealed from

them; unto whom although they reveal the visible design, yet
do they commonly conceal the capital intention. And therefore
have they ever been the instruments of great designes, yet
seldom understood the true intention of any, accomplishing the
drifts of wiser heads, as inanimate and ignorant Agents, the
general design of the World; who though in some Latitude of
sense, and in a natural cognition perform their proper actions,
yet do they unknowingly concurr unto higher ends, and blindly
advance the great intention of Nature. Now how far they may
be kept in ignorance a greater example there is in the people of
Rome; who never knew the true and proper name of their own
City. For, beside that common appellation received by the Citizens, it had a proper and secret name concealed from them: *Cujus
alterum nomen discere secretis Ceremoniarum nefas habetur*, saith Plinie;
lest the name thereof being discovered unto their enemies, their
Penates and Patronal Gods might be called forth by charms and
incantations. For according unto the tradition of Magitians, the
tutelary Spirits will not remove at common appellations, but at
the proper names of things whereunto they are Protectors.

The people
of Rome,
why never
suffered to
know the
right name of
their City.

Thus having been deceived by themselves, and continually
deluded by others, they must needs be stuffed with Errors,
and even over-run with these inferiour falsities; whereunto
whosoever shall resign their reasons, either from the Root of
deceit in themselves, or inability to resist such trivial deceptions[3] from others, although their condition and fortunes may
place them many Spheres above the multitude, yet are they
still within the line of Vulgarity, and Democratical enemies of
truth.

CHAP. IV

*Of the nearer and more Immediate Causes of popular Errors, both in the
wiser and common sort, Misapprehension, Fallacy, or false deduction,
Credulity, Supinity, adherence unto Antiquity, Tradition and
Authority.*

THE first is a mistake, or a misconception of things, either
in their first apprehensions, or secondary relations. So
Eve mistook the Commandment, either from the immediate injunction of God, or from the secondary narration of

her Husband. So might the Disciples mistake our Saviour, in his answer unto Peter concerning the death of John, as is delivered, John 21: Peter *seeing* John *said unto* Jesus, *Lord, and what shall this man do?* Jesus *saith, If I will, that he tarry till I come, what is that unto thee? Then went this saying abroad among the brethren, that that Disciple should not die.* Thus began the conceit and

The belief of Centaures whence occasioned. opinion of the Centaures: that is, in the mistake of the first beholders, as is declared by Servius; when some young Thessalians on horseback were beheld afar off, while their horses watered, that is, while their heads, were depressed, they were conceived by the first Spectators, to be but one animal; and answerable hereunto have their pictures been drawn ever since.

And, as simple mistakes commonly beget fallacies, so men rest not in false apprehensions, without absurd and inconsequent deductions; from fallacious foundations and misapprehended mediums, erecting conclusions no way inferrible from their premises. Now the fallacys whereby men deceive others, and are deceived themselves, the Ancients have divided into Verbal and Real. Of the Verbal, and such as conclude from mistakes of the Word, although there be no less than six, yet are there but two thereof worthy our notation, and unto which the rest

Equivocation and Amphibologie, how they differ. may be referred; that is the fallacy of Equivocation and Amphibologie which conclude from the ambiguity of some one word, or the ambiguous Syntaxis of many put together. From this fallacy arose that calamitous Error of the Jews, misapprehending the Prophesies of their Messias, and expounding them always unto literal and temporal expectations. By this way many

Pythagoras his Allegorical precepts moralized. Errors crept in and perverted the Doctrin of Pythagoras, whilst men received his Precepts in a different sense from his intention; converting Metaphors into proprieties, and receiving as literal expressions, obscure and involved truths. Thus when he enjoyned his Disciples an abstinence from Beans, many conceived they were with severity debarred the use of that pulse; which notwithstanding could not be his meaning; for as Aristoxenus, who wrote his life averreth, he delighted much in that kind of food himself. But herein, as Plutarch observeth, he had no other intention than to dissuade men from Magistracy, or undertaking the publick offices of state; for by beans was the Magistrate elected in some parts of Greece; and, after his daies, we read in Thucydides, of the Council of the bean in Athens. The same word also in Greek doth signifie a Testicle, and hath been thought by some an injunction only of Continency, as Aul. Gellius hath expounded, and as Empedocles may also be interpreted: that is, *Testiculis miseri dextras subducite*; and might be the original intention of Pythagoras; as having a notable hint hereof in Beans, from the natural signature of the venereal organs of both Sexes. Again, his injunction is, not to harbour Swallows in our Houses: Whose advice notwithstanding we do not contemn, who daily admit and cherish them: For herein a caution is only implied, not to entertain ungrateful and thankless persons, which like the Swallow are no way commodious unto us; but having made use of our habitations, and served their own turns, forsake us. So he commands to deface the Print of a Cauldron in the ashes, after it hath boiled. Which strictly to observe were condemnable superstition: But hereby he covertly adviseth us not to persevere in anger; but after our choler hath boiled, to retain no impression thereof. In the like sense are to be received, when he adviseth his Disciples to give the right hand but to few, to put no viands in a Chamber-pot, not to pass over a Balance, not to rake up fire with a Sword, or piss against the Sun. Which ænigmatical deliveries comprehend useful verities, but being mistaken by literal Expositors at the first, they have been mis-understood by most since, and may be occasion of Error to Verbal capacities for ever.

πὰν δειλοὶ κυαμῶν ἀπὸ χεῖρας ἔχεσθε.

This fallacy in the first delusion Satan put upon Eve, and his whole tentation might be the same continued;[4] so when he said, *Ye shall not die*, that was, in his equivocation, ye shall not incurr a present death, or a destruction immediately ensuing your transgression. *Your eyes shall be opened*, that is, not to the enlargement of your knowledg, but discovery of your shame and proper confusion; *You shall know good and evil*, that is, you shall have knowledge of good by its privation, but cognisance of evil by sense and visible experience. And the same fallacy or way of deceit, so well succeeding in Paradise, he continued in his Oracles through all the World. Which had not men more warily understood, they might have performed many acts inconsistent with his intention. Brutus might have made haste with Tarquine to have kissed his own Mother. The Athenians might have built them woodden Walls, or doubled the Altar at Delphos.

The circle of this fallacy is very large; and herein may be comprised all Ironical mistakes for intended expressions receiving inverted significations; all deductions from Metaphors, Parables, Allegories, unto real and rigid interpretations. Whereby have risen not only popular Errors in Philosophy, but vulgar and sensless Heresies in Divinity; as will be evident unto any that shall examine their foundations, as they stand related by Epiphanius, Austin, or Prateolus.

De hæres-
ibus.   Other waies there are of deceit; which consist not in false apprehension of Words, that is, Verbal expressions or sentential significations, but fraudulent deductions, or inconsequent illations, from a false conception of things. Of these extradictionary and real fallacies, Aristotle and Logicians make in number six, but we observe that men are most commonly deceived by four thereof: those are, *Petitio principii*, *A dicto secundum quid ad dictum simpliciter*, *A non causa pro causa*; And, *fallacia consequentis*.

The first is, *Petitio principii*. Which fallacy is committed, when a question is made a medium, or we assume a medium as granted, whereof we remain as unsatisfied as of the question. Briefly, where that is assumed as a Principle to prove another thing, which is not conceded as true it self. By this fallacy was Eve deceived, when she took for granted, a false assertion of the Devil; *Ye shall not surely die; for God doth know that in the day ye shall eat thereof, your eyes shall be opened, and you shall be as Gods.* Which was but a bare affirmation of Satan, without proof or probable inducement, contrary unto the command of God, and former belief of her self. And this was the Logick of the Jews when they accused our Saviour unto Pilate; who demanding a reasonable impeachment, or the allegation of some crime worthy of Condemnation, they only replied, *If he had not been worthy of Death, we would not have brought Him before thee.* Wherein there was neither accusation of the person, nor satisfaction of the Judg; who well understood, a bare accusation was not presumption of guilt, and the clamours of the people no accusation at all. The same Fallacy is sometime used in the dispute between Job and his friends; they often taking that for granted which afterward he disproveth.

The second is, *A dicto secundum quid ad dictum simpliciter*,
when from that which is but true in a qualified sense, an
inconditional and absolute verity is inferred; transferring the
special consideration of things unto their general acceptions,
or concluding from their strict acception unto that without all
limitation. This fallacy men commit when they argue from a
particular to a general; as when we conclude the vices or qualities of a few upon a whole Nation. Or from a part unto the whole.
Thus the Devil argues with our Saviour: and by this, he would
perswade Him he might be secure, if he cast himself from the
Pinnacle: For, said he, it is written, *He shall give his Angels* Psal. 91.
charge concerning thee, and in their hands they shall bear thee up, lest
at any time thou dash thy foot against a stone. But this illation was
fallacious, leaving one part of the Text, *He shall keep thee in all*
thy wayes; that is, in the wayes of righteousness, and not of rash
attempts: so he urged a part for the whole, and inferred more
in the conclusion, than was contained in the premises. By the
same fallacy we proceed, when we conclude from the sign unto
the thing signified. By this incroachment, Idolatry first crept
in, men converting the symbolical use of Idols into their proper
Worship, and receiving the representation of things as the substance and thing it self. So the Statue of Belus at first erected in
his memory, was in after-times adored as a Divinity. And so   The Original
also in the Sacrament of the Eucharist, the Bread and Wine   of Idolatry.
which were but the signals or visible signs, were made the
things signified, and worshipped as the Body of Christ. And
hereby generally men are deceived that take things spoken
in some Latitude without any at all. Hereby the Jews were
deceived concerning the commandment of the Sabbath, accusing our Saviour for healing the sick, and his Disciples for pluck-
ing the ears of Corn upon that day. And by this deplorable
mistake they were deceived unto destruction, upon the assault
of Pompey the great, made upon that day; by whose superstitious observation they could not defend themselves, or perform
any labour whatever.

The third is, *A non causa pro causa*, when that is pretended   The Alcoran
for a cause which is not, or not in that sense which is inferred.   endures
Upon this consequence the law of Mahomet forbids the use of   neither Wine
Wine; and his Successors abolished Universities. By this also   nor Universities.

many Christians have condemned literature, misunderstanding the councel of Saint Paul, who adviseth no further than to beware of Philosophy. On this Foundation were built the conclusions of Southsayers in their Augurial, and Tripudiary divinations; collecting presages from voice or food of Birds, and conjoyning Events unto causes of no connection. Hereupon also are grounded the gross mistakes, in the cure of many diseases; not only from the last medicine and sympathetical Receipts, but Amulets, Charms, and all incantatory applications; deriving effects not only from inconcurring causes, but things devoid of all efficiency whatever.

The fourth is, the Fallacy of the Consequent; which if strictly taken, may be a fallacious illation in reference unto antecedency, or consequency; as to conclude from the position of the antecedent to the position of the consequent, or from the remotion of the consequent to the remotion of the antecedent. This is usually committed, when in connexed Propositions the Terms adhere contingently. This is frequent in Oratory illations; and thus the Pharisees, because He conversed with Publicans and Sinners, accused the holiness of Christ. But if this Fallacy be largely taken, it is committed in any vicious illation, offending the rules of good consequence; and so it may be very large, and comprehend all false illations against the setled Laws of Logick: But the most usual inconsequencies are from particulars, from negatives, and from affirmative conclusions in the second figure, wherein indeed offences are most frequent, and their discoveries not difficult.

CHAP. V

Of Credulity and Supinity

A THIRD cause of common Errors is the Credulity of men, that is, an easie assent to what is obtruded, or a believing at first ear, what is delivered by others. This is a weakness in the understanding, without examination assenting unto things, which from their Natures and Causes do carry no perswasion; whereby men often swallow falsities for truths,

CHAP. X

Of the last and common Promoter of false Opinions, the endeavours
of Satan

BUT beside the infirmities of humane Nature, the seed of
Error within our selves, and the several ways of delusion
from each other, there is an invisible Agent, and secret
promoter without us, whose activity is undiscerned, and plays
in the dark upon us; and that is the first contriver of Error, and
professed opposer of Truth, the Devil. For though permitted
unto his proper principles, Adam perhaps would have sinned
without the suggestion of Satan: and from the transgressive
infirmities of himself might have erred alone, as well as the
Angels before him: And although also there were no Devil at
all, yet there is now in our Natures a confessed sufficiency unto
corruption, and the frailty of our own Oeconomie, were able
to betray us out of Truth, yet wants there not another Agent,
who taking advantage hereof proceedeth to obscure the diviner
part, and efface all tract of its traduction. To attempt a particular of all his wiles, is too bold an Arithmetick for man: what
most considerably concerneth his popular and practised ways
of delusion, he first deceiveth mankind in five main points concerning God and himself.

And first his endeavours have ever been, and they cease not
yet to instill a belief in the mind of Man, there is no God at all.
And this he principally endeavours to establish in a direct and
literal apprehension; that is, that there is no such reality existent,
that the necessity of his entity dependeth upon ours, and is
but a Political Chymera; that the natural truth of God is an
artificial erection of Man, and the Creator himself but a subtile
invention of the Creature. Where he succeeds not thus high, he
labours to introduce a secondary and deductive Atheism; that
although men concede there is a God, yet should they deny his
providence. And therefore assertions have flown about, that he
intendeth only the care of the species or common natures, but
letteth loose the guard of individuals, and single existencies
therein: that he looks not below the Moon, but hath designed
the regiment of sublunary affairs unto inferiour deputations.

To promote which apprehensions, or empuzzel their due conceptions, he casteth in the notions of fate, destiny, fortune, chance, and necessity; terms commonly misconceived by vulgar heads, and their propriety sometime perverted by the wisest. Whereby extinguishing in minds the compensation of vertue and vice, the hope and fear of Heaven or Hell; they comply in their actions unto the drift of his delusions, and live like creatures without the capacity of either.

Now hereby he not onely undermineth the Base of Religion, and destroyeth the principle preambulous unto all belief; but puts upon us the remotest Error from Truth. For Atheism is the greatest falsity, and to affirm there is no God, the highest lie in Nature. And therefore strictly taken, some men will say his labour is in vain; For many there are, who cannot conceive there was ever any absolute Atheist; or such as could determine there was no God, without all check from himself, or contradiction from his other opinions. And therefore those few so called by elder times, might be the best of Pagans; suffering that name rather in relation to the gods of the Gentiles, then the true Creator of all. A conceit that cannot befal his greatest enemy, or him that would induce the same in us; who hath a sensible apprehension hereof, for he believeth with trembling. To speak yet more strictly and conformably unto some Opinions, no creature can wish thus much; nor can the Will which hath a power to run into velleities, and wishes of impossibilities, have any *utinam* of this. For to desire there were no God, were plainly to unwish their own being; which must needs be annihilated in the substraction of that essence which substantially supporteth them, and restrains them from regression into nothing. And if, as some contend, no creature can desire his own annihilation, that Nothing is not appetible, and not to be at all, is worse then to be in the miserablest condition of something; the Devil himself could not embrace that motion, nor would the enemy of God be freed by such a Redemption.

But coldly thriving in this design, as being repulsed by the principles of humanity, and the dictates of that production, which cannot deny its original, he fetcheth a wider circle; and when he cannot make men conceive there is no God at all, he endeavours to make them believe there is not one, but many:

wherein he hath been so successful with common heads, that
he hath led their belief thorow all the Works of Nature.

Now in this latter attempt, the subtilty of his circumvention,
hath indirectly obtained the former. For although to opinion
there be many gods, may seem an excess in Religion, and such
as cannot at all consist with Atheism, yet doth it deductively
and upon inference include the same, for Unity is the insepar-
able and essential attribute of Deity; and if there be more then
one God, it is no Atheism to say there is no God at all. And
herein though Socrates only suffered, yet were Plato and
Aristotle guilty of the same Truth; who demonstratively understanding the simplicity of perfection, and the indivisible condition of the first causator, it was not in the power of Earth, or
Areopagy of Hell to work them from it. For holding an Apodic-
tical* knowledge, and assured science of its verity, to perswade
their apprehensions unto a plurality of gods in the world, were
to make Euclide believe there were more then one Center in a
Circle, or one right Angle in a Triangle; which were indeed a
fruitless attempt, and inferreth absurdities beyond the evasion
of Hell. For though Mechanick and vulgar heads ascend not
unto such comprehensions, who live not commonly unto half
the advantage of their principles; yet did they not escape the
eye of wiser Minerva's, and such as made good the genealogie
of Jupiter's brains; who although they had divers stiles for God,
yet under many appellations acknowledged one divinity: rather
conceiving thereby the evidence or acts of his power in several
ways and places, then a multiplication of Essence, or real
distraction of unity in any one.

Again, To render our errors more monstrous (and what unto
miracle sets forth the patience of God,) he hath endeavoured to
make the world believe, that he was God himself; and failing
of his first attempt to be but like the highest in Heaven, he
hath obtained with men to be the same on Earth. And hath
accordingly assumed the annexes of Divinity, and the preroga-
tives of the Creator, drawing into practice the operation of
miracles, and the prescience of things to come. Thus hath he
in a specious way wrought cures upon the sick: played over the
wondrous acts of Prophets, and counterfeited many miracles
of Christ and his Apostles. Thus hath he openly contended with

Areopagus
the severe
Court of
Athens.

* Demon-
strative.

God, and to this effect his insolency was not ashamed to play a solemn prize with Moses; wherein although his performance were very specious, and beyond the common apprehension of any power below a Deity; yet was it not such as could make good his Omnipotency. For he was wholly confounded in the conversion of dust into lice. An act Philosophy can scarce deny to be above the power of Nature, nor upon a requisite predisposition beyond the efficacy of the Sun. Wherein notwithstanding the head of the old Serpent was confessedly too weak for Moses' hand, and the arm of his Magicians too short for the finger of God.

Thus hath he also made men believe that he can raise the dead, that he hath the key of life and death, and a prerogative above that principle which makes no regression from privations. The Stoicks that opinioned the souls of wise men dwelt about the Moon, and those of fools wandred about the Earth, advantaged the conceit of this effect; wherein the Epicureans, who held that death was nothing, nor nothing after death, must contradict their principles to be deceived. Nor could the Pythagorian or such as maintained the transmigration of souls give easie admittance hereto: for holding that separated souls successively supplied other bodies, they could hardly allow the raising of souls from other worlds, which at the same time, they

The Author's
opinion,
touching
Necromancy
and appari-
tions of the
spirits of men
departed.

conceived conjoyned unto bodies in this. More inconsistent with these Opinions, is the Error of Christians, who holding the dead do rest in the Lord, do yet believe they are at the lure of the Devil; that he who is in bonds himself commandeth the fetters of the dead, and dwelling in the bottomless lake, the blessed from Abraham's bosome, that can believe the real resurrection of Samuel: or that there is any thing but delusion in the practice of Necromancy* and popular raising of Ghosts.

* Divination
by the dead.

He hath moreover endeavoured the opinion of Deity, by the delusion of Dreams, and the discovery of things to come in sleep, above the prescience of our waked senses. In this expectation he perswaded the credulity of elder times to take up their lodging before his temple, in skins of their own sacrifices: till his reservedness had contrived answers, whose accomplishments were in his power, or not beyond his presagement. Which way, although it hath pleased Almighty God, sometimes to reveal

himself, yet was the proceeding very different. For the revelations of Heaven are conveyed by new impressions, and the
immediate illumination of the soul, whereas the deceiving spirit,
by concitation of humours, produceth his conceited phantasms,
or by compounding the species already residing, doth make up
words which mentally speak his intentions.

But above all he most advanced his Deity in the solemn
practice of Oracles, wherein in several parts of the World, he
publikely professed his Divinity; but how short they flew of
that spirit, whose omniscience they would resemble, their weakness sufficiently declared. What jugling there was therein, the
Orator plainly confessed, who being good at the same game
himself, could say that Pythia Philippised. Who can but laugh
at the carriage of Ammon unto Alexander, who addressing unto
him as a god, was made to believe, he was a god himself? How
openly did he betray his Indivinity unto Crœsus, who being
ruined by his Amphibology, and expostulating with him for so
ungrateful a deceit, received no higher answer then the excuse
of his impotency upon the contradiction of fate, and the setled
law of powers beyond his power to controle! What more then
sublunary directions, or such as might proceed from the Oracle
of humane Reason, was in his advice unto the Spartans in the
time of a great Plague; when for the cessation thereof, he wisht
them to have recourse unto a Fawn, that is in open terms, unto
one Nebrus, a good Physitian of those days? From no diviner a
spirit came his reply unto Caracalla, who requiring a remedy
for his gout, received no other counsel then to refrain cold
drink; which was but a dietetical caution, and such as without
a journey unto Æsculapius, culinary prescription and kitchin
Aphorisms might have afforded at home. Nor surely if any truth
there were therein, of more then natural activity was his counsel
unto Democritus; when for the Falling sickness he commended
the Maggot in a Goat's head. For many things secret are true:
sympathies and antipathies are safely authentick unto us, who
ignorant of their causes may yet acknowledge their effects.
Beside, being a natural Magician he may perform many acts in
ways above our knowledge, though not transcending our natural
power, when our knowledge shall direct it. Part hereof hath
been discovered by himself, and some by humane indagation:

which though magnified as fresh inventions unto us, are stale unto his cognition. I hardly believe he hath from elder times unknown the verticity of the Loadstone; surely his perspicacity discerned it to respect the North, when ours beheld it indeterminately. Many secrets there are in Nature of difficult discovery unto man, of easie knowledge unto Satan: whereof some his vain glory cannot conceal, others his envy will not discover.

Again, Such is the mysterie of his delusion, that although he labour to make us believe that he is God, and supremest nature whatsoever, yet would he also perswade our beliefs, that he is less then Angels or men; and his condition not onely subjected unto rational powers, but the actions of things which have no efficacy on our selves. Thus hath he inveigled no small part of the world into a credulity of artificial Magick: That there is an Art, which without compact commandeth the powers of Hell; whence some have delivered the polity of spirits, and left an account even to their Provincial Dominions: that they stand in awe of Charms, Spels, and Conjurations; that he is afraid of letters and characters, of notes and dashes, which set together do signifie nothing, not only in the dictionary of man, but the subtiler vocabulary of Satan. That there is any power in Bitumen, Pitch, or Brimstone, to purifie the air from his uncleanness; that any vertue there is in Hipericon to make good the name of *fuga Dæmonis*,★ any such Magick as is ascribed unto the Root Baaras by Josephus, or Cynospastus by Ælianus, it is not easie to believe; nor is it naturally made out what is delivered of Tobias, that by the fume of a Fish's liver, he put to flight Asmodeus. That they are afraid of the pentangle of Solomon,★ though so set forth with the body of man, as to touch and point out the five places wherein our Saviour was wounded, I know not how to assent. If perhaps he hath fled from holy Water, if he cares not to hear the sound of Tetragrammaton,★ if his eye delight not in the sign of the Cross; and that sometimes he will seem to be charmed with words of holy Scripture, and to flie from the letter and dead verbality, who must onely start at the life and animated interiors thereof: It may be feared they are but Parthian flights, Ambuscado retreats, and elusory tergiversations: Whereby to confirm our credulities, he will

★ St. John's wort, so called by Magicians.

★ 3 triangles intersected and made of five lines.

★ Implying Iehovah, which in Hebrew consisteth of four letters.

comply with the opinion of such powers, which in themselves have no activities. Whereof having once begot in our minds an assured dependance, he makes us relie on powers which he but precariously obeys; and to desert those true and only charms which Hell cannot withstand.

Lastly, To lead us farther into darkness, and quite to lose us in this maze of Error, he would make men believe there is no such creature as himself: and that he is not only subject unto inferiour creatures, but in the rank of nothing. Insinuating into men's minds there is no Devil at all, and contriveth accordingly, many ways to conceal or indubitate his existency. Wherein beside that, he annihilates the blessed Angels and Spirits in the rank of his Creation; he begets a security of himself, and a careless eye unto the last remunerations. And therefore hereto he inveigleth, not only Sadduces and such as retain unto the Church of God: but is also content that Epicurus, Democritus, or any Heathen should hold the same. And to this effect he maketh men believe that apparitions, and such as confirm his existence are either deceptions of sight, or melancholly depravements of phansie. Thus when he had not onely appeared but spake unto Brutus; Cassius the Epicurian was ready at hand to perswade him, it was but a mistake in his weary imagination, and that indeed there were no such realities in nature. Thus he endeavours to propagate the unbelief of Witches, whose concession infers his co-existency; by this means also he advanceth the opinion of total death, and staggereth the immortality of the soul; for, such as deny there are spirits subsistent without bodies, will with more difficulty affirm the separated existence of their own.

Now to induce and bring about these falsities, he hath laboured to destroy the evidence of Truth, that is the revealed verity and written Word of God. To which intent he hath obtained with some to repudiate the Books of Moses, others those of the Prophets, and some both: to deny the Gospel and authentick Histories of Christ; to reject that of John, and to receive that of Judas; to disallow all, and erect another of Thomas. And when neither their corruption by Valentinus and Arrius, their mutilation by Marcion, Manes, and Ebion could satisfie his design, he attempted the ruine and total destruction thereof; as he sedulously endeavoured, by the power and subtilty of Julian, Maximinus, and Dioclesian.

But the longevity of that piece, which hath so long escaped the common fate, and the providence of that Spirit, which ever waketh over it, may at last discourage such attempts; and if not make doubtful its Mortality, at least indubitably declare; this is a stone too big for Satan's mouth, and a bit indeed Oblivion cannot swallow.

And thus how strangely he possesseth us with Errors may clearly be observed, deluding us into contradictory and inconsistent falsities; whilest he would make us believe, That there is no God. That there are many. That he himself is God. That he is less then Angels or Men. That he is nothing at all.

Nor hath he onely by these wiles depraved the conception of the Creator, but with such Riddles hath also entangled the Nature of our Redeemer. Some denying his Humanity, and that he was one of the Angels, as Ebion; that the Father and Son were but one person, as Sabellius. That his body was phantastical, as Manes, Basilides, Priscillian, Jovinianus; that he only passed through Mary, as Utyches and Valentinus. Some denying his Divinity; that he was begotten of humane principles, and the seminal Son of Joseph, as Carpocras, Symmachus, Photinus: that he was Seth the Son of Adam, as the Sethians: that he was less then Angels, as Cherinthus: that he was inferiour unto Melchisedec, as Theodotus: that he was not God, but God dwelt in him, as Nicholaus: and some embroyled them both. So did they which converted the Trinity into a Quaternity, and affirmed two persons in Christ, as Paulus Samosatenus: that held he was Man without a Soul, and that the Word performed that office in him, as Apollinaris: that he was both Son and Father, as Montanus: that Jesus suffered, but Christ remained impatible, as Cherinthus. Thus he endeavours to entangle Truths: And when he cannot possibly destroy its substance, he cunningly confounds its apprehensions; that from the inconsistent and contrary determinations thereof, collective impieties, and hopeful conclusions may arise, there's no such thing at all.

CHAP. VI

Of sundry Tenets concerning Vegetables or Plants,
which examined, prove either false or dubious.

MANY Mola's and false conceptions there are of Mandrakes, the first from great Antiquity, conceiveth the Root thereof resembleth the shape of Man; which is a conceit not to be made out by ordinary inspection, or any other eyes, then such as regarding the Clouds, behold them in shapes conformable to pre-apprehensions.

Now whatever encouraged the first invention, there have not been wanting many ways of its promotion. The first a Catachrestical and far derived similitude it holds with Man; that is, in a bifurcation or division of the Root into two parts, which some are content to call Thighs; whereas notwithstanding they are oft-times three, and when but two, commonly so complicated and crossed, that men for this deceit are fain to effect their design in other plants; And as fair a resemblance is often found in Carrots, Parsnips, Briony, and many others. There are, I confess, divers Plants which carry about them not only the shape of parts, but also of whole Animals, but surely not all thereof, unto whom this conformity is imputed. Whoever shall peruse the signatures of Crollius, or rather the *Phytognomy* of Porta, and strictly observe how vegetable Realities are commonly forced into Animal Representations, may easily perceive in very many, the semblance is but postulatory, and must have a more assimilating phansie then mine to make good many thereof.

Illiterate heads have been led on by the name, which in the first syllable expresseth its Representation; but others have better observed the Laws of Etymology, and deduced it from a word of the same language, because it delighteth to grow in obscure and shady places; which derivation, although we shall not stand to maintain, yet the other seemeth answerable unto the Etymologies of many Authors, who often confound such nominal Notations. Not to enquire beyond our own profession, the Latine Physitians which most adhered unto the Arabick way, have often failed herein; particularly Valescus de Tarranta,

a received Physitian, in whose *Philonium* or *Medical practice* these may be observed; *Diarhea*, saith he, *Quia pluries venit in die. Herisepela, quasi hærens pilis. Emorrhois, ab emach, sanguis, & morrhois, quod est cadere. Lithargia à Litos, quod est oblivio, & Targus, morbus. Scotomia à Scotus, quod est videre, & mias, musca. Opthalmia ab opus Græce, quod est succus, & Talmon, quod est occulus. Paralisis, quasi læsio partis. Fistula à fos sonus, & stolon, quod est emissio, quasi emissio soni vel vocis.* Which are derivations as strange indeed as the other, and hardly to be parallel'd elsewhere; confirming not only the words of one language with another, but creating such as were never yet in any.

The received distinction and common Notation by Sexes, hath also promoted the conceit; for true it is, that Herbalists from ancient times, have thus distinguished them; naming that the Male, whose leaves are lighter, and Fruit and Apples rounder; but this is properly no generative division, but rather some note of distinction in colour, figure or operation. For though Empedocles affirm, there is a mixt, and undivided Sex

in Vegetables; and Scaliger upon Aristotle, doth favourably explain that opinion; yet will it not consist with the common and ordinary acception, nor yet with Aristotle's definition. For if that be Male which generates in another, that Female which procreates in it self; if it be understood of Sexes conjoined, all Plants are Female; and if of disjoined and congressive generation, there is no Male or Female in them at all.

But the Atlas or main Axis which supported this opinion, was dayly experience, and the visible testimony of sense. For many there are in several parts of Europe, who carry about Roots and sell them unto ignorant people, which handsomely make out the shape of Man or Woman. But these are not productions of Nature, but contrivances of Art, as divers have noted, and Mathiolus plainly detected, who learned this way of Trumpery from a vagabond cheater lying under his cure for the French disease. His words are these, and may determine the point, *Sed profecto vanum & fabulosum, &c.* But this is vain and fabulous, which ignorant people, and simple women believe; for the roots which are carried about by impostors to deceive unfruitful women, are made of the roots of Canes, Briony and other plants: for in these yet fresh and virent, they carve out the figures of men and women, first sticking therein the grains of Barley or Millet, where they intend the hair should grow; then bury them in sand until the grains shoot forth their roots, which at the longest will happen in twenty days; they afterward clip and trim those tender strings in the fashion of beards and other hairy tegument. All which like other impostures once discovered is easily effected, and in the root of white Briony may be practised every spring.

What is therefore delivered in favour thereof, by Authors ancient or modern, must have its root in tradition, imposture, far derived similitude, or casual and rare contingency. So may we admit of the Epithet of Pythagoras, who calls it *Anthropomorphus*; and that of Columella, who terms it *Semihomo*; more appliable unto the Man-*Orchis*, whose flower represents a Man. Thus is Albertus to be received when he affirmeth, that Mandrakes represent man-kind with the distinction of either Sex. Under these restrictions may those Authors be admitted, which for this opinion are introduced by Drusius; nor shall we need to question the monstrous root of Briony described in Aldrovandus.[21]

Orchis Anthropomorphus cujus Icon in Kircheri Magia parastatica.

*De mandragora.
De monstris.*

The second assertion concerneth its production, That it naturally groweth under Gallowses and places of execution, arising from fat or urine that drops from the body of the dead; a story somewhat agreeable unto the fable of the Serpent's teeth sowed in the earth by Cadmus; or rather the birth of Orion from the urine of Jupiter, Mercury, and Neptune. Now this opinion seems grounded on the former, that is, a conceived similitude it hath with man; and therefore from him in some way they would make out its production: Which conceit is

not only erroneous in the foundation, but injurious unto Philosophy in the superstruction. Making putrifactive generations, correspondent unto seminal productions, and conceiving
in equivocal effects an univocal conformity unto the efficient.
Which is so far from being verified of animals in their corruptive
mutations into Plants, that they maintain not this similitude in
their nearer translation into animals. So when the Oxe cor-
rupteth into Bees, or the Horse into Hornets, they come not
forth in the image of their originals. So the corrupt and excre-
mentous humours in man are animated into Lice; and we may
observe, that Hogs, Sheep, Goats, Hawks, Hens and others,
have one peculiar and proper kind of vermine; not resembling
themselves according to seminal conditions, yet carrying a
setled and confined habitude unto their corruptive originals.
And therefore come not forth in generations erratical, or different from each other: but seem specifically and in regular
shapes to attend the corruption of their bodies, as do more
perfect conceptions, the rule of seminal productions.

Generations equivocal, are yet commonly regular and of a determinate form or species.

The third affirmeth the roots of Mandrakes do make a noise,
or give a shriek upon eradication; which is indeed ridiculous,
and false below confute; arising perhaps from a small and stridu-
lous noise, which being firmly rooted, it maketh upon divulsion
of parts. A slender foundation for such a vast conception: for
such a noise we sometime observe in other Plants, in Parsenips,
Liquorish, Eringium, Flags, and others.

The last concerneth the danger ensuing, That there follows
an hazard of life to them that pull it up, that some evil fate
pursues them, and they live not very long after. Therefore the
attempt hereof among the Ancients, was not in ordinary way;
but as Pliny informeth, when they intended to take up the root
of this Plant, they took the wind thereof, and with a sword
describing three circles about it, they digged it up, looking
toward the west. A conceit not only injurious unto truth, and
confutable by daily experience, but somewhat derogatory unto
the providence of God; that is, not only to impose so destructive
a quality on any Plant, but to conceive a Vegetable, whose parts
are useful unto many, should in the only taking up prove mortal
unto any. To think he suffereth the poison of Nubia to be
gathered, *Napellus*, Aconite, and *Thora*, to be eradicated, yet this

Granum Nubiæ.

not to be moved. That he permitteth Arsenick and mineral poisons to be forced from the bowels of the Earth, yet not this from the surface thereof. This were to introduce a second forbidden fruit, and inhance the first malediction, making it not only mortal for Adam to taste the one, but capital unto his posterity to eradicate or dig up the other.

Now what begot, at least promoted so strange conceptions, might be the magical opinion hereof; this being conceived the Plant so much in use with Circe, and therefore named *Circea*, as Dioscorides and Theophrastus have delivered, which being the eminent Sorcerers of elder story, and by the magick of simples believed to have wrought many wonders: some men were apt to invent, others to believe any tradition or magical promise thereof.

Analogous relations concerning other plants, and such as are of near affinity unto this, have made its currant smooth, and pass more easily among us. For the same effect is also delivered by Josephus, concerning the root *Baaras*; by Ælian of Cynospastus; and we read in Homer the very same opinion concerning Moly,

> Μῶλυ δέ μιν καλέουσι θεοὶ, χαλεπὸν δέ τ' ὀρύσσειν ,
> 'Ανδράσι γε θνητοῖσι, θεοὶ δέ τε πάντα δύνανται.

The Gods it Moly call, whose Root to dig away,
Is dangerous unto Man; but Gods, they all things may.

Now parallels or like relations alternately relieve each other, when neither will pass asunder, yet are they plausible together; their mutual concurrences supporting their solitary instabilities.

Signaturists have somewhat advanced it; who seldom omitting what Ancients delivered; drawing into inference received distinction of sex, not willing to examine its humane resemblance; and placing it in the form of strange and magical simples, have made men suspect there was more therein, then ordinary practice allowed; and so became apt to embrace whatever they heard or read conformable unto such conceptions.

Lastly, The conceit promoteth it self: for concerning an effect whose trial must cost so dear, it fortifies it self in that invention; and few there are whose experiment it need to fear. For (what is most contemptible) although not only the reason of any head, but experience of every hand may well convict it, yet will it not by divers be rejected; for prepossessed heads will ever doubt it, and timorous beliefs will never dare to trie it. So these Traditions how low and ridiculous soever, will find suspition in some, doubt in others, and serve as tests or trials of Melancholy and superstitious tempers for ever.

2. That Cinamon, Ginger, Clove, Mace, and Nutmeg, are but the several parts and fruits of the same tree, is the common belief of those which daily use them. Whereof to speak distinctly, Ginger is the root of neither Tree nor Shrub, but of an herbaceous Plant, resembling the Water Flower-De-luce, as Garcias first described; or rather the common Reed, as Lobelius since affirmed. Very common in many parts of India, growing either from Root or Seed, which in December and January they take up, and gently dried, roll it up in earth, whereby occluding the pores, they conserve the natural humidity, and so prevent corruption.

Cinamon is the inward bark of a Cinamon Tree, whereof the best is brought from Zeilan; this freed from the outward bark, and exposed unto the Sun, contracts into those folds wherein we commonly receive it. If it have not a sufficient insolation it looketh pale, and attains not its laudable colour; if it be sunned too long, it suffereth a torrefaction, and descendeth somewhat below it.

Clove seems to be either the rudiment of a fruit, or the fruit it self growing upon the Clove tree, to be found but in few Countries. The most commendable is that of the Isles of Molucca; it is first white, afterward green, which beaten down, and dried in the Sun, becometh black, and in the complexion we receive it.

Nutmeg is the fruit of a Tree differing from all these, and as Garcias describeth it, somewhat like a Peach; growing in divers places, but fructifying in the Isle of Banda. The fruit hereof consisteth of four parts; the first or outward part is a thick and carnous covering like that of a Wal-nut. The second a dry and flosculous coat, commonly called Mace. The third a harder tegument or shell, which lieth under the Mace. The fourth a Kernel included in the shell, which is the same we call Nutmeg. All which both in their parts and order of disposure, are easily discerned in those fruits, which are brought in preserves unto us.

Now if because Mace and Nutmegs proceed from one Tree, the rest must bear them company; or because they are all from the East Indies, they are all from one Plant: the Inference is precipitous, nor will there such a Plant be found in the Herbal of Nature.

3. That *Viscus Arboreus* or Misseltoe is bred upon Trees, from seeds which Birds, especially Thrushes and Ring-doves let fall thereon, was the Creed of the Ancients, and is still believed among us, is the account of its production, set down by Pliny, delivered by Virgil, and subscribed by many more. If so, some reason must be assigned, why it groweth onely upon certain Trees, and not upon many whereon these Birds do light. For as Exotick observers deliver, it groweth upon Almond-trees, Chesnut, Apples, Oaks, and Pine-trees. As we observe in England very commonly upon Apple, Crabs, and White-thorn; sometimes upon Sallow, Hazel, and Oak: rarely upon Ash, Lime-tree, and Maple; never, that I could observe, upon Holly, Elm, and many more. Why it groweth not in all Countries and places where these Birds are found; for so Brassavolus affirmeth, it is not to be found in the Territory of Ferrara, and was fain to supply himself from other parts of Italy. Why if it ariseth from a seed, if sown it will not grow again, as Pliny affirmeth, and as by setting the Berries thereof, we have in vain attempted its production; why if it cometh from seed that falleth upon the tree, it groweth often downwards, and puts forth under the bough, where seed can neither fall nor yet remain. Hereof beside some others, the Lord Verulam hath taken notice. And they surely speak probably who make it an arboreous excrescence, or rather super-plant, bred of a viscous and super-fluous sap which the tree it self cannot assimilate. And there- What the Misseltoe in some Trees is. fore sprouteth not forth in boughs and surcles of the same shape, and similary unto the Tree that beareth it; but in a different form, and secondary unto its specifical intention, wherein once failing, another form succeedeth: and in the first place that of Misseltoe, in Plants and Trees disposed to its production. And therefore also where ever it groweth, it is of constant shape, and maintains a regular figure; like other supercrescences, and such as living upon the stock of others, are termed parasitical Plants, as Polypody, Moss, the smaller Capillaries, and many more: So

that several regions produce several Misseltoes; India one, America another, according to the law and rule of their degenerations.

Now what begot this conceit, might be the enlargement of some part of truth contained in its story. For certain it is, that some Birds do feed upon the berries of this Vegetable, and we 'Ιξρβόρος. meet in Aristotle with one kind of Thrush called the Missel Thrush, or feeder upon Misseltoe. But that which hath most promoted it, is a received proverb, *Turdus sibi malum cacat*; appliable unto such men as are authors of their own misfortune. For according unto ancient tradition and Plinie's relation, the Bird not able to digest the fruit whereon she feedeth; from her inconverted muting ariseth this Plant, of the Berries whereof Birdlime is made, wherewith she is after entangled. But although Proverbs be popular principles, yet is not all true that is proverbial; and in many thereof, there being one thing delivered, and another intended; though the verbal expression be false, the Proverb is true enough in the verity of its intention.

Paganish superstition about the Misseltoe of the Oak. As for the Magical vertues in this Plant, and conceived efficacy unto veneficial intentions, it seemeth a Pagan relique derived from the ancient Druides, the great admirers of the Oak, especially the Misseltoe that grew thereon; which according unto the particular of Pliny, they gathered with great solemnity. For after sacrifice the Priest in a white garment ascended the tree, cut down the Misseltoe with a golden hook, and received it in a white coat; the vertue whereof was to resist all poisons, and make fruitful any that used it. Vertues not expected from Classical practice; and did they fully answer their promise which are so commended, in Epileptical intentions, we would abate these qualities. Country practice hath added another, to provoke the after-birth, and in that case the decoction is given unto Cows. That the Berries are poison as some conceive, we are so far from averring, that we have safely given them inwardly, and can confirm the experiment of Brassavolus, that they have some purgative quality.

4. The Rose of Jericho, that flourishes every year just about Christmas Eve, is famous in Christian reports; which notwithstanding we have some reason to doubt, and are plainly informed

by Bellonius, it is but a Monastical imposture, as he hath delivered in his observations, concerning the Plants in Jericho. That which promoted the conceit or perhaps begot its continuance, was a propriety in this Plant. For though it be dry, yet will it upon imbibition of moisture dilate its leaves, and explicate its flowers contracted, and seemingly dried up. And this is to be effected not only in the Plant yet growing, but in some manner also in that which is brought exuccous and dry unto us. Which quality being observed, the subtilty of contrivers did commonly play this shew upon the Eve of our Saviour's Nativity, when by drying the Plant again, it closed the next day, and so pretended a double mystery: referring unto the opening and closing of the womb of Mary.

There wanted not a specious confirmation from a text in Ecclesiasticus, *Quasi palma exaltata sum in Cades, & quasi plantatio Rosæ in Jericho:* I was exalted like a Palm-tree in Engaddi, and as a Rose in Jericho. The sound whereof in common ears, begat an extraordinary opinion of the Rose of that denomination. But herein there seemeth a mistake: for by the Rose in the Text, is implied the true and proper Rose, as first the Greek, and ours accordingly rendreth it. But that which passeth under this name, and by us is commonly called the Rose of Jericho, is properly no Rose, but a small thorny shrub or kind of Heath, bearing little white flowers, far differing from the Rose; whereof Bellonius, a very inquisitive Herbalist, could not find any in his travels thorow Jericho. A Plant so unlike a Rose, it hath been mistaken by some good Simplist for *Amomum*; which truly understood is so unlike a Rose, that as Dioscorides delivers, the flowers thereof are like the white Violet, and its leaves resemble Briony.

Suitable unto this relation almost in all points is that of the Thorn at Glassenbury, and perhaps the daughter hereof; herein our endeavours as yet have not attained satisfaction, and cannot therefore enlarge. Thus much in general we may observe, that strange effects, are naturally taken for miracles by weaker heads, and artificially improved to that apprehension by wiser. Certainly many precocious Trees, and such as spring in the Winter, may be found in most parts of Europe, and divers also in England. For most Trees do begin to sprout in the Fall of the

Cap. 24.
Φύτα τοῦ
ῥόδου.

Such a Thorn there is in Parham Park in Suffolk, and elsewhere.

leaf or Autumn, and if not kept back by cold and outward causes, would leaf about the Solstice. Now if it happen that any be so strongly constituted, as to make this good against the power of Winter, they may produce their leaves or blossoms in that season. And perform that in some singles, which is observable in whole kinds; as in Ivy, which blossoms and bears at least twice a year, and once in the Winter; as also in Furz, which flowereth in that season.

5. That *ferrum Equinum*, or *Sferra Cavallo* hath a vertue attractive of Iron, a power to break locks, and draw off the shoes of a Horse that passeth over it: whether you take it for one kind of *Securidaca*, or will also take in *Lunaria*, we know it to be false: and cannot but wonder at Mathiolus, who upon a parallel in Pliny was staggered into suspension. Who notwithstanding in the imputed vertue to open things, close and shut up, could laugh himself at that promise from the herb *Æthiopis* or Æthiopian mullen; and condemn the judgment of Scipio, who having such a picklock, would spend so many years in battering the Gates of Carthage. Which strange and Magical conceit, seems to have no deeper root in reason, then the figure of its seed; for therein indeed it somewhat resembles a Horse-shoe; which notwithstanding Baptista Porta hath thought too low a signification, and raised the same unto a Lunary representation.

6. That Bayes will protect from the mischief of Lightning and Thunder, is a quality ascribed thereto, common with the Fig-tree, Eagle, and skin of a Seal. Against so famous a quality, Vicomercatus produceth experiment of a Bay-tree blasted in Italy. And therefore although Tiberius for this intent, did wear a Lawrel upon his Temples; yet did Augustus take a more probable course, who fled under arches and hollow vaults for protection. And though Porta conceive, because in a streperous eruption, it riseth against fire, it doth therefore resist lightning, yet is that no emboldning Illation. And if we consider the three-fold effect of Jupiter's Trisulk, to burn, discuss, and terebrate; and if that be true which is commonly delivered, that it will melt the blade, yet pass the scabbard; kill the child, yet spare the mother; dry up the wine, yet leave the hogshead entire: though it favour the amulet, it may not spare us; it will be unsure to rely on any preservative, 'tis no security to be dipped

in Styx, or clad in the armour of Ceneus. Now that Beer, Wine, and other Liquors, are spoiled with lightning and thunder, we conceive it proceeds not onely from noise and concussion of the air, but also noxious spirits, which mingle therewith, and draw them to corruption; whereby they become not only dead themselves, but sometime deadly unto others, as that which Seneca mentioneth; whereof whosoever drank, either lost his life, or else his wits upon it.

BOOK II
Chapter 6
How Beer and Wine come to be spoiled by Lightning.

7. It hath much deceived the hope of good fellows, what is commonly expected of bitter Almonds, and though in Plutarch confirmed from the practice of Claudius his Physitian, that Antidote against ebriety hath commonly failed. Surely men much versed in the practice do err in the theory of inebriation; conceiving in that disturbance the brain doth only suffer from exhalations and vaporous ascensions from the stomack, which fat and oyly substances may suppress. Whereas the prevalent intoxication is from the spirits of drink dispersed into the veins and arteries; from whence by common conveyances they creep into the brain, insinuate into its ventricles, and beget those vertigoes, accompanying that perversion. And therefore the same effect may be produced by a Glister, the Head may be intoxicated by a medicine at the Heel. So the poisonous bites of Serpents, although on parts at distance from the head, yet having entered the veins, disturb the animal faculties, and produce the effects of drink, or poison swallowed. And so as the Head may be disturbed by the skin, it may the same way be relieved; as is observable in balneations, washings, and fomentations, either of the whole body, or of that part alone.

How drinks intoxicate or overcome men.

THE THIRD BOOK

Of divers popular and received Tenets concerning Animals,
which examined, prove either false or dubious

CHAP. I

Of the Elephant

THE first shall be of the Elephant, whereof there generally passeth an opinion it hath no joints; and this absurdity is seconded with another, that being unable to lie down, it sleepeth against a Tree; which the Hunters observing, do saw it almost asunder; whereon the Beast relying, by the fall of the Tree, falls also down it self, and is able to rise no more. Which conceit is not the daughter of later times, but an old and gray-headed error, even in the days of Aristotle, as he delivereth in his Book, *De incessu Animalium*, and stands successively related by several other Authors: by Diodorus Siculus, Strabo, Ambrose, Cassiodore, Solinus, and many more. Now herein methinks men much forget themselves, not well considering the absurdity of such assertions.

For first, they affirm it hath no joints, and yet concede it walks and moves about; whereby they conceive there may be a progression or advancement made in Motion without inflexion How pro-
gression is
made in
animals. of parts. Now all progression or Animals' locomotion being (as Aristotle teacheth) performed *tractu & pulsu*; that is, by drawing on, or impelling forward some part which was before in station, or at quiet; where there are no joints or flexures, neither can there be these actions. And this is true, not onely in Quadrupedes, Volatils, and Fishes, which have distinct and prominent Organs of Motion, Legs, Wings, and Fins; but in such also as perform their progression by the Trunk as Serpents, Worms, and Leeches. Whereof though some want bones, and all extended

articulations, yet have they arthritical Analogies, and by the
motion of fibrous and musculous parts, are able to make progression. Which to conceive in bodies inflexible, and without
all protrusion of parts, were to expect a Race from Hercules his
pillars; or hope to behold the effects of Orpheus his Harp, when
trees found joints, and danced after his Musick.

BOOK III
Chapter I
Joint-like
parts.

Again, While men conceive they never lie down, and enjoy
not the position of rest, ordained unto all pedestrious Animals,
hereby they imagine (what Reason cannot conceive) that an
Animal of the vastest dimension and longest duration, should
live in a continual motion, without that alternity and vicissitude
of rest whereby all others continue; and yet must thus much
come to pass, if we opinion they lye not down and enjoy no
decumbence at all. For station is properly no rest, but one kind
of motion, relating unto that which Physitians (from Galen) do
name extensive or tonical; that is, an extension of the muscles
and organs of motion maintaining the body at length or in its
proper figure.

Extensive or
Tonical Mo-
tion, what?

Wherein although it seem to be unmoved, it is not without
all Motion; for in this position the muscles are sensibly extended,
and labour to support the body; which permitted unto its
proper gravity, would suddenly subside and fall unto the earth;
as it happeneth in sleep, diseases, and death. From which occult
action and invisible motion of the muscles in station (as Galen
declareth) proceed more offensive lassitudes then from ambula-
tion. And therefore the Tyranny of some have tormented men
with long and enforced station, and though Ixion and Sisiphus
which always moved, do seem to have the hardest measure;
yet was not Titius favoured, that lay extended upon Caucasus;
and Tantalus suffered somewhat more then thirst, that stood
perpetually in Hell. Thus Mercurialis in his *Gymnasticks* justly
makes standing one kind of exercise: and Galen when we lie
down, commends unto us middle figures, that is, not to lye
directly, or at length, but somewhat inflected, that the muscles
may be at rest; for such as he termeth *Hypobolemaioi* or figures
of excess, either shrinking up or stretching out, are wearisome
positions, and such as perturb the quiet of those parts. Now
various parts do variously discover these indolent and quiet
positions, some in right lines, as the wrists: some at right angles,

as the cubit: others at oblique angles, as the fingers and the
knees: all resting satisfied in postures of moderation, and none
enduring the extremity of flexure or extension.

Moreover men herein do strangely forget the obvious relations of history, affirming they have no joints, whereas they
dayly read of several actions which are not performable without
them. They forget what is delivered by Xiphilinus, and also
by Suetonius in the lives of Nero and Galba, that Elephants
have been instructed to walk on ropes, in publick shews before
the people. Which is not easily performed by man, and requireth
not only a broad foot, but a pliable flexure of joints, and com-
mandible disposure of all parts of progression. They pass by
that memorable place in Curtius, concerning the Elephant of
King Porus, *Indus qui Elephantem regebat, descendere eum ratus, more
solito procumbere jussit in genua, cæteri quoque (ita enim instituti erant)
demisere corpora in terram.* They remember not the expression
De rebus of Osorius, when he speaks of the Elephant presented to Leo
gestis the tenth, *Pontificem ter genibus flexis, & demisso corporis habitu
Emanuelis.* *venerabundus salutavit.* But above all, they call not to mind that
memorable shew of Germanicus, wherein twelve Elephants
danced unto the sound of Musick, and after laid down in the
Tricliniums, or places of festival Recumbency.

Γόνυ from   They forget the Etymologie of the Knee, approved by some
γωνία. Grammarians. They disturb the position of the young ones in
the womb: which upon extension of legs is not easily conceiv-
able; and contrary unto the general contrivance of Nature.
Nor do they consider the impossible exclusion thereof, upon
extension and rigour of the legs.

Lastly, they forget or consult not experience, whereof not many
years past, we have had the advantage in England, by an Elephant
shewn in many parts thereof, not only in the posture of standing,
but kneeling and lying down. Whereby although the opinion at
present be well suppressed, yet from some strings of tradition, and
fruitful recurrence of errour, it is not improbable, it may revive in
the next generation again. This being not the first that hath been
seen in England; for (besides some others) as Polydore Virgil relateth, Lewis the French King sent one to Henry the third, and
Emanuel of Portugal another to Leo the tenth into Italy, where
notwithstanding the errour is still alive and epidemical, as with us.

The hint and ground of this opinion might be the gross and somewhat Cylindrical composure of the legs, the equality and less perceptible disposure of the joints, especially in the former legs of this Animal; they appearing when he standeth, like Pillars of flesh, without any evidence of articulation. The different flexure and order of the joints might also countenance the same, being not disposed in the Elephant, as they are in other quadrupedes, but carry a nearer conformity unto those of Man; that is, the bought of the fore-legs, not directly backward, but laterally and somewhat inward; but the hough or suffraginous flexure behind rather outward. Somewhat different unto many other quadrupedes, as Horses, Camels, Deer, Sheep, and Dogs; for their forelegs bend like our legs, and their hinder legs like our arms, when we move them to our shoulders. But quadrupedes oviparous, as Frogs, Lizards, Crocodiles, have their joints and motive flexures more analogously framed unto ours: and some among viviparous, that is, such thereof as can bring their fore-feet and meat therein unto their mouths, as most can do that have the clavicles or coller-bones: whereby their brests are broader, and their shoulders more asunder, as the Ape, the Monkey, the Squirrel and some others. If therefore any shall affirm the joints of Elephants are differently framed from most of other quadrupedes, and more obscurely and grosly almost then any, he doth herein no injury unto truth. But if *à dicto secundum quid ad dictum simpliciter*, he affirmeth also they have no articulations at all, he incurs the controulment of reason, and cannot avoid the contradiction also of sense.

As for the manner of their venation, if we consult historical experience, we shall find it to be otherwise then as is commonly presumed, by sawing away of Trees. The accounts whereof are to be seen at large in Johannes Hugo, Edwardus Lopez, Garcias ab Horto, Cadamustus, and many more.

Other concernments there are of the Elephant, which might admit of discourse; and if we should question the teeth of Elephants, that is, whether they be properly so termed, or might not rather be called horns: it were no new enquiry of mine, but a Paradox as old as Oppianus.* Whether as Pliny and divers since affirm it, that Elephants are terrified, and make away upon the grunting of Swine, Garcias ab Horto may decide,

* *Cyneget.*
lib. 2.

T

who affirmeth upon experience, they enter their stalls, and live
promiscuously in the Woods of Malavar. That the situation of
the genitals is averse, and their copulation like that which some
believe of Camels, as Pliny hath also delivered, is not to be
received; for we have beheld that part in a different position;
and their coition is made by supersaliency, like that of horses,
as we are informed by some who have beheld them in that act.
That some Elephants have not only written whole sentences, as
Ælian ocularly testifieth, but have also spoken, as Oppianus
delivereth, and Christophorus à Costa particularly relateth;
although it sound like that of Achilles' Horse in Homer, we do
not conceive impossible. Nor beside the affinity of reason in this
Animal any such intollerable incapacity in the organs of divers
Some Brutes quadrupedes, whereby they might not be taught to speak, or
tolerably well become imitators of speech like Birds. Strange it is how the
organized for
speech and curiosity of men that have been active in the instruction of
approaching Beasts, have never fallen upon this artifice; and among those,
to reason. many paradoxical and unheard of imitations, should not attempt
to make one speak. The Serpent that spake unto Eve, the Dogs
and Cats that usually speak unto Witches, might afford some
encouragement. And since broad and thick chops are required
in Birds that speak, since lips and teeth are also organs of speech;
from these there is also an advantage in quadrupedes, and a
proximity of reason in Elephants and Apes above them all.
Since also an Echo will speak without any mouth at all, articu-
lately returning the voice of man, by only ordering the vocal
spirit in concave and hollow places; whether the musculous
and motive parts about the hollow mouths of Beasts, may not
dispose the passing spirit into some articulate notes, seems a
query of no great doubt.

CHAP. IV

Of the Bever

THAT a Bever to escape the Hunter, bites off his testicles   BOOK III
or stones, is a Tenet very ancient; and hath had thereby
advantage of propagation. For the same we find in the
Hieroglyphicks of the Egyptians, in the Apologue of Æsop, an   Æsop's
Author of great Antiquity, who lived in the beginning of the   Apologues
Persian Monarchy, and in the time of Cyrus: the same is touched   antiquity.
by Aristotle in his *Ethicks* but seriously delivered by Ælian,
Pliny, and Solinus: the same we meet with in Juvenal, who by
an handsome and.Metrical expression more welcomly engrafts
it in our junior Memories:

> ——— *imitatus Castora, qui se*
> *Eunuchum ipse facit, cupiens evadere damno*
> *Testiculorum, adeo medicatum intelligit inguen;*

it hath been propagated by Emblems: and some have been so
bad Grammarians as to be deceived by the Name, deriving
Castor a castrando, whereas the proper Latine word is *Fiber,* and
Castor but borrowed from the Greek, so called *quasi γάστωρ,* that
is, *Animal ventricosum,* from his swaggy and prominent belly.

Herein therefore to speak compendiously, we first presume to
affirm that from strict enquiry, we cannot maintain the evulsion
or biting off any parts, and this is declarable from the best and
most professed Writers: for though some have made use hereof
in a Moral or Tropical way, yet have the professed Discoursers
by silence deserted, or by experience rejected this assertion.
Thus was it in ancient times discovered, and experimentally
refuted by one Sestius a Physitian, as it stands related by Pliny;
by Dioscorides, who plainly affirms that this tradition is false;
by the discoveries of Modern Authors, who have expressly
discoursed hereon, as Aldrovandus, Mathiolus, Gesnerus,
Bellonius; by Olaus Magnus, Peter Martyr, and others, who
have described the manner of their Venations in America; they
generally omitting this way of their escape, and have delivered
several other, by which they are daily taken.

The original of the conceit was probably Hieroglyphical,

which after became Mythological unto the Greeks, and so set down by Æsop; and by process of tradition, stole into a total verity, which was but partially true, that is in its covert sense and Morality. Now why they placed this invention upon the Bever (beside the Medical and Merchantable commodity of *Castoreum*, or parts conceived to be bitten away) might be the sagacity and wisdom of that Animal, which from the works it performs, and especially its Artifice in building, is very strange, and surely not to be matched by any other. Omitted by Plutarch, *De solertia Animalium*, but might have much advantaged the drift of that Discourse.

If therefore any affirm a wise man should demean himself like the Bever, who to escape with his life, contemneth the loss of his genitals, that is in case of extremity, not strictly to endeavour the preservation of all, but to sit down in the enjoyment of the greater good, though with the detriment and hazard of the lesser; we may hereby apprehend a real and useful Truth. In this latitude of belief, we are content to receive the Fable of Hippomanes, who redeemed his life with the loss of a Golden Ball; and whether true or false, we reject not the Tragœdy of Absyrtus, and the dispersion of his Members by Medea, to perplex the pursuit of her Father. But if any shall positively affirm this act, and cannot believe the Moral, unless he also credit the Fable; he is surely greedy of delusion, and will hardly avoid deception in theories of this Nature. The Error therefore and Alogy in this opinion, is worse then in the last; that is, not to receive Figures for Realities, but expect a verity in Apologues; and believe, as serious affirmations, confessed and studied Fables.

Again, If this were true, and that the Bever in chase makes some divulsion of parts, as that which we call *Castoreum*; yet are not the same[23] to be termed Testicles or Stones; for these Cods or Follicles are found in both Sexes, though somewhat more protuberant in the Male. There is hereto no derivation of the seminal parts, nor any passage from hence, unto the Vessels of Ejaculation: some perforations onely in the part it self, through which the humour included doth exudate: as may be observed in such as are fresh, and not much dried with age. And lastly, The Testicles properly so called, are of a lesser magnitude, and seated inwardly upon the loins: and therefore it were not only

a fruitless attempt, but impossible act, to Eunuchate or castrate
themselves: and might be an hazardous practice of Art, if at all
attempted by others.

Now all this is confirmed from the experimental Testimony
of five very memorable Authors: Bellonius, Gesnerus, Amatus,
Rondeletius, and Mathiolus: who receiving the hint hereof
from Rondeletius in the Anatomy of two Bevers, did find all
true that had been delivered by him, whose words are these in
his learned Book *De Piscibus*: *Fibri in inguinibus geminos tumores
habent, utrinque unicum, ovi Anserini magnitudine, inter hos est mentula
in maribus, in fœminis pudendum, hi tumores testes non sunt, sed folliculi
membrana contecti, in quorum medio singuli sunt meatus è quibus exudat
liquor pinguis & cerosus, quem ipse Castor sæpe admoto ore lambit &
exugit, postea veluti oleo, corporis partes oblinit; Hos tumores testes
non esse hinc maxime colligitur, quod ab illis nulla est ad mentulam via
neque ductus quo humor in mentulæ meatum derivetur, & foras emittatur;
præterea quod testes intus reperiuntur, eosdem tumores Moscho animali
inesse puto, è quibus odoratum illud plus emanat.* Then which words
there can be no plainer, nor more evidently discovering the
impropriety of this appellation. That which is included in the
cod or visible bag about the groin, being not the Testicle, or
any spermatical part; but rather a collection of some superfluous matter deflowing from the body, especially the parts of
nutrition as unto their proper emunctories; and as it doth in
Musk and Civet Cats, though in a different and offensive odour;
proceeding partly from its food, that being especially Fish;
whereof this humour may be a garous excretion and olidous[24]
separation.

Most therefore of the Moderns before Rondeletius, and all
the Ancients excepting Sestius, have misunderstood this part,
conceiving *Castoreum* the Testicles of the Bever; as Dioscorides,
Galen, Ægineta, Ætius, and others have pleased to name it.
The Egyptians also failed in the ground of their Hieroglyphick,
when they expressed the punishment of Adultery by the Bever
depriving himself of his testicles, which was amongst them the
penalty of such incontinency. Nor is Ætius perhaps, too strictly
to be observed, when he prescribeth the stones of the Otter, or
River-dog, as succedaneous unto *Castoreum*. But most inexcusable
of all is Pliny; who having before him in one place the experiment

of Sestius against it, sets down in another, that the Bevers of Pontus bite off their testicles: and in the same place affirmeth the like of the Hyena. Which was indeed well joined with the Bever, as having also a bag in those parts; if thereby we understand the *Hyena odorata,* or Civet Cat, as is delivered and graphi-cally described by Castellus.

Now the ground of this mistake might be the resemblance and situation of these tumours about those parts, wherein we observe the testicles in other animals. Which notwithstanding is no well founded illation, for the testicles are defined by their office, and not determined by place or situation; they having one office in all, but different seats in many. For, beside that no Serpent, or Fishes oviparous, that neither biped nor quadruped oviparous have testicles exteriourly, or prominent in the groin; some also that are viviparous contain these parts within, as beside this Animal, the Elephant and the Hedg-hog.

If any therefore shall term these testicles, intending meta-phorically, and in no strict acception; his language is tolerable, and offends our ears no more then the Tropical names of Plants: when we read in Herbals, of Dog's,[25] Fox, and Goat-stones. But if he insisteth thereon, and maintaineth a propriety in this language: our discourse hath overthrown his assertion, nor will Logick permit his illation; that is, from things alike, to conclude a thing the same; and from an accidental convenience, that is a similitude in place or figure, to infer a specifical congruity or substantial concurrence in Nature.

CHAP. V

Of the Badger

THAT a Brock or Badger hath the legs on one side shorter then of the other, though an opinion perhaps not very ancient, is yet very general; received not only by Theorists and unexperienced believers, but assented unto by most who have the opportunity to behold and hunt them daily. Which notwithstanding upon enquiry I find repugnant unto the three Determinators of Truth, Authority, Sense, and Reason.

For first, Albertus Magnus speaks dubiously, confessing he could not confirm the verity hereof; but Aldrovandus plainly affirmeth, there can be no such inequality observed. And for my own part, upon indifferent enquiry, I cannot discover this difference, although the regardable side be defined, and the brevity by most imputed unto the left.

Again, It seems no easie affront unto Reason, and generally repugnant unto the course of Nature; for if we survey the total set of Animals, we may in their legs, or Organs of progression, observe an equality of length, and parity of Numeration; that is, not any to have an odd legg, or the supporters and movers of one side not exactly answered by the other. Although the hinder may be unequal unto the fore and middle legs, as in Frogs, Locusts, and Grashoppers; or both unto the middle, as in some Beetles and Spiders, as is determined by Aristotle; *De incessu Animalium.* Perfect and viviparous quadrupeds, so standing in their position of proneness, that the opposite joints of Neighbour-legs consist in the same plane; and a line descending from their Navel intersects at right angles the axis of the Earth. It happeneth often I confess that a Lobster hath the Chely or great claw of one side longer then the other; but this is not properly their leg, but a part of apprehension, and whereby they hold or seize upon their prey; for the legs and proper parts of progression are inverted backward, and stand in a position opposite unto these.

De incessu Animalium.

Lastly, The Monstrosity is ill contrived, and with some disadvantage; the shortness being affixed unto the legs of one side, which might have been more tolerably placed upon the thwart or Diagonial Movers. For the progression of quadrupeds being performed *per Diametrum,* that is the cross legs moving or resting together, so that two are always in motion, and two in station at the same time; the brevity had been more tolerable in the cross legs. For then the Motion and station had been performed by equal legs; whereas herein they are both performed by unequal Organs, and the imperfection becomes discoverable at every hand.

Diagonion, a line drawn from the cross angles.

CHAP. VI

Of the Bear

THAT a Bear brings forth her young informous and un-shapen, which she fashioneth after by licking them over, is an opinion not only vulgar, and common with us at present: but hath been of old delivered by ancient Writers. Upon this foundation it was an Hieroglyphick with the Egyptians: Aristotle seems to countenance it; Solinus, Pliny, and Ælian directly affirm it, and Ovid smoothly delivereth it:

> *Nec catulus partu quem reddidit ursa recenti*
> *Sed male viva caro est, lambendo mater in artus*
> *Ducit, & in formam qualem cupit ipsa reducit.*

Which notwithstanding is not only repugnant unto the sense of every one that shall enquire into it, but the exact and deliberate experiment of three Authentick Philosophers. The first of Mathiolus in his Comment on Dioscorides, whose words are to this effect. In the Valley of Anania about Trent, in a Bear which the Hunters eventerated or opened, I beheld the young ones with all their parts distinct: and not without shape, as many conceive: giving more credit unto Aristotle and Pliny, then experience and their proper senses. Of the same assurance was Julius Scaliger in his *Exercitations, Ursam fœtus informes potius ejicere, quam parere, si vera dicunt, quos postea linctu effingat: Quid hujusce fabulæ authoribus fidei habendum ex hac historia cognosces; In nostris Alpibus venatores fœtam Ursam cepere, dissecta ea fœtus plane formatus intus inventus est.* And lastly, Aldrovandus who from the testimony of his own eyes affirmeth, that in the Cabinet of the Senate of Bononia, there was preserved in a Glass a Cub taken out of a Bear perfectly formed, and compleat in every part.

It is moreover injurious unto Reason, and much impugneth the course and providence of Nature, to conceive a birth should be ordained before there is a formation. For the conformation of parts is necessarily required, not onely unto the pre-requisites and previous conditions of birth, as Motion and Animation: but also unto the parturition or very birth it self: Wherein not only the Dam, but the younglings play their parts; and the cause

and act of exclusion proceedeth from them both. For the exclusion of Animals is not meerly passive like that of Eggs, nor
the total action of delivery to be imputed unto the Mother:
but the first attempt beginneth from the Infant: which at the
accomplished period attempteth to change his Mansion: and
strugling to come forth, dilacerates and breaks those parts
which restrained him before.

Beside (what few take notice of) Men hereby do in an high
measure vilifie the works of God, imputing that unto the tongue
of a Beast, which is the strangest Artifice in all the acts of
Nature; that is the formation of the Infant in the Womb, not
only in Mankind, but all viviparous Animals. Wherein the
plastick or formative faculty, from matter appearing Homo-
geneous, and of a similary substance, erecteth Bones, Membranes, Veins, and Arteries: and out of these contriveth every
part in number, place, and figure, according to the law of its
species. Which is so far from being fashioned by any outward
agent, that once omitted or perverted by a slip of the inward
Phidias, it is not reducible by any other whatsoever. And therefore *Mirè me plasmaverunt manus tuæ*, though it originally respected
the generation of Man, yet is it appliable unto that of other
Animals; who entring the Womb in bare and simple Materials,
return with distinction of parts, and the perfect breath of life.
He that shall consider these alterations without, must needs
conceive there have been strange operations within; which to
behold, it were a spectacle almost worth one's beeing, a sight
beyond all; except that Man had been created first, and might
have seen the shew of five days after.

Now as the opinion is repugnant both unto sense and Reason,
so hath it probably been occasioned from some slight ground in
either. Thus in regard the Cub comes forth involved in the
Chorion, a thick and tough Membrane obscuring the formation,
and which the Dam doth after bite and tear asunder; the beholder
at first sight conceives it a rude and informous lump of flesh,
and imputes the ensuing shape unto the Mouthing of the Dam;
which addeth nothing thereunto, but only draws the curtain,
and takes away the vail which concealed the Piece before. And
thus have some endeavoured to enforce the same from Reason;
that is, the small and slender time of the Bear's gestation, or

going with her young; which lasting but few days (a Month some say) the exclusion becomes precipitous, and the young ones consequently informous; according to that of Solinus, *Trigesimus dies uterum liberat ursæ; unde evenit ut præcipitata fœcunditas informes creet partus.* But this will overthrow the general Method of Nature in the works of generation. For therein the conformation is not only antecedent, but proportional unto the exclusion; and if the period of the birth be short, the term of conformation will be as sudden also. There may I confess from this narrow time of gestation ensue a Minority or smalness in the exclusion; but this however inferreth no informity, and it still receiveth the Name of a natural and legitimate birth; whereas if we affirm a total informity, it cannot admit so forward a term as an Abortment, for that supposeth conformation. So we must call this constant and intended act of Nature, a slip ῎Εκρυσις. or effluxion, that is an exclusion before conformation: before the birth can bear the name of the Parent, or be so much as properly called an Embryon.

CHAP. VII

Of the Basilisk

Chapter 7

MANY Opinions are passant concerning the Basilisk or little King of Serpents, commonly called the Cockatrice: some affirming, others denying, most doubting the relations made hereof. What therefore in these incertainties we may more safely determine: that such an Animal there is, if we evade not the testimony of Scripture and humane Writers, we cannot safely deny. So is it said, Psalm 91, *Super Aspidem & Basiliscum ambulabis,* wherein the Vulgar Translation retaineth the Word of the Septuagint, using in other places the Latine expression *Regulus,* as Proverbs 23, *Mordebit ut coluber, & sicut Regulus venena diffundet:* and Jeremy 8, *Ecce ego mittam vobis serpentes Regulos, &c.* That is, as ours translate it, *Behold I will send Serpents, Cockatrices among you which will not be charmed, and they shall bite you.* And as for humane Authors, or such as have discoursed of Animals, or Poisons, it is to be found almost in all: in Dioscorides, Galen, Pliny, Solinus, Ælian, Ætius, Avicen, Ardoynus, Grevinus, and many more. In Aristotle I confess we find no mention thereof, but Scaliger in his *Comment and enumeration of Serpents*, hath made supply; and in his *Exercitations* delivereth that a Basilisk was found in Rome, in the days of Leo the fourth. The like is reported by Sigonius; and some are so far from denying one, that they have made several kinds thereof: for such is the *Catobleplas* of Pliny conceived to be by some, and the *Dryinus* of Ætius by others.

But although we deny not the existence of the Basilisk, yet whether we do not commonly mistake in the conception hereof, and call that a Basilisk which is none at all, is surely to be questioned. For certainly that which from the conceit of its generation we vulgarly call a Cockatrice, and wherein (but under a different name) we intend a formal Identity and adequate conception with the Basilisk; is not the Basilisk of the Ancients, whereof such wonders are delivered. For this of ours is generally described with legs, wings, a Serpentine and winding tail, and a crist or comb somewhat like a Cock. But the Basilisk of elder times was a proper kind of Serpent, not above three palms long, as some account; and differenced from other Serpents by advancing his head, and some white marks or coronary spots upon the crown, as all authentick Writers have delivered.

Nor is this Cockatrice only unlike the Basilisk, but of no real shape in Nature; and rather an Hieroglyphical fansie, to express different intentions, set forth in different fashions. Sometimes with the head of a Man, sometimes with the head of an Hawk, as Pierius hath delivered; and as with addition of legs the Heralds and Painters still describe it. Nor was it only of old a symbolical and allowable invention, but is now become a manual contrivance of Art, and artificial imposture; whereof besides others, Scaliger hath taken notice: *Basilisci formam mentiti sunt vulgo Gallinaceo similem, & pedibus binis; neque enim absimiles sunt cæteris serpentibus, nisi macula quasi in vertice candida, unde illi nomen Regium;* that is, men commonly counterfeit the form of a Basilisk with another like a Cock, and with two feet; whereas they differ not from other serpents, but in a white speck upon their Crown. Now although in some manner it might be counterfeited in

Indian Cocks, and flying Serpents, yet is it commonly contrived out of the skins of Thornbacks, Scaits, or Maids, as Aldrovand hath observed, and also graphically described in his excellent *Book of Fishes*; and for satisfaction of my own curiosity I have caused some to be thus contrived out of the same Fishes.

Nor is onely the existency of this animal considerable, but many things delivered thereof, particularly its poison and its generation. Concerning the first, according to the doctrine of the Ancients, men still affirm, that it killeth at a distance, that it poisoneth by the eye, and by priority of vision. Now that deleterious it may be at some distance, and destructive without corporal contaction, what uncertainty soever there be in the effect, there is no high improbability in the relation. For if Plagues or pestilential Atoms have been conveyed in the Air from different Regions, if men at a distance have infected each other, if the shadows of some trees be noxious, if Torpedoes deliver their opium at a distance, and stupifie beyond themselves; we cannot reasonably deny, that (beside our gross and restrained poisons requiring contiguity unto their actions) there may proceed from subtiller seeds, more agile emanations, which contemn those Laws, and invade at distance unexpected.

That this venenation shooteth from the eye, and that this way a Basilisk may empoison, although thus much be not agreed upon by Authors, some imputing it unto the breath, others unto the bite, it is not a thing impossible. For eyes receive offensive impressions from their objects, and may have influences
destructive to each other. For the visible species of things strike not our senses immaterially, but streaming in corporal raies, do carry with them the qualities of the object from whence they flow, and the medium through which they pass. Thus through a green or red Glass all things we behold appear of the same colours; thus sore eyes affect those which are sound, and themselves also by reflection, as will happen to an inflamed eye that beholds it self long in a Glass; thus is fascination made out, and
thus also it is not impossible, what is affirmed of this animal, the visible rayes of their eyes carrying forth the subtilest portion of their poison, which received by the eye of man or beast, infecteth first the brain, and is from thence communicated unto the heart.

But lastly, That this destruction should be the effect of the
first beholder, or depend upon priority of aspection, is a point
not easily to be granted, and very hardly to be made out upon
the principles of Aristotle, Alhazen, Vitello, and others, who
hold that sight is made by Reception, and not by extramission;
by receiving the raies of the object into the eye, and not by
sending any out. For hereby although he behold a man first, the
Basilisk should rather be destroyed, in regard he first receiveth
the rayes of his Antipathy, and venomous emissions which
objectively move his sense; but how powerful soever his own
poison be, it invadeth not the sense of man, in regard he beholdeth him not. And therefore this conceit was probably begot by
such as held the opinion of sight by extramission; as did Pythagoras, Plato, Empedocles, Hipparchus, Galen, Macrobius,
Proclus, Simplicius, with most of the Ancients, and is the postulate of Euclide in his Opticks, but now sufficiently convicted
from observations of the Dark Chamber.

As for the generation of the Basilisk, that it proceedeth from
a Cock's egg hatched under a Toad or Serpent, it is a conceit
as monstrous as the brood it self. For if we should grant that   *The genera-*
Cocks growing old, and unable for emission, amass within them-   *tion of the*
selves some seminal matter, which may after conglobate into   *Cock's egg.*
the form of an egg, yet will this substance be unfruitful. As
wanting one principle of generation, and a commixture of both
sexes, which is required unto production, as may be observed
in the eggs of Hens not trodden; and as we have made trial in
some which are termed Cocks' eggs. It is not indeed impossible   *Ovum Cente-*
that from the sperm of a Cock, Hen, or other Animal, being   *minum, or the*
once in putrescence, either from incubation or otherwise, some   *last egg,*
                                                                  which is a
generation may ensue; not univocal and of the same species, but   *very little*
some imperfect or monstrous production, even as in the body   *one.*
of man from putrid humours, and peculiar ways of corruption;
there have succeeded strange and unseconded shapes of worms;
whereof we have beheld some our selves, and read of others in
medical observations. And so may strange and venomous Serpents be several ways engendered; but that this generation
should be regular, and alway produce a Basilisk, is beyond our
affirmation, and we have good reason to doubt.

Again, It is unreasonable to ascribe the equivocacy of this

form unto the hatching of a Toad, or imagine that diversifies the production. For Incubation alters not the species, nor if we observe it, so much as concurs either to the sex or colour: as appears in the eggs of Ducks or Partridges hatched under a Hen, there being required unto their exclusion only a gentle and continued heat: and that not particular or confined unto the species or parent. So have I known the seed of Silk-worms hatched on the bodies of women: and Pliny reports that Livia the wife of Augustus hatched an egg in her bosome. Nor is only an animal heat required hereto, but an elemental and artificial warmth will suffice: for as Diodorus delivereth, the Ægyptians were wont to hatch their eggs in Ovens, and many eye-witnesses confirm that practice unto this day. And therefore this generation of the Basilisk, seems like that of Castor and Helena: he that can credit the one, may easily believe the other: that is, that these two were hatched out of the egg which Jupiter in the form of a Swan, begat on his Mistress Leda.

The occasion of this conceit might be an Ægyptian tradition concerning the Bird Ibis: which after became transferred unto Cocks. For an opinion it was of that Nation, that the Ibis feeding upon Serpents, that venomous food so inquinated their oval conceptions, or eggs within their bodies, that they sometimes came forth in Serpentine shapes, and therefore they always brake their eggs, nor would they endure the Bird to sit upon them. But how causeless their fear was herein, the daily incubation of Ducks, Pea-hens, and many other testifie, and the Stork might have informed them; which Bird they honoured and cherished, to destroy their Serpents.

That which much promoted it, was a misapprehension in holy Scripture upon the Latine translation in Esa. 59, *Ova aspidum ruperunt, & telas Aranearum texuerunt, qui comedent de ovis eorum morietur, & quod confotum est, erumpet in Regulum.* From whence notwithstanding, beside the generation of Serpents from eggs, there can be nothing concluded; and what kind of Serpents are meant, not easie to be determined, for Translations are very different: Tremellius rendering the Asp *Hæmorrhous*, and the Regulus or Basilisk a Viper, and our translation for the Asp sets down a Cockatrice in the Text, and an Adder in the margin.

Another place of Esay doth also seem to countenance it,

Chap. 14. *Ne læteris Philistæa quoniam diminuta est virga percus-*
soris tui, de radice enim colubri egredietur Regulus, & semen ejus
absorbens volucrem; which ours somewhat favourably rendereth:
Out of the Serpent's Root shall come forth a Cockatrice, and his fruit
shall be a fiery flying Serpent. But Tremellius, *è radice Serpentis*
prodit Hæmorrhous, & fructus illius præster volans; wherein the words
are different, but the sense is still the same; for therein are
figuratively intended Uzziah and Ezechias; for though the
Philistines had escaped the minor Serpent Uzziah, yet from his
stock a fiercer Snake should arise, that would more terribly
sting them, and that was Ezechias.

But the greatest promotion it hath received from a misunderstanding of the Hieroglyphical intention. For being conceived to be the Lord and King of Serpents, to awe all others,
nor to be destroyed by any; the Ægyptians hereby implied
Eternity, and the awful power of the supreme Deitie: and therefore described a crowned Asp or Basilisk upon the heads of their
gods. As may be observed in the Bembine Table, and other
Ægyptian Monuments.

CHAP. VIII

Of the Wolf

SUCH a Story as the Basilisk is that of the Wolf concerning
priority of vision, that a man becomes hoarse or dumb, if
a Wolf have the advantage first to eye him. And this is a
plain language affirmed by Pliny: *In Italia ut creditur, Luporum*
visus est noxius, vocemque homini, quem prius contemplatur adimere; so
is it made out what is delivered by Theocritus, and after him by
Virgil:

> ——— *Vox quoque Mœrim*
> *Jam fugit ipsa, Lupi Mœrim videre priores.*

Thus is the Proverb to be understood, when during the discourse, if the party or subject interveneth, and there ensueth a
sudden silence, it is usually said, *Lupus est in fabula.* Which conceit being already convicted, not only by Scaliger, Riolanus,
and others; but daily confutable almost every where out of
England, we shall not further refute.

The ground or occasional original hereof, was probably the amazement and sudden silence the unexpected appearance of Wolves do often put upon Travellers; not by a supposed vapour, or venomous emanation, but a vehement fear which naturally produceth obmutescence; and sometimes irrecoverable silence. Thus Birds are silent in presence of an Hawk, and Pliny saith that Dogs are mute in the shadow of an Hiæna. But thus could not the mouths of worthy Martyrs be silenced, who being exposed not onely unto the eyes, but the merciless teeth of Wolves, gave loud expressions of their faith, and their holy clamours were heard as high as Heaven.

That which much promoted it beside the common Proverb, was an expression in Theocritus, a very ancient Poet, οὐ φθεγξῇ λύκον εἶδες, *Edere non poteris vocem, Lycus est tibi visus*; which Lycus was Rival unto another, and suddenly appearing stopped the mouth of his Corrival: now Lycus signifying also a Wolf, occasioned this apprehension; men taking that appellatively, which was to be understood properly, and translating the genuine acception. Which is a fallacy of Æquivocation, and in some opinions begat the like conceit concerning Romulus and Remus, that they were fostered by a Wolf; the name of the Nurse being Lupa, and founded the Fable of Europa, and her carriage over Sea by a Bull, because the Ship or Pilot's name was Taurus. And thus have some been startled at the Proverb, *Bos in lingua*, confusedly apprehending how a man should be said to have an Oxe in his tongue, that would not speak his mind; which was no more then that a piece of money had silenced him: for by the Oxe was onely implied a piece of coin stamped with that figure, first currant with the Athenians, and after among the Romans.

CHAP. XXVII

Compendiously of sundry Tenents concerning other Animals, which examined, prove either false or dubious

I. AND first from great Antiquity, and before the Melody of Syrens, the Musical note of Swans hath been commended, and that they sing most sweetly before their death. For thus we read in Plato, that from the opinion of *Metempsuchosis*, or transmigration of the souls of men into the bodies of beasts most sutable unto their humane condition, after his death, Orpheus the Musician became a Swan. Thus was it the bird of Apollo the god of Musick by the Greeks; and an Hieroglyphick of musick among the Egyptians, from whom the Greeks derived the conception; hath been the affirmation of many Latines, and hath not wanted assertors almost from every Nation. Chapter 27

All which notwithstanding, we find this relation doubtfully received by Ælian, as an hear-say account by Bellonius, as a false one by Pliny, expresly refuted by Myndius in *Athenæus*; and severely rejected by Scaliger; whose words unto Cardan are these: *De Cygni vero cantu suavissimo quem cum parente mendaciorum Græcia jactare ausus es, ad Luciani tribunal, apud quem novi aliquid dicas, statuo.* Authors also that countenance it, speak not satisfactorily of it; Some affirming they sing not till they die; some that they sing, yet die not. Some speak generally, as though this note were in all; some but particularly, as though it were only in some; some in places remote, and where we can have no trial of it; others in places where every experience can refute it; as Aldrovandus upon relation delivered, concerning the Musick of the Swans on the river of Thames near London. Of Swans, and their singing before death.

Now that which countenanceth, and probably confirmeth this opinion, is the strange and unusual conformation of the wind pipe, or vocal organ in this animal: observed first by The figuration to be found in Elks, and not in common Swans.

U

Aldrovandus, and conceived by some contrived for this intention. For in its length it far exceedeth the gullet; and hath in the
chest a sinuous revolution, that is, when it ariseth from the
lungs, it ascendeth not directly unto the throat, but descending first into a capsulary reception of the breast bone; by a Serpentine and Trumpet recurvation it ascendeth again into the
neck; and so by the length thereof a great quantity of air is
received, and by the figure thereof a Musical modulation effected.
But to speak indifferently, this formation of the Weazon, is not
peculiar unto the Swan, but common also unto the *Platea* or
Shovelard, a bird of no Musical throat; And as Aldrovandus
confesseth, may thus be contrived in the Swan to contain a
larger stock of air, whereby being to feed on weeds at the bottom, they might the longer space detain their heads under
water. But were this formation peculiar, or had they unto this
effect an advantage from this part: yet have they a known and
open disadvantage from another; that is, a flat bill. For no
Latirostrous animal (whereof nevertheless there are no slender
numbers) were ever commended for their note, or accounted
among those animals which have been instructed to speak.

When therefore we consider the dissention of Authors, the
falsity of relations, the indisposition of the Organs, and the
immusical note of all we ever beheld or heard of; if generally
taken and comprehending all Swans, or of all places, we cannot
assent thereto. Surely he that is bit with a Tarantula, shall
never be cured by this Musick; and with the same hopes we
expect to hear the harmony of the Spheres.

2. That there is a special propriety in the flesh of Peacocks,
roast or boiled, to preserve a long time incorrupted, hath been
the assertion of many; stands yet confirmed by Austin, *De Civi-
tate Dei*; by Gygas Sempronius, in Aldrovandus; and the same
experiment we can confirm our selves, in the brawn or fleshly
parts of Peacocks so hanged up with thred, that they touch no
place whereby to contract a moisture; and hereof we have made
trial both in summer and winter. The reason, some, I perceive,
attempt to make out from the siccity and driness of its flesh,
and some are content to rest in a secret propriety thereof. As
for the siccity of the flesh, it is more remarkable in other animals,
as Eagles, Hawks, and birds of prey; That it is a propriety or

agreeable unto none other, we cannot, with reason admit: for
the same preservation, or rather incorruption we have observed
in the flesh of Turkeys, Capons, Hares, Partridge, Venison,
suspended freely in the air, and after a year and a half, dogs have
not refused to eat them.

As for the other conceit, that a Peacock is ashamed when he
looks on his legs, as is commonly held, and also delivered by
Cardan; beside what hath been said against it by Scaliger; let
them believe that hold specificial deformities; or that any part
can seem unhandsome to their eyes, which hath appeared good
and beautiful unto their makers. The occasion of this conceit,
might first arise from a common observation, that when they
are in their pride, that is, advance their train, if they decline
their neck to the ground, the hinder grow too weak, and suffer
the train to fall. And the same in some degree is also observable
in Turkeys.

3. That Storks are to be found, and will only live, in Repub-
likes or free States, is a petty conceit to advance the opinion of
popular policies, and from Antipathies in nature, to disparage
Monarchical government. But how far agreeable unto truth, let
them consider who read in Pliny, that among the Thessalians
who were governed by Kings, and much abounded with Serpents, it was no less then capital to kill a Stork. That the Ancient
Egyptians honoured them, whose government was from all
times Monarchical. That Bellonius affirmeth, men make them
nests in France. That relations make them common in Persia, and
the dominions of the great Turk. And lastly, how Jeremy the
Prophet delivered himself unto his countreymen, whose government was at that time Monarchical: *The Stork in the heaven knowing her appointed time, the Turtile, Crane, and Swallow observe the
time of their coming, but my people know not the judgment of the Lord.*
Wherein to exprobate their stupidity, he induceth the providence of Storks. Now if the bird had been unknown, the illustration had been obscure, and the exprobation not so proper.

4. That a Bittor maketh that mugient noise, or as we term it
Bumping, by putting its bill into a reed as most believe, or as
Bellonius and Aldrovandus conceive, by putting the same in
water or mud, and after a while retaining the air by suddenly
excluding it again, is not so easily made out. For my own part,

though after diligent enquiry, I could never behold them in this motion; Notwithstanding by others whose observations we have expressly requested, we are informed, that some have beheld them making this noise on the shore, their bills being far enough removed from reed or water; that is, first strongly attracting the air, and unto a manifest distention of the neck, and presently after with great contention and violence excluding the same again. As for what Authors affirm of putting their bill in water or mud, it is also hard to make out. For what may be observed from any that walketh the Fens, there is little intermission, nor any observable pawse, between the drawing in and sending forth of their breath. And the expiration or breathing forth doth not only produce a noise, but the inspiration or hailing in of the air, affordeth a sound that may be heard almost a flight-shot.

Now the reason of this strange and peculiar noise, is deduced from the conformation of the wind-pipe, which in this bird is different from other volatiles. For at the upper extream it hath no fit Larinx, or throttle to qualify the sound, and at the other end, by two branches deriveth it self into the lungs. Which division consisteth only of Semicircular fibers, and such as attain but half way round the part; By which formation they are dilatable into larger capacities, and are able to contain a fuller proportion of air; which being with violence sent up the weazon, and finding no resistance by the Larinx, it issueth forth in a sound like that from caverns, and such as sometimes subterraneous erup-Sect. 15. tions from hollow rocks afford. As Aristotle observeth in a Problem, and is observable in pitchers, bottles, and that instrument which Aponensis upon that Problem describeth, wherewith in Aristotle's time Gardiners affrighted birds.

Whether the large perforations of the extremities of the weazon, in the abdomen, admitting large quantity of ayr within the cavity of its membrans, as it doth in Frogs; may not much assist this mugiency or boation, may also be considered. For such as have beheld them making this noise out of the water, observe a large distention in their bodies; and their ordinary note is but like that of a Raven.

Of Whelps.   5. That whelps are blind nine days and then begin to see, is the common opinion of all, and some will be apt enough to descend unto oaths upon it. But this I find not answerable unto experience, for upon a strict observation of many, I have scarce found any that see the ninth day, few before the twelth, and the eyes of some not open before the fourteenth day. And this is agreeable unto the determination of Aristotle: who computeth the time of their anopsie or non-vision by that of their gestation. For some, saith he, do go with their young the sixt part of a year, two days over or under, that is, about sixty days or nine weeks; and the whelps of these see not till twelve days. Some go the fifth part of a year, that is, seventy one days, and these saith he, see not before the fourteenth day. Others do go the fourth part of the year, that is, three whole months, and these, saith he, are without sight no less then seventeen days. Wherein although the accounts be different, yet doth the least thereof exceed the term of nine days, which is so generally received. And this compute of Aristotle doth generally overthrow the common cause alleadged for this effect, that is, a precipitation or over-hasty exclusion before the birth be perfect, according unto the vulgar Adage, *Festinans canis cæcos parit catulos*: for herein the whelps of longest gestation, are also the latest in vision. The manner hereof is this. At the first littering, their eyes are fastly closed, that is, by coalition or joining together of the eyelids, and so continue untill about the twelfth day; at which time they begin to separate, and may be easily divelled or parted asunder; they open at the inward Canthis or greater Angle of the eye, and so by degrees dilate themselves quite open. An effect very strange, and the cause of much obscurity, wherein as yet men's enquiries are blind, and satisfaction not easily acquirable. What ever it be, thus much we may observe, those animals are only excluded without sight, which are multiparous and multifidous, that is, which have many at a litter, and have also their feet divided into many portions. For the Swine, although multiparous, yet being bisulcous, and only cloven hoofed, is not excluded in this manner, but farrowed with open eyes, as other bisulcous animals.

6. The antipathy between a Toad and a Spider, and that they poisonously destroy each other, is very famous, and solemn stories have been written of their combats; wherein most commonly the victory is given unto the Spider. Of what Toads and Spiders it is to be understood would be considered. For the

Phalangium and deadly Spiders, are different from those we generally behold in England. However the verity hereof, as also of many others, we cannot but desire; for hereby we might be surely provided of proper Antidotes in cases which require them; But what we have observed herein, we cannot in reason conceal; who having in a Glass included a Toad with several Spiders, we beheld the Spiders without resistance to sit upon his head and pass over all his body; which at last upon advantage he swallowed down, and that in few hours, unto the number of seven. And in the like manner will Toads also serve Bees, and are accounted enemies unto their Hives.

Of a Lion and a Cock. 7. Whether a Lion be also afraid of a Cock, as is related by many, and believed by most, were very easie in some places to make trial. Although how far they stand in fear of that Animal, we may sufficiently understand, from what is delivered by Camerarius, whose words in his *Symbola* are these; *Nostris temporibus in Aula serenissimi Principis Bavariæ, unus ex Leonibus miris saltibus in vicinam cujusdam domus aream sese dimisit, ubi Gallinaciorum cantum aut clamores nihil reformidans, ipsos unà cum plurimis gallinis devoravit.* That is, In our time in the Court of the Prince of Bavaria, one of the Lions leaped down into a Neighbour's yard, where nothing regarding the crowing or noise of the Cocks, he eat them up with many other Hens. And therefore a very unsafe defensative it is against the fury of this animal (and *De sacrificiis & magia.* surely no better then Virginity or bloud Royal) which Pliny doth place in Cock broth: For herewith, saith he whoever is anointed (especially if Garlick be boiled therein) no Lion or Panther will touch him. But of an higher nature it were, and more exalted Antipathy, if that were certain which Proclus delivers, that solary Dæmons, and such as appear in the shape of Lions, will disappear and vanish, if a Cock be presented upon them.

8. It is generally conceived, an Ear-wig hath no Wings, and is reckoned amongst impennous insects by many; but he that shall narrowly observe them, or shall with a needle put a side the short and sheathy cases on their back, may extend and draw forth two wings of a proportionable length for flight, and larger then in many flies. The experiment of Pennius is yet more perfect, who with a Rush or Bristle so pricked them as to make them flie.

9. That Worms are exanguious Animals, and such as have no bloud at all, is the determination of Phylosophy, the general opinion of Scholars, and I know not well to dissent from thence my self. If so, surely we want a proper term whereby to express that humour in them which so strictly resembleth bloud: and we refer it unto the discernment of others what to determine of that red and sanguineous humor, found more plentifully about the Torquis or carneous Circle of great Worms in the Spring, affording in Linnen or Paper an indiscernable tincture from bloud. Or wherein that differeth from a vein, which in an apparent blew runneth along the body, and if dexterously pricked with a lancet, emitteth a red drop, which pricked on either side it will not readily afford.

In the upper parts of Worms, there are likewise found certain white and oval Glandulosities, which Authors term Eggs, and in magnifying Glasses, they also represent them; how properly, may also be enquired; since if in them there be distinction of Sexes, these Eggs are to be found in both. For in that which is presumed to be their coition, that is, their usual complication, or lateral adhesion above the ground, dividing suddenly with two Knives the adhering parts of both, I have found these Eggs in either.

10. That Flies, Bees, &c., Do make that noise or humming sound by their mouth, or as many believe with their wings only, would be more warily asserted, if we consulted the determination of Aristotle, who as in sundry other places, so more expresly in his book of respiration, affirmeth this sound to be made by the illision of an inward spirit upon a pellicle or little membrane about the precinct or pectoral division of their body. If we also consider that a Bee or Flie, so it be able to move the body, will buz, though its head be off; that it will do the like if deprived of wings, reserving the head, whereby the body may be the better moved. And that some also which are big and lively will hum without either head or wing.

Nor is it only the beating upon this little membrane, by the inward and con-natural spirit as Aristotle determines, or the outward air as Scaliger conceiveth, which affordeth this humming noise, but most of the other parts may also concur hereto; as will be manifest, if while they hum we lay our finger on the

back or other parts; for thereupon will be felt a serrous or jarring motion like that which happeneth while we blow on the
teeth of a comb through paper; and so if the head or other parts
of the trunk be touched with oyl, the sound will be much impaired, if not destroyed: for those being also dry and membranous parts, by attrition of the spirit do help to advance the
noise: And therefore also the sound is strongest in dry weather,
and very weak in rainy season, and toward winter; for then the
air is moist, and the inward spirit growing weak, makes a languid and dumb allision upon the parts.

Of a Tainct.   11. There is found in the Summer a kind of Spider called a
'Tainct, of a red colour, and so little of body that ten of the
largest will hardly outway a grain; this by Country people is
accounted a deadly poison unto Cows and Horses; who, if they
suddenly die, and swell thereon, ascribe their death hereto, and
will commonly say, they have licked a Tainct. Now to satisfie
the doubts of men we have called this tradition unto experiment; we have given hereof unto Dogs, Chickens, Calves and
Horses, and not in the singular number; yet never could find
the least disturbance ensue. There must be therefore other
causes enquired of the sudden death and swelling of cattle; and
perhaps this insect is mistaken, and unjustly accused for some
other. For some there are which from elder times have been
observed pernicious unto cattle, as the *Buprestis* or Burstcow,
the *Pityocampe* or *Eruca Pinuum,* by Dioscorides, Galen and Ætius,
the *Staphilinus* described by Aristotle and others, or those red
Phalangious Spiders like *Cantharides* mentioned by Muffetus.
Now although the animal may be mistaken and the opinion also
false, yet in the ground and reason which makes men most to
doubt the verity hereof, there may be truth enough, that is, the
inconsiderable quantity of this insect. For that a poison cannot
destroy in so small a bulk; we have no reason to affirm. For if as
Leo Africanus reporteth, the tenth part of a grain of the poison
granum Nubiæ. of Nubia, will dispatch a man in two hours; if the bite of a
Viper and sting of a Scorpion, is not conceived to impart so
much; if the bite of an Asp will kill within an hour, yet the
impression scarce visible, and the poison communicated not pon-
derable; we cannot as impossible reject this way of destruction;
or deny the power of death in so narrow a circumscription.

12. Wondrous things are promised from the Glow-worm; from
thence perpetual lights are pretended, and waters said to be distilled which afford a lustre in the night; and this is asserted by Cardan, Albertus, Gaudentinus, Mizaldus, and many more. But hereto we cannot with reason assent: for the light made by this animal depends much upon its life. For when they are dead they shine not, nor alwaies while they live; but are obscure or light, according to the protrusion of their luminous parts, as observation will instruct us. For this flammeous light is not over all the body, but only visible on the inward side; in a small white part near the tail. When this is full and seemeth protruded, there ariseth a flame of a circular figure and Emerald green colour; which is discernable in any dark place in the day; but when it falleth and seemeth contracted, the light disappeareth, and the colour of the part only remaineth. Now this light, as it appeareth and disappeareth in their life, so doth it go quite out at their death. As we have observed in some, which preserved in fresh grass have lived and shined eighteen days; but as they declined, and the luminous humor dryed, their light grew languid, and at last went out with their lives. Thus also the Torpedo, which alive hath a power to stupifie at a distance, hath none upon contaction being dead, as Galen and Rondeletius particularly experimented. And this hath also disappointed the mischief of those intentions, which study the advancement of poisons; and fancy destructive compositions from Asp's or Viper's teeth, from Scorpion's or Hornet stings. For these omit their efficacy in the death of the individual, and act but dependantly on their forms. And thus far also those Philosophers concur with us, which held the Sun and Stars were living creatures, for they conceived their lustre depended on their lives; but if they ever died, their light must also perish.

It were a Notable piece of Art to translate the light from the Bononian Stone into another Body; he that would attempt to make a shining Water from Glow-worms, must make trial when the Splendent part is fresh and turgid. For even from the great American Glow-worms, and Flaming Flies, the light declineth as the luminous humor dryeth.

Now whether the light of animals, which do not occasionally shine from contingent causes, be of Kin unto the light of Heaven;

whether the invisible flame of life received in a convenient matter, may not become visible, and the diffused ætherial light make little Stars by conglobation in idoneous parts of the *compositum*: whether also it may not have some original in the seed and spirit analogous unto the Element of Stars, whereof some glympse is observable in the little refulgent humor, at the first attempts of formation: Philosophy may yet enquire.

True it is, that a Glow-worm will afford a faint light, almost a day's space when many will conceive it dead; but this is a mistake in the compute of death, and term of disanimation; for indeed, it is not then dead, but if it be distended will slowly contract it self again, which when it cannot do, it ceaseth to shine any more. And to speak strictly, it is no easie matter to determine the point of death in Insects and Creatures who have not their vitalities radically confined unto one part; for they are not dead when they cease to move or afford the visible evidences of life; as may be observed in Flies, who, when they appear even desperate and quite forsaken of their forms, by vertue of the Sun or warm ashes will be revoked unto life, and perform its functions again.

Now whether this lustre, a while remaining after death, dependeth not still upon the first impression, and light communicated or raised from an inward spirit, subsisting a while in a moist and apt recipient, nor long continuing in this, or the more remarkable Indian Glow-worm; or whether it be of another Nature, and proceedeth from different causes of illumination; yet since it confessedly subsisteth so little a while after their lives, how to make perpetual lights, and sublunary moons thereof as is pretended, we rationally doubt, though not so sharply deny, with Scaliger and Muffetus.

13. The wisdom of the Pismire is magnified by all, and in the Panegyricks of their providence we alwaies meet with this, that to prevent the growth of Corn which they store up, they bite off the end thereof: And some have conceived that from hence they have their name in Hebrew: From whence ariseth a conceit that Corn will not grow if the extreams be cut or broken. But herein we find no security to prevent its germination; as having made trial in grains, whose ends cut off have notwithstanding suddenly sprouted, and accordingly to the Law of their

Nemalah a Namal circumcidit.

kinds; that is, the roots of barley and oats at contrary ends, of wheat and rye at the same. And therefore some have delivered that after rainy weather they dry these grains in the Sun; which if effectual, we must conceive to be made in a high degree and above the progression of Malt; for that Malt will grow, this year hath informed us, and that unto a perfect ear.

And if that be true which is delivered by many, and we shall further experiment, that a decoction of Toad-stools if poured upon earth, will produce the same again: If Sow-thistles will abound in places manured with dung of Hogs, which feeds much upon that plant: If Horse-dung reproduceth oats; If winds and rains will transport the seminals of plants; it will not be easie to determine where the power of generation ceaseth. The forms of things may lie deeper then we conceive them; seminal principles may not be dead in the divided atoms of plants; but wandering in the ocean of nature, when they hit upon proportionable materials, may unite, and return to their visible selves again.

But the prudence of this animal is by knawing, piercing, or otherwise to destroy the little nebbe or principle of germination. Which notwithstanding is not easily discoverable; it being no ready business to meet with such grains in Anthills; and he must dig deep, that will seek them in the Winter.

CHAP. VI

Of Swimming and Floating

Chapter 6   THAT Men swim naturally, if not disturbed by fear; that Men being drowned and sunk, do float the ninth day when their gall breaketh; that Women drowned, swim prone, but Men supine, or upon their backs; are popular affirmations, whereto we cannot assent. And first, that man should swim naturally, because we observe it is no lesson unto other Animals, we are not forward to conclude; for other Animals swim in the same manner as they go, and need no other way of motion for natation in the water, then for progression upon the land. And this is true whether they move *per latera*, that is, two legs of one side together, which is Tollutation or ambling; or *per diametrum*, lifting one foot before, and the cross foot behind, which is succussation or trotting; or whether *per frontem* or *quadratum*, as Scaliger terms it, upon a square base, the legs of both sides moving together, as Frogs and salient Animals, which is properly called leaping. For by these motions they are able to support and impel themselves in the water, without alteration in the stroak of their legs, or position of their bodies.

But with Man it is performed otherwise: for in regard of site he alters his natural posture and swimmeth prone; whereas he walketh erect. Again, in progression the arms move parallel to

the legs, and the arms and legs unto each other; but in natation
they intersect and make all sorts of angles. And lastly, in progressive motion, the arms and legs do move successively, but in natation both together; all which aptly to perform, and so as to support and advance the body, is a point of Art, and such as some in their young and docile years could never attain. But although swimming be acquired by art, yet is there somewhat more of nature in it then we observe in other habits, nor will it strictly fall under that definition; for once obtained, it is not to be removed; nor is there any who from disuse did ever yet forget it.

Secondly, That persons drowned arise and float the ninth day when their gall breaketh, is a questionable determination both in the time and cause. For the time of floating, it is uncertain according to the time of putrefaction, which shall retard or accelerate according to the subject and season of the year, for as we have observed, Cats and Mice will arise unequally, and at different times, though drowned at the same. Such as are fat do commonly float soonest, for their bodies soonest ferment, and that substance approacheth nearest unto air; and this is one of Aristotle's reasons why dead Eels will not float, because saith he, they have but slender bellies, and little fat.

As for the cause, it is not so reasonably imputed unto the
breaking of the gall as the putrefaction or corruptive fermentation of the body, whereby the unnatural heat prevailing, the putrifying parts do suffer a turgescence and inflation, and becoming aery and spumous affect to approach the air, and ascend unto the surface of the water. And this is also evidenced in Eggs, whereof the sound ones sink, and such as are addled swim, as do also those which are termed hypenemia or wind-eggs; and this is also a way to separate seeds, whereof such as are corrupted and steril, swim; and this agreeth not only unto the seed of plants lockt up and capsulated in their husks, but also unto the sperm and seminal humour of Man; for such a passage hath Aristotle upon the Inquisition and test of its fertility.

That the breaking of the gall is not the cause hereof, experience hath informed us. For opening the abdomen, and taking out the gall in Cats and Mice, they did notwithstanding arise. And because we had read in Rhodiginus of a Tyrant, who to

prevent the emergency of murdered bodies, did use to cut off
their lungs, and found Men's minds possessed with this reason;
we committed some unto the water without lungs, which notwithstanding floated with the others. And to compleat the
experiment, although we took out the guts and bladder, and
also perforated the Cranium, yet would they arise, though in a
longer time. From these observations in other Animals, it may
not be unreasonable to conclude the same in Man, who is too
noble a subject on whom to make them expressly, and the
casual opportunity too rare almost to make any. Now if any
should ground this effect from gall or choler, because it is the
highest humour and will be above the rest; or being the fiery
humour will readiest surmount the water, we must confess in
the common putrescence it may promote elevation, which the
breaking of the bladder of gall, so small a part in Man, cannot
considerably advantage.

Lastly, That Women drowned float prone, that is, with their
bellies downward, but Men supine or upward, is an assertion
wherein the *hoti* or point it self is dubious; and were it true, the
reason alledged for it, is of no validity. The reason yet current
was first expressed by Pliny, *veluti pudori defunctorum parcente
naturâ*, nature modestly ordaining this position to conceal the
shame of the dead; which hath been taken up by Solinus, Rhodiginus, and many more. This indeed (as Scaliger termeth it) is
ratio civilis non philosophica, strong enough for morality of Rheto-
ricks, not for Philosophy or Physicks. For first, in nature the
concealment of secret parts is the same in both sexes, and the
shame of their reveal equal: so Adam upon the tast of the fruit
was ashamed of his nakedness as well as Eve. And so likewise
in America and Countries unacquainted with habits, where
modesty conceals these parts in one sex, it doth it also in the
other; and therefore had this been the intention of nature, not
only Women but Men also had swimmed downwards; the posture in reason being common unto both, where the intent is also
common.

Again, While herein we commend the modesty, we condemn
the wisdom of nature: for that prone position we make her contrive unto the Woman, were best agreeable unto the Man, in
whom the secret parts are very anteriour and more discoverable

in a supine and upward posture. And therefore Scaliger declining this reason, hath recurred unto another from the difference of parts in both sexes; *Quod ventre vasto sunt mulieres plenoque intestinis, itaque minus impletur & subsidet, inanior maribus quibus nates præponderant*: If so, then Men, with great bellies will float downward, and only *Callipygæ*, and Women largely composed behind, upward. But Anatomists observe, that to make the larger cavity for the Infant, the hanch bones in Women, and consequently the parts appendant, are more protuberant then they are in Men. They who ascribe the cause unto the breasts of Women, take not away the doubt; for they resolve not why children float downward, who are included in that sex, though not in the reason alleadged. But hereof we cease to discourse, lest we undertake to afford a reason of the golden tooth,* that is, to invent or assign a cause, when we remain unsatisfied or unassured of the effect.

* Of the cause whereof much dispute was made, and at last proved an imposture.

That a Mare will sooner drown then a Horse, though commonly opinion'd, is not I fear experienced: nor is the same observed, in the drowning of whelps and Kitlins. But that a Man cannot shut or open his eyes under water, easie experiment may convict. Whether Cripples and mutilated Persons, who have lost the greatest part of their thighs, will not sink but float, their lungs being abler to waft up their bodies, which are in others overpoised by the hinder legs; we have not made experiment. Thus much we observe, that Animals drown downwards, and the same is observable in Frogs, when the hinder legs are cut off. But in the air most seem to perish headlong from high place; however Vulcan thrown from Heaven, be made to fall on his feet.

THE FIFTH BOOK

Of many things questionable as they are commonly described in Pictures

CHAP. I

Of the Picture of the Pelecan

BOOK V
Chapter I

ᴀɴᴅ first in every place we meet with the picture of the Pelecan, opening her breast with her bill, and feeding her young ones with the blood distilling from her. Thus is it set forth not only in common Signs, but in the Crest and Scutcheon of many Noble families; hath been asserted by many holy Writers, and was an Hierogliphick of piety and pitty among the Ægyptians; on which consideration, they spared them at their tables.

Notwithstanding upon enquiry we find no mention hereof in Ancient Zoographers, and such as have particularly discoursed upon Animals, as Aristotle, Elian, Pliny, Solinus and many more; who seldom forget proprieties of such a nature, and have been very punctual in less considerable Records. Some ground hereof I confess we may allow, nor need we deny a remarkable affection in Pelecans toward their young; for Elian discoursing of Storks, and their affection toward their brood, whom they instruct to fly, and unto whom they re-deliver up the provision of their Bellies, concludeth at last, that Herons and Pelecans do the like.

As for the testimonies of Ancient Fathers, and Ecclesiastical Writers, we may more safely conceive therein some Emblematical than any real Story: so doth Eucherius confess it to be the Emblem of Christ. And we are unwilling literally to receive that account of Jerom, that perceiving her young ones destroyed by Serpents, she openeth her side with her bill, by the blood whereof they revive and return unto life again. By which relation they might indeed illustrate the destruction of man by the old Serpent, and his restorement by the blood of Christ: and in this sense we shall not dispute the like relations of Austine, Isidore, Albertus, and many more, and under an Emblematical intention, we accept it in coat-armour.

As for the Hieroglyphick of the Egyptians, they erected the same upon another consideration, which was parental affection; manifested in the protection of her young ones, when her nest was set on fire. For as for letting out her blood, it was not the assertion of the Egyptians, but seems translated unto the Pelecan from the Vulture, as Pierius hath plainly delivered. *Sed quod Pelicanum (ut etiam aliis plerisque persuasum est) rostro pectus dissecantem pingunt, ita ut suo sanguine filios alat, ab Ægyptiorum historiâ valde alienum est, illi enim vulturem tantum id facere tradiderunt.*

And lastly, as concerning the picture, if naturally examined, and not Hieroglyphically conceived, it containeth many improprieties, disagreeing almost in all things from the true and proper description. For, whereas it is commonly set forth green or yellow, in its proper colour, it is inclining to white; excepting the extremities or tops of the wing feathers, which are brown. It is described in the bigness of a Hen, whereas it approacheth and sometimes exceedeth the magnitude of a Swan. It is commonly painted with a short bill; whereas that of the Pelecan attaineth sometimes the length of two spans. The bill is made acute or pointed at the end; whereas it is flat and broad, though somewhat inverted at the extream. It is described like fissipedes, or birds which have their feet or claws divided; whereas it is palmipedous, or fin-footed like Swans and Geese; according to the method of nature, in latirostrous or flat-bild birds; which being generally swimmers, the organ is wisely contrived unto the action, and they are framed with fins or oars upon their feet; and therefore they neither light, nor build on trees, if we except Cormorants, who make their nests like Herons. Lastly, there is one part omitted more remarkable than any other, that is, the chowle or crop adhering unto the lower side of the bill, and so descending by the throat: a bag or sachel very observable, and of a capacity almost beyond credit;

The bigness of a Pelecan.

Of her Crop.

X

which notwithstanding, this animal could not want; for therein[50] it receiveth Oysters, Cochles, Scollops, and other testaceous animals; which being not able to break, it retains them until they open, and vomiting them up, takes out the meat contained. This is that part preserved for a rarity and wherein (as Sanctius delivers) in one dissected, a Negro child was found.

A possibility there may be of opening and bleeding their breast; for this may be done by the uncous and pointed extremity of their bill: and some probability also that they sometimes do it, for their own relief, though not for their young ones; that is by nibling and biting themselves on their itching part of their breast, upon fullness or acrimony of blood. And the same may be better made out, if (as some relate) their feathers on that part are sometimes observed to be red and tincted with blood.

CHAP. II

Of the Picture of Dolphins

THAT Dolphins are crooked, is not only affirmed by the hand of the Painter, but commonly conceived their natural and proper figure; which is not only the opinion of our times, but seems the belief of elder times before us. For, beside the expressions of Ovid and Pliny, their Pourtraicts in some ancient Coyns are framed in this figure, as will appear in some thereof in Gesner, others in Goltsius, and Lævinus Hulsius in his discription of Coyns, from Julius Cæsar unto Rhodulphus the second.

Notwithstanding, to speak strictly in their natural figure they are streight, nor have their spine convexed, or more considerably embowed, than Sharks, Porposes, Whales, and other Cetaceous animals, as Scaliger plainly affirmeth: *Corpus habet non magis curvum quam reliqui pisces.* As ocular enquiry informeth; and as unto such as have not had the opportunity to behold them, their proper pourtraicts will discover in Rondeletius, Gesner, and Aldrovandus. And as indeed is deducible from pictures themselves; for though they be drawn repandous, or convexedly crooked in one piece, yet the Dolphin that carrieth Arion is concavously inverted, and hath its spine depressed in another. And answerably hereto may we behold them differently bowed in medalls, and the Dolphins of Varus and Julius do make another flexure from that of Commodus and Agrippa.

And therefore what is delivered of their incurvity, must either be taken Emphatically, that is, not really but in appearance; which happeneth, when they leap above water, and suddenly shoot down again; which is a fallacy in vision, whereby straight bodies in a sudden motion protruded obliquely downward, appear unto the eye crooked; and this is the construction of Bellonius. Or if it be taken really, it must not universally and perpetually; that is, not when they swim and remain in their proper figures, but only when they leap, or impetuously whirl their bodies any way; and this is the opinion of Gesnerus. Or lastly, It may be taken neither really nor emphatically, but only Emblematically: for being the Hieroglyphick of celerity, and swifter than other animals, men best expressed their velocity by incurvity, and under some figure of a bow: and in this sense probably do Heralds also receive it, when from a Dolphin extended, they distinguish a Dolphin embowed.

And thus also must that picture be taken of a Dolphin clasping an Anchor: that is, not really, as is by most conceived out of affection unto man, conveighing the Anchor unto the ground: but emblematically, according as Pierius hath expressed it, The swiftest animal conjoyned with that heavy body, implying that common moral, *Festina lentè*: and that celerity should always be contempered with cunctation.

CHAP. III

Of the Picture of a Grasshopper

THERE is also among us a common description and picture of a Grashopper, as may be observed in the pictures of Emblematists, in the coats of several families, and as the word *Cicada* is usually translated in Dictionaries. Wherein to speak strictly, if by this word Grashopper, we understand that animal which is implied by τέττιξ with the

Greeks, and by *Cicada* with the Latines; we may with safety affirm the picture is widely mistaken, and that for ought enquiry can inform, there is no such insect in England. Which how paradoxical soever, upon a strict enquiry, will prove undeniable truth.

For first, That animal which the French term *Sauterelle*, we a Grashopper, and which under this name is commonly described by us, is named Ἀκρὶς by the Greeks, by the Latines *Locusta*, and by our selves in proper speech a Locust; as in the diet of John Baptist, and in our Translation, *the Locusts have no King, yet go they forth all of them by bands.* Again, Between the *Cicada* and that we call a Grashopper, the differences are very many, as may be observed in themselves, or their descriptions in Matthiolus, Aldrovandus and Muffetus. For first, They are differently cucullated or capuched upon the head and back, and in the *Cicada* the eyes are more prominent: the Locusts have Antennæ or long horns before, with a long falcation or forcipated tail behind; and being ordained for saltation, their hinder legs do far exceed the other. The Locust or our Grashopper hath teeth, the *Cicada* none at all; nor any mouth according unto Aristotle: the *Cicada* is most upon trees; and lastly, the *fritinnitus*[51] or proper note thereof, is far more shril than that of the Locust; and its life so short in Summer, that for provision it needs not have recourse unto the providence of the Pismire in Winter.

And therefore where the *Cicada* must be understood, the pictures of Heralds and Emblematists are not exact, nor is it safe to adhere unto the interpretation of Dictionaries; and we must with candour make out our own Translations: for in the Plague of Ægypt, Exodus 10. the word Ἀκρὶς is translated a Locust, but in the same sense and subject, Wisdom 16. it is translated a Grashopper, *For them the bitings of Grasshoppers and flies killed*: whereas we have declared before, the *Cicáda* hath no teeth, but is conceived to live upon dew; and the possibility of its subsistence is disputed by Licetus. Hereof I perceive Muffetus hath taken notice, dissenting from Langius and Lycostenes, while they deliver, the *Cicada's* destroyed the fruits in Germany, where that insect is not found; and therefore concludeth, *Tam ipsos quam alios deceptos fuisse autumno, dum locustas cicadas esse vulgari errore crederent.*

And hereby there may be some mistake in the due dispensation of Medicines desumed from this animal; particularly of Diatettigon commended by Ætius in the affections of the kidneys. It must be likewise understood with some restriction what hath been affirmed by Isidore, and yet delivered by many, that *Cicada's* are bred out of Cuccow spittle or Woodsear; that is, that spumous, frothy dew or exudation, or both, found upon Plants, especially about the joints of Lavinder and Rosemary, observable with us about the latter end of May. For here the true *Cicada* is not bred, but certain it is, that out of this, some kind of Locust doth proceed; for herein may be discovered a little insect of a festucine or pale green, resembling in all parts a Locust, or what we call a Grashopper.

Lastly, The word it self is improper, and the term of Grashopper not appliable unto the *Cicada*; for therein the organs of motion are not contrived for saltation, nor are the hinder legs of such extension, as is observable in salient animals, and such as move by leaping. Whereto the Locust is very well conformed; for therein the legs behind are longer than all the body, and make at the second joynt acute angles, at a considerable advancement above their backs.

The mistake therefore with us might have its original from a defect in our language; for having not the insect with us, we have not fallen upon its proper name, and so make use of a term common unto it and the Locust; whereas other countries have proper expressions for it. So the Italian calls it *Cicala*, the Spaniard *Cigarra*, and the French *Cigale*; all which appellations conform unto the original, and properly express this animal. Whereas our word is borrowed from the Saxon *Gœrsthopp*, which our forefathers, who never beheld the *Cicada*, used for that insect which we yet call a Grashopper.

CHAP. IV

Of the Picture of the Serpent tempting Eve

IN the Picture of Paradise, and delusion of our first Parents, the Serpent is often described with humane visage; not unlike unto Cadmus or his wife, in the act of their Metamorphosis. Which is not a meer pictorial contrivance or invention of the Picturer, but an ancient tradition and conceived reality, as it stands delivered by Beda and Authors of some antiquity; that is, that Sathan appeared not unto Eve in the naked form of a Serpent, but with a Virgin's head, that thereby he might become more acceptable, and his temptation find the easier entertainment.[52] Which nevertheless is a conceit not to be admitted, and the plain and received figure, is with better reason embraced.

For first, as Pierius observeth from Barcephas, the assumption of humane shape had proved a disadvantage unto Sathan; affording not only a suspicious amazement in Eve, before the fact, in beholding a third humanity beside her self and Adam; but leaving some excuse unto the woman, which afterward the man took up with lesser reason; that is, to have been deceived by another like her self.

Again, There was no inconvenience in the shape assumed, or any considerable impediment that might disturb that performance in the common form of a Serpent. For whereas it is conceived the woman must needs be afraid thereof, and rather flie than approach it; it was not agreeable unto the condition of Paradise and state of innocency therein; if in that place as most determine, no creature was hurtful or terrible unto man, and those destructive effects they now discover succeeded the curse, and came in with thorns and briars. And therefore Eugubinus (who affirmeth this Serpent was a Basilisk) incurreth no absurdity, nor need we infer that Eve should be destroyed immediately upon that Vision. For noxious animals could offend them no more in the Garden, than Noah in the Ark: as they peaceably received their names, so they friendly possessed their natures: and were their conditions destructive unto each other, they were not so unto man, whose constitutions then were antidotes, and needed not fear poisons.[53] And if (as most conceive) there were but two created of every kind, they could not at that time destroy either man or themselves; for this had frustrated the command of multiplication, destroyed a species, and imperfected the Creation. And therefore also if Cain were the first man born, with him entred not only the act, but the first power of murther; for before that time neither could the Serpent nor Adam destroy Eve, nor Adam and Eve each other; for that had

overthrown the intention of the world, and put its Creator to
act the sixt day over again.

Moreover, Whereas in regard of speech, and vocal conference
with Eve, it may be thought he would rather assume an humane
shape and organs, then the improper form of a Serpent; it
implies no material impediment. Nor need we to wonder how
he contrived a voice out of the mouth of a Serpent, who hath
done the like out of the belly of a Pythonissa, and the trunk of
an Oak; as he did for many years at Dodona.

Lastly, Whereas it might be conceived that an humane shape
was fitter for this enterprise; it being more than probable she   Why Eve
would be amazed to hear a Serpent speak; some conceive she   wondered
not at the
might not yet be certain that only man was priviledged with   serpent's
speech; and being in the novity of the Creation, and inexperi-   speaking.
ence of all things, might not be affrighted to hear a Serpent
speak. Beside she might be ignorant of their natures, who was
not versed in their names, as being not present at the general
survey of Animals, when Adam assigned unto every one a name
concordant unto its nature. Nor is this my opinion, but the
determination of Lombard and Tostatus; and also the reply of
Cyrill unto the objection of Julian, who compared this story
unto the fables of the Greeks.

CHAP. V

Of the Picture of Adam and Eve with Navels

ANOTHER mistake there may be in the Picture of our first   Chapter 5
Parents, who after the manner of their posterity are
both delineated with a Navel. And this is observable not
only in ordinary and stained pieces, but in the Authentick
draughts of Urbin, Angelo and others. Which notwithstanding
cannot be allowed, except we impute that unto the first cause,
which we impose not on the second; or what we deny unto
nature, we impute unto Naturity it self; that is, that in the first
and most accomplished piece, the Creator affected superflui-   What the
ties, or ordained parts without use or office.   Navel is, and
For the use of the Navel is to continue the Infant unto the   for what use.

Mother, and by the vessels thereof to convey its aliment and sustentation. The vessels whereof it consisteth, are the umbilical vein, which is a branch of the Porta, and implanted in the Liver of the Infant; two Arteries likewise arising from the Iliacal branches, by which the Infant receiveth the purer portion of blood and spirits from the mother; and lastly, the Urachos or ligamental passage derived from the bottom of the bladder, whereby it dischargeth the waterish and urinary part of its aliment. Now upon the birth, when the Infant forsaketh the womb, although it dilacerate, and break the involving membranes, yet do these vessels hold, and by the mediation thereof the Infant is connected unto the womb, not only before, but a while also after the birth. These therefore the midwife cutteth off, contriving them into a knot close unto the body of the Infant; from whence ensueth that tortuosity or complicated nodosity we usually call the Navel; occasioned by the colliga-

tion of vessels before mentioned. Now the Navel being a part, not precedent, but subsequent unto generation, nativity or parturition, it cannot be well imagined at the creation or extraordinary formation of Adam, who immediately issued from the Artifice of God; nor also that of Eve; who was not solemnly begotten, but suddenly framed, and anomalously proceeded from Adam.

And if we be led into conclusions that Adam had also this part, because we behold the same in our selves, the inference is not reasonable; for if we conceive the way of his formation, or of the first animals, did carry in all points a strict conformity unto succeeding productions, we might fall into imaginations that Adam was made without Teeth; or that he ran through those notable alterations in the vessels of the heart, which the Infant suffereth after birth: we need not dispute whether the egg or bird were first; and might conceive that Dogs were created blind, because we observe they are littered so with us. Which to affirm, is to confound, at least to regulate creation unto generation, the first Acts of God, unto the second of Nature; which were determined in that general indulgence, Encrease and Multiply, produce or propagate each other; that is, not answerably in all points, but in a prolonged method according to seminal progression. For the formation of things at first was different from their generation after; and although it had nothing to precede it, was aptly contrived for that which should succeed it. And therefore though Adam were framed without this part, as having no other womb than that of his proper principles, yet was not his posterity without the same: for the seminality of his fabrick contained the power thereof; and was endued with the science of those parts whose pre-destinations upon succession it did accomplish.

All the Navel therefore and conjunctive part we can suppose in Adam, was his dependency on his Maker, and the connexion he must needs have unto heaven, who was the Son of God. For holding no dependence on any preceding efficient but God; in the act of his production there may be conceived some connexion, and Adam to have been in a momental Navel with his Maker. And although from his carnality and corporal existence, the conjunction seemeth no nearer than of causality and effect; yet in his immortal and diviner part he seemed to hold a nearer coherence, and an umbilicality even with God himself. And so indeed although the propriety of this part be found but in some animals, and many species there are which have no Navel at all; yet is there one link and common connexion, one general ligament, and necessary obligation of all what ever unto God. Whereby although they act themselves at distance, and seem to be at loose; yet do they hold a continuity with their Maker. Which catenation or conserving union when ever his pleasure shall divide, let go, or separate; they shall fall from their exist-ence, essence, and operations: in brief, they must retire unto their primitive nothing, and shrink into their Chaos again.

They who hold the egg was before the Bird, prevent this doubt in many other animals, which also extendeth unto them: For birds are nourished by umbilical vessels, and the Navel is manifest sometimes a day or two after exclusion. The same is probable in oviparous exclusions, if the lesser part of eggs must serve for the formation, the greater part for nutriment. The same is made out in the eggs of Snakes; and is not improbable in the generation of Porwiggles or Tadpoles, and may be also true in some vermiparous exclusions: although (as we have observed in the daily progress in some) the whole Maggot is little enough to make a Fly, without any part remaining.

CHAP. VI

Of the Pictures of Eastern Nations, and the Jews at their
Feasts, especially our Saviour at the Passover

CONCERNING the Pictures of the Jews, and Eastern
Nations at their Feasts, concerning the gesture of our
Saviour at the Passover, who is usually described sitting
upon a stool or bench at a square table, in the middest of the
twelve, many make great doubt; and (though they concede a
table-gesture) will hardly allow this usual way of Session.

Wherein restraining no man's enquiry, it will appear that
accubation, or lying down at meals was a gesture used by very
many Nations. That the Persians used it, beside the testimony
of humane Writers, is deducible from that passage in Esther,

that when *the King returned into the place of the banquet of wine,*
Haman was fallen upon the bed whereon Esther was. That the Parthians used it, is evident from Athenæus, who delivereth out of
Posidonius, that their King lay down at meals, on an higher bed
than others. That Cleopatra thus entertained Anthony, the same
Author manifesteth when he saith, she prepared twelve Tricliniums. That it was in use among the Greeks, the word Triclinium implieth, and the same is also declarable from many
places in the *Symposiacks* of Plutarch. That it was not out of
fashion in the days of Aristotle, he declareth in his politicks;
when among the Institutionary rules of youth, he adviseth they
might not be permitted to hear Iambicks and Tragedies before
they were admitted unto discumbency or lying along with
others at their meals. That the Romans used this gesture at
repast, beside many more, is evident from Lipsius, Mercurialis,
Salmasius and Ciaconius, who have expresly and distinctly
treated hereof.

Now of their accumbing places, the one was called Stibadion
and Sigma, carrying the figure of an half Moon, and of an uncertain capacity, whereupon it received the name of Hexa-
clinon, Octaclinon, according unto that of Martial,

Accipe lunata scriptum testudine Sigma:
Octo capit: veniat, quisquis amicus erit.

Hereat in several ages the left and right horn were the principal places, and the most honorable person, if he were not master of the feast, possessed one of those rooms. The other was termed Triclinium, that is, Three beds about a table, as may be seen in the figures thereof, and particularly in the Rhamnusian Triclinium, set down by Mercurialis. The customary use hereof was probably deduced from the frequent use of bathing, after which they commonly retired to bed, and refected themselves with repast; and so that custom by degrees changed their cubicularly beds into discubitory, and introduced a fashion to go from the bathes unto these.

As for their gesture or position, the men lay down leaning on their left elbow, their back being advanced by some pillow or soft substance: the second lay so with his back towards the first, that his head attained about his bosome; and the rest in the same order. For women, they sat sometimes distinctly with their sex, sometime promiscuously with men, according to affection or favour, as is delivered by Juvenal,

Gremio jacuit nova nupta mariti.

And by Suetonius of Caligula, that at his feasts he placed his sisters, with whom he had been incontinent, successively in order below him.

Again, As their beds were three, so the guests did not usually exceed that number in every one; according to the ancient Laws, and proverbial observations to begin with the Graces, and make up their feasts with the Muses. And therefore it was remarkable in the Emperour Lucius Verus, that he lay down with twelve: which was, saith Julius Capitolinus, *præter exempla majorum*, not according to the custom of his Predecessors, except it were at publick and nuptial suppers. The regular number was also exceeded in the last supper, whereat there were no less than thirteen, and in no place fewer than ten, for, as Josephus delivereth, it was not lawful to celebrate the Passover with fewer than that number.

Lastly, For the disposing and ordering of the persons: The first and middle beds were for the guests, the third and lowest for the Master of the house and his family; he always lying in the first place of the last bed, that is, next the middle bed; but if

BOOK V
Chapter 6
Who the
Umbræ
were at
banquets.

Jul. Scalig.
familiarium
exercita-
tionum
Problema 1.

the wife or children were absent, their rooms were supplied by the Umbræ ,or hangers on, according to that of Juvenal*—*Locus est & pluribus Umbris.* For the guests, the honourablest place in every bed was the first, excepting the middle or second bed; wherein the most honourable Guest of the feast was placed in the last place, because by that position he might be next the Master of the feast. For the Master lying in the first of the last bed, and the principal Guest in the last place of the second, they must needs be next each other; as this figure doth plainly declare, and whereby we may apprehend the feast of Perpenna made unto Sertorius, described by Salustius, whose words we shall thus read with Salmasius: *Igitur discubuere, Sertorius inferior in medio lecto, supra Fabius; Antonius in summo; Infra Scriba Sertorii Versius; alter scriba Mæcenas in Imo, medius inter Tarquitium & Dominum Perpennam.*

At this feast there were but seven; the middle places of the highest and middle bed being vacant; and hereat was Sertorius the General and principal guest slain. And so may we make out what is delivered by Plutarch in his life, that lying on his back, and raising himself up, Perpenna cast himself upon his stomack;

* *Juvenal* is an error for *Horace* [*Ep.* 1, v, 28].

which he might very well do, being Master of the feast, and lying next unto him. And thus also from this Tricliniary disposure, we may illustrate that obscure expression of Seneca; That the Northwind was in the middle, the North-East on the higher side, and the North-West on the lower. For as appeareth in the circle of the winds, the North-East will answer the bed of Antonius, and the North-West that of Perpenna.

That the custom of feasting upon beds was in use among the Hebrews, many deduce from Ezekiel, *Thou satest upon a stately* Ezek. 23. *bed, and a table prepared before it.* The custom of Discalceation or putting off their shoes at meals, is conceived to confirm the same; as by that means keeping their beds clean; and therefore they had a peculiar charge to eat the Passover with their shooes on; which Injunction were needless, if they used not to put them off. However it were in times of high antiquity, probable it is that in after ages they conformed unto the fashions of the Assyrians and Eastern Nations, and lastly of the Romans, being reduced by Pompey unto a Provincial subjection.

That this discumbency at meals was in use in the days of our Saviour, is conceived probable from several speeches of his expressed in that phrase, even unto common Auditors, as Luke 14. *Cum invitatus fueris ad nuptias, non discumbas in primo loco,* and besides many more, Matthew 23. When reprehending the Scribes and Pharises, he saith, *Amant protoclisias, id est, primos recubitus in cœnis, & protocathedrias, sive, primas cathedras, in Synagogis*: wherein the terms are very distinct, and by an Antithesis do plainly distinguish the posture of sitting, from this of lying on beds. The consent of the Jews with the Romans in other ceremonies and rites of feasting, makes probable their conformity in this. The Romans washed, were anointed, and wore a cenatory garment: and that the same was practised by the Jews, is Luke 7. deduceable from that expostulation of our Saviour with Simon, that he washed not his feet, nor anointed his head with oyl, the common civilities at festival entertainments: and that expression of his concerning the cenatory or wedding garment; and Matth. 22: as some conceive of the linnen garment of the young man or St. John, which might be the same he wore the night before at the last Supper.

That they used this gesture at the Passover, is more than

probable from the testimony of Jewish Writers, and particularly of Ben-maimon recorded by Scaliger *De emendatione
temporum.* After the second cup according to the Institution, The

Son asketh, *what meaneth this service?* Then he that maketh the
declaration, saith, How different is this night from all other
nights? for all other nights we wash but once, but this night
twice; all other we eat leavened or unleavened bread, but this
only unleavened;[54] all other we eat flesh roasted, boyled or baked,
but this only roasted; all other nights we eat together lying or
sitting, but this only lying along. And this posture they used
as a token of rest and security which they enjoyed, far different
from that, at the eating of the Passover in Ægypt.

That this gesture was used when our Saviour eat the Passe-
over, is not conceived improbable from the words whereby
the Evangelists express the same, that is, ἀναπίπτειν, ἀνακεῖσθαι,
κατακεῖσθαι, ἀνακλειθῆναι, which terms do properly signifie this
Gesture in Aristotle, Athenæus, Euripides, Sophocles, and all
humane Authors; and the like we meet with in the paraphras-
tical expression of Nonnus.

Lastly, If it be not fully conceded, that this gesture was used
at the Passover, yet that it was observed at the last supper,
seems almost incontrovertible; for at this feast or cenatory con-
vention, learned men make more than one supper, or at least
many parts thereof. The first was that Legal one of the Passover, or eating of the Paschal Lamb with bitter herbs, and cere-

monies described by Moses. Of this it is said, *then when the even
was come he sat down with the twelve.* This is supposed when it is
said, that the supper being ended, our Saviour arose, took a
towel and washed the disciples' feet. The second was common
and Domestical, consisting of ordinary and undefined provisions; of this it may be said, that our Saviour took his garment,
and sat down again, after he had washed the Disciples' feet, and
performed the preparative civilities of suppers; at this 'tis conceived the sop was given unto Judas, the Original word implying some broath or decoction, not used at the Passover. The
third or latter part was Eucharistical, which began at the breaking and blessing of the bread, according to that of Matthew,
and as they were eating, Jesus took bread and blessed it.

Now although at the Passover or first supper, many have

doubted this Reclining posture, and some have affirmed that
our Saviour stood; yet that he lay down at the other, the same men have acknowledged, as Chrysostom, Theophylact, Austin, and many more. And if the tradition will hold, the position is unquestionable; for the very Triclinium is to be seen at Rome, brought thither by Vespasian, and graphically set forth by
Casalius.

Thus may it properly be made out; what is delivered, John 13.

Erat recumbens unus ex Discipulis ejus in sinu Jesu quem diligebat; Now there was leaning on Jesus' bosom one of his Disciples whom Jesus loved; which gesture will not so well agree unto the position of sitting, but is natural, and cannot be avoided in the Laws of accubation. And the very same expression is to be found in Pliny, concerning the Emperour Nerva and Veiento whom he favoured; *Cœnebat Nerva cum paucis, Veiento recumbebat proprius atque etiam in sinu;* and from this custom arose the word ἐπιστήθιος, that is, a near and bosom friend. And therefore Casaubon justly rejecteth Theo- phylact; who not considering the ancient manner of decum- bency, imputed this gesture of the beloved Disciple unto Rusticity, or an act of incivility. And thus also have some con- ceived, it may be more plainly made out what is delivered of Mary Magdalen, *That she stood at Christ's feet behind him weeping,* *and began to wash his feet with tears, and did wipe them with the hairs of her head.* Which actions, if our Saviour sat, she could not per- form standing, and had rather stood behind his back, than at his feet. And therefore it is not allowable, what is observable in many pieces, and even of Raphael Urbin; wherein Mary Mag- dalen is pictured before our Saviour, washing his feet on her knees; which will not consist with the strict description and letter of the Text.

Now whereas this position may seem to be discountenanced by our Translation, which usually renders it sitting, it cannot have that illation, for the French and Italian Translations ex- pressing neither position of session or recubation, do only say that he placed himself at the table; and when ours expresseth the same by sitting, it is in relation unto our custom, time, and apprehension. The like upon occasion is not unusual: so when it is said, Luke 4. πτύξας τὸ βιβλίον, and the Vulgar renders it, *Cum plicuisset librum,* ours translateth it, he shut or *closed the book;*

which is an expression proper unto the paginal books of our times, but not so agreeable unto volumes or rolling books in use among the Jews, not only in elder times, but even unto this day. So when it is said, the Samaritan delivered unto the host two pence for the provision of the Levite; and when our Saviour agreed with the Labourers for a penny a day; in strict translation it should be seven pence half penny; and is not to be conceived our common penny, the sixtieth part of an ounce. For the word in the Original is δηνάριον, in Latine, *Denarius*, and with the Romans did value the eight part of an ounce, which after five shillings the ounce amounteth unto seven pence half penny of our money.

What *Denari-
us*, or the
penny in the
Gospel is.

Lastly, Whereas it might be conceived that they eat the Passover standing rather than sitting, or lying down, according to the Institution, Exod. 12. *Thus shall you eat, with your loins girded, your shooes on your feet, and your staff in your hand;* the Jews themselves reply, this was not required of succeeding generations, and was not observed, but in the Passover of Ægypt. And so also many other injunctions were afterward omitted, as the taking up of the Paschal Lamb from the tenth day, the eating of it in their houses dispersed, the striking of the blood on the door posts, and the eating thereof in hast. Solemnities and Ceremonies primitively enjoyned, afterward omitted; as was also this of station, for the occasion ceasing, and being in security, they applied themselves unto gestures in use among them.

Now in what order of recumbency Christ and the Disciples were disposed, is not so easily determined. Casalius from the Lateran Triclinium will tell us, that there being thirteen, five lay down in the first bed, five in the last, and three in the middle bed; and that our Saviour possessed the upper place thereof. That John lay in the same bed seems plain, because he leaned on our Saviour's bosom. That Peter made the third in that bed, conjecture is made, because he beckened unto John, as being next him, to ask of Christ, who it was that should betray him. That Judas was not far off seems probable, not only because he dipped in the same dish, but because he was so near, that our Saviour could hand the sop unto him.

CHAP. VII

Of the Picture of our Saviour with long hair

ANOTHER Picture there is of our Saviour described with long hair, according to the custom of the Jews, and his description sent by Lentulus unto the Senate. Wherein indeed the hand of the Painter is not accusable, but the judgement of the common Spectator; conceiving he observed this fashion of his hair, because he was a Nazarite, and confounding a Nazarite by vow with those by birth or education.

The Nazarite by vow is declared Numb. 6. and was to refrain three things, drinking of Wine, cutting the hair, and approaching unto the dead; and such a one was Sampson. Now that our Saviour was a Nazarite after this kind, we have no reason to determine; for he drank Wine, and was therefore called by the Pharisees, a Wine-bibber; he approached also the dead, as when he raised from death Lazarus, and the daughter of Jairus.

The other Nazarite was a Topical appellation, and appliable unto such as were born in Nazareth, a City of Galilee, and in the Tribe of Napthali. Neither if strictly taken was our Saviour in this sense a Nazarite; for he was born in Bethlehem in the Tribe of Judah; but might receive that name, because he abode in that City, and was not only conceived therein, but there also passed the silent part of his life, after his return from Ægypt; as is delivered by Matthew, *And he came and dwelt in a City called Nazareth, that it might be fulfilled which was spoken by the Prophet, He shall be called a Nazarene.* Both which kinds of Nazarites, as they are distinguishable by Zain, and Tsade in the Hebrew, so in the Greek, by Alpha and Omega; for as Jansenius observeth, where the votary Nazarite is mentioned, it is written, Ναζαραῖος, as Levit. 6. and Lament. 4. Where it is spoken of our Saviour, we read it, Ναζωρεῖος, as in Matthew, Luke and John; only Mark who writ his Gospel at Rome, did Latinize, and wrote it Ναζαρηνός.

BOOK V
Chapter 7

Jans. *Concordia Evangelica.*

CHAP. VIII

Of the Picture of Abraham sacrificing Isaac

IN the Picture of the Immolation of Isaac, or Abraham sacrificing his son, Isaac is described as a little boy; which notwithstanding is not consentaneous unto the authority of Expositors, or the circumstance of the Text. For therein it is delivered that Isaac carried on his back the wood for the sacrifice; which being an holocaust or burnt offering to be consumed unto ashes, we cannot well conceive a burthen for a boy; but such a one unto Isaac, as that which it typified was unto Christ, that is, the wood or cross whereon he suffered; which was too heavy a load for his shoulders, and was fain to be relieved therein by Simon of Cyrene.

Again, he was so far from a boy, that he was a man grown, and at his full stature, if we believe Josephus, who placeth him in the last of Adolescency, and makes him twenty five years old. And whereas in the Vulgar Translation he is termed *puer*, it must not be strictly apprehended (for that age properly endeth in puberty, and extendeth but unto fourteen) but respectively unto Abraham, who was at that time above sixscore. And therefore also herein he was not unlike unto him, who was after led dumb unto the slaughter, and commanded by others, who had legions at command; that is, in meekness and humble submission. For had he resisted, it had not been in the power of his aged parent to have enforced; and many at his years have performed such acts, as few besides at any. David was too strong for a Lion and a Bear; Pompey had deserved the name of Great; Alexander of the same cognomination was Generalissimo of Greece; and Anibal but one year after, succeeded Asdruball in that memorable War against the Romans.

CHAP. XXII

*Compendiously of many questionable Customs, Opinions,
Pictures, Practices, and Popular Observations*

IF an Hare cross the high way, there are few above threescore years that are not perplexed thereat; which notwithstanding is but an Augurial terror, according to that
received expression, *Inauspicatum dat iter oblatus Lepus.* And the
ground of the conceit was probably no greater than this, that
a fearful animal passing by us, portended unto us some thing
to be feared: as upon the like consideration, the meeting of a
Fox presaged some future imposture; which was a superstitious observation prohibited unto the Jews, as is expressed in
the Idolatry of Maimonides, and is referred unto the sin of an
observer of Fortunes, or one that abuseth events unto good or
bad signs, forbidden by the Law of Moses; which notwithstanding sometimes succeeding, according to fears or desires, have
left impressions and timerous expectations in credulous minds
for ever.

BOOK V
Chapter 22

The ground
of many vain
observations.
Deut. 18.

2. That Owls and Ravens are ominous appearers, and pre-
signifying unlucky events, as Christians yet conceit, was also
an Augurial conception. Because many Ravens were seen when
Alexander entred Babylon, they were thought to pre-ominate
his death; and because an Owl appeared before the battle, it
presaged the ruin of Crassus. Which though decrepite supersti-
tions, and such as had their nativity in times beyond all history,
are fresh in the observation of many heads, and by the credulous
and feminine party still in some Majesty among us. And therefore the Emblem of Superstition was well set out by Ripa, in
the picture of an Owl, an Hare, and an Old Woman. And it no
way confirmeth the Augurial consideration, that an Owl is a
forbidden food in the Law of Moses; or that Jerusalem was
threatened by the Raven and the Owl, in that expression of
Esay 34. That it should be a court for Owls, that the Cor-
morant and the Bittern should possess it, and the Owl and the
Raven dwell in it. For thereby was only implied their ensuing
desolation, as is expounded in the words succeeding; *He shall
draw upon it the line of confusion, and the stones of emptiness.*

The Emblem
of super-
stition.
*Iconologia de
Cæsare Ripa.*

3. The falling of Salt is an authentick presagement of ill luck, nor can every temper contemn it; from whence notwithstanding nothing can be naturally feared: nor was the same a general prognostick of future evil among the Ancients, but a particular omination concerning the breach of friendship. For Salt as incorruptible, was the Symbole of friendship, and before the other service was offered unto their guests; which if it casually fell, was accounted ominous, and their amity of no duration. But whether Salt were not only a Symbole of friendship with man, but also a figure of amity and reconciliation with God, and was therefore observed in sacrifices; is an higher speculation.

4. To break the egg shell after the meat is out, we are taught in our childhood, and practise it all our lives; which nevertheless is but a superstitious relict, according to the judgment of Pliny, *Huc pertinet ovorum, ut exsorbuerit quisque, calices protinus frangi, aut eosdem coclearibus perforari*; and the intent hereof was to prevent witchcraft; for lest witches should draw or prick their names therein, and veneficiously mischief their persons, they broke the shell, as Dalecampius hath observed.

5. The true Lover's knot is very much magnified, and still retained in presents of Love among us; which though in all points it doth not make it out, had perhaps its original from the *Nodus Herculanus*, or that which was called Hercules his knot, resembling the snaky complication in the *caduceus* or rod of Hermes; and in which form the Zone or woollen girdle of the Bride was fastned, as Turnebus observeth in his *Adversaria*.

6. When our cheek burneth or ear tingleth, we usually say that some body is talking of us, which is an ancient conceit, and ranked among superstitious opinions by Pliny. *Absentes tinnitu aurium præsentire sermones de se receptum est*; according to that distick noted by Dalecampius:

> *Garrula quid totis resonas mihi noctibus auris?*
> *Nescio quem dicis nunc meminisse mei.*

Which is a conceit hardly to be made out without the concession of a signifying Genius, or universal Mercury; conducting sounds unto their distant subjects, and teaching us to hear by touch.

7. When we desire to confine our words, we commonly say

they are spoken under the Rose; which expression is commendable, if the Rose from any natural property may be the Symbole
of silence, as Nazianzene seems to imply in these translated
verses:

BOOK V
Chapter 22
The original
of the pro-
verb, *Under
the Rose be it,*
&c.

> *Utque latet Rosa Verna suo putamine clausa,*
> *Sic os vincla ferat, validisque arctetur habenis,*
> *Indicatque suis prolixa silentia labris:*

And is also tolerable, if by desiring a secrecy to words spoke
under the Rose, we only mean in society and compotation,
from the ancient custom in Symposiack meetings, to wear chap-
lets of Roses about their heads: and so we condemn not the
German custom, which over the Table describeth a Rose in the
cieling. But more considerable it is, if the original were such as
Lemnius, and others have recorded; that the Rose was the
flower of Venus, which Cupid consecrated unto Harpocrates,
the God of silence, and was therefore an Emblem thereof, to conceal the pranks of Venery; as is declared in this Tetrastick;

> *Est Rosa flos veneris, cujus quo facta laterent,*
> *Harpocrati matris, dona dicavit Amor;*
> *Inde Rosam mensis hospes suspendit Amicis,*
> *Convivæ ut sub eâ dicta tacenda sciant.*

8. That smoak doth follow the fairest, is an usual saying
with us, and in many parts of Europe; whereof although there
seem no natural ground, yet is it the continuation of a very
ancient opinion, as Petrus Victorius and Casaubon have observed
from a passage in Athenæus, wherein a Parasite thus describeth
himself:

> To every Table first I come,
> Whence Porridg I am cal'd by some:
> A Capaneus at Stares I am,
> To enter any Room a Ram;
> Like whips and thongs to all I ply,
> Like smoake unto the Fair I fly.

9. To sit cross leg'd, or with our fingers pectinated or shut
together, is accounted bad, and friends will perswade us from
it. The same conceit religiously possessed the Ancients, as is
observable from Pliny, *Poplites alternis genibus imponere nefas olim;*

and also from Athenæus, that it was an old veneficious practice, and Juno is made in this posture to hinder the delivery of Alcmæna. And therefore, as Pierius observeth, in the Medal of Julia Pia, the right hand of Venus was made extended with the inscription of *Venus Genetrix*; for the complication or pectination of the fingers was an Hieroglyphick of impediment, as in that place he declareth.

10. The set and statary times of paring of nails, and cutting of hair, is thought by many a point of consideration; which is perhaps but the continuation of an ancient superstition. For piaculous it was unto the Romans to pare their nails upon the Nundinæ, observed every ninth day; and was also feared by others in certain daies of the week, according to that of Ausonius, *Ungues Mercurio, Barbam Jove, Cypride Crines*; and was one part of the wickedness that filled up the measure of Manasses, when 'tis delivered that he observed times.

2 Chron. 33.

11. A common fashion it is to nourish hair upon the mouls of the face; which is the perpetuation of a very ancient custom; and though innocently practised among us, may have a superstitious original, according to that of Pliny, *Nævos in facie tondere religiosum habent nunc multi*. From the like might proceed the fears of poling Elvelocks or complicated hairs of the head, and also of locks longer than the other hair; they being votary at first, and dedicated upon occasion; preserved with great care, and accordingly esteemed by others, as appears by that of Apuleius, *Adjuro per dulcem capilli tui nodulum*.

12. A custom there is in most parts of Europe to adorn Aqueducts, spouts and Cisterns with Lions' heads: which though no illaudable ornament, is of an Egyptian genealogy,[59] who practised the same under a symbolical illation. For because the Sun being in Leo, the flood of *Nilus* was at the full, and water became conveyed into every part, they made the spouts of their Aqueducts through the head of a Lion. And upon some cœlestial respects it is not improbable the great Mogul or Indian King doth bear for his Arms a Lion and the Sun.

Symbolical
significations
of the girdle.

13. Many conceive there is somewhat amiss, and that as we usually say, they are unblest until they put on their girdle. Wherein (although most know not what they say) there are involved unknown considerations. For by a girdle or cincture

are symbolically implied Truth, Resolution, and Readiness unto
action, which are parts and vertues required in the service of
God. According whereto we find that the Israelites did eat the
Paschal Lamb with their loins girded; and the Almighty challenging Job, bids him gird up his loins like a man. So runneth
the expression of Peter, *Gird up the loins of your minds, be sober and
hope to the end*: so the high Priest was girt with the girdle of fine
linnen: so is it part of the holy habit to have our loines girt
about with truth; and so is it also said concerning our Saviour,
Righteousness shall be the girdle of his loins, and faithfulness the girdle Isa. 11.
of his reins.

Moreover by the girdle, the heart and parts which God requires are divided from the inferior and concupiscential organs;[60]
implying thereby a memento unto purification and cleanness of
heart, which is commonly defiled from the concupiscence and
affection of those parts; and therefore unto this day the Jews do
bless themselves when they put on their zone or cincture. And
thus may we make out the doctrin of Pythagoras, to offer sacrifice with our feet naked, that is, that our inferiour parts and
farthest removed from reason might be free, and of no impediment unto us. Thus Achilles, though dipped in Styx, yet having
his heel untouched by that water, although he were fortified
elsewhere, he was slain in that part, as only vulnerable in the
inferiour and brutal part of Man. This is that part of Eve and
her posterity the devil still doth bruise, that is, that part of the
soul which adhereth unto earth, and walks in the paths thereof.
And in this secondary and symbolical sense it may be also
understood, when the Priests in the Law washed their feet
before the sacrifice; when our Saviour washed the feet of his
Disciples, and said unto Peter, *If I wash not thy feet thou hast no
part in me.* And thus is it symbolically explainable, and implyeth
purification and cleanness, when in the burnt offerings the
Priest is commanded to wash the inwards and legs thereof in
water; and in the peace and sin-offerings, to burn the two kidneys, the fat which is about the flanks, and as we translate it,
the Caul above the Liver. But whether the Jews when they
blessed themselves, had any eye unto the words of Jeremy, Jer. 13.
wherein God makes them his Girdle; or had therein any reference unto the Girdle, which the Prophet was commanded to

hide in the hole of the rock of Euphrates, and which was the type of their captivity, we leave unto higher conjecture.

Certain
Hereticks
who
ascribed
humane
figure unto
God, after
which they
conceived
he created
man in his
likeness.
14. The Picture of the Creator, or God the Father in the shape of an old Man, is a dangerous piece, and in this Fecundity of sects may revive the Anthropomorphites; which although maintained from the expression of Daniel, *I beheld where the Ancient of dayes did sit, whose hair of his head was like the pure wool*, yet may it be also derivative from the Hieroglyphical description of the Ægyptians; who to express their Eneph, or Creator of the world, described an old man in a blew mantle, with an egg in his mouth; which was the Emblem of the world. Surely those heathens, that notwithstanding the exemplary advantage in heaven, would endure no pictures of Sun or Moon, as being visible unto all the world, and needing no representation; do evidently accuse the practice of those pencils, that will describe invisibles. And he that challenged the boldest hand unto the picture of an Echo, must laugh at this attempt, not only in the description of invisibility, but circumscription of Ubiquity, and fetching under lines incomprehensible circularity.

The Pictures of the Ægyptians were more tolerable, and in their sacred letters more veniably expressed the apprehension of Divinity. For though they implied the same by an eye upon a Scepter, by an Ægle's head, a Crocodile, and the like: yet did these manual descriptions pretend no corporal representations; nor could the people misconceive the same unto real correspondencies. So though the Cherub carried some apprehension of Divinity, yet was it not conceived to be the shape thereof: and so perhaps because it is metaphorically predicated of God, that he is a consuming fire, he may be harmlessly described by a flaming representation. Yet if, as some will have it, all mediocrity of folly is foolish, and because an unrequitable evil may ensue, an indifferent convenience must be omitted, we shall not urge such representments; we could spare the holy Lamb for the picture of our Saviour, and the Dove or fiery Tongues to represent the holy Ghost.

15. The Sun and Moon are usually described with humane faces; whether herein there be not a Pagan imitation, and those visages at first implied Apollo and Diana, we may make some doubt; and we find the *statua* of the Sun was framed with raies

about the head, which were the indiciduous and unshaven locks of Apollo. We should be too Iconomical to question the pictures of the winds, as commonly drawn in humane heads, and with their cheeks distended; which notwithstanding we find condemned by Minutius, as answering poetical fancies, and the gentile description of Æolus, Boreas, and the feigned Deities of winds.

BOOK V
Chapter 22
Or quarrel-
som with
Pictures.
Dion. Ep. 7.
a, ad Policar.
& Pet. Hall
not. in vit. S.
Dionys.

16. We shall not, I hope, disparage the Resurrection of our Redeemer, if we say the Sun doth not dance on Easter day. And though we would willingly assent unto any sympathetical exultation, yet cannot conceive therein any more than a Tropical expression. Whether any such motion there were in that day wherein Christ arised, Scripture hath not revealed, which hath been punctual in other records concerning solary miracles: and the Areopagite that was amazed at the Eclipse, took no notice of this. And if metaphorical expressions go so far, we may be bold to affirm, not only that one Sun danced, but two arose that day: That light appeared at his nativity, and darkness at his death, and yet a light at both; for even that darkness was a light unto the Gentiles, illuminated by that obscurity. That 'twas the first time the Sun set above the Horizon; that although there were darkness above the earth, there was light beneath it, nor dare we say that hell was dark if he were in it.

17. Great conceits are raised of the involution or membranous covering, commonly called the Silly-how, that sometimes is found about the heads of children upon their birth; and is therefore preserved with great care, not only as medical in diseases, but effectual in success, concerning the Infant and others; which is surely no more than a continued superstition. For hereof we read in the life of Antoninus delivered by Spartianus, that children are born sometimes with this natural cap; which Midwives were wont to sell unto credulous Lawyers, who had an opinion it advantaged their promotion.

But to speak strictly, the effect is natural, and thus may be conceived: Animal conceptions have largely taken three teguments, or membranous films which cover them in the womb, that is, the Corion, Amnios, and Allantois; the Corion is the outward membrane wherein are implanted the Veins, Arteries and umbilical vessels, whereby its nourishment is conveyed; the

Allantois a thin coat seated under the Corion, wherein are received the watery separations conveyed by the Urachus, that the acrimony thereof should not offend the skin; the Amnios is a general investment, containing the sudorus or thin serosity perspirable through the skin. Now about the time when the Infant breaketh these coverings, it sometimes carrieth with it about the head a part of the Amnios or nearest coat; which saith Spiegelius, either proceedeth from the toughness of the membrane or weakness of the Infant that cannot get clear thereof. And therefore herein significations are natural and concluding upon the Infant, but not to be extended unto magical signalities, or any other person.

18. That 'tis good to be drunk once a moneth, is a common flattery of sensuality, supporting it self upon Physick, and the healthful effects of inebriation. This indeed seems plainly affirmed by Avicenna, a Physitian of great authority, and whose religion prohibiting Wine, could less extenuate ebriety. But Averroes a man of his own faith was of another belief; restraining his ebriety unto hilarity, and in effect making no more thereof than Seneca commendeth, and was allowable in Cato; that is, a sober incalescence and regulated æstuation from wine; or what may be conceived between Joseph and his brethren, when the text expresseth they were merry, or drank largely, and whereby indeed the commodities set down by Avicenna, that is, alleviation of spirits, resolution of superfluities, provocation of sweat and urine, may also ensue. But as for dementation, sopition of reason, and the diviner particle from drink; though American religion approve, and Pagan piety of old hath practised it, even at their sacrifices; Christian morality and the doctrine of Christ will not allow. And surely that religion which excuseth the fact of Noah, in the aged surprizal of six hundred years, and unexpected inebriation from the unknown effects of wine, will neither acquit ebriosity nor ebriety, in their known and intended perversions.

And indeed, although sometimes effects succeed which may relieve the body, yet if they carry mischief or peril unto the soul, we are therein restrainable by Divinity, which circumscribeth Physick, and circumstantially determines the use thereof. From natural considerations, Physick commendeth the use

of venery; and happily, incest, adultery, or stupration may
prove as Physically advantagious, as conjugal copulation; which
notwithstanding must not be drawn into practise. And truly
effects, consequents, or events which we commend, arise oft-
times from wayes which we all condemn. Thus from the fact
of Lot, we derive the generation of Ruth, and blessed Nativity
of our Saviour; which notwithstanding did not extenuate the
incestuous ebriety of the generator. And if, as is commonly
urged, we think to extenuate ebriety from the benefit of vomit
oft succeeding, Egyptian sobriety will condemn us, which
purged both wayes twice a moneth, without this perturbation:
and we foolishly contemn the liberal hand of God, and ample
field of medicines which soberly produce that action.

19. A conceit there is, that the Devil commonly appeareth
with a cloven hoof; wherein although it seem excessively ridiculous, there may be somewhat of truth; and the ground thereof
at first might be his frequent appearing in the shape of a Goat,
which answers that description. This was the opinion of ancient
Christians concerning the apparition of Panites, Fauns and
Satyres; and in this form we read of one that appeared unto
Antony in the wilderness. The same is also confirmed from
expositions of holy Scripture; for whereas it is said, *Thou shalt
not offer unto Devils*, the Original word is *Seghnirim*, that is, rough
and hairy Goats, because in that shape the Devil most often
appeared; as is expounded by the Rabbins, as Tremellius hath
also explained; and as the word *Ascimah*, the god of Emath, is
by some conceived. Nor did he only assume this shape in elder
times, but commonly in later dayes, especially in the place of
his worship, if there be any truth in the confession of Witches,
and as in many stories it stands confirmed by Bodinus. And
therefore a Goat is not improperly made the Hieroglyphick of
the devil, as Pierius hath expressed it. So might it be the
Emblem of sin, as it was in the sin-offering; and so likewise of
wicked and sinful men, according to the expression of Scripture
in the method of the last distribution, when our Saviour shall
separate the Sheep from the Goats, that is, the Sons of the Lamb
from the children of the devil.

Why the devil
is commonly
said to appear
with a cloven
foot.

Levit. 17.

In his *Dæmo-
nomania.*

THE SIXTH BOOK

Of sundry common opinions Cosmographical and Historical

The first Discourse comprehended in several Chapters

CHAP. I

Concerning the beginning of the World, that the time thereof is not precisely to be known, as men generally suppose: Of men's enquiries in what season or point of the Zodiack it began. That as they are generally made they are in vain, and as particularly applied uncertain. Of the division of the seasons and four quarters of the year, according to Astronomers and Physitians. That the common compute of the Ancients, and which is yet retained by most, is unreasonable and erroneous. Of some Divinations and ridiculous diductions from one part of the year to another. And of the Providence and Wisdom of God in the site and motion of the Sun

BOOK VI
Chapter I
The age of
the world not
certainly de-
terminable.

CONCERNING the World and its temporal circumscriptions, who ever shall strictly examine both extreams, will easily perceive there is not only obscurity in its end, but its beginning; that as its period is inscrutable, so is its nativity indeterminable: That as it is presumption to enquire after the one, so is there no rest or satisfactory decision in the other. And hereunto we shall more readily assent, if we examine the informations, and take a view of the several difficulties in this point; which we shall more easily do, if we consider the different conceits of men, and duly perpend the imperfections of their discoveries.

And first, The histories of the Gentiles afford us slender satisfaction, nor can they relate any story, or affix a probable point to its beginning. For some thereof (and those of the wisest

amongst them) are so far from determining its beginning, that
they opinion and maintain it never had any at all; as the doctrin of Epicurus implieth, and more positively Aristotle in his
books *De Cælo* declareth, endeavouring to confirm it with arguments of reason, and those appearingly demonstrative; wherein
his labours are rational, and uncontroulable upon the grounds
assumed, that is, of Physical generation, and a Primary or first
matter, beyond which no other hand was apprehended. But
herein we remain sufficiently satisfied from Moses, and the Doctrin delivered of the Creation; that is, a production of all things
out of nothing, a formation not only of matter, but of form, and
a materiation even of matter it self.

Others are so far from defining the Original of the World or
of mankind, that they have held opinions not only repugnant
unto Chronology, but Philosophy; that is, that they had their
beginning in the soil where they inhabited; assuming or receiving appellations conformable unto such conceits. So did the
Athenians term themselves αὐτόχθονες or Aborigines, and in
testimony thereof did wear a golden Insect on their heads: the
same name is also given unto the Inlanders, or Midland inhabitants of this Island by Cæsar. But this is a conceit answerable
unto the generation of the Giants; not admittable in Philosophy, much less in Divinity, which distinctly informeth we are
all the seed of Adam, that the whole world perished unto eight
persons before the flood, and was after peopled by the Colonies
of the sons of Noah. There was therefore never *Autochthon*, or
man arising from the earth, but Adam; for the Woman being
formed out of the rib, was once removed from earth, and framed
from that Element under incarnation. And so although her production were not by copulation, yet was it in a manner seminal:
For if in every part from whence the seed doth flow, there be
contained the Idea of the whole; there was a seminality and contracted Adam in the rib, which by the information of a soul,
was individuated into Eve. And therefore this conceit applied
unto the Original of man, and the beginning of the world, is
more justly appropriable unto its end. For then indeed men shall
rise out of the earth: the graves shall shoot up their concealed
seeds, and in that great Autumn, men shall spring up, and awake
from their Chaos again.

Others have been so blind in deducing the Original of things, or delivering their own beginnings, that when it hath fallen into controversie, they have not recurred unto Chronologie or the Records of time: but betaken themselves unto probabilities, and the conjecturalities of Philosophy. Thus when the two ancient Nations, Egyptians, and Scythians contended for antiquity, the Egyptians pleaded their antiquity from the fertility of their soil, inferring that men there first inhabited, where they were with most facility sustained; and such a land did they conceive was Egypt.

The Scythians, although a cold and heavier Nation urged more acutely, deducing their arguments from the two active Elements and Principles of all things, Fire and Water. For if of all things there was first an union, and that Fire over-ruled the rest: surely that part of earth which was coldest, would first get free, and afford a place of habitation. But if all the earth were first involved in Water, those parts would surely first appear, which were most high, and of most elevated situation, and such was theirs. These reasons carried indeed the antiquity from the Egyptians, but confirmed it not in the Scythians: for as Herodotus relateth from Targitaus, their first King unto Darius, they accounted but one thousand years.

As for the Egyptians they invented another way of trial; for as the same Author relateth, Psammitichus their King attempted this decision by a new and unknown experiment, bringing up two Infants with Goats, and where they never heard the voice of man; concluding that to be the ancientest Nation, whose language they should first deliver. But herein he forgot that speech was by instruction not instinct, by imitation, not by nature, that men do speak in some kind but like Parrets, and as they are instructed, that is, in simple terms and words, expressing the open notions of things; which the second act of Reason compoundeth into propositions, and the last into Syllogisms and Forms of ratiocination. And howsoever the account of Manethon the Egyptian Priest run very high, and it be evident that Mizraim peopled that Country (whose name with the Hebrews it beareth unto this day) and there be many things of great antiquity related in Holy Scripture, yet was their exact account not very ancient; for Ptolomy their Country-man

beginneth his Astronomical compute no higher than Nabo-
nasser, who is conceived by some the same with Salmanasser.
As for the argument deduced from the Fertility of the soil, duly
enquired, it rather overthroweth than promoteth their antiquity; if that Country whose Fertility they so advance, was in
ancient times no firm or open land, but some vast lake or part
of the Sea, and became a gained ground by the mud and limous
matter brought down by the River Nilus, which setled by
degrees into a firm land. According as is expressed by Strabo,
and more at large by Herodotus, both from the Egyptian tradition and probable inducements from reason, called therefore
fluvii donum, an accession of earth, or tract of land acquired by the
River.

Lastly, Some indeed there are, who have kept Records of
time, and of a considerable duration, yet do the exactest thereof
afford no satisfaction concerning the beginning of the world, or
any way point out the time of its creation. The most authentick
Records and best approved antiquity are those of the Chaldeans; yet in the time of Alexander the Great, they attained
not so high as the flood. For as Simplicius relateth, Aristotle
required of Calisthenes, who accompanied that Worthy in his
Expedition, that at his arrive at Babylon, he would enquire of
the antiquity of their Records; and those upon compute he
found to amount unto 1903 years; which account notwithstanding ariseth no higher than 95 years after the flood. The Arca-
dians I confess, were esteemed of great antiquity, and it was
usually said they were before the Moon, according unto that of
Seneca, *Sydus post veteres Arcades editum*; and that of Ovid, *Lunâ
gens prior illa fuit.* But this as Censorinus observeth, must not be
taken grosly, as though they were existent before that Luminary; but were so esteemed, because they observed a set course
of year, before the Greeks conformed their year unto the course
and motion of the Moon.

Thus the Heathens affording no satisfaction herein, they are
most likely to manifest this truth, who have been acquainted
with Holy Scripture, and the sacred Chronology delivered by
Moses, who distinctly sets down this account, computing by
certain intervals, by memorable Æras, Epoches, or terms of
time. As from the Creation unto the flood; from thence unto

BOOK VI
Chapter 1

Different
counts upon
Scripture
concerning
the Age of
the World.
Abraham, from Abraham unto the departure from Egypt, &c. Now in this number have only been Samaritans, Jews and Christians. For the Jews they agree not in their accounts, as Bodine in his method of History hath observed out of Baal Seder, Rabbi Nassom, Gersom, and others; in whose compute the age of the World is not yet 5400 years. The same is more evidently observable from the two most learned Jews, Philo and Josephus; who very much differ in the accounts of time, and variously sum up these Intervalls assented unto by all. Thus Philo from the departure out of Egypt unto the building of the Temple, accounts but 920 years, but Josephus sets down 1062. Philo from the building of the Temple to its destruction 440. Josephus 470. Philo from the Creation to the Destruction of the Temple 3373. but Josephus 3513. Philo from the Deluge to the Destruction of the Temple 1718. but Josephus 1913. In which Computes there are manifest disparities, and such as much divide the concordance and harmony of times.

For the Samaritans, their account is different from these or any others; for they account from the Creation to the Deluge, but 1302 years; which cometh to pass upon the different account of the ages of the Patriarks set down when they begat children. For whereas the Hebrew, Greek and Latin texts account Jared 162 when he begat Enoch, they account but 62, and so in others. Now the Samaritans were no incompetent Judges of times and the Chronology thereof; for they embraced the five books of Moses, and as it seemeth, preserved the Text with far more integrity then the Jews; who as Tertullian, Chrysostom, and others observe, did several wayes corrupt the same, especially in passages concerning the prophesies of Christ; So that as Jerom professeth, in his translation he was fain sometime to relieve himself by the Samaritan Pentateuch; as amongst others in that Text, Deuteronomy 27. *Maledictus omnis qui non permanserit in omnibus quæ scripta sunt in libro Legis.* From hence Saint Paul inferreth there is no justification by the Law, and urgeth

Gal. 3. the Text according to the Septuagint. Now the Jews to afford a latitude unto themselves, in their copies expunged the word כל or Syncategorematical term *omnis*: wherein lieth the strength of the Law, and of the Apostle's argument; but the Samaritan Bible retained it right, and answerable unto what the Apostle had urged.

As for Christians from whom we should expect the exactest and most concurring account, there is also in them a manifest disagreement, and such as is not easily reconciled. For first, the Latins accord not in their account: to omit the calculation of the Ancients, of Austin, Bede, and others, the Chronology of the Moderns doth manifestly dissent. Josephus Scaliger, whom Helvicus seems to follow, accounts the Creation in 765 of the Julian period; and from thence unto the Nativity of our Saviour alloweth 3947 years; But Dionysius Petavius a learned Chronologer dissenteth from this compute almost 40 years, placing the Creation in the 730 of the Julian period, and from thence unto the Incarnation accounteth 3983 years.

For the Greeks, their accounts are more anomalous; for if we recur unto ancient computes, we shall find that Clemens Alexandrinus, an ancient Father and Præceptor unto Origen, accounted from the Creation unto our Saviour, 5664 years; for in the first of his Stromaticks, he collecteth the time from Adam unto the death of Commodus to be 5858 years; now the death of Commodus he placeth in the year after Christ 194, which number deducted from the former, there remaineth 5664. Theophilus Bishop of Antioch accounteth unto the Nativity of Christ 5515, deduceable from the like way of compute, for in his first book *ad Autolychum*, he accounteth from Adam unto Aurelius Verus 5695 years; now that Emperour died in the year of our Lord 180, which deducted from the former sum, there remaineth 5515. Julius Africanus an ancient Chronologer, accounteth somewhat less, that is, 5500. Eusebius, Orosius and others dissent not much from this, but all exceed five thousand.

The latter compute of the Greeks, as Petavius observeth, hath been reduced unto two or three accounts. The first accounts unto our Saviour 5501, and this hath been observed by Nicephorus, Theophanes, and Maximus. The other accounts 5509; and this of all at present is generally received by the Church of Constantinople, observed also by the Moscovite, as I have seen in the date of the Emperor's letters; wherein this year of ours 1645 is from the year of the world 7154, which doth exactly agree unto this last account 5509, for if unto that sum be added 1645, the product will be 7154, by this Chronology are many Greek Authors to be understood; and thus is Martinus Crusius to be made out, when in his Turcogrecian history he delivers, the City of Constantinople was taken by the Turks in the year σϠξα; that is, 6961. Now according unto these Chronologists, the Prophecy of Elias the Rabbin, so much in request with the Jews, and in some credit also with Christians, that the world should last but six thousand years; unto these I say, it hath been long and out of memory disproved, for the Sabbatical and 7000 year wherein the world should end (as did the Creation on the seventh day) unto them is long ago expired; they are proceeding in the eight thousand year, and numbers exceeding those days which men have made the types and shadows of these. But certainly what Marcus Leo the Jew conceiveth of the end of the heavens, exceedeth the account of all that ever shall be; for though he conceiveth the Elemental frame shall end in the Seventh or Sabbatical Millenary, yet cannot he opinion the heavens and more durable part of the Creation shall perish before seven times seven, or 49, that is, the Quadrant of the other seven, and perfect Jubilee of thousands.

Thus may we observe the difference and wide dissent of men's opinions, and thereby the great incertainty in this establishment. The Hebrews not only dissenting from the Samaritans, the Latins from the Greeks, but every one from another. Insomuch that all can be in the right it is impossible; that any one is so, not with assurance determinable. And therefore as Petavius confesseth, to effect the same exactly without inspiration it is impossible, and beyond the Arithmetick of any but God himself. And therefore also what satisfaction may be obtained from those violent disputes, and eager enquirers in what day of the month the world began either of March or October; likewise in what face or position of the Moon, whether at the prime or full, or soon after, let our second and serious considerations determine.

The cause of
so different
accounts
about the age
of the world. Now the reason and ground of this dissent, is the unhappy difference between the Greek and Hebrew Editions of the Bible, for unto these two Languages have all Translations conformed; the holy Scripture being first delivered in Hebrew, and first translated into Greek. For the Hebrew, it seems the primitive and surest text to rely on, and to preserve the same entire and uncorrupt, there hath been used the highest caution humanity

could invent. For as R. Ben. Maimon hath declared, if in the BOOK VI

copying thereof one letter were written twice, or if one letter Chapter 1
but touched another, that copy was not admitted into their
Synagogues, but only allowable to be read in Schools and private families. Neither were they careful only in the exact num- Corruption
ber of their Sections of the Law, but had also the curiosity to even in the
number every word, and affixed the account unto their several Hebrew Text
books. Notwithstanding all which, divers corruptions ensued, of the Bible.
and several depravations slipt in, arising from many and manifest grounds, as hath been exactly noted by Morinus in his
preface unto the Septuagint.

   As for the Septuagint, it is the first and most ancient Translation; and of greater antiquity than the Chaldee version; occasioned by the request of Ptolomeus Philadelphus King of Egypt,
for the ornament of his memorable Library; unto whom the high
Priest addressed six Jews out of every Tribe, which amounteth
unto 72; and by these was effected that Translation we usually
term the Septuagint, or Translation of seventy. Which name, The Credit
however it obtain from the number of their persons, yet in of the
respect of one common Spirit, it was the Translation but as it Septuagint
were of one man; if as the story relateth, although they were translation.
set apart and severed from each other, yet were their Translations found to agree in every point, according as is related by Aristeas *ad*
Philo and Josephus; although we find not the same in Aristeas, *Philocratorem*
who hath expresly treated thereof. But of the Greek compute *de 72 interpre-*
tibus.
there have passed some learned dissertations not many years
ago, wherein the learned Isaac Vossius makes the nativity of the
world to anticipate the common account one thousand four
hundred and forty years.

   This Translation in ancient times was of great authority, by
this many of the Heathens received some notions of the Creation and the mighty works of God. This in express terms is
often followed by the Evangelists, by the Apostles, and by our
Saviour himself in the quotations of the Old Testmanent. This
for many years was used by the Jews themselves, that is, such
as did Hellenize and dispersedly dwelt out of Palestine with the
Greeks; and this also the succeeding Christians and ancient
Fathers observed; although there succeeded other Greek versions, that is, of Aquila, Theodosius and Symmachus; for the

Latin translation of Jerom called now the Vulgar, was about 800 years after the Septuagint; although there was also a Latin translation before, called the Italick version. Which was after lost upon the general reception of the translation of Saint Jerom. *Præfat. in Paralipom.* Which notwithstanding (as he himself acknowledgeth) had been needless, if the Septuagint copys had remained pure, and as they were first translated. But, (beside that different copys were used, that Alexandria and Egypt followed the copy of Hesychius, Antioch and Constantinople that of Lucian the Martyr, and others that of Origen) the Septuagint was much depraved, not only from the errors of Scribes, and the emergent corruptions of time, but malicious contrivance of the Jews; as Justin Martyr hath declared, in his learned dialogue with *De Hebræi & Græci textus sinceritate.* Tryphon, and Morinus hath learnedly shewn from many confirmations.

Whatsoever Interpretations there have been since, have been especially effected with reference unto these, that is, the Greek and Hebrew text, the Translators sometimes following the one, sometimes adhering unto the other, according as they found them consonant unto truth, or most correspondent unto the rules of faith. Now however it cometh to pass, these two are very different in the enumeration of Genealogies, and particular accounts of time; for in the second intervall, that is, between the Flood and Abraham, there is by the Septuagint introduced one Cainan to be the son of Arphaxad and father of Salah; whereas in the Hebrew there is no mention of such a person, but Arphaxad is set down to be the father of Salah. But in the first intervall, that is, from the Creation unto the Flood, their disagreement is more considerable; for therein the Greek exceedeth the Hebrew and common account almost 600 years. And 'tis indeed a thing not very strange, to be at the difference of a third part, in so large and collective an account, if we consider how differently they are set forth in minor and less mistakable numbers. So in the Prophesie of Jonah, both in the Hebrew and Latin text, it is said, Yet forty dayes and Ninevy shall be overthrown: But the Septuagint saith plainly, and that in letters at length, $\tau\rho\epsilon\hat{\iota}s$ $\dot{\eta}\mu\acute{\epsilon}\rho\alpha s$, that is, yet three dayes and Ninevy shall be destroyed. Which is a difference not newly crept in, but an observation very ancient, discussed by Austin and Theodoret, and was conceived an error committed by the Scribe. Men therefore have raised different computes of time, according as they have followed their different texts; and so have left the history of times far more perplexed than Chronology hath reduced.

Again, However the texts were plain, and might in their numerations agree, yet were there no small difficulty to set down a determinable Chronology, or establish from hence any fixed point of time. For the doubts concerning the time of the Judges are inexplicable; that of the Reigns and succession of Kings is as perplexed; it being uncertain whether the years both of their lives and reigns ought to be taken as compleat, or in their beginning and but currant accounts. Nor is it unreasonable to make some doubt whether in the first ages and long lives of our fathers, Moses doth not sometime account by full and round numbers, whereas strictly taken they might be some few years above or under; as in the age of Noah, it is delivered to be just five hundred when he begat Sem; whereas perhaps he might be somewhat above or below that round and compleat number. For the same way of speech is usual in divers other expressions: Thus do we say the Septuagint, and using the full and articulate number, do write the Translation of Seventy; whereas we have shewn before, the precise number was Seventy two. So is it said that Christ was three days in the grave; according to that of Mathew, *as Jonas was three days and three nights in the Whale's belly, so shall the Son of man be three days and three nights in the heart of the earth*: which notwithstanding must be taken Synecdochically; or by understanding a part for an whole day; for he remained but two nights in the grave; for he was buried in the afternoon of the first day; and arose very early in the morning on the third; that is, he was interred in the eve of the Sabbath, and arose the morning after it.

Moreover although the number of years be determined and rightly understood, and there be without doubt a certain truth herein; yet the text speaking obscurely or dubiously, there is oft-times no slender difficulty at what point to begin or terminate the account. So when it is said Exod. 12. *the sojourning of the children of Israel who dwelt in Egypt was 430 years*, it cannot be taken strictly, and from their first arrival into Egypt, for their habitation in that land was far less; but the account must begin from the Covenant of God with Abraham, and must also comprehend their sojourn in the land of Canaan, according as is expressed, Gal. 3. *The Covenant that was confirmed before of God in Christ, the Law which was 430 years after cannot disanul.* Thus hath it also happened in the account of the 70 years of their captivity, according to that of Jeremy. *This whole land shall be a desolation, and these Nations shall serve the King of Babylon 70 years.* Now where to begin or end this compute, ariseth no small difficulties; for there were three remarkable captivities, and deportations of the Jews. The first was in the third or fourth year of Joachim, and first of Nabuchodonozor, when Daniel was carried away; the second in the reign of Jeconiah, and the eighth year of the same King; the third and most deplorable in the reign of Zedechias, and in the nineteenth year of Nabuchodonozor, whereat both the Temple and City were burned. Now such is the different conceit of these times, that men have computed from all; but the probablest account and most concordant unto the intention of Jeremy, is from the first of Nabuchodonozor unto the first of King Cyrus over Babylon; although the Prophet Zachary ac- counteth from the last, *O Lord of hosts, How Long! Wilt thou not have mercy on Jerusalem, against which thou hast had indignation these threescore and ten years?* for he maketh this expostulation in the second year of Darius Histaspes, wherein he prophesied, which is about eighteen years in account after the other.

Thus also although there be a certain truth therein, yet is there no easie doubt concerning the seventy weeks, or seventy times seven years of Daniel; whether they have reference unto the nativity or passion of our Saviour, and especially from whence, or what point of time they are to be computed. For thus is it delivered by the Angel Gabriel: *Seventy weeks are determined upon the people*; and again in the following verse: *Know therefore and understand, that from the going forth of the Commandment to restore and to build Jerusalem unto the Messias the Prince, shall be seven weeks, and threescore and two weeks, the street shall be built again, and the wall even in troublesome times; and after threescore and two weeks shall Messiah be cut off.* Now the going out of the Commandment to build the City, being the point from whence to compute, there is no slender controversie when to begin. For

AND COMMON ERRORS 343

there are no less then four several Edicts to this effect, the one in the first year of Cyrus, the other in the second of Darius, the third and fourth in the seventh, and in the twentieth of Artaxerxes Longimanus; although as Petavius accounteth, it best accordeth unto the twenty year of Artaxerxes, from whence Nehemiah deriveth his Commission. Now that computes are made uncertainly with reference unto Christ, it is no wonder, since I perceive the time of his Nativity is in controversie, and no less his age at his Passion, For Clemens and Tertullian conceive he suffered at thirty; but Ireneus, a Father neerer his time, is further off in his account, that is, between forty and fifty.

Longomontanus a late Astronomer, endeavours to discover this secret from Astronomical grounds, that is, the Apogeum of the Sun; conceiving the Excentricity invariable, and the Apogeum yearly to move one scruple, two seconds, fifty thirds, &c. Wherefore if in the time of Hipparchus, that is, in the year of the Julian period 4557. it was in the fifth degree of Gemini, and in the daies of Tycho Brahe, that is in the year of our Lord 1588. or of the world 5554. the same was removed unto the fift degree of Cancer; by the proportion of its motion, it was at the Creation first in the beginning of Aries, and the Perigeum or nearest point in Libra. But this conceit how ingenious or subtile soever, is not of satisfaction; it being not determinable, or yet agreed in what time precisely the Apogeum absolveth one degree, as Petavius hath also delivered.

Lastly, However these or other difficulties intervene, and that we cannot satisfie our selves in the exact compute of time, yet may we sit down with the common and usual account; nor are these differences derogatory unto the Advent or Passion of Christ, unto which indeed they all do seem to point, for the Prophecies concerning our Saviour were indefinitely delivered before that of Daniel; so was that pronounced unto Eve in paradise, that after of Balaam, those of Isaiah and the Prophets, and that memorable one of Jacob, *the Scepter shall not depart from Israel* untill Shilo come*; which time notwithstanding it did not define at all. In what year therefore soever, either from the destruction of the Temple, from the re-edifying thereof, from the flood, or from the Creation he appeared, certain it is, that

* *Israel* is an error for *Judah*.

BOOK VI
Chapter 1

Of our Bless. Saviour's age at his Passion.

De Doctrina temporum l. 4.

in the fulness of time he came. When he therefore came is not so considerable, as that he is come: in the one there is consolation, in the other no satisfaction. The greater Quere is, when he will come again; and yet indeed it is no Quere at all: for that is never to be known, and therefore vainly enquired: 'tis a professed and authentick obscurity, unknown to all but to the omiscience of the Almighty. Certainly the ends of things are wrapt up in the hands of God, he that undertakes the knowledge thereof, forgets his own beginning, and disclaims his principles of earth. No man knows the end of the world, nor assuredly of any thing in it: God sees it, because unto his Eternity it is present; he knoweth the ends of us, but not of himself: and because he knows not this, he knoweth all things, and his knowledge is endless, even in the object of himself.

THE SEVENTH BOOK

*Concerning many Historical Tenents generally received,
and some deduced from the history of holy Scripture*

CHAP. I

Of the Forbidden Fruit

THAT the Forbidden fruit of Paradise was an Apple, is commonly believed, confirmed by Tradition, perpetuated by Writings, Verses, Pictures; and some have been so bad Prosodians, as from thence to derive the Latine word *malum*, because that fruit was the first occasion of evil; wherein notwithstanding determinations are presumptuous, and many I perceive are of another belief. For some have conceived it a Vine; in the mystery of whose fruit lay the expiation of the transgression: Goropius Becanus, reviving the conceit of Barcephas, peremptorily concludeth it to be the Indian Fig-tree; and by a witty Allegory labours to confirm the same. Again, some fruits pass under the name of Adam's apples, which in common acception admit not that appellation; the one described by Mathiolus under the name of *Pomum Adami*, a very fair fruit, and not unlike a Citron, but somewhat rougher, chopt and cranied, vulgarly conceived the marks of Adam's teeth. Another, the fruit of that plant which Serapion termeth *Musa*, but the Eastern Christians commonly the Apples of Paradise; not resembling an apple in figure, and in taste a Melon or Cowcomber. Which fruits although they have received appellations suitable unto the tradition, yet can we not from thence infer they were this fruit in question: no more then *Arbor vitæ*, so commonly called, to obtain its name from the tree of life in Paradise, or *Arbor Judæ*, to be the same which supplied the gibbet unto Judas.

Again, There is no determination in the Text; wherein is

only particulared that it was the fruit of a tree good for food, and pleasant unto the eye, in which regards many excell the Apple; and therefore learned men do wisely conceive it inexplicable; and Philo puts determination unto despair, when he affirmeth the same kind of fruit was never produced since. Surely, were it not requisite to have been concealed, it had not passed unspecified; nor the tree revealed which concealed their nakedness, and that concealed which revealed it; for in the same chapter mention is made of fig-leaves. And the like particulars, although they seem uncircumstantial, are oft set down in holy Scripture; so is it specified that Elias sat under a juniper tree, Absolom hanged by an Oak, and Zacheus got up into a Sycomore.

And although to condemn such Indeterminables unto him that demanded on what hand Venus was wounded, the Philosopher thought it a sufficient resolution to reinquire upon what leg King Philip halted; and the Jews, not undoubtedly resolved *Jacob's* of the Sciatica-side of Jacob, do cautelously in their diet abstain *Sciatica, see* from the sinews of both: yet are there many nice particulars *Gen. 32. 25,* which may be authentically determined. That Peter cut off the *31, 32.* right ear of Malchus, is beyond all doubt. That our Saviour eat the Passover in an upper room, we may determine from the Text. And some we may concede which the Scripture plainly defines not. That the Dyal of Ahaz was placed upon the West side of the Temple, we will not deny, or contradict the description of Adricomius. That Abraham's servant put his hand under his right thigh, we shall not question; and that the Thief on the right hand was saved, and the other on the left reprobated, to make good the Method of the last judicial dismission, we are ready to admit. But surely in vain we enquire of what wood was Moses' rod, or the tree that sweetned the waters. Or though tradition or humane History might afford some light, whether the Crown of thorns was made of Paliurus; Whether the cross *Pes cedrus est,* of Christ were made of those four woods in the Distick of *truncus cupres-* Durantes, or only of Oak, according unto Lipsius and Goropius, *sus, oliva su-* we labour not to determine. For though hereof prudent Sym- *premum,* *Palmaque* bols and pious Allegories be made by wiser Conceivers; yet *transversum* common heads will flie unto superstitious applications, and *Christi sunt in* *cruce lignum.* hardly avoid miraculous or magical expectations.

Now the ground or reason that occasioned this expression by an Apple, might be the community of this fruit, and which is often taken for any other. So the Goddess of Gardens is termed *Pomona*; so the Proverb expresseth it to give Apples unto Alcinous; so the fruit which Paris decided was called an Apple; so in the garden of Hesperides (which many conceive a fiction drawn from Paradise) we read of golden Apples guarded by the Dragon. And to speak strictly in this apellation, they placed it more safely then any other; for beside the great variety of Apples, the word in Greek comprehendeth Orenges, Lemmons, Citrons, Quinces; and as Ruellius defineth, such fruits as have no stone within, and a soft covering without; excepting the Pomegranate. And will extend much farther in the acception of Spigelius, who comprehendeth all round fruits under the name of apples, not excluding Nuts and Plumbs.

It hath been promoted in some constructions from a passage in the Canticles, as it runs in the vulgar translation, *Sub arbore malo suscitavi te, ibi corrupta est mater tua, ibi violata est genetrix tua;* Which words notwithstanding parabolically intended, admit no literal inference, and are of little force in our translation, *I raised thee up under the Apple-tree, there thy mother brought thee forth, there she brought thee forth that bare thee.* So when from a basket of summer fruits or apples, as the vulgar rendreth them, God by Amos foretold the destruction of his people; we cannot say they had any reference unto the fruit of Paradise, which was the destruction of man; but thereby was declared the propinquity of their desolation, and that their tranquility was of no longer duration then those horary or soon decaying fruits of Summer. Nor when it is said in the same translation, *Poma desiderii animæ tuæ discesserunt à te,* the apples that thy soul lusted after are departed from thee, is there any allusion therein unto the fruit of Paradise. But thereby is threatned unto Babylon, that the pleasures and delights of their Palate should forsake them. And we read in Pierius, that an Apple was the Hieroglyphick of Love, and that the Statua of Venus was made with one in her hand. So the little Cupids in the figures of Philostratus do play with apples in a garden; and there want not some who have symbolized the Apple of Paradise unto such constructions.

Since therefore after this fruit, curiosity fruitlesly enquireth,

and confidence blindly determineth, we shall surcease our Inquisition; rather troubled that it was tasted, then troubling our
selves in its decision; this only we observe, when things are
left uncertain, men will assure them by determination. Which
Opinions of
what kind the
Serpent was,
&c.
is not only verified concerning the fruit, but the Serpent that
perswaded; many defining the kind or species thereof. So Bona-
venture and Comestor affirm it was a Dragon, Eugubinus a
Basilisk, Delrio a Viper, and others a common snake. Wherein
men still continue the delusion of the Serpent, who having
deceived Eve in the main, sets her posterity on work to mistake
in the circumstance, and endeavours to propagate errors at any
hand. And those he surely most desireth which concern either
God or himself; for they dishonour God who is absolute truth
and goodness; but for himself, who is extreamly evil, and the
worst we can conceive, by aberration of conceit they may
extenuate his depravity, and ascribe some goodness unto him.

CHAP. II

That a Man hath one Rib less then a Woman

Chapter 2
THAT a Man hath one Rib less then a Woman, is a common conceit derived from the History of Genesis, wherein it stands delivered, that Eve was framed out of a Rib
of Adam; whence 'tis concluded the sex of man still wants that
rib our Father lost in Eve. And this is not only passant with the
many, but was urged against Columbus in an Anatomy of his
at Pisa, where having prepared the Sceleton of a woman that
chanced to have thirteen ribs on one side, there arose a party
that cried him down, and even unto oaths affirmed, this was the
rib wherein a woman exceeded. Were this true, it would ocularly[73] silence that dispute out of which side Eve was framed;
it would determine the opinion of Oleaster, that she was made
out of the ribs of both sides, or such as from the expression of
Os ex ossibus
meis.
the Text maintain there was a plurality of ribs required; and
might indeed decry the parabolical exposition of Origen, Cajetan, and such as fearing to concede a monstrosity, or mutilate
the integrity of Adam, preventively conceive the creation of
thirteen ribs.

BOOK VII
Chapter 2
How many
ribs common-
ly in men and
women.

But this will not consist with reason or inspection. For if we survey the Sceleton of both sexes, and therein the compage of bones, we shall readily discover that men and women have four and twenty ribs, that is, twelve on each side, seven greater annexed unto the Sternon, and five lesser which come short thereof. Wherein if it sometimes happen that either sex exceed, the conformation is irregular, deflecting from the common rate or number, and no more inferrible upon mankind, then the monstrosity of the son of Rapha, or the vitious excess in the number of fingers and toes. And although some difference there be in figure and the female *os innominatum* be somewhat more protuberant, to make a fairer cavity for the Infant; the coccyx sometime more reflected to give the easier delivery, and the ribs themselves seem a little flatter, yet are they equal in number. And therefore while Aristotle doubteth the relations made of Nations, which had but seven ribs on a side, and yet delivereth, that men have generally no more then eight; as he rejecteth their history, so can we not accept of his Anatomy.

Again, Although we concede there wanted one rib in the Sceleton of Adam, yet were it repugnant unto reason and common observation that his posterity should want the same. For we observe that mutilations are not transmitted from father unto son; the blind begetting such as can see, men with one eye children with two, and cripples mutilate in their own persons do come out perfect in their generations. For the seed conveyeth with it not only the extract and single Idea of every part, whereby it transmits their perfections or infirmities, but double and over again; whereby sometimes it multipliciously delineates the same, as in Twins, in mixed and numerous generations. Parts of the seed do seem to contain the Idea and power of the whole; so parents deprived of hands, beget manual issues, and the defect of those parts is supplied by the Idea of others. So in one grain of corn appearing similary and insufficient for a plural germination, there lyeth dormant the virtuality of many other; and from thence sometimes proceed above an hundred ears. And thus may be made out the cause of multiparous productions; for though the seminal materials disperse and separate in the matrix, the formative operator will not delineate a part, but endeavour the formation of the whole;

effecting the same as far as the matter will permit, and from divided materials attempt entire formations. And therefore, though wondrous strange, it may not be impossible what is confirmed at Lausdun concerning the Countess of Holland, nor what Albertus reports of the birth of an hundred and fifty. And if we consider the magnalities of generation in some things, we shall not controvert its possibilities in others: nor easily question that great work, whose wonders are only second unto those of the Creation, and a close apprehension of the one, might perhaps afford a glimmering light, and crepusculous glance of the other.

CHAP. III

Of Methuselah

WHAT hath been every where opinioned by all men, and in all times, is more then paradoxical to dispute; and so that Methuselah was the longest liver of all the posterity of Adam, we quietly believe: but that he must needs be so, is perhaps below paralogy to deny. For hereof there is no determination from the Text; wherein it is only particulared he was the longest Liver of all the Patriarchs whose age is there expressed; but that he outlived all others, we cannot well conclude. For of those nine whose death is mentioned before the flood, the Text expresseth that Enoch was the shortest Liver; who saw but three hundred sixty five years. But to affirm from hence, none of the rest, whose age is not expressed, did die before that time, is surely an illation whereto we cannot assent.

Again, Many persons there were in those days of longevity, of whose age notwithstanding there is no account in Scripture; as of the race of Cain, the wives of the nine Patriarchs, with all the sons and daughters that every one begat: whereof perhaps some persons might out-live Methuselah; the Text intending only the masculine line of Seth, conduceable unto the Genealogy of our Saviour, and the antediluvian Chronology. And therefore we must not contract the lives of those which are left in silence by Moses; for neither is the age of Abel expressed in the Scripture, yet is he conceived far elder then commonly opinioned; and if we allow the conclusion of his Epitaph as made by Adam, and so set down by Salian, *Posuit mærens pater, cui à filio justius positum foret, Anno ab ortu rerum* 130. *ab Abele nato* 129. we shall not need to doubt. Which notwithstanding Cajetan and others confirm, nor is it improbable, if we conceive that Abel was born in the second year of Adam, and Seth a year after the death of Abel: for so it being said, that Adam was an hundred and thirty years old when he begat Seth, Abel must perish the year before, which was one hundred twenty nine.

And if the account of Cain extend unto the Deluge, it may not be improbable that some thereof exceeded any of Seth. Nor is it unlikely in life, riches, power and temporal blessings, they might surpass them in this world, whose lives related unto the next. For so when the seed of Jacob was under affliction and captivity, that of Ismael and Esau flourished and grew mighty, there proceeding from the one twelve Princes, from the other no less then fourteen Dukes and eight Kings. And whereas the age of Cain and his posterity is not delivered in the Text, some do salve it from the secret method of Scripture, which sometimes wholly omits, but seldom or never delivers the entire duration of wicked and faithless persons, as is observable in the history of Esau, and the Kings of Israel and Judah. And therefore when mention is made that Ismael lived 137 years, some conceive he adhered unto the faith of Abraham; for so did others who were not descended from Jacob; for Job is thought to be an Idumean, and of the seed of Esau.

Job thought
by some to
be of the race
of Esau.

Lastly (although we rely not thereon) we will not omit that conceit urged by learned men, that Adam was elder then Methuselah; inasmuch as he was created in the perfect age of man, which was in those days 50 or 60 years, for about that time we read that they begat children; so that if unto 930 we add 60 years, he will exceed Methuselah. And therefore if not in length of days, at least in old age he surpassed others; he was older then all, who was never so young as any. For though he knew old age, he was never acquainted with puberty, youth or Infancy; and so in a strict account he begat children at one year old. And if the usual compute will hold, that men are of the same age which are born within compass of the same year; Eve was as old as her husband and parent Adam, and Cain their son coetaneous unto both.

Now that conception, that no man did ever attain unto a thousand years, because none should ever be one day old in the sight of the Lord, unto whom according to that of David, *A thousand years are but as one day*; doth not advantage Methuselah. And being deduced from a popular expression, which will not stand a Metaphysical and strict examination, is not of force to divert a serious enquirer. For unto God a thousand years are no more then one moment, and in his sight Methuselah lived no nearer one day then Abel, for all parts of time are alike unto him, unto whom none are referrible; and all things present, unto whom nothing is past or to come. And therefore, although we be measured by the Zone of time, and the flowing and continued instants thereof, do weave at last a line and circle about the eldest: yet can we not thus commensurate the sphere of Trismegistus; or sum up the unsuccessive and stable duration of God.

CHAP. IV

That there was no Rain-bow before the Flood

THAT there shall no Rain-bow appear forty years before the end of the world, and that the preceding drought unto that great flame shall exhaust the materials of this Meteor, was an assertion grounded upon no solid reason: but that there was not any in sixteen hundred years, that is, before the flood, seems deduceable from holy Scripture, Gen. 9. *I do set my bow in the clouds, and it shall be for a token of a Covenant between me and the earth.* From whence notwithstanding we cannot conclude the nonexistence of the Rain-bow; nor is that Chronology naturally established, which computeth the antiquity of effects arising from physical and setled causes, by additionall impositions from voluntary determinators. Now by the decree of reason and Philosophy, the Rain-bow hath its ground in Nature, as caused by the rayes of the Sun, falling upon a roride and opposite cloud: whereof some reflected, others refracted, beget that semi-circular variety we generally call the Rain-bow; which

must succeed upon concurrence of causes and subjects aptly
predisposed. And therefore, to conceive there was no Rain-bow
before, because God chose this out as a token of the Covenant,
is to conclude the existence of things from their signalities, or
of what is objected unto the sense, a coexistence with that which
is internally presented unto the understanding. With equall
reason we may infer there was no water before the institution
of Baptism, nor bread and wine before the holy Eucharist.

Again, while men deny the antiquity of one Rain-bow, they
anciently concede another. For, beside the solary Iris which God
shewed unto Noah, there is another Lunary, whose efficient is
the Moon, visible only in the night, most commonly at full
Moon, and some degrees above the Horizon. Now the existence
hereof men do not controvert, although effected by a different
Luminary in the same way with the other. And probably
appeared later, as being of rare appearance and rarer observation,
and many there are which think there is no such thing in Nature.
And therefore by casual spectators they are lookt upon like
prodigies, and significations made, not signified by their natures.

Lastly, We shall not need to conceive God made the Rain-
bow at this time, if we consider that in its created and predisposed nature, it was more proper for this signification then any
other Meteor or celestial appearancy whatsoever. Thunder and
lightning had too much terrour to have been tokens of mercy;
Comets or blazing Stars appear too seldom to put us in mind of
a Covenant to be remembered often: and might rather signifie
the world should be once destroyed by fire, then never again by
water. The Galaxia or milky Circle had been more probable;
for (beside that unto the latitude of thirty, it becomes their
Horizon twice in four and twenty hours, and unto such as live
under the Æquator, in that space the whole Circle appeareth)
part thereof is visible unto any situation; but being only discoverable in the night, and when the ayr is clear, it becomes of
unfrequent and comfortless signification. A fixed Star had not
been visible unto all the Globe, and so of too narrow a signality
in a Covenant concerning all. But Rain-bows are seen unto all
the world, and every position of sphere. Unto our own elevation they may appear in the morning, while the Sun hath attained about forty five degrees above the Horizon (which is

conceived the largest semi-diameter of any Iris), and so in the afternoon when it hath declined unto that altitude again; which height the Sun not attaining in winter, rain-bows may happen with us at noon or any time. Unto a right position of sphere they may appear three hours after the rising of the Sun, and three before its setting; for the Sun ascending fifteen degrees an hour, in three attaineth forty five of altitude. Even unto a parallel sphere, and such as live under the pole, for half a year some segments may appear at any time and under any quarter, the Sun not setting, but walking round about them.

The natural signification of the rain-bow.
But the propriety of its Election most properly appeareth in the natural signification and prognostick of it self; as containing a mixt signality of rain and fair weather. For being in a roride cloud and ready to drop, it declareth a pluvious disposure in the air; but because when it appears the Sun must also shine, there can be no universal showrs, and consequently no Deluge. Thus when the windows of the great deep were open, in vain men lookt for the Rain-bow: for at that time it could not be seen, which after appeared unto Noah. It might be therefore existent before the flood, and had in nature some ground of its addition. Unto that of nature God superadded an assurance of his Promise, that is, never to hinder its appearance, or so to replenish the heavens again, as that we should behold it no more. And thus without disparaging the promise, it might rain at the same time when God shewed it unto Noah; thus was there more therein then the heathens understood, when they
Risus plorantis Olympi.
called it the *Nuncia* of the gods, and the laugh of weeping Heaven; and thus may it be elegantly said, I put my bow, not my arrow in the clouds, that is, in the menace of rain and mercy of fair weather.

Isa. 34. 4.
Cabalistical heads, who from that expression in Esay, do make a book of heaven, and read therein the great concernments of earth, do literally play on this, and from its semicircular figure, resembling the Hebrew letter כ Caph, whereby is signified the uncomfortable number of twenty, at which years Joseph was sold, which Jacob lived under Laban, and at which men were to go to war: do note a propriety in its signification; as thereby declaring the dismal Time of the Deluge. And Christian conceits do seem to strain as high, while from the irradiation of the

Sun upon a cloud, they apprehend the mysterie of the Sun of
Righteousness in the obscurity of flesh; by the colours green
and red, the two destructions of the world by fire and water;
or by the colours of blood and water, the mysteries of Baptism,
and the holy Eucharist.

Laudable therefore is the custom of the Jews, who upon the
appearance of the Rain-bow, do magnifie the fidelity of God in
the memory of his Covenant; according to that of Syracides,
Look upon the Rain-bow, and praise him that made it. And though
some pious and Christian pens have only symbolized the same
from the mysterie of its colours, yet are there other affections
which might admit of Theological allusions. Nor would he find
a more improper subject, that should consider that the colours
are made by refraction of Light, and the shadows that limit that
light; that the Center of the Sun, the Rainbow, and the eye of
the Beholder must be in one right line; that the spectator must
be between the Sun and the Rain-bow; that sometime three Thaumancias.
appear, sometime one reversed. With many others, considerable in Meteorological Divinity, which would more sensibly
make out the Epithite of the Heathens; and the expression of
the son of Syrach, *Very beautifull is the Rain-bow, it compasseth the
heaven about with a glorious circle, and the hands of the most High have
bended it.*

CHAP. V

Of Sem, Ham and Japhet

CONCERNING the three sons of Noah, Sem, Ham and   Chapter 5
Japhet, that the order of their nativity was according to
that of numeration, and Japhet the youngest son, as most
believe, as Austin and others account, the sons of Japhet and
Europeans need not grant: nor will it so well concord unto the
letter of the Text, and its readiest Interpretations. For, so is it
said in our Translation, *Sem the father of all the sons of Heber the
brother of Japhet the elder*: so by the Septuagint, and so by that of
Tremelius. And therefore when the Vulgar reads it, *Fratre Japhet
majore*, the mistake as Junius observeth, might be committed
by the neglect of the Hebrew accent; which occasioned Jerom

so to render it, and many after to believe it. Nor is that Argument contemptible which is deduced from their Chronology; for probable it is that Noah had none of them before, and begat them from that year when it is said he was five hundred years old, and begat Sem, Ham and Japhet. Again it is said he was six hundred years old at the flood, and that two years after Sem was but an hundred; therefore Sem must be born when Noah was five hundred and two, and some other before in the year of five hundred and one.

Now whereas the Scripture affordeth the priority of order unto Sem, we cannot from thence infer his primogeniture. For in Sem the holy line was continued: and therefore however born, his genealogy was most remarkable. So is it not unusuall in holy Scripture to nominate the younger before the elder: so is it said, That *Tarah begat Abraham, Nachor and Haram*: whereas Haram was the eldest. So Rebecca is termed the mother of Jacob and Esau. Nor is it strange the younger should be first in nomination, who have commonly had the priority in the blessings of God, and been first in his benediction. So Abel was accepted before Cain, Isaac the younger preferred before Ishmael the elder, Jacob before Esau, Joseph was the youngest of twelve, and David the eleventh son and minor cadet of Jesse.

Lastly, though Japhet were not elder then Sem, yet must we not affirm that he was younger then Cham, for it is plainly delivered, that after Sem and Japhet had covered Noah, he awaked, and knew what his youngest son had done unto him υἱὸς ὁ νεώτερος, is the expression of the Septuagint, *Filius minor* of Jerom, and *minimus* of Tremelius. And upon these grounds perhaps Josephus doth vary from the Scripture enumeration, and nameth them Sem, Japhet and Cham; which is also observed by the Annian Berosus; *Noah cum tribus filiis, Semo, Japeto, Chem.* And therefore although in the priority of Sem and Japhet, there may be some difficulty, though Cyril, Epiphanius and Austin have accounted Sem the elder, and Salian the Annalist, and Petavius the Chronologist contend for the same; yet Cham is more plainly and confessedly named the youngest in the Text.

And this is more conformable unto the Pagan history and Gentile account hereof, unto whom Noah was Saturn, whose symbol was a ship, as relating unto the Ark, and who is said to

Gen. 11.
Gen. 28.

In divine
benedictions
the younger
often pre-
ferred.

That Noah
and Saturn
were the same
person.

have divided the world between his three sons. Ham is conceived to be Jupiter, who was the youngest son; worshipped by the name of Hamon, which was the Egyptian and African name for Jupiter, who is said to have cut off the genitals of his father, derived from the history of Ham, who beheld the nakedness of his, and by no hard mistake might be confirmed from the Text, as Bochartus hath well observed.

BOOK VII
Chapter 5
Gen. 9. 22.
Reading
Veiaggod &
abscidit for
Veiegged &
nunciavit.
Bochartus
*de Geographiâ
sacrâ.*

CHAP. XVI

Of divers other Relations

Chapter 16

THE relation of Averroes, and now common in every mouth, of the woman that conceived in a bath, by attracting the sperm or seminal effluxion of a man admitted to bathe in some vicinity unto her, I have scarce faith to believe; and had I been of the Jury, should have hardly thought I had found the father in the person that stood by her. 'Tis a new and unseconded way in History to fornicate at a distance, and much offendeth the rules of Physick, which say, there is no generation without a joynt emission, nor only a virtual, but corporal and carnal contaction. And although Aristotle and his adherents do cut off the one, who conceive no effectual ejaculation in women, yet in defence of the other they cannot be introduced. For, if as he believeth, the inordinate longitude of the organ, though in its proper recipient, may be a means to improlificate the seed; surely the distance of place, with the commixture of an aqueous body, must prove an effectual impediment, and utterly prevent the success of a conception. And therefore that conceit concerning the daughters of Lot, that they were impregnated by their sleeping father, or conceived by seminal pollution received at distance from him, will hardly be admitted. And therefore what is related of devils, and the contrived delusions of spirits, that they steal the seminal emissions of man, and transmit them into their votaries in coition, is much to be suspected; and altogether to be denied, that there ensue conceptions thereupon; however husbanded by Art,

Generations by the Devil very improbable.

and the wisest menagery of that most subtile imposter. And
therefore also that our magnified Merlin, was thus begotten by the devil, is a groundless conception; and as vain to think from thence to give the reason of his prophetical spirit. For if a generation could succeed, yet should not the issue inherit the faculties of the devil, who is but an auxiliary, and no univocal Actor; nor will his nature substantially concur to such productions.

And although it seems not impossible, that impregnation may succeed from seminal spirits, and vaporous irradiations containing the active principle, without material and gross immissions; as it happeneth sometimes in imperforated persons, and rare conceptions of some much under pubertie or fourteen. As may be also conjectured in the coition of some insects, wherein the female makes intrusion into the male; and from the continued ovation in Hens, from one single tread of a cock, and little stock laid up near the vent, sufficient for durable prolification. And although also in humane generation the gross and corpulent seminal body may return again, and the great business be acted by what it caryeth with it: yet will not the same suffice to support the story in question, wherein no corpulent immission is acknowledged; answerable unto the fable of the Talmudists, in the storie of Benzira, begotten in the same manner on the daughter of the Prophet Jeremie.

2. The Relation of Lucillius, and now become common, concerning Crassus the grand-father of Marcus the wealthy Roman, that he never laughed but once in all his life, and that was at an Ass eating thistles, is something strange. For, if an indifferent and unridiculous object could draw his habitual austereness unto a smile: it will be hard to believe he could with perpetuity resist the proper motives thereof. For the act of Laughter which is evidenced by a sweet contraction of the muscles of the face, and a pleasant agitation of the vocal Organs, is not meerly voluntary, or totally within the jurisdiction of our selves: but as it may be constrained by corporal contaction in any, and hath been enforced in some even in their death; so the new unusual or unexpected jucundities, which present themselves to any man in his life, at some time or other will have activity enough to excitate the earthiest soul, and raise a

smile from most composed tempers. Certainly the times were dull when these things happened, and the wits of those Ages short of these of ours; when men could maintain such immutable faces, as to remain like statues under the flatteries of wit and persist unalterable at all efforts of Jocularity. The spirits in hell, and Pluto himself, whom Lucian makes to laugh at passages upon earth, will plainly condemn these Saturnines, and make ridiculous the magnified Heraclitus, who wept preposterously, and made a hell on earth; for rejecting the consolations of life, he passed his days in tears, and the uncomfortable attendments of hell.

3. The same conceit there passeth concerning our blessed Saviour, and is sometimes urged as an high example of gravity. And this is opinioned, because in holy Scripture it is recorded he sometimes wept, but never that he laughed. Which howsoever granted, it will be hard to conceive how he passed his younger years and child-hood without a smile, if as Divinity affirmeth, for the assurance of his humanity unto men, and the concealment of his Divinity from the devil, he passed this age like other children, and so proceeded untill he evidenced the same. And surely herein no danger there is to affirm the act or performance of that, whereof we acknowledge the power and essential property; and whereby indeed he most nearly convinced the doubt of his humanity. Nor need we be afraid to ascribe that unto the incarnate Son, which sometimes is attributed unto the uncarnate Father; of whom it is said, *He that dwelleth in the heavens shall laugh the wicked to scorn.* For a laugh there is of contempt or indignation, as well as of mirth and Jocosity; And that our Saviour was not exempted from the ground hereof, that is, the passion of anger, regulated and rightly ordered by reason, the schools do not deny: and besides the experience of the money-changers, and Dove-sellers in the *Zelus domus* Temple, is testified by St. John, when he saith, the speech of *tuæ comedit me.* David was fulfilled in our Saviour.

Now the Alogie of this opinion consisteth in the illation; it being not reasonable to conclude from Scripture negatively in points which are not matters of faith, and pertaining unto salvation. And therefore, although in the description of the creation there be no mention of fire, Christian Philosophy did

not think it reasonable presently to annihilate that element, or
positively to decree there was no such thing at all. Thus whereas in the brief narration of Moses there is no record of wine before the flood, we cannot satisfactorily conclude that Noah was the first that ever tasted thereof. And thus because the word Brain is scarce mentioned once, but Heart above an hundred times in holy Scripture; Physitians that dispute the principality of parts are not from hence induced to bereave the animal Organ of its priority. Wherefore the Scriptures being serious, and commonly omitting such Parergies, it will be unreasonable from hence to condemn all Laughter, and from considerations inconsiderable to discipline a man out of his nature. For this is by a rustical severity to banish all urbanity; whose harmless and confined condition, as it stands commended by morality; so is it consistent with Religion, and doth not offend Divinity.

4. The custom it is of Popes to change their name at their creation; and the Author thereof is commonly said to be *Bocca di porco,* or Swine's face; who therefore assumed the stile of Sergius the second, as being ashamed so foul a name should dishonour the chair of Peter; wherein notwithstanding, from Montacutius and others I find there may be some mistake. For Massonius who writ the lives of Popes, acknowledgeth he was not the first that changed his name in that See; nor as Platina affirmeth, have all his Successors precisely continued that custom; for Adrian the sixt, and Marcellus the second, did still retain their Baptismal denominations. Nor is it proved, or probable, that Sergius changed the name of *Bocca di Porco,* for this was his sirname or gentilitious appellation: nor was it the custom to alter that with the other; but he commuted his Christian name Peter for Sergius, because he would seem to decline the name of Peter the second. A scruple I confess not thought considerable in other Sees, whose Originals and first Patriarchs have been less disputed; nor yet perhaps of that reality as to prevail in points of the same nature. For the names of the Apostles, Patriarchs and Prophets have been assumed even to affectation; the name of Jesus hath not been appropriate; but some in precedent ages have born that name, and many since have not refused the Christian name of Emmanuel. Thus

are there few names more frequent then Moses and Abraham among the Jews; The Turks without scruple affect the name of Mahomet, and with gladness receive so honourable cognomination.

And truly in humane occurrences there ever have been many well directed intentions, whose rationalities will never bear a rigid examination, and though in some way they do commend their Authors, and such as first began them, yet have they proved insufficient to perpetuate imitation in such as have succeeded them. Thus was it a worthy resolution of Godfrey, and most Christians have applauded it, That he refused to wear a Crown of Gold where his Saviour had worn one of thorns. Yet did not his Successors durably inherit that scruple, but some were anointed, and solemnly accepted the Diadem of regality. Thus Julius, Augustus and Tiberius with great humility or popularity refused the name of *Imperator*, but their Successors have challenged that title, and retain the same even in its titularity. And thus to come nearer our subject, the humility of Gregory the Great, would by no means admit the stile of Universal Bishop; but the ambition of Boniface made no scruple thereof, nor of more queasie resolutions have been their Successors ever since.

Turkish
History. 5. That Tamerlane was a Scythian Shepherd, from Mr. Knolls and others, from Alhazen a learned Arabian who wrote his life, and was Spectator of many of his exploits, we have reasons to deny. Not only from his birth, for he was of the blood of the Tartarian Emperours, whose father Og had for his possession the Country of Sagathy; which was no slender Territory, but comprehended all that tract wherein were contained Bactriana, Sogdiana, Margiana, and the nation of the Massagetes, whose capital City was Samarcand; a place though now decaid, of great esteem and trade in former ages. But from his regal Inauguration; for it is said, that being about the age of fifteen, his old father resigned the Kingdom and men of war unto him. And also from his education, for as the storie speaks it, he was instructed in the Arabian learning, and afterward exercised himself therein. Now Arabian learning was in a manner all the liberal Sciences, especially the Mathematicks, and natural Philosophy; wherein not many ages before him there flourished

Avicenna, Averroes, Avenzoar, Geber, Almanzor and Alhazen,
cognominal unto him that wrote his History, whose Chronology indeed, although it be obscure, yet in the opinion of his
Commentator, he was contemporary unto Avicenna, and hath
left sixteen books of Opticks, of great esteem with ages past,
and textuary unto our days.

Now the ground of this mistake was surely that which the
Turkish Historian declareth. Some, saith he, of our Historians
will needs have Tamerlane to be the Son of a Shepherd. But this
they have said, not knowing at all the custom of their Country;
wherein the principal revenews of the King and Nobles consisteth in cattle; who despising gold and silver, abound in all
sorts thereof. And this was the occasion that some men call
them Shepherds, and also affirm this Prince descended from
them. Now, if it be reasonable, that great men whose possessions are chiefly in cattle, should bear the name of Shepherds,
and fall upon so low denominations; then may we say that
Abraham was a Shepherd, although too powerful for four Kings:
that Job was of that condition, who beside Camels and Oxen
had seven thousand Sheep: and yet is said to be the greatest
man in the East. Thus was Mesha King of Moab a Shepherd,
who annually paid unto the Crown of Israel, an hundred thousand Lambs, and as many Rams. Surely it is no dishonourable
course of life which Moses and Jacob have made exemplary:
'tis a profession supported upon the natural way of acquisition,
and though contemned by the Egyptians, much countenanced
by the Hebrews, whose sacrifices required plenty of Sheep and
Lambs. And certainly they were very numerous; for, at the
consecration of the Temple, beside two and twenty thousand
Oxen, King Solomon sacrificed an hundred and twenty thousand
Sheep: and the same is observable from the daily provision of his
house: which was ten fat Oxen, twenty Oxen out of the pastures,
and an hundred Sheep, beside row Buck, fallow Deer, and fatted
Fowls. Wherein notwithstanding (if a punctual relation thereof Description
do rightly inform us) the grand Seignior doth exceed: the daily of the Turk-
provision of whose Seraglio in the reign of Achmet, beside ish Seraglio,
Beeves, consumed two hundred Sheep, Lambs and Kids when since printed.
they were in season one hundred, Calves ten, Geese fifty, Hens The daily
provision of
two hundred, Chickens one hundred, Pigeons an hundred pair. the Seraglio.

BOOK VII
Chapter 17
Rog. Bacon.
minorita,
Oxoniensis vir
doctissimus.
a brazen head to speak these words, *Time is.* Which though there want not the like relations, is surely too literally received, and was but a mystical fable concerning the Philosopher's great work, wherein he eminently laboured: implying no more by the copper head, then the vessel wherein it was wrought, and by the words it spake, then the opportunity to be watched, about the *Tempus ortus*, or birth of the mystical child, or Philosophical King of Lullius: the rising of the *Terra foliata* of Arnoldus, when the earth sufficiently impregnated with the water, ascendeth white and splendent. Which not observed, the work is irre-coverably lost; according to that of Petrus Bonus. *Ibi est operis perfectio aut annihilatio; quoniam ipsa die, immo horâ, oriuntur elementa simplicia depurata, quæ egent statim compositione, antequam volent ab igne.*

Now letting slip this critical opportunity, he missed the intended treasure. Which had he obtained, he might have made out the tradition of making a brazen wall about England. That is, the most powerfull defence, and strongest fortification which Gold could have effected.

8. Who can but pitty the vertuous Epicurus, who is commonly conceived to have placed his chief felicity in pleasure and sensual delights, and hath therefore left an infamous name behind him? How true, let them determine who read that he lived seventy years, and wrote more books then any Philosopher but Chrysippus, and no less then three hundred, without borrowing from any Author. That he was contented with bread and water, and when he would dine with Jove, and pretend unto epulation, he desired no other addition then a piece of Cytheridian cheese. That shall consider the words of Seneca, *Non dico, quod plerique nostrorum, sectam Epicuri flagitiorum magistrum esse: sed illud dico, malè audit infamis est, & immerito.* Or shall read his life, his Epistles, his Testament in Laertius, who plainly names them Calumnies, which are commonly said against them.

The ground hereof seems a mis-apprehension of his opinion, who placed his Felicity not in the pleasures of the body, but the mind, and tranquility thereof, obtained by wisdom and vertue, as is clearly determined in his Epistle unto Menæceus. Now how this opinion was first traduced by the Stoicks, how it afterwards became a common belief, and so taken up by Authors

of all ages, by Cicero, Plutarch, Clemens, Ambrose and others;
the learned Pen of Gassendus hath discovered.

CHAP. XVIII

More briefly of some others

OTHER relations there are, and those in very good Chapter 18
Authors, which though we do not positively deny, yet
have they not been unquestioned by some, and at least
as improbable truths have been received[74] by others. Unto
some it hath seemed incredible what Herodotus reporteth of
the great Army of Xerxes, that drank whole rivers dry. And
unto the Author himself it appeared wondrous strange, that
they exhausted not the provision of the Countrey, rather then
the waters thereof. For as he maketh the account, and Budeus
de Asse correcting the mis-compute of Valla, delivereth it; if
every man of the Army had had a chenix of Corn a day, that is,
a sextary and half, or about two pints and a quarter, the Army
had daily expended ten hundred thousand and forty Medimna's,
or measures containing six Bushels. Which rightly considered,
the Abderites had reason to bless the Heavens, that Xerxes eat
but one meal a day; and Pythius his noble Host, might with less
charge and possible provision entertain both him and his Army.
And yet may all be salved, if we take it hyperbolically, as wise
men receive that expression in Job, concerning Behemoth or the
Elephant; *Behold, he drinketh up a river and hasteth not, he trusteth
that he can draw up Jordan into his mouth.*

2. That Annibal eat or brake through the Alps with Vinegar,
may be too grosly taken, and the Author of his life annexed
unto Plutarch, affirmeth only he used this artifice upon the
tops of some of the highest mountains. For as it is vulgarly
understood, that he cut a passage for his Army through those
mighty mountains, it may seem incredible, not only in the
greatness of the effect, but the quantity of the efficient; and
such as behold them, may think an Ocean of Vinegar too little
for that effect. 'Twas a work indeed rather to be expected from
earthquakes and inundations, then any corrosive waters, and
much condemneth the Judgement of Xerxes, that wrought
through Mount Athos with Mattocks.

3. That Archimedes burnt the ships of Marcellus, with speculums of parabolical figures, at three furlongs, or as some will have it, at the distance of three miles, sounds hard unto reason, and artificial experience: and therefore justly questioned by Kircherus, who after long enquiry could find but one made *De luce &* by Manfredus Septalius that fired at fifteen paces. And there-
umbra. fore more probable it is, that the ships were nearer the shore, or about some thirty paces: at which distance notwithstanding the effect was very great. But whereas men conceive the ships were more easily set on flame, by reason of the pitch about them, it seemeth no advantage. Since burning glasses will melt pitch or make it boyl, not easily set it on fire.

4. The story of the *Fabii*, whereof three hundred and six marching against the Veientes, were all slain, and one child alone to support the family remained; is surely not to be paralleld, nor easie to be conceived, except we can imagine, that of three hundred and six, but one had children below the service of war; that the rest were all unmarried, or the wife but of one impregnated.

5. The received story of Milo, who by daily lifting a Calf, attained an ability to carry it being a Bull, is a witty conceit, and handsomly sets forth the efficacy of Assuefaction. But surely the account had been more reasonably placed upon some person not much exceeding in strength, and such a one as without the assistance of custom could never have performed that act; which some may presume that Milo without precedent artifice or any other preparative, had strength enough to perform. For as relations declare, he was the most pancratical man of Greece, and as Galen reporteth, and Mercurialis in his *Gymnasticks* representeth, he was able to persist erect upon an oyled plank, and not to be removed by the force or protrusion of three men. And if that be true which Athenæus reporteth, he was little beholding to custom for this ability. For in the Olympick games, for the space of a furlong, he carried an Ox of four years upon his shoulders; and the same day he carried it in his belly: for as it is there delivered he eat it up himself. Surely *In Rabelais.* he had been a proper guest at Grandgousier's feast, and might have matcht his throat that eat six pilgrims for a Salad.

Who writ in the praise of 6. It much disadvantageth the Panegyrick of Synesius, and is *baldness.* no small disparagement unto baldness, if it be true what is related by Ælian concerning Æschilus, whose bald-pate was mistaken for a rock, and so was brained by a Tortoise which an Æagle let fall upon it. Certainly it was a very great mistake in the perspicacity of that Animal. Some men critically disposed, would from hence confute the opinion of Copernicus, never conceiving how the motion of the earth below, should not wave him from a knock perpendicularly directed from a body in the air above.

7. It crosseth the Proverb, and Rome might well be built in a day; if that were true which is traditionally related by Strabo; that the great Cities Anchiale and Tarsus, were built by Sardanapalus both in one day, according to the inscription of his monument, *Sardanapalus Anacyndaraxis filius, Anchialem & Tarsum unâ die edificavi, Tu autem hospes Ede, Lude, Bibe, &c.* Which if strictly taken, that is, for the finishing thereof, and not only for the beginning; for an artificial or natural day, and not one of Daniel's weeks, that is, seven whole years; surely their hands were very heavy that wasted thirteen years in the private house of Solomon: It may be wondred how forty years were spent in the erection of the Temple of Jerusalem, and no less than an hundred in that famous one of Ephesus. Certainly it was the greatest Architecture of one day, since that great one of six; an Art quite lost with our Mechanicks, a work not to be made out, but like the walls of Thebes, and such an Artificer as Amphion.

8. It had been a sight only second unto the Ark to have beheld the great *Syracusia*, or mighty ship of Hiero, described in Athenæus; and some have thought it a very large one, wherein were to be found ten stables for horses, eight Towers, besides Fish-ponds, Gardens, Tricliniums, and many fair rooms paved with Agath, and precious Stones. But nothing was impossible unto Archimedes, the learned Contriver thereof; nor shall we question his removing the earth, when he finds an immoveable base to place his Engine upon it.

9. That the Pamphilian Sea gave way unto Alexander in his intended March toward Persia, many have been apt to credit, and Josephus is willing to believe, to countenance the passage of the Israelites through the Red Sea. But Strabo who writ before him delivereth another account; that the Mountain Climax

adjoyning to the Pamphilian Sea, leaves a narrow passage between the Sea and it, which passage at an ebb and quiet Sea all men take; but Alexander coming in the Winter, and eagerly pursuing his affairs, would not wait for the reflux or return of the Sea; and so was fain to pass with his Army in the water, and march up to the navel in it.

A List of some
historical
Errata's in
this and the
following
Sections. 10. The relation of Plutarch of a youth of Sparta, that suffered a Fox concealed under his robe to tear out his bowels, before he would either by voice or countenance betray his theft; and the other of the Spartan Lad, that with the same resolution suffered a coal from the Altar to burn his arm, although defended by the Author that writes his life, is I perceive mistrusted by men of Judgment, and the Author with an *aiunt*, is made to salve himself. Assuredly it was a noble Nation that could afford an hint to such inventions of patience, and upon whom, if not such verities, at least such verisimilities of fortitude were placed. Were the story true, they would have made the only Disciples for Zeno, and the Stoicks, and might perhaps have been perswaded to laugh in Phaleris his Bull.

11. If any man shall content his belief with the speech of Balaam's Ass, without a belief of that of Mahomet's Camel, or Livie's Ox: If any man make a doubt of Giges' ring in Justinus, or conceives he must be a Jew that believes the Sabbatical river in Josephus: If any man will say he doth not apprehend how the tayl of an African Weather out-weighteth the body of a good Calf, that is, an hundred pound, according unto Leo Africanus, or desires before belief, to behold such a creature as is the Ruck in Paulus Venetus, for my part I shall not be angry with his incredulity.

12. If any one shall receive as stretcht or fabulous accounts what is delivered of Cocles, Scævola and Curtius, the sphere of Archimedes, the story of the Amazons, the taking of the City *Farfalloni* of Babylon, not known to some therein three days after; that *Historici.* the nation was deaf which dwelt at the fall of Nilus, the laughing and weeping humour of Heraclitus and Democritus, with many more, he shall not want some reason and the authority of Lancellotti.

13. If any man doubt of the strange Antiquities delivered by Historians, as of the wonderful corps of Antæus untombed a

thousand years after his death by Sertorius. Whether there were
no deceit in those fragments of the Ark so common to be seen in the days of Berosus; whether the Pillar which Josephus beheld long ago, Tertullian long after, and Bartholomeus de Salig-niaco, and Borchardus long since, be the same with that of Lot's wife; whether this were the hand of Paul, or that which is commonly shewn the head of Peter, if any doubt, I shall not much dispute with their suspicions. If any man shall not believe the Turpentine Tree, betwixt Jerusalem and Bethlem, under which the Virgin suckled our Saviour, as she passed between those Cities; or the fig-tree of Bethany shewed to this day, whereon Zacheus ascended to behold our Saviour; I cannot tell
how to enforce his belief, nor do I think it requisite to attempt it. For, as it is no reasonable proceeding to compel a religion, or think to enforce our own belief upon another, who cannot without the concurrence of God's spirit, have any indubitable evidence of things that are obtruded: So is it also in matters of common belief; whereunto neither can we indubitably assent, without the co-operation of our sense or reason, wherein con-sists the principles of perswasion. For, as the habit of Faith in Divinity is an Argument of things unseen, and a stable assent unto things inevident, upon authority of the Divine Revealer: So the belief of man which depends upon humane testimony, is but a staggering assent unto the affirmative, not without some fear of the negative. And as there is required the Word of God, or infused inclination unto the one, so must the actual sensation of our senses, at least the non-opposition of our reasons procure our assent and acquiescence in the other. So when Eusebius an holy Writer affirmeth, there grew a strange and unknown plant near the statue of Christ, erected by his Hæmorrhoidal patient in the Gospel, which attaining unto the hem of his vesture, acquired a sudden faculty to cure all diseases; although he saith he saw the statua in his days, yet hath it found in many men so much as humane belief? Some believing, others opinioning, a third suspecting it might be otherwise. For indeed, in matters of belief the understanding assenting unto the relation, either for the authority of the person, or the probability of the object, although there may be a confidence of the one, yet if there be not a satisfaction in the other, there will arise suspensions; nor

can we properly believe until some argument of reason, or of our proper sense convince or determine our dubitations.

And thus it is also in matters of certain and experimented truth: for if unto one that never heard thereof, a man should undertake to perswade the affections of the Load-stone, or that Jet and Amber attracteth straws and light bodies, there would be little Rhetorick in the authority of Aristotle, Pliny, or any other. Thus, although it be true that the string of a Lute or Viol will stir upon the stroak of an Unison or Diapazon in another of the same kind; that Alcanna being green, will suddenly infect the nails and other parts with a durable red; that a Candle out of a Musket will pierce through an Inch-board, or an urinal force a nail through a Plank; yet can few or none believe thus much without a visible experiment. Which notwithstanding falls out more happily for knowledge; for these relations leaving unsatisfaction in the Hearers, do stir up ingenuous dubiosities unto experiment, and by an exploration of all, prevent delusion in any.

CHAP. XIX

Of some Relations whose truth we fear

Chapter 19 Lastly, As there are many Relations whereto we cannot assent, and make some doubt thereof, so there are divers others whose verities we fear, and heartily wish there were no truth therein.

1. It is an unsufferable affront unto filiall piety, and a deep discouragement unto the expectation of all aged Parents, who shall but read the story of that barbarous Queen; who after she had beheld her royall Parent's ruin, lay yet in the arms of his assassine, and carowsed with him in the skull of her father. For my part, I should have doubted the operation of antimony, where such a potion would not work; 'twas an act me thinks beyond Anthropophagy, and a cup fit to be served up only at the Table of Atreus.

2. While we laugh at the story of Pygmaleon, and receive as a fable that he fell in love with a statua; we cannot but fear it

may be true, what is delivered by Herodotus concerning
Egyptian Pollinctors, or such as annointed the dead; that some
thereof were found in the act of carnality with them. From wits
that say 'tis more then incontinency for Hylas to sport with
Hecuba, and youth to flame in the frozen embraces of age, we
require a name for this: wherein Petronius or Martial cannot
relieve us. The tyrannie of Mezentius did never equall the
vitiosity of this Incubus, that could embrace corruption, and
make a Mistress of the grave; that could not resist the dead
provocations of beauty, whose quick invitements scarce excuse
submission. Surely, if such depravities there be yet alive, deformity need not despair; nor will the eldest hopes be ever
superannuated, since death hath spurs, and carcasses have been
courted.

3. I am heartily sorry, and wish it were not true, what to the
dishonour of Christianity is affirmed of the Italian; who after he
had inveigled his enemy to disclaim his faith for the redemption
of his life, did presently poyniard him, to prevent repentance,
and assure his eternal death. The villany of this Christian
exceeded the persecution of Heathens, whose malice was never
so Longimanous as to reach the soul of their enemies; or to
extend unto the exile of their Elysiums. And though the blindness of some ferities have savaged on the bodies of the dead, and
been so injurious unto worms, as to disenter the bodies of the
deceased; yet had they therein no design upon the soul: and
have been so far from the destruction of that, or desires of a
perpetual death, that for the satisfaction of their revenge they
wisht them many souls, and were it in their power would have
reduced them unto life again. It is a great depravity in our
natures, and surely an affection that somewhat savoureth of
hell, to desire the society, or comfort our selves in the fellowship of others that suffer with us; but to procure the miseries
of others in those extremities, wherein we hold an hope to
have no society our selves, is me thinks a strain above Lucifer,
and a project beyond the primary seduction of hell.

4. I hope it is not true, and some indeed have probably
denied, what is recorded of the Monk that poysoned Henry the
Emperour, in a draught of the holy Eucharist. 'Twas a scandalous wound unto Christian Religion, and I hope all Pagans will

forgive it, when they shall read that a Christian was poysoned in a cup of Christ, and received his bane in a draught of his salvation. Had he believed Transubstantiation, he would[75] have doubted the effect; and surely the sin it self received an aggravation in that opinion. It much commendeth the innocency of our forefathers, and the simplicity of those times, whose Laws could never dream so high a crime as parricide: whereas this at the least may seem to out-reach that fact, and to exceed the regular distinctions of murder. I will not say what sin it was to act it; yet may it seem a kind of martyrdom to suffer by it. For, although unknowingly, he died for Christ his sake, and lost his life in the ordained testimony of his death. Certainly, had they known it, some noble zeales would scarcely have refused it; rather adventuring their own death, then refusing the memorial of his.

Hujus farinæ multa in historia horribili. Many other accounts like these we meet sometimes in history, scandalous unto Christianity, and even unto humanity; whose verities not only, but whose relations honest minds do deprecate. For of sins heteroclital, and such as want either name or president, there is oft times a sin even in their histories. We desire no records of such enormities; sins should be accounted new, that so they may be esteemed monstrous. They omit of monstrosity as they fall from their rarity; for, men count it veniall to err with their forefathers, and foolishly conceive they divide a sin in its society. The pens of men may sufficiently expatiate without these singularities of villany; For, as they encrease the hatred of vice in some, so do they enlarge the theory of wickedness in all. And this is one thing that may make latter ages worse then were the former; For, the vicious examples of Ages past, poyson the curiosity of these present, affording a hint of sin unto seduceable spirits, and soliciting those unto the imitation of them, whose heads were never so perversly principled as to invent them. In this kind we commend the wisdom and goodness of Galen, who would not leave unto the world too subtile a Theory of poisons; unarming thereby the malice of venemous spirits, whose ignorance must be contented with Sublimate and Arsenick. For, surely there are subtiler venenations, such as will invisibly destroy, and like the Basilisks of heaven. In things of this nature silence commendeth

history: 'tis the veniable part of things lost; wherein there must
never rise a Pancirollus, nor remain any Register but that of hell.

And yet, if as some Stoicks opinion, and Seneca himself disputeth, these unruly affections that make us sin such prodigies, and even sins themselves, be animals; there is an history of Africa and story of Snakes in these. And if the transanimation of Pythagoras or method thereof were true, that the souls of men transmigrated into species answering their former natures: some men must surely live over many Serpents, and cannot escape that very brood whose sire Satan entered. And though the objection of Plato should take place, that bodies subjected unto corruption, must fail at last before the period of all things, and growing fewer in number, must leave some souls apart unto themselves; the spirits of many long before that time will find but naked habitations: and meeting no assimilables wherein to react their natures, must certainly anticipate such natural desolations.

LACTANT.

Primus sapientiæ gradus est, falsa intelligere.

FINIS

OF HAWKS AND FALCONRY

ANCIENT & MODERN

Sir,

TRACT V
[Brit. Mus.
MS Sloane
1827, another
version] In vain you expect much information, *de Re Accipitraria*, of Falconry, Hawks or Hawking, from very ancient Greek or Latin Authours; for that Art being either unknown or so little advanced among them, that it seems to have proceeded no higher than the daring of Birds: which makes so little thereof to be found in Aristotle, who onely mentions some rude practice thereof in Thracia; as also in Ælian, who speaks something of Hawks and Crows among the Indians; little or nothing of true Falconry being mention'd before Julius Firmicus, in the days of Constantius, Son to Constantine the Great.

Yet if you consult the accounts of latter Antiquity left by Demetrius the Greek, by Symmachus and Theodosius, and by Albertus Magnus, about five hundred years ago, you, who have been so long acquainted with this noble Recreation, may better compare the ancient and modern practice, and rightly observe how many things in that Art are added, varied, disused or retained in the practice of these days.

In the Diet of Hawks, they allowed of divers Meats which we should hardly commend. For beside the Flesh of [Lamb, mutton,][1] Beef, they admitted of Goat, Hog, Deer, Whelp and Bear. And how you will approve the quantity and measure thereof, I make some doubt; while by weight they allowed half a pound of Beef, seven ounces of Swines Flesh, five of Hare, eight ounces of Whelp, as much of Deer, and ten ounces of He-Goats Flesh.

In the time of Demetrius they were not without the practice of Phlebotomy or Bleeding, which they used in the Thigh and Pounces; they plucked away the Feathers on the Thigh, and

[1] MS Sloane 1827.

rubbed the part, but if the Vein appeared not in that part, they
opened the Vein of the fore Talon.

In the days of Albertus, they made use of Cauteries in divers places: to advantage their sight they seared them under the inward angle of the eye; above the eye in distillations and diseases of the Head; in upward pains they seared above the Joint of the Wing, and at the bottom of the Foot, against the Gout; and the chief time for these cauteries they made to be the month of March.

In great coldness of Hawks they made use of Fomentations, some of the steam or vapour of artificial and natural Baths, some wrapt them up in hot Blankets, giving them Nettle Seeds and Butter.

No Clysters are mention'd, nor can they be so profitably used; but they made use of many purging Medicines. They purged with Aloe, which, unto larger Hawks, they gave in the bigness of a Greek Bean; unto less, in the quantity of a *Cicer*, which notwithstanding I should rather give washed, and with a few drops of Oil of Almonds: for the Guts of flying Fowls are tender and easily scratched by it; and upon the use of Aloe both in Hawks and Cormorants I have sometimes observed bloody excretions.

In phlegmatick causes they seldom omitted Stavesaker, but they purged sometimes with a Mouse, and the Food of boiled Chickens, sometimes with good Oil and Honey.

They used also the Ink of Cuttle Fishes, with Smallage, Betony, Wine and Honey. They made use of stronger Medicines than present practice doth allow. For they were not afraid to give *Coccus Baphicus* [or mezerion];[1] beating up eleven of its Grains unto a *Lentor*, which they made up into five Pills wrapt up with Honey and Pepper: and, in some of their old Medicines, we meet with Scammony and *Euphorbium*. Whether, in the tender Bowels of Birds, infusions of Rhubarb, Agaric and *Mechoachan* be not of safer use, as to take of Agary two Drachms, of Cinnamon half a Drachm, of Liquorish a Scruple, and, infusing them in Wine, to express a part into the mouth of the Hawk, may be considered by present practice.

Few Mineral Medicines were of inward use among them: yet

[1] MS Sloane 1827.

TRACT V sometimes we observe they gave filings of Iron in the straitness of the Chest, as also Lime in some of their pectoral Medicines.

But they commended Unguents of Quick-silver against the Scab: and I have safely given six or eight Grains of *Mercurius Dulcis* unto Kestrils and Owls, as also crude and current Quick-silver, giving the next day small Pellets of Silver or Lead till they came away uncoloured: and this, if any, may probably destroy that obstinate Disease of the Filander or Backworm.

A peculiar remedy they had against the consumption of Hawks. For, filling a Chicken with Vinegar, they closed up the Bill, and hanging it up untill the Flesh grew tender, they fed the Hawk therewith: and to restore and well Flesh them, they commonly gave them Hogs Flesh, with Oil, Butter and Honey; and a decoction of Cumfory to bouze[1] [; and had a notable medicine against the inflammation of the eyes, by juice of purslain, opium, and saffron].[2]

They disallowed of salt Meats and Fat; but highly esteemed of Mice in most indispositions; and in the falling Sickness had great esteem of boiled Batts: and in many Diseases, of the Flesh of Owls which feed upon those Animals. In Epilepsies they also gave the Brain of a Kid drawn thorough a gold Ring; and, in Convulsions, made use of a mixture of Musk and *Stercus humanum aridum*.

For the better preservation of their Health they strowed Mint and Sage about them; and for the speedier mewing of their Feathers, they gave them the Slough of a Snake, or a Tortoise out of the Shell, or a green Lizard cut in pieces.

If a Hawk were unquiet, they hooded him, and placed him in a Smith's Shop for some time, where, accustomed to the continual noise of hammering, he became more gentle and tractable.

They used few terms of Art, plainly and intelligibly expressing the Parts affected, their Diseases and Remedies. This heap of artificial terms first entring with the French Artists: who seem to have been the first and noblest Falconers in the Western part of Europe; although, in their Language, they have no word which in general expresseth an Hawk.

They carried their Hawks in the left hand, and let them flie

---

[1] *bouze*] drink (MS Sloane 1827).   [2] MS Sloane 1827.

from the right. They used a Bell, and took great care that their
Jesses should not be red, lest Eagles should flie at them. Though
they used Hoods, we have no clear description of them, and
little account of their Lures.

The ancient Writers left no account of the swiftness of Hawks
or measure of their flight: but Heresbachius* delivers that   *De Re
William Duke of Cleve had an Hawk which, in one day, made a   *Rustica.*
flight out of Westphalia into Prussia. And, upon good account,
an Hawk in this Country of Norfolk, made a flight at a Wood-
cock near thirty miles in one hour. How far the Hawks, Mer-
lins and wild Fowl which come unto us with a North-west wind
in the Autumn, flie in a day, there is no clear account; but coming over Sea their flight hath been long, or very speedy. For I
have known them to light so weary on the coast, that many have
been taken with Dogs, and some knock'd down with Staves and
Stones.

Their Perches seem not so large as ours; for they made them
of such a bigness that their Talons might almost meet: and they
chose to make them of Sallow, Poplar or Lime Tree.

They used great clamours and hollowing in their flight, which
they made by these words, *ou loi, la, la, la*; and to raise the
Fowls, made use of the sound of a Cymbal.

Their recreation seemed more sober and solemn than ours at
present, so improperly attended with Oaths and Imprecations.
For they called on God at their setting out, according to the
account of Demetrius, τὸν θεὸν ἐπικαλέσαντες, *in the first place
calling upon God.*

The learned Rigaltius thinketh, that if the Romans had well
known this airy Chase, they would have left or less regarded
their Circensial Recreations. The Greeks understood Hunting
early, but little or nothing of our Falconry. If Alexander had
known it, we might have found something of it and more of
Hawks in Aristotle; who was so unacquainted with that way,
that he thought that Hawks would not feed upon the Heart
of Birds. Though he hath mention'd divers Hawks, yet Julius
Scaliger, an expert Falconer, despaired to reconcile them unto
ours. And 'tis well if, among them, you can clearly make out a
Lanner, a Sparrow Hawk and a Kestril, but must not hope to
find your Gier Falcon there, which is the noble Hawk; and I

TRACT V wish you one no worse than that of Henry King of Navarre; which Scaliger saith, he saw strike down a Buzzard, two wild Geese, divers Kites, a Crane and a Swan.

Nor must you expect from high Antiquity the distinctions of Eyess and Ramage Hawks, of Sores and Entermewers, of Hawks of the Lure and the Fist; nor that material distinction into short and long winged Hawks; from whence arise such differences in their taking down of Stones; in their flight, their striking down or seizing of their Prey, in the strength of their Talons, either in the Heel and fore-Talon, or the middle and the Heel: nor yet what Eggs produce the different Hawks, or when they lay three Eggs, that the first produceth a Female and large Hawk, the second of a midler sort, and the third a smaller Bird, Tercellene, or Tassel, of the Masle Sex; which Hawks being onely observed abroad by the Ancients, were looked upon as Hawks of different kinds and not of the same Eyrie or Nest. As for what Aristotle affirmeth that Hawks and Birds of prey drink not; although you know that it will not strictly hold, yet I kept an Eagle two years, which fed upon Kats, Kittlings, Whelps and Ratts, without one drop of Water.

If any thing may add unto your knowledge in this noble Art, you must pick it out of later Writers than those you enquire of. You may peruse the two Books of Falconry writ by that renowned Emperour Frederick the Second; as also the Works of the noble Duke Belisarius, of Tardiffe, Francherius, of Francisco Sforzino of Vicensa; and may not a little inform or recreate your self with that elegant Poem of Thuanus.* I leave you to divert your self by the perusal of it, having, at present, no more to say but that I am, &c.

★ *De Re Accipitraria*, in 3 Books. 'Or, more of late, by P. Rapinus in verse.' J. Evelyn.

OF THE

ANSWERS OF THE ORACLE
OF APOLLO

AT DELPHOS TO

CRŒSUS KING OF LYDIA

Sir,

[Men looked upon ancient oracles as natural, artificial, demoniacal, or all. They conceived something natural of them, as being in places affording exhalations, which were found to operate upon the brains of persons unto raptures, strange utterances and divinations; which being observed and admired by the people, an advantage was taken thereof; an artificial contrivance made by subtle crafty persons confederating to carry on a practice of divination; pretending some power of divinity therein; but because they sometimes made very strange predictions, and above the power of human reason, men were inclined to believe some demoniacal co-operation, and that some evil spirit ruled the whole scene; having so fair an opportunity to delude mankind and to advance his own worship; and were thought to proceed from the spirit of Apollo or other Heathen deities; so that these oracles were not only apprehended to be natural, human, or artificial, but also demoniacal, according to common opinion, and also of learned men; as Vossius hath declared, *Constitere quidem oracula fraudibus vatum, sed non solis; solertia humana, sed sæpe etiam diabolica. Cum multa predixerint, ad quæ nulla ratione humana mentis acumen perligisset in natura humana non est subsistendum, sed assurgendum ad causas superioris naturæ, quales sunt dæmones.* According to which sense and opinion we shall enlarge upon this following oracle of Delphos.][1]

TRACT XI

[Brit. Mus. MS Sloane 1827, 1839, other versions.]

[1] MS Sloane 1839.

TRACT XI
* See *Vulg.*
Err. l. 7. *c.* 12.
* Herod. *l.* 1,
46, 47, &c.
90, 91.
Among the Oracles* of Apollo there are none more cele-
brated than those which he delivered unto Crœsus King of
Lydia,* who seems of all Princes to have held the greatest depen-
dence on them. But most considerable are his plain and intel-
ligible replies which he made unto the same King, when he sent
his Chains of Captivity unto Delphos, after his overthrow by
Cyrus, with sad expostulations why he encouraged him unto
that fatal War by his Oracle, saying, προλέγουσαι Κροίσῳ, ἢν
* Herod.
Ibid. 54. στρατεύηται ἐπὶ Πέρσας, μεγάλην ἀρχήν μιν καταλύσειν*
Crœsus, if he Wars against the Persians, shall dissolve a great Empire.
Why, at least, he prevented not that sad infelicity of his devoted
and bountifull Servant, and whether it were fair or honourable
for the Gods of Greece to be ingratefull: which being a plain
and open delivery of Delphos, and scarce to be parallel'd in any
ancient story, it may well deserve your farther consideration.

1. His first reply was, That Crœsus suffered not for himself;
but paid the transgression of his fifth predecessour, who kill'd
his Master and usurp'd the dignity unto which he held no title.

Now whether Crœsus suffered upon this account or not,
hereby he plainly betrayed his insufficiency to protect him; and
also obliquely discovered he had a knowledge of his misfortune;
for knowing that wicked act lay yet unpunished, he might well
divine some of his successours might smart for it: and also
understanding he was like to be the last of that race, he might
justly fear and conclude this infelicity upon him.

Hereby he also acknowledged the inevitable justice of God;
that though Revenge lay dormant, it would not always sleep;
and consequently confessed the just hand of God punishing
unto the third and fourth generation, nor suffering such iniquities to pass for ever unrevenged. [The devil, who sees how things
of this nature go on in kingdoms, nations, and families, is able
to saye much in this poynt; whereas, wee, that understand not
the reserved judgments of God, or the due time of their execu-
tions, are fayn to bee doubtfully silent, which makes Riddles unto
us in the tragicall ends of many noble persons & families. In this
Answer he also obliquely discovered his knowledge of Crœsus
his affliction for knowing that wicked act lay yet unpunished,
he might justly expect that sonne of Gyges his posteritie would
smart for it; and finding that his successors, Argis, Sardiattes

and Halyattes had escaped he might reasonably conclude that
Crœsus must be the man and knowing also from other conjectures that Crœsus was like to be last of that race, might
justly conclude this infelicity upon him.][1]

Hereby he flatteringly encouraged him in the opinion of his
own merits, and that he onely suffered for other mens transgressions: mean while he concealed Crœsus his pride, elation of
mind and secure conceit of his own unparallel'd felicity, together
with the vanity, pride and height of luxury of the Lydian
Nation, which the Spirit of Delphos knew well to be ripe and
ready for destruction.

2. A Second excuse was, That it is not in the power of God
to hinder the Decree of Fate. A general evasion for any falsified
prediction founded upon the common opinion of Fate, which
impiously subjecteth the power of Heaven unto it; widely discovering the folly of such as repair unto him concerning future
events: which, according unto this rule, must go on as the Fates
have ordered, beyond his power to prevent or theirs to avoid;
and consequently teaching that his Oracles had onely this use
to render men more miserable by foreknowing their misfortunes;
whereof Crœsus himself had a sensible experience in that Dæ-
moniacal Dream concerning his eldest Son, That he should be
killed by a Spear, which, after all care and caution, he found
inevitably to befall him.

3. In his Third Apology he assured him that he endeavoured
to transfer the evil Fate and to pass it upon his Children;
and did however procrastinate his infelicity, and deferred the
destruction of Sardis and his own Captivity three years longer
than was fatally decreed upon it.

Wherein while he wipes off the stain of Ingratitude, he leaves
no small doubt whether, it being out of his power to contradict
or transfer the Fates of his Servants, it be not also beyond it to
defer such signal events, and whereon the Fates of whole
Nations do depend.

As also, whether he intended or endeavoured to bring to pass
what he pretended, some question might be made. For that he
should attempt or think he could translate his infelicity upon
his Sons, it could not consist with his judgment, which attempts

[1] MS Sloane 1839.

not impossibles or things beyond his power; nor with his knowledge of future things, and the Fates of succeeding Generations: for he understood that Monarchy was to expire in himself, and could particularly foretell the infelicity of his Sons, and hath also made remote predictions unto others concerning the fortunes of many succeeding descents; as appears in that answer unto Attalus,

> *Be of good courage, Attalus, thou shalt reign*
> *And thy Sons' Sons, but not their Sons again.*

As also unto Cypselus King of Corinth,

> *Happy is the Man who at my Altar stands,*
> *Great Cypselus who Corinth now commands.*
> *Happy is he, his Sons shall happy be,*
> *But for their Sons, unhappy days they'll see.*

Now, being able to have so large a prospect of future things, and of the fate of many Generations, it might well be granted he was not ignorant of the Fate of Crœsus his Sons, and well understood it was in vain to think to translate his misery upon them.

4. In the Fourth part of his reply, he clears himself of Ingratitude which Hell it self cannot hear of; alledging that he had saved his life when he was ready to be burnt, by sending a mighty Showre, in a fair and cloudless day, to quench the Fire already kindled, which all the Servants of Cyrus could not do. Though this Shower might well be granted, as much concerning his honour, and not beyond his power [when countenanced by divine permission or decree];[1] yet whether this mercifull Showre fell not out contingently or were not contrived by an higher power, which hath often pity upon Pagans, and rewardeth their vertues sometimes with extraordinary temporal favours; also, in no unlike case, who was the authour of those few fair minutes, which, in a showry day, gave onely time enough for the burning of Sylla's Body, some question might be made.

5. The last excuse devolveth the errour and miscarriage of the business upon Crœsus, and that he deceived himself by an inconsiderate misconstruction of his Oracle, that if he had

---

[1] MS Sloane 1839.

doubted, he should not have passed it over in silence, but consulted again for an exposition of it. Besides, he had neither
discussed, nor well perpended his Oracle concerning Cyrus,
whereby he might have understood not to engage against him.

Wherein, to speak indifferently, the deception and miscarriage seems chiefly to lie at Crœsus his door, who, if not infatu-
ated with confidence and security, might justly have doubted
the construction: besides, he had received two Oracles before,
which clearly hinted an unhappy time unto him: the first concerning Cyrus.

> *When ever a Mule shall o'er the Medians reign,*
> *Stay not, but unto Hermus fly amain.*

Herein though he understood not the Median Mule of Cyrus,
that is, of his mixed descent, and from Assyrian and Median
Parents, yet he could not but apprehend some misfortune from
that quarter.

Though this prediction seemed a notable piece of Divination, yet did it not so highly magnify his natural sagacity or
knowledge of future events as was by many esteemed; he having no small assistance herein from the Prophecy of Daniel concerning the Persian Monarchy, and the Prophecy of Jeremiah
and Isaiah, wherein he might reade the name of Cyrus who
should restore the Captivity of the Jews, and must, therefore,
be the great Monarch and Lord of all those Nations.

The same misfortune was also foretold when he demanded of
Apollo if ever he should hear his dumb Son speak.

> *O foolish Crœsus who hast made this choice,*
> *To know when thou shalt hear thy dumb Son's voice;*
> *Better he still were mute, would nothing say,*
> *When he first speaks, look for a dismal day.*

This, if he contrived not the time and the means of his
recovery, was no ordinary divination: yet how to make out the
verity of the story some doubt may yet remain. For though the
causes of deafness and dumbness were removed, yet since words
are attained by hearing, and men speak not without instruction,
how he should be able immediately to utter such apt and signi- Herod. *l.* 1.
cant words, as Ἄνθρωπε, μὴ κτεῖνε κροῖσον, *O man slay not* 85.

TRACT XI *Crœsus*, it cannot escape some doubt, since the Story also delivers, that he was deaf and dumb, that he then first began to speak, and spake all his life after.

Now, [not withstanding this plausible apologie and evasion],[1] if Crœsus had consulted again for a clearer exposition of what was doubtfully delivered, whether the Oracle would have spake out the second time or afforded a clearer answer, some question might be made from the examples of his practice upon the like demands.

So, when the Spartans had often fought with ill success against the Tegeates, they consulted the Oracle what God they should appease, to become victorious over them. The answer was, *that they should remove the Bones of Orestes*. Though the words were plain, yet the thing was obscure, and like finding out the Body of Moses. And therefore they once more demanded in what place they should find the same; unto whom he returned this answer.

> *When in the Tegean Plains a place thou find'st*
> *Where blasts are made by two impetuous Winds,*
> *Where that that strikes is struck, blows follow blows,*
> *There doth the Earth Orestes Bones enclose.*

Which obscure reply the wisest of Sparta could not make out, and was casually unriddled by one talking with a Smith who had found large Bones of a Man buried about his House; the Oracle importing no more than a Smith's Forge, expressed by a double Bellows, the Hammer and Anvil therein.

Now, why the Oracle should place such consideration upon the Bones of Orestes the Son of Agamemnon, a mad man and a murtherer, if not to promote the idolatry of the Heathens, and maintain a superstitious veneration of things of no activity, it may leave no small obscurity.

Or why, in a business so clear in his knowledge, he should affect so obscure expressions it may also be wondred; if it were not to maintain the wary and evasive method in his answers: for, speaking obscurely in things beyond doubt within his knowledge, he might be more tolerably dark in matters beyond his prescience.

[1] MS Sloane 1827, 1839.

Though E I were inscribed over the Gate of Delphos, yet was there no uniformity in his deliveries. Sometimes with that obscurity as argued a fearfull prophecy; sometimes so plainly as might confirm a spirit of divinity; sometimes morally, deterring from vice and villany; another time vitiously, and in the spirit of bloud and cruelty: observably modest in his civil enigma and periphrasis of that part which old Numa would plainly name,★ and Medea would not understand, when he ★ Plut. in advised Ægeus not to draw out his foot before, untill he arriv'd Thes. upon the Athenian ground; whereas another time he seemed too literal in that unseemly epithet unto Cyanus King of Cyprus,★ ★ v. Herod. and put a beastly trouble upon all Ægypt to find out the Urine of a true Virgin [to cure the King's eyes][1]. Sometimes, more beholding unto memory than invention, he delighted to express himself in the bare Verses of Homer. But that he principally affected Poetry, and that the Priest not onely or always composed his prosal raptures into Verse, seems plain from his necromantical Prophecies, whilst the dead Head in Phlegon delivers a long Prediction in Verse; and at the raising of the Ghost of Commodus unto Caracalla, when none of his Ancestours would speak, the divining Spirit versified his infelicities; corresponding herein to the apprehensions of elder times, who conceived not onely a Majesty but something of Divinity in Poetry, and as in ancient times the old Theologians delivered their inventions.

Some critical Readers might expect in his oraculous Poems a more than ordinary strain and true spirit of Apollo; not content to find that Spirits make Verses like Men, beating upon the filling Epithet, and taking the licence of dialects and lower helps, common to humane Poetry; wherein, since Scaliger, who hath spared none of the Greeks, hath thought it wisdom to be silent, we shall make no excursion.

Others may wonder how the curiosity of elder times, having this opportunity of his Answers, omitted Natural Questions; or how the old Magicians discovered no more Philosophy; and if they had the assistance of Spirits, could rest content with the bare assertions of things, without the knowledge of their causes; whereby they had made their Acts iterable by sober hands, and a standing part of Philosophy. Many wise Divines hold a reality

[1] MS Sloane, 1827, 1839.

in the wonders of the Ægyptian Magicians, and that those *magnalia* which they performed before Pharaoh were not mere delusions of Sense. Rightly to understand how they made Serpents out of Rods; Froggs and Bloud of Water, were worth half Porta's Magick.

Hermolaus Barbarus was scarce in his wits, when, upon conference with a Spirit, he would demand no other question than the explication of Aristotle's Entelecheia. Appion the Grammarian, that would raise the Ghost of Homer to decide the Controversie of his Country, made a frivolous and pedantick use of Necromancy. Philostratus did as little, that call'd up the Ghost of Achilles for a particular of the Story of Troy. Smarter curiosities would have been at the great Elixir, the Flux and Reflux of the Sea, with other noble obscurities in Nature; but probably all in vain: in matters cognoscible and framed for our disquisition, our Industry must be our Oracle, and Reason our Apollo.

Not to know things without the Arch of our intellectuals, or what Spirits apprehend, is the imperfection of our nature not our knowledge, and rather inscience than ignorance in man. Revelation might render a great part of the Creation easie which now seems beyond the stretch of humane indagation, and welcome no doubt from good hands might be a true Almagest, and great celestial construction: a clear Systeme of the planetical Bodies of the invisible and seeming useless Stars unto us, of the many Suns in the eighth Sphere, what they are, what they contain and to what more immediately those stupendious Bodies are serviceable. But being not hinted in the authentick Revelation of God, nor known how far their discoveries are stinted; if they should come unto us from the mouth of evil Spirits, the belief thereof might be as unsafe as the enquiry, [and how far to credit the father of darkness and great obscurer of truth, might yet be obscure unto us].[1]

This is a copious Subject; but, having exceeded the bounds of a Letter, I will not, now, pursue it farther. I am,

Yours, &c.

[1] MS Sloane 1827, 1839.

MUSÆUM CLAUSUM, OR
BIBLIOTHECA ABSCONDITA:

CONTAINING SOME REMARKABLE BOOKS,
ANTIQUITIES, PICTURES *&* RARITIES
OF SEVERAL KINDS, SCARCE OR NEVER
SEEN BY ANY MAN NOW LIVING

Sir,

With many thanks I return that noble Catalogue of Books, TRACT XIII
Rarities and Singularities of Art and Nature, which you were [Brit. Mus.
pleased to communicate unto me. There are many Collections MS Sloane
of this kind in Europe. And, besides the printed accounts of the 1874, another
version.]
Musæum Aldrovandi, Calceolarianum Moscardi, Wormianum; the
Casa Abbellita at Loretto, and *Threasor* of S. Dennis, the Reposi-
tory of the Duke of Tuscany, that of the Duke of Saxony, and
that noble one of the Emperour at Vienna, and many more are
of singular note. Of what in this kind I have by me I shall make
no repetition, and you having already had a view thereof, I am
bold to present you with the List of a Collection, which I may
justly say you have not seen before.

The Title is, as above,

Musæum Clausum, or *Bibliotheca Abscondita*: containing some
remarkable Books, Antiquities, Pictures and Rarities of several
kinds, scarce or never seen by any man now living.

1. Rare and generally unknown Books.

1. A Poem of Ovidius Naso, written in the Getick Lan-
guage,★ during his exile at Tomos, found wrapt up in Wax at ★ *Ab pudet &*
Sabaria, on the Frontiers of Hungary, where there remains a *scripsi Getico
sermone*
tradition that he died, in his return towards Rome from Tomos, *Libellum.*
either after his pardon or the death of Augustus.

2. The Letter of Quintus Cicero, which he wrote in answer

TRACT XIII to that of his Brother Marcus Tullius, desiring of him an account of Britany, wherein are described the Country, State and Manners of the Britains of that Age.

3. An Ancient British Herbal, or description of divers Plants of this Island, observed by that famous Physician Scribonius Largus, when he attended the Emperour Claudius in his Expedition into Britany.

4. An exact account of the Life and Death of Avicenna[1] confirming the account of his Death by taking nine Clysters together in a fit of the Colick; and not as Marius[2] the Italian Poet delivereth, by being broken upon the Wheel; left with other Pieces by Benjamin Tudelensis, as he travelled from Saragossa to Jerusalem, in the hands of Abraham Jarchi, a famous Rabbi of Lunell near Montpelier, and found in a Vault when the Walls of that City were demolished by Lewis the Thirteenth.

5. A punctual relation of Hannibal's march out of Spain into Italy, and far more particular than that of Livy, where about he passed the River Rhodanus or Rhosne; at what place he crossed the Isara or L'isere; when he marched up toward the confluence of the Sone and the Rhone, or the place where the City Lyons was afterward built; how wisely he decided the difference between King Brancus and his Brother, at what place he passed the Alpes, what Vinegar he used, and where he obtained such quantity to break and calcine the Rocks made hot with Fire.

6. A learned Comment upon the Periplus of Hanno the Carthaginian, or his Navigation upon the Western Coast of Africa, with the several places he landed at; what Colonies he settled, what Ships were scattered from his Fleet near the Æquinoctial Line, which were not afterward heard of, and which probably fell into the Trade Winds, and were carried over into the Coast of America.

7. A particular Narration of that famous Expedition of the English into Barbary in the ninety fourth year of the Hegira, so shortly touched by Leo Africanus, whither called by the Goths they besieged, took and burnt the City of Arzilla possessed by the Mahometans, and lately the seat of Gayland; with many other exploits delivered at large in Arabick, lost in the Ship of

---

[1] Avicenna *is probably an error for* Averrhoes (cf. Browne's fragment *De Peste*, p. 250).   [2] Marius *is probably an error for* Marini (cf. ibid.).

Books and Rarities which the King of Spain took from Siddy TRACT XIII
Hamet King of Fez, whereof a great part were carried into the
Escurial, and conceived to be gathered out of the relations of
Hibnu Nachu, the best Historian of the African Affairs.

8. A Fragment of Pytheas that ancient Traveller of Mar-
seille; which we suspect not to be spurious, because, in the
description of the Northern Countries, we find that passage of
Pytheas mentioned by Strabo, that all the Air beyond Thule is
thick, condensed and gellied, looking just like Sea Lungs.

9. A *Sub Marine* Herbal, describing the several Vegetables
found on the Rocks, Hills, Valleys, Meadows at the bottom of
the Sea, with many sorts of *Alga, Fucus, Quercus, Polygonum,
Gramens* and others not yet described.

10. Some Manuscripts and Rarities brought from the Libraries
of Æthiopia, by Zaga Zaba, and afterward transported to Rome,
and scattered by the Souldiers of the Duke of Bourbon, when
they barbarously sacked that City.

11. Some Pieces of Julius Scaliger, which he complains to
have been stoln from him, sold to the Bishop of Mende in
Languedock, and afterward taken away and sold in the Civil
Wars under the Duke of Rohan.

12. A Comment of Dioscorides upon Hyppocrates, procured
from Constantinople by Amatus Lusitanus, and left in the hands
of a Jew of Ragusa.

13. Marcus Tullius Cicero his Geography; as also a part of
that magnified Piece of his *De Republica*, very little answering
the great expectation of it, and short of Pieces under the same
name by Bodinus and Tholosanus.

14. King Mithridates his Oneirocritica.

Aristotle *de Precationibus.*

Democritus *de his quæ fiunt apud Orcum, & Oceani circumnavigatio.*

[A defence of Arnoldus de Villa Nova, whom the learned
Postellus conceived to be the author of *De Tribus Impostoribus.*

A learned explanation of the receit to make a divell:

    ℞ *Judaei bis furti*
     Itali cornuti
     Angli Italionati
     misce fiat diabolus][1]

[1] MS Sloane 1874, f. 98, v.

Epicurus *de Pietate.*

A Tragedy of Thyestes, and another of Medea, writ by Diogenes the Cynick.

King Alfred upon *Aristotle de Plantis.*

Seneca's Epistles to S. Paul.

King Solomon *de Umbris Idæarum,* which Chicus Asculanus, in his Comment upon Johannes de Sacrobosco, would make us believe he saw in the Library of the Duke of Bavaria.

15. *Artemidori Oneirocritici Geographia.*

Pythagoras *de Mari Rubro.*

The Works of Confutius the famous Philosopher of China, translated into Spanish.

16. Josephus in Hebrew, written by himself.

17. The Commentaries of Sylla the Dictatour.

18. A Commentary of Galen upon the Plague of Athens described by Thucydides.

19. *Duo Cæsaris Anti-Catones,* or the two notable Books writ by Julius Cæsar against Cato; mentioned by Livy, Salustius and Juvenal; which the Cardinal of Liege told Ludovicus Vives were in an old Library of that City.

Mazhapha Einok, or, the Prophecy of Enoch, which Ægidius Lochiensis, a learned Eastern Traveller, told Peireschius that he had found in an old Library at Alexandria containing eight thousand Volumes.

20. A Collection of Hebrew Epistles, which passed between the two learned Women of our age, Maria Molinea of Sedan, and Maria Schurman of Utrecht.

A wondrous Collection of some Writings of Ludovica Saracenica, Daughter of Philibertus Saracenicus a Physician of Lyons, who at eight years of age had made a good progress in the Hebrew, Greek and Latin Tongues.

2. Rarities in Pictures.

1. A Picture of the three remarkable Steeples or Towers in Europe built purposely awry and so as they seem falling. Torre Pisana at Pisa, Torre Garisenda in Bononia, and that other in the City of Colein.

2. A Draught of all sorts of Sistrums, Crotaloes, Cymbals, Tympans, &c. in use among the Ancients.

3. Large Submarine Pieces, well delineating the bottom of TRACT XIII
the Mediterranean Sea, the Prerie or large Sea-meadow upon the
Coast of Provence, the Coral Fishing, the gathering of Sponges,
the Mountains, Valleys and Desarts, the Subterraneous Vents
and Passages at the bottom of that Sea.[1] Together with a lively
Draught of Cola Pesce, or the famous Sicilian Swimmer, diving
into the Voragos and broken Rocks by Charybdis, to fetch up
the golden Cup, which Frederick, King of Sicily, had purposely
thrown into that Sea.

4. A Moon Piece, describing that notable Battel between
Axalla, General of Tamerlane, and Camares the Persian, fought
by the light of the Moon.

5. Another remarkable Fight of Inghirami the Florentine with
the Turkish Galleys by Moon-light, who being for three hours
grappled with the Basha Galley, concluded with a signal Victory.

6. A delineation of the great Fair of Almachara in Arabia,
which, to avoid the great heat of the Sun, is kept in the Night,
and by the light of the Moon.

7. A Snow Piece, of Land and Trees covered with Snow and
Ice, and Mountains of Ice floating in the Sea, with Bears, Seals,
Foxes, and variety of rare Fowls upon them.

8. An Ice Piece describing the notable Battel between the
Jaziges and the Romans, fought upon the frozen Danubius, the
Romans settling one foot upon their Targets to hinder them
from slipping, their fighting with the Jaziges when they were
fallen, and their advantages therein by their art in volutation and
rolling contention or wrastling, according to the description of
Dion.

9. Sosia, or a Draught of three persons notably resembling
each other. Of King Henry the Fourth of France, and a Miller
of Languedock; of Sforza Duke of Milain and a Souldier; of Mala-
testa Duke of Rimini and Marchesinus the Jester.*

10. A Picture of the great Fire which happened at Constantinople in the Reign of Sultan Achmet. The Janizaries in the mean
time plundring the best Houses, Nassa Bassa the Vizier riding
about with a Cimetre in one hand and a Janizary's Head in the

* 'Of Charles
the First, and
one Osborn,
an hedger,
whom I often
employd.'
J. Evelyn.

[1] *the Subterraneous Vents . . . Sea*] the passage of Kircherus in his *Iter Sub-
marinum* when he went down about Egypt, and rose again in the Red Sea
(MS Sloane 1874).

other to deter them; and the Priests attempting to quench the Fire, by pieces of Mahomet's Shirt dipped in holy Water and thrown into it.

11. A Night Piece of the dismal Supper and strange Entertain of the Senatours by Domitian, according to the description of Dion.

12. A Vestal Sinner in the Cave with a Table and a Candle.

13. An Elephant dancing upon the Ropes with a Negro Dwarf upon his Back.

14. Another describing the mighty Stone falling from the Clouds into Ægospotamos or the Goats River in Greece, which Antiquity could believe that Anaxagoras was able to foretell half a year before.

15. Three noble Pieces; of Vercingetorix the Gaul submitting his person unto Julius Cæsar; of Tigranes King of Armenia humbly presenting himself unto Pompey; and of Tamerlane ascending his Horse from the Neck of Bajazet.

16. Draughts of three passionate Looks; of Thyestes when he was told at the Table that he had eaten a piece of his own Son; of Bajazet when he went into the Iron Cage; of Œdipus when he first came to know that he had killed his Father, and married his own Mother.

17. Of the Cymbrian Mother in Plutarch who, after the overthrow by Marius, hanged her self and her two Children at her feet.

18. Some Pieces delineating singular inhumanities in Tortures. The Scaphismus of the Persians. The living truncation of the Turks. The hanging Sport at the Feasts of the Thracians. The exact method of flaying men alive, beginning between the Shoulders, according to the description of Thomas Minadoi, in his Persian War. Together with the studied tortures of the French Traitours at Pappa in Hungaria: as also the wild and enormous torment invented by Tiberius, designed according unto the description of Suetonius. *Excogitaverunt inter genera cruciatûs, ut largâ meri potione per fallaciam oneratos repentè veretris deligatis fidicularum simul urinæque tormento distenderet.*

19. A Picture describing how Hannibal forced his passage over the River Rhosne with his Elephants, Baggage and mixed Army; with the Army of the Gauls opposing him on the contrary Shore, and Hanno passing over with his Horse much above to fall upon the Rere of the Gauls.

20. A neat Piece describing the Sack of Fundi by the Fleet and Souldiers of Barbarossa the Turkish Admiral, the confusion of the people and their flying up to the Mountains, and Julia Gonzaga the beauty of Italy flying away with her Ladies half naked on Horseback over the Hills.

21. A noble Head of Franciscus Gonzaga, who, being imprisoned for Treason, grew grey in one night, with this Inscription,

O nox quam longa est quæ facit una senem.

22. A large Picture describing the Siege of Vienna by Solyman the Magnificent, and at the same time the Siege of Florence by the Emperour Charles the Fifth and Pope Clement the Seventh, with this Subscription,

Tum vacui capitis populum Phæaca putares?

23. An exquisite Piece properly delineating the first course of Metellus his Pontificial Supper, according to the description of Macrobius; together with a Dish of *Pisces Fossiles*, garnished about with the little Eels taken out of the backs of Cods and Perches; as also with the Shell Fishes found in Stones about Ancona.

24. A Picture of the noble Entertain and Feast of the Duke of Chausne at the Treaty of Collen, 1673, when in a very large Room, with all the Windows open, and at a very large Table he sate himself, with many great persons and Ladies; next about the Table stood a row of Waiters, then a row of Musicians, then a row of Musketiers.

25. Miltiades, who overthrew the Persians at the Battel of Marathon and delivered Greece, looking out of a Prison Grate in Athens, wherein he died, with this Inscription,

Non hoc terribiles Cymbri non Britones unquam,
Sauromatæve truces aut immanes Agathyrsi.

26. A fair English Lady drawn *Al Negro*, or in the Æthiopian hue excelling the original White and Red Beauty, with this Subscription,

Sed quandam volo nocte Nigriorem.

27. Pictures and Draughts in *Caricatura*, of Princes, Cardinals and famous men; wherein, among others, the Painter hath

singularly hit the signatures of a Lion and a Fox in the face of Pope Leo the Tenth.

28. Some Pieces *A la ventura*, or Rare Chance Pieces, either drawn at random, and happening to be like some person, or drawn for some and happening to be more like another; while the Face, mistaken by the Painter, proves a tolerable Picture of one he never saw.

29. A Draught of famous Dwarfs with this Inscription,

Nos facimus Bruti puerum nos Lagona vivum.

30. An exact and proper delineation of all sorts of Dogs upon occasion of the practice of Sultan Achmet; who in a great Plague at Constantinople transported all the Dogs therein unto Pera, and from thence into a little Island, where they perished at last by Famine: as also the manner of the Priests curing of mad Dogs by burning them in the forehead with Saint Bellin's Key.

31. A noble Picture of Thorismund King of the Goths as he was killed in his Palace at Tholouze, who being let bloud by a Surgeon, while he was bleeding, a stander by took the advantage to stab him.

32. A Picture of rare Fruits with this Inscription,

Credere quæ possis surrepta sororibus Afris.

33. An handsome Piece of Deformity expressed in a notable hard Face, with this Inscription,

—Ora
Julius in Satyris qualia Rufus habet.

34. A noble Picture of the famous Duel between Paul Manessi and Caragusa the Turk in the time of Amurath the Second; the Turkish Army and that of Scanderbeg looking on; wherein Manessi slew the Turk, cut off his Head and carried away the Spoils of his Body.

3. Antiquities and Rarities of several sorts.

1. Certain ancient Medals with Greek and Roman Inscriptions, found about Crim Tartary; conceived to be left in those parts by the Souldiers of Mithridates, when overcome by Pompey, he marched round about the North of the Euxine to come about into Thracia.

2. Some ancient Ivory and Copper Crosses found with many others in China; conceived to have been brought and left there by the Greek Souldiers who served under Tamerlane in his Expedition and Conquest of that Country.

3. Stones of strange and illegible Inscriptions, found about the great ruines which Vincent le Blanc describeth about Cephala in Africa, where he opinion'd that the Hebrews raised some Buildings of old, and that Solomon brought from thereabout a good part of his Gold.

4. Some handsome Engraveries and Medals, of Justinus and Justinianus, found in the custody of a Bannyan in the remote parts of India, conjectured to have been left there by the Friers mentioned in Procopius, who travelled those parts in the Reign of Justinianus, and brought back into Europe the discovery of Silk and Silk Worms.

5. An original Medal of Petrus Aretinus, who was called *Flagellum Principum*, wherein he made his own Figure on the Obverse part with this Inscription,

Il Divino Aretino.

On the Reverse sitting on a Throne, and at his Feet Ambassadours of Kings and Princes bringing presents unto him, with this Inscription,

I Principi tributati da i Popoli tributano il Servitor loro.

6. *Mummia Tholosana;* or, The complete Head and Body of Father Crispin, buried long ago in the Vault of the Cordeliers at Tholouse, where the Skins of the dead so drie and parch up without corruption that their persons may be known very long after, with this Inscription,

Ecce iterum Crispinus.

7. A noble *Quandros* or Stone taken out of a Vulture's Head.

8. A large Ostridge's Egg, whereon is neatly and fully wrought that famous Battel of Alcazar, in which three Kings lost their lives.

9. An *Etiudros Alberti* or Stone that is apt to be always moist: usefull unto drie tempers, and to be held in the hand in Fevers instead of Crystal, Eggs, Limmons, Cucumbers.

10. A small Viol of Water taken out of the Stones therefore called *Enhydri*, which naturally include a little Water in them, in like manner as the *Ætites* or Aëgle Stone doth another Stone.

11. A neat painted and gilded Cup made out of the *Confiti di Tivoli* and formed with powder'd Egg-shells; as Nero is conceived to have made his *Piscina admirabilis*, singular against Fluxes to drink often therein.

12. The Skin of a Snake bred out of the Spinal Marrow of a Man.

13. Vegetable Horns mentioned by Linschoten, which set in the ground grow up like Plants about Goa.

14. An extract of the Inck of Cuttle Fishes reviving the old remedy of Hippocrates in Hysterical Passions.

15. Spirits and Salt of Sargasso made in the Western Ocean covered with that Vegetable; excellent against the Scurvy.

16. An extract of *Cachundè* or *Liberans* that famous and highly magnified Composition in the East Indies against Melancholy.

17. *Diarhizon mirificum*; or an unparallel'd Composition of the most effectual and wonderfull Roots in Nature.

℞. *Rad. Butuæ Cuamensis.*
Rad. Moniche Cuamensis.
Rad. Mongus Bazainensis.
Rad. Casei Bazainensis.
Rad. Columbæ Mozambiguensis.
Gim. Sem. Sinicæ.
Fo. Lim. lac. Tigridis dictæ.
Fo. seu Cort. Rad. Soldæ.
Rad. Ligni Solorani.
Rad. Malacensis madrededios dictæ an. ℥ ij.

M. fiat pulvis, qui cum gelatinâ Cornu cervi Moschati Chinensis formetur in massas oviformes.

18. A transcendent Perfume made of the richest Odorates of both the Indies, kept in a Box made of the Muschie Stone of Niarienburg, with this Inscription,

—*Deos rogato*
Totum ut te faciant, Fabulle, Nasum.

19. A *Clepselæa*, or Oil Hour-glass, as the Ancients used those of Water.

20. A Ring found in a Fishes Belly taken about Gorro; con- ceived to be the same wherewith the Duke of Venice had wedded the Sea.

21. A neat Crucifix made out of the cross Bone of a Frog's Head.

22. A large Agath containing a various and careless Figure, which looked upon by a Cylinder representeth a perfect Centaur. By some such advantages King Pyrrhus might find out Apollo and the nine Muses in those Agaths of his whereof Pliny maketh mention.

23. *Batrachomyomachia*, or the Homerican Battel between Frogs and Mice, neatly described upon the Chizel Bone of a large Pike's Jaw.

24. *Pyxis Pandoræ*, or a Box which held the *Unguentum Pestiferum*, which by anointing the Garments of several persons begat the great and horrible Plague of Milan.

25. A Glass of Spirits made of Æthereal Salt, Hermetically sealed up, kept continually in Quick-silver; of so volatile a nature that it will scarce endure the Light, and therefore onely to be shown in Winter, or by the light of a Carbuncle, or Bononian Stone.

He who knows where all this Treasure now is, is a great Apollo. I'm sure I am not He. However, I am,

Sir, Yours, &c.

FINIS

ON DREAMS

[Mus. Brit.
MS Sloane
1879, ff. 2–10.
Wilkin, iv.
355.]

Half our dayes wee passe in the shadowe of the earth, and the brother of death exacteth a third part of our lives. A good part of our sleepes is peeced out with visions, and phantasticall objects wherin wee are confessedly deceaved. The day supplyeth us with truths, the night with fictions and falshoods, which unconfortably divide the natural account of our beings. And therefore having passed the day in sober labours and rationall enquiries of truth, wee are fayne to betake ourselves unto such a state of being, wherin the soberest heads have acted all the monstrosities of melancholy, and which unto open eyes are no better then folly and madnesse.

Happy are they that go to bed with grave musick like Pythagoras, or have wayes to compose the phantasticall spirit, whose unrulie wandrings takes of inward sleepe, filling our heads with St. Antonies visions, and the dreams of Lipara* in the sober chambers of rest.

*somnia
Liparitana,
turbulent
dreames as
men were
observed to
have in the
Isle of Lipara,
abounding in
sulphurous &
minerall exhalations,
sounds,
smoakes &
fires.

Virtuous thoughts of the day laye up good treasors for the night, whereby the impressions of imaginarie formes arise into sober similitudes, acceptable unto our slumbring selves, and preparatory unto divine impressions: hereby Solomons sleepe was happy. Thus prepared, Jacob might well dreame of Angells upon a pillowe of stone, and the first sleepe of Adam might bee the best of any after.

That there should bee divine dreames seemes unreasonably doubted by Aristotle. That there are demonicall dreames wee have little reason to doubt. Why may there not bee Angelicall? If there bee Guardian spirits, they may not bee unactively about us in sleepe, butt may sometimes order our dreames, and many strange hints, instigations, or discoveries which are so amazing unto us, may arise from such foundations.

Butt the phantasmes of sleepe do commonly walk in the great roade of naturall & animal dreames; wherin the thoughts or

actions of the day are acted over and ecchoed in the night. Who
can therefore wonder that Chrysostome should dreame of St.
Paul who dayly read his Epistles; or that Cardan whose head
was so taken up about the starres should dreame that his soul
was in the moone! Pious persons whose thoughts are dayly
buisied about heaven & the blessed state thereof, can hardly
escape the nightly phantasmes of it, which though sometimes
taken for illuminations or divine dreames, yet rightly perpended
may prove butt animal visions and naturall night scenes of their
waking contemplations.

Many dreames are made out by sagacious exposition & from
the signature of their subjects; carying their interpretation in
their fundamentall sence & mysterie of similitude, whereby hee
that understands upon what naturall fundamentall every
notionall dependeth, may by symbolicall adaptation hold a
readie way to read the characters of Morpheus. In dreames of
such a nature Artemidorus, Achmet, and Astrampsychus, from
Greeck, Ægyptian, and Arabian oneirocriticisme, may hint
some interpretation, who, while wee read of a ladder in Jacobs
dreame, will tell us that ladders and scalarie ascents signifie
preferment, & while wee consider the dreame of Pharaoh, do
teach us, that rivers overflowing speake plentie, leane oxen
famin and scarcitie, and therefore it was butt reasonable in
Pharaoh to demand the interpretation from his magitians, who
being Ægyptians, should have been well versed in symbols &
the hieroglyphicall notions of things. The greatest tyrant in
such divinations was Nabuchodonosor, while beside the interpretation hee demanded the dreame itself; which being probably determin'd by divine immission, might escape the common
roade of phantasmes, that might have been traced by Satan.

When Alexander going to beseidge Tyre dreampt of a Satyre, σατυρος.
it was no hard exposition for a Grecian to say, Tyre will bee
thine. Hee that dreamed that hee sawe his father washed by
Jupiter and annoynted by the sunne, had cause to feare that hee
might bee crucified, whereby his body would bee washed by
the rayne & drop by the heat of the sunne. The dreame of
Vespasian was of harder exposition, as also that of the Emperour
Mauritius concerning his successor Phocas. And a man might
have been hard putt to it to interpret the languadge of

Æsculapius, when to a consumptive person hee held forth his fingers, implying thereby that his cure laye in dates, from the
Dactylus. homonomie of the Greeck which signifies dates & fingers.

Wee owe unto dreames that Galen was a physitian, Dion an historian, and that the world hath seen some notable peeces of Cardan, yet hee that should order his affayres by dreames, or make the night a rule unto the day, might bee ridiculously deluded. Wherin Cicero is much to bee pittied; who having excellently discoursed of the vanitie of dreames, was yet undone by the flatterie of his owne, which urged him to apply himself unto Augustus.

However dreames may bee fallacious concerning outward events, yet may they bee truly significant at home, & whereby wee may more sensibly understand ourselves. Men act in sleepe with some conformity unto their awaked senses, & consolations or discoureagments may bee drawne from dreames, which intimately tell us ourselves. Luther was not like to feare a spiritt in the night, when such an apparition would not terrifie him in the daye. Alexander would hardly have runne away in the sharpest combates of sleepe, nor Demosthenes have stood stoutly to it, who was scarce able to do it in his prepared senses. Persons of radicall integritie will not easily bee perverted in their dreames, nor noble minds do pitifully things in sleepe. Crassus would have hardly been bountifull in a dreame, whose fist was so close awake. Butt a man might have lived all his life upon the sleeping hand of Antonius.

There is an Art to make dreames as well as their interpretations, and physitians will tell us that some food makes turbulent, some gives quiet dreames. Cato who doated upon cabbadge might find the crude effects thereof in his sleepe; wherin the Ægyptians might find some advantage by their superstitious abstinence from onyons. Pythagoras might have more calmer sleepes if hee totally abstained from beanes. Even Daniel, that great interpreter of dreames, in his leguminous dyet seemes to have chosen no advantageous food for quiet sleepes according to Græcian physick.

To adde unto the delusion of dreames, the phantasticall objects seeme greater then they are, and being beheld in the vaporous state of sleepe, enlarge their diameters unto us;

whereby it may prove more easie to dreame of Gyants then pygmies. Democritus might seldome dreame of Atomes, who so often thought of them. Helmont might dreame himself a bubble extending unto the eigth sphere. A little water makes a sea, a small puff of wind a Tempest, a graine of sulphur kindled in the blood may make a flame like Ætna, and a small spark in the bowells of Olympias a lightning over all the chamber.

Butt beside these innocent delusions there is a sinfull state of dreames; death alone, not sleepe is able to putt an end unto sinne, & there may bee a night booke of our Iniquities; for beside the transgressions of the day, casuists will tell us of mortall sinnes in dreames arising from evill precogitations; meanewhile human lawe regards not noctambulos; and if a night walker should breake his neck, or kill a man, takes no notice of it.

Dionysius was absurdly tyrannicall to kill a man for dreaming that hee had killed him, and really to take away his life who had butt fantastically taken away his. Lamia was ridiculously unjust to sue a yong man for a reward, who had confessed that pleasure from her in a dreame, wch shee had denyed unto his awaking senses, conceaving that shee had merited somewhat from his phantasticall fruition & shadowe of herself. If there bee such debts, wee owe deeply unto sympathies, butt the common spirit of the world must bee judg in such arreareges. *Plutarch.*

If some have swounded they may have also dyed in dreames, since death is butt a confirmed swounding. Whether Plato dyed in a dreame, as some deliver,* hee must rise agayne to informe us. That some have never dreamed is as improbable as that some have never laughed. That children dreame not the first half yeare, that men dreame not in some countries, with many more, are unto mee sick mens dreames, dreames out of the Ivorie gate, and visions before midnight.

* Tertullian.

Sunt geminæ somni portæ. The Ivory & the horny gate; false dreames out of the ivory gate, true out of the horny.

MISCELLANEOUS
POETICAL PIECES

[Mus. Brit.
MS Sloane
1869, ff. 5–8.] To give you the precise time when Mr. T. M. dyed, It is now
so long ago that I dare not undertake it, but thus much I
remember, it was in the dog dayes by these four verses which
were part of a coppy wch I made upon his death:

> And if the Dogstarre up hath dranck
> The streames that wash the Elyzian banck;
> Wee'le waft him 'ore with teares, for sorrowe
> Shall of our eyes a River borrowe.

* * *

Of those upon a Tempest I was in on the Irish seas I can call
to mind only these:

> Whether yee angrie winds? What breath
> is this that $\begin{cases} \text{soundeth} \\ \text{whisleth} \end{cases}$ nought butt death?
> The waves swell high, the surges reare,
> as though each man a Jonas were
> what paynes thou takst great god to kill
> those who are nothing, at thy will
> The watery element doth aspire
> As though it would bee next to fire,
> And mounts aloft at every flash
> As though twould give the sunne a dash.
> Great Stagerite hee that this did see
> A meteour would it make with thee.
> All things by the wind were throwne
> As though the thirtie two had blowne.
> The fearfull steeresman lookes about
> whether he bee or his compasse out,

And fearfully beholds in's glasse
how his latest hower doth passe.
The rest I have utterly forgott.[1]

*   *   *

The other verses upon a different subject were these:

Wee scorne those judgements which adore
the sunne & moone, yet wee do more,
And foolishly fall downe to features
not half so glorious as these creatures.
Virtue tis whose lovely face
hath in my affection place.
Shee knowes no age nor scarre whereby
to dull the passion of myne eye,
Quencheth all voluptuous fires,
addes to chast acts & chast desires,
makes mee to endure those rayes
Cupid from their browes displayes,
And with as chast an eye behold
as Tulip, rose, or marigold.
O that reason had an eye
that could herself like these descrie;
Or could one soule another see,
No love there would of bodies bee.
Butt now on them our love wee cast
whom wee shall abhorre at last,
And love those faces which our lust
Shall loath & start at in their dust.
A richer sanguine then these weare
doth every rose & poppy beare.
This sweet vermillion wee adore
seemes ugly to the Jetty moore.
There is no face so divine
wee all adore, great god, butt thine,
Bee thou my paramour: o lett mee
not looke on these butt gaze on thee.

*   *   *

[1] For the whole poem see pp. 404–5.

Diseases are the armes whereby
wee naturally do fall & dye;
what furie ist to take deaths part
& rather then by nature, dye by Art.
Men for mee agayne shall clime
to Jared or Methusala's time.
That thred of life the fates do twyne
their gentle hand shall clip, not myne.
o let mee never know the cruell
& heedlesse villany of duell,
or if I must that fate sustayne
Let mee bee Abel & not Cain.

*　　*　　*

The courteous Sunne with dust & lowlie mire
Voutsafes to joyne his generative fire.
Disdaine not then my armes, scorne not to Joyne
thy heavenly substance to this earth of myne.

*　　*　　*

The Almond flourisheth, the Birch trees flowe,
the sad Mezereon Cheerefully doth Blowe.
The flourie sonnes[1] before their fathers seen,
and snayles beginne to Crop the Mandrake[2] green.
The vernall sunne with Crocus gardens fills,
with Hyacinths, Anemones and Daffodills:
the Hazell Catskins now delate and fall,
and Paronychions[3] peep upon each wall.

UPON A TEMPEST AT SEA

Whither yea angry winds! what breath
is this that whistles nought but death?
what furie or malicious hagge
hath now let Loose the Aeolian bag?

[1] i.e. *Filius ante Patrem*, the Mede-Saffron (Gerard) or Autumn Crocus, which produces leaves in February, seed in May, and flowers in September (J. Britton, *The Times Lit. Sup.* 18 Sept. 1919).

[2] i.e. *Bryonia dioica*, the White Bryony, which according to Gerard was often mistaken for the true Mandrakes (ibid.).

[3] i.e. *Erophila verna*, the Whitlow Grass, and *Saxifraga tridactylites*, the Rue-leaved Saxifrage, both styled Paronychia by Gerard (ibid.).

the waves swell high, the surges reare
as though each man a Jonas were:
the watry Element doth Aspire
as tho it would be next to fire,
and mounts aloft at every flash
as tho t'would give the Sun a dash.
no more could doubt who this did see
whither sea or Land the highest bee,
but Laugh at that Poetick knack
of Arion on a Dolphins back.
all things by the wind were throwne
as tho the thirtie two had blowne.
what Paines thou takest, great god, to drowne
those who are nothing at thy frowne.
the Careful steersman Looks about
whither hee be or his Compas out,
And fearfully beholds in's glass
how his Latest hower doth Pass.
In vayne we do the Pilot coart:
the bottome of the sea's our Port.
no Anckers in the sea wee cast;
our Ancker is in heaven fast.
our only hopes on him wee Laye
to whom both Seas and winds obeye.

     writt by my Father at the Crowe Inne
in Chester at his Coming from Ireland.[1]

⋆   ⋆   ⋆

AN EPITAPH ON MONSIEUR POLIANDER
Ob. c. 1645.

Here lys deposited in trust
Poliander's reverend dust;
not one man so much as many,
not one virtue more then any.
Plainess like the baptist way,
Justice like that of the great day,
Wisdome so like that from above,
you saw no serpent for the Dove.

[Mus. Brit.
MS Addl.
19253.
Copy.]

His looks were awfull, like to one
of those that fall before the Throne:
yet so chearfull that their song
seem'd in his face as on their Toung.
Meeke hee was to dull sharpe words,
no downe brake halfe soe many swords;
yet so valliant as to dread
To breake with balme the Royall head.

Hee preacht duty many a yeare
more then most men lived to heare,
and so used to say and doe
the Preacher was the sermon too—
and men that understood not Books
were catechised by his looks;
whilst life and learning made one dam
to wash the Eliphant and the Lamb.

Sinn hee reprov'd with so much Art
that hee both smote and strok'd the hart;
and men seem'd fond of their backslyding
for the pleasure of a chiding.
Difference in Church or State
hee did calmely Temperate,
and quarrell'd with the same mind
with which other men are kind.

Shap's and disguises hee defied,
desembling only when hee dy'd,
his soule so softly prison broke
as ever hart of Lover spoke:
to Rich and poore an equall freind
who lov'd all, yet lov'd none for end.
Peace hee gave oft the wounded Mind:
Peace now lett his Ashes find.

Dr and Mrs Browne to their son Thomas
at sea

[Jan. 1, 1664-5.]

Honest Tom,

God blesse & protect thee & mercifully lead you through the
wayes of his providence. I am much greived you have such a
cold, sharpe & hard introduction, wch addes newe feares unto
mee for your health, whereof pray bee carefull & as good an
husband as possible, wch will gayne you credit & make you
better trusted in all affayres. I am sorry you went unprovided
with bookes without which you cannot well spend time in
those great shipps. If you have a globe you may easily learne the
starres as also by bookes. Waggoner[1] you will not bee without
wch will teach the particular coasts, depths of roades & how the
land riseth upon severall poynts of the compasse. Observe the
variation of the compasse. Blundevill[2] or Moxon[3] will teach you
severall things. I see the little Comet or blazing starre every
cleare evening; the last time I observed it about 42 degrees of
hight about 7 aclock in the constellation of Cetus or the whale,
in the head thereof. It moveth west & northerly, so that it
moveth toward Piscis or Linum Septentrionale piscis. Ten
degrees is the utmost extent of the tayle. Anno 1580 there was
a comet seen in the same place & a dimme one like this dis-
cribed by Mæstlinus. That wch I sawe 1618 began in Libra &
moved northward, ending about the tayle of ursa major. It was
farre brighter then this & the tayle extended 40 degrees, lasted
little above a moneth. This now seen hath lasted above a moneth
alread[ie] so that I beleeve from the motion that it began in
Eridanus or Fluvius. If they have quadrants, crossestaffes & other
instruments learne the practicall use thereof, the names of all
parts & roupes about the shippe, what proportion the masts must
hold to the length & depth of a shippe & also the sayles. I hope
you receaved my letters from Nancy after you were gone

[Mus. Brit.
MS Sloane
1847, f. 101
Wilkin,
i. 117.]

[1] *Speculum Nauticum* by L. J. E. Wagenær, transl. into English by Ant.
Ashley, as *The Mariner's Mirrour*, 1588.

[2] Thomas Blundeville, of Newton Flotman in Norfolk, author of astronomical works.

[3] *Concerning the Use of Globes*, by Joseph Moxon, F.R.S., 1659.

wherein was a plaine electuary agaynst the scurvie. ℞. conservæ
Absynthii conservæ cochleareiæ ʒij. cons. berber ʒiij santali
citrivi ℈j sp. sulph. gutt vj syr. de suc. Aurantiorum qs. fiat
elect. capiat mane quantitatem Juglandis et hora 4ta pomeri-
diana.

Mr. Curteen stayd butt one night; pray salute him sometimes. My humble service to Captain Brooke whom I take the
boldnesse to Salute upon the title of my long acquaintance
with his worthy brother Sr Robert & his Lady. God blesse you.

Your loving father,
Tho Browne

Jan. 1, Norwich

Forget not French & Latin. No such defence agaynst extreme
cold as a woollen or flannell wascoat next the skinne.

Dear Tom,
I am in much care and fares for you. I besich god of his marcy
bles you; trust in him for it his marcys only can suport you.
Bee as god a husband as you can posable, for you know what
great charges wee ar now att. Your sisters present thar trew
loves to you and Franke prayes for her prity brothar dayly, so
dooes

your affectionat
Mothar, D. B.

Mis Corbat and the Hothams and the rest of your frinds
present thar loves to you.

For Mr Thomas Browne

Dr Browne to his son Thomas at Plymouth

[February, 1667.]

[Mus. Brit.
MS Sloane
1745, f. 11.
Copy by the
writer.
Wilkin, i.
143.]
I receaved yours & would not deferre to send unto you before
you sayled, wch I hope will come unto you; for in this wind,
nether can Reare Admirall Kempthorne come to you, nor you
beginne your voyage. I am glad you like Lucan so well; I
wish more military men could read him. In this passage you

mention there are noble straynes & such as may well affect
generous minds. Butt I hope you are more taken with the verses
then the subject, and rather embrace the expression then the
example. And this I the rather hint unto you, because the like,
though in another waye, is sometimes practised in the Kings
shipps; when in desperate cases they blowe up the same. For
though I know you are sober & considerative, yet knowing you
also to bee of great resolution; & having also heard from ocular
testimonies with what undaunted & persevering courage you
have demeaned yourself in great difficulties, & knowing your
Captaine to bee a stout & resolute man, & withall the cordiall
freindshippe that is between you, I cannot omitt my earnest
prayers unto god to deliver you from such a temptation. Hee
that goes to warre, must patiently submitt unto the various
accidents thereof. To bee made prisoner by an unequall and
overruling power, after a due resistance, is no disparagement,
butt upon a carelesse surprizall or faynt opposition. And you
have so good a memorie that you cannot forgett many examples
thereof, even of the worthiest commanders, in your beloved
Plutark. God hath given you a stout, butt a generous and
mercifull heart withall, & in all your life you could never behold
any person in miserie butt with compassion & releif; wch hath
been notable in you from a child. So have you layd up a good
foundation for gods mercy, & if such a disaster should happen
hee will without doubt mercifully remember you. However let
god that brought you in the world in his owne good time, lead
you thorough it, & in his owne season bring you out of it, &
without such wayes as are displeasing unto him. When you are
at Cales, see if you can get a box of the Jesuits powder at easie
rate & bring it in the bark, not in powder. I am glad you have
receaved the bill of exchange for Cales, if you should find occasion to make use thereof. Enquire farther at Tangier of the
minerall water you told mee wch was neere the toune & whereof many made use. Take notice of such plants as you meet with
ether upon the Spanish or African coast & if you knowe them
not, putt some leaves into a booke, though carelessely, and not
with that neatenesse as in your booke at Norwich.

Enquire after any one who hath been at Fez, and learne what
you can of the present state of that place, wch hath been so

famous in the discription of Leo & others. The mercifull providence of god go with you. *Impellant animæ lintea Thraciæ.*

Your loving father,
Thomas Browne

For Mr Thomas Browne, Lieutenant of his Majesties shippe the Marie Rose, *riding in Plimmouth sound*

Dr Browne to his son Thomas at Portsmouth

[May or June, 1667.]

Dear Sonne,

[Bibl. Bodl. MS Rawl. D 391, f. 28. Copy by the writer. Wilkin, i. 149.]

I am very glad you are returned from the strayghts mouth once more in health and safetie. God continue his mercifull providence over you. I hope you maintaine a thankfull heart and daylie blesse him for your great deliverances in so many fights, and dangers of the sea, whereto you have been exposed upon severall seas and in all seasons of the yeare. When you first undertooke this service, you cannot butt remember that I caused you to read the discription of all the sea fights of note in Plutark, the Turkish history, and others; and withall gave you the discription of fortitude left by Aristotle, *Fortitudinis est inconcussum* δύσπληκτον *a mortis metu et constantem in malis et intrepidum ad pericula esse, et malle honestè mori quam turpiter servari et victoriæ causam præstare. Præterea autem fortitudinis est laborare et tolerare. Accedit autem fortitudini audacia et animi præstantia et fiducia, et confidentia, ad hæc industria et tolerantia.* That which I then proposed for your example, I now send you for your commendation. For to give you your due, in the whole cours of this warre, both in fights and other sea affayres, hazards and perills, you have very well fullfilled this character in yourself. And allthough you bee not forward in commending yourself, yett others have not been backward to do it for you, and have so earnestly expressed your courage, valour, and resolution; your sober and studious and observing cours of life; your generous and obliging disposition, and the notable knowledge you have obtayned in military and all kind of sea affayres, that it affoordeth no small comfort unto mee. And I would by no meanes omitt to declare the same unto yourself, that you may not

want that encouragement which you so well deserve. They
that do well need not commend themselves; others will bee
readie enough to do it for them. And because you may understand how well I have heard of you, I would not omitt to communicate this unto you. Mr Scudamore, your sober and learned
chaplaine, in your voyage with Sir Jeremie Smith,[1] gives you no
small commendations for a sober, studious, courageous, and
diligent person; that hee had not met with any of the fleet like
you, so civill, observing, and diligent to your charge, with the
reputation and love of all the shippe; and that without doubt
you would make a famous man, and a reputation to your
country. Captain Fenne, a meere rough seaman, sayd, that if
hee were to choose, hee would have your company before any
hee knewe. Mr W. B. of Lynne, a stout volunteer in the Dread-
nought, sayd in my hearing that you were a deserving person
and of as good a reputation as any yong man in the fleet.
Another, who was with you at Schellinck, highly commended
your sobrietie, carefullnesse, undaunted and lasting courage
through all the cours of the warre; that you had acquired no
small knowledge in navigation as well as the military part.
That you understood any thing that belonged unto a shippe;
and had been so strict and criticall an observer of the shipps in
the fleet, that you could name any shippe sayling at some distance; and by some private mark and observation which you
had made, would hardly mistake one, if seventie shippes should
sayle at a reasonable distance by you. You are much obliged to
Sir Thomas Allen, who upon all occasions speakes highly of
you; . . .[2] 'and is to be held to the fleet by encouragement and
preferment: for I would not have him leave the sea, which
otherwise probably hee might, having parts to make himself
considerable by divers other wayes.' Mr I. told mee you were
compleately constituted to do your country service, honour,
and reputation, as being exceeding faythfull, valiant, diligent,
generous, vigilant, observing, very knowing, and a schollar.
How you behaved yourself in the Foresight, at the hard service
at Bergen in Norway,[3] captain Brooke the commander expressed unto many before his death not long after in Suffolk;

[1] In the Mediterranean during the winter of 1665–6.
[2] Some words here are deleted and illegible.   [3] In 1665.

and particularly unto my Lord of Sandwich, then Admiral, which thoughe you would not tell mee yourself, yet was I informed from a person of no ordinary qualitie, C. Harbord,[1] who when you came aboard the admiral after the taking of the East India shippes, heard my Lord of Sandwich to speake thus unto you. 'Sir, you are a person whom I am glad to see, and must bee better acquainted with you, upon the account which captain Brooke gave mee of you. I must encourage such persons and give them their due, which will stand so firmly and courageously unto it upon extremities, wherein true valour is best discovered.' Hee told mee you were the only man that stuck closely and boldly to him unto the Last, and that after so many of his men and his Lieutenant was slayne, hee could not have well knowne what to have done without you. Butt beside these I must not fayle to tell you how well I like it, that you are not only *Marti* butt *Mercurio*, and very much pleased to find how good a student you have been at sea, and particularly with what successe you have read divers bookes there, especially Homer and Juvenal, with Lubines notes. Being much surprized to find you so perfect therein that you had them in a manner without booke, and could proceed in any verse I named unto you. I am glad you can overcome Lucan. The other bookes which I sent are I perceive not hard unto you, and having such industrie adjoyned unto your apprehension and memorie, you are like to prove not only a noble navigator butt a great scholler, which will bee much more to your honour and my satisfaction and content. I am much pleased to find that you take the draughts of remarkable things where ere you goe; for that may bee very usefull, and will fasten themselves the better in your memorie. You are mightily improved in your violin, butt I would by no meanes have you practise upon the trumpet for many reasons. Your fencing in the shippe may bee good against the scurvie, butt that knowledge is of little advantage in actions of the sea.

Superscribed, *For Mr Tho Browne Lieutenant of his majesties shippe the* Marie Rose *at Portsmouth*

[1] Charles Harbord, son of Sir Charles Harbord of Stanning hall, Norfolk, Surveyor General to Charles I and II (see R. W. Ketton-Cremer, *Norfolk Assembly*, 1957).

Dr Browne to Dr Henry Power

[1646.]

ἐκ βιβλίου κυβερνῆτα is grown into a proverb; and no less [Kippis, Biogr. Britan. 1780, ii. 633.] ridiculous are they who think out of book to become Physicians. I shall therefore mention such as tend less to ostentation than use, for the directing a novice to observation and experience, without which you cannot expect to be other than ἐκ βιβλίου κυβερνήτης. Galen and Hippocrates must be had as fathers and fountains of the faculty. And, indeed, Hippocrates's *Aphorisms* should be conned for the frequent use which may be made of them. Lay your foundation in Anatomy, wherein αὐτοψία must be your *fidus Achates*. The help that books can afford you may expect, besides what is delivered *sparsim* from Galen and Hippocrates, Vesalius, Spigelius, and Bartholinus. And be sure you make yourself master of Dr Harvey's piece *De Circul. Sang.*; which discovery I prefer to that of Columbus. The knowledge of Plants, Animals, and Minerals, (whence are fetched the *Materia Medicamentorum*) may be your πάρεργον; and, so far as concerns physic, is attainable in gardens, fields, Apothecaries' and Druggists' shops. Read Theophrastus, Dioscorides, Matthiolus, Dodonæus, and our English Herbalists: Spigelius's *Isagoge in rem herbariam* will be of use. Wecker's *Antidotarium speciale*, Renodæus for composition and preparation of medicaments. See what Apothecaries do. Read Morelli *Formulas medicas*, Bauderoni *Pharmacopœa, Pharmacopœa Augustana*. See chymical operations in hospitals, private houses. Read Fallopius, Aquapendente, Paræus, Vigo, &c. Be not a stranger to the useful part of Chymistry. See what Chymistators do in their officines. Begin with *Tirocinium Chymicum*, Crollius, Hartmannus, and so by degrees march on. *Materia Medicamentorum*, Surgery, and Chymistry, may be your diversions and recreations; Physic is your business. Having, therefore, gained perfection in Anatomy, betake yourself to Sennertus's *Institutions*, which read with care and diligence two or three times over, and assure yourself that when you are a perfect master of these Institutes you will seldom meet with any point in Physic to which you will not be able to speak like a man. This done, see how Institutes are applicable to practice, by reading upon diseases in Sennertus, Fernelius, Mercatus, Hollerius, Riverius, in particular treatises, in counsels, and consultations, all which are of singular benefit. But in reading upon diseases satisfy yourself not so much with the remedies set down (although I would not have these altogether neglected) as with the true understanding the nature of the disease, its causes, and proper indications for cure. For by this knowledge, and that of the instruments you are to work by, the *Materia Medicamentorum*, you will often conquer with ease those difficulties, through which books will not be able to bring you; *secretum medicorum est judicium*. Thus have I briefly pointed out the way which, closely pursued, will lead to the highest pitch of the art you aim at. Although I mention but few books (which, well digested, will be *instar omnium*) yet it is not my intent to confine you. If at one view you would see who hath written, and upon what diseases, by way of counsel and observation, look upon Moronus's *Directorium Medico-practicum*. You may look upon all, but dwell upon few. I need not tell you the great use of the Greek tongue in Physic; without it nothing can be done to perfection. The words of art you may learn from Gorræus's *Definitiones Medicæ*. This, and many good wishes,

From your loving friend,

T. B.

about it a few Flowers pickt out of your own Garden: This *Royall Vale*, which like him (*qui suam Iotam profert*) speaks my good will to draw on the Reader to a due Commendation of your imparted *Improvements*; The first Flower that offers it self to my hand, is a *Violet*, (a lively Emblem of your self) which though it be odoriferous and as well usefull as pleasant, yet being small, is usually covered with a great leaf; and so obscured, that Passers by cannot easily discern it, till the Sense of *Smelling* Summon them to contemplate the Virtue of it: There needs no *Clavis* to illustrate the parallel; your Worth hath been vail'd till *Time* the next Flower in this Garden makes a most pleasant discovery of it. I have a *Rose* that is grown up above the pricks, shewing how your self hath been fenced and preserved amongst the Briars, till your riper years should bloom this fragrancie, that it had been hard, nay pity too, any one should have nipt the bud without a bloody finger. The next are *Gillyflowers* of various and most choice Complexions; should I name them all, I must be beholding to *France* for some affected and fictitious terms, to expresse their beauties; These, stuck in *Camomill*, strewed round the foot-pace of this Monument, will adde to the Fragrancie; for the more Spectators tread and trample, the greater perfume do they make: Of these and other choice blossoms, from your own Garden, conglutinated with gratitude, will I also compose a Coronet most worthily to adorn your Temples, in token of praise, for this *Herculean Labour*, in collecting and composing this Book, so eminently Beneficiall to your Country-men: which I hope will be acknowledged by All, as well as by

> Your old Acquaintance, and
> true Friend,
>> Tho: Brown.

Dr Browne to Mr Daniel King

[1656.]

To His endeared Friend, Mr Daniel King, the Ingenious Author of
that worthily to be commended Work and acurate Piece of the Geographi-
call and Historicall Description of the Vale-Royall of England, or
County Palatine of Chester, most Artificially adorned
with Typographie and Sculpture.

[King's *Vale-Royall of England*, 1656. Wilkin, i. xcix.]

Dear Friend,

Though it will be acknowledged, that you have fallen upon
a most worthy Subject, yet it may be started for a Question,
Whether owe a greater Duty, you unto your Country (wherof
I also am a more unworthy member) or your Country, unto
you? For it may be truly said, that therein you drew your first
breath, that it hath been a fosterer of you, and your Fathers
Father; nay more, that you had Education there, and that
therefore *cum animo revertendi*, you owe all your pains and Labour
to illustrate beautifie and adorn the place; but though it be my
way sometimes to put Cases, yet should I be injurious to have
made this Quaery without a resolve; for I shall Answer for you,
that though you had your beginning in this Countrey, yet like
a Plant removed, you have elsewhere grown up to more compleat Man, and to that perfection which speaks it self in this
work. Had you still kept home, its more then probable you
had not prospered so well in your own soyl, nor born such
pleasant fruit, as herein your Countrey-men may Taste and
refresh themselves withall; and therefore in that you hold out
your hand to your own Countrey-men, and bend your studies,
nay, I may say, stoop and incline to do them grace; I may
well conclude, that your Countrey owes more to you, then you
to it: By this *work* you have not onely done an Honour to your
Countrey, but also raised a glorious Monument of your own
Worth, upon which although I am not able to build Turrets of
Silver, to make it more famous and perspicuous, yet will I strew